Ch 2: p28 : Recovery and human rights

p32 : Community acceptance and recovery

Ch 7 : p98 : Therapeutic jurisprudence

p119 : Deficits of opportunity in communities
Key issues in community transitions

Ch 17 : p245 : Women's desistance from crime

p246 : Community predictors of reintegration

p253 : Circles of support

This book gives full recognition that people who offend against the law often do so because of a myriad of individual and social problems, and in careful, thoughtful and insightful fashion the authors give attention to the need for better links between mental health, welfare and criminal justice systems. The contributors question and challenge received wisdom, law and policy in relation to people who offend, and set out a new paradigm for effective work between forensic mental health and human support services. This is an excellent, authoritative and thought-provoking collection of essays.

Loraine Gelsthorpe, *Institute of Criminology, University of Cambridge and President of the British Society of Criminology, UK*

Practitioners, policymakers and researchers will all find this book valuable. The editors of this text define forensic mental health matters broadly and have assembled an international, interdisciplinary team of contributors. What results is a sharing of perspectives, paradigms and strategies that is unmatched by any other publication devoted to forensic mental health administration, policy and practice.

Randy K. Otto, *Associate Professor, Departments of Mental Health Law and Policy, Psychology, and Criminology, University of South Florida, USA*

Working within the Forensic Paradigm

Forensic work occurs across the criminal justice sector and the legal and health professions and intersects with work in a range of areas, such as child protection, family welfare, mental health, offending, disability, addictions, family violence programmes, juvenile justice and sexual assault centres. This book offers contemporary perspectives on forensic policy and practice from the range of practitioners working with people within the forensic domain and canvasses ideas about risk and offending behaviours together with ideas about effective responses to rehabilitation and recovery.

The contributors to this book are drawn from the practitioners, policy contributors, advocates and researchers in mental health, welfare, law, criminology, policing and health. Negligible attention has been paid to forensic policy and practice; this book offers cross-national attention to how mental health, welfare and justice systems intersect, who they affect, and how practitioners structure effective responses for vulnerable people within the forensic domain.

A particular strength of the book is its international focus, making it relevant to academics and practitioners who work in this field around the world.

Rosemary Sheehan is Associate Professor in the Department of Social Work, Monash University, Australia. Her published research has looked at child welfare and the law, mental health and judicial and corrections responses to offenders, with particular reference to women offenders. Her recent research developed a specialist list project in the Children's Court of Victoria to hear matters involving child sexual abuse; she recently completed a major study of women exiting prison.

James Ogloff is the Professor and Director of Forensic Behavioural Science at Swinburne University and Director of Psychological Services and Research at the Victorian Institute of Forensic Mental Health (Forensicare). He is trained as a psychologist and lawyer, a Fellow of the Canadian, American and Australian psychological societies. His research addresses violence risk prediction, psychopathy and jury decision-making, and long-term outcomes for children who have been sexually abused.

Routledge Frontiers of Criminal Justice

Working within the Forensic Paradigm

Cross-discipline approaches for policy and practice

Edited by Rosemary Sheehan and James Ogloff

Routledge
Taylor & Francis Group

LONDON AND NEW YORK

First published 2015
by Routledge
2 Park Square, Milton Park, Abingdon, Oxon OX14 4RN

and by Routledge
711 Third Avenue, New York, NY 10017

Routledge is an imprint of the Taylor & Francis Group, an informa business

British Library Cataloguing-in-Publication Data
A catalogue record for this book is available from the British Library.

Library of Congress Cataloging-in-Publication Data
Working within the forensic paradigm : cross-discipline approaches for policy and practice / edited by Rosemary Sheehan, James Ogloff.
    pages cm. – (Routledge frontiers of criminal justice ; 22)
    1. Forensic sciences. 2. Criminal investigation. I. Sheehan, Rosemary.
    II. Ogloff, James R. P.
    HV8073.W667 2014
    363.25–dc23   2014020855

ISBN: 978-1-138-01758-0 (hbk)
ISBN: 978-1-315-78039-9 (ebk)

Typeset in Times New Roman
by Wearset Ltd, Boldon, Tyne and Wear

MIX
Paper from
responsible sources
FSC   FSC® C013056
www.fsc.org

Printed and bound in Great Britain by
TJ International Ltd, Padstow, Cornwall

Contents

Figures

Tables

Contributors

Peta Barry is a social worker working with offenders in prisons and community corrections in the Western Australian Department of Corrective Services, as Clinical Supervisor of the Offender Management and Professional Development Branch. She is currently pursuing doctoral studies and developing a model of resilience and offender rehabilitation for corrections staff.

David Best is Associate Professor of Addiction Studies at Monash University, Australia, and Head of Research and Workforce Development for Turning Point Alcohol and Drug Centre. He has conducted extensive research into treatment effectiveness and the link between substance use and offending, and around recovery from alcohol and drug dependence.

Jacqueline Blatt works with the chronically homeless with addiction and trauma issues and developed the first Arts Psychotherapy programme in the Philadelphia County Prison System in the US. She also has a post at Drexel University, Philadelphia.

Amanda Brazil is a project manager at the Addictions Research Centre, Correctional Service of Canada. She previously worked in social programming at the federal women's prison, Nova Institution, located in Truro, Nova Scotia, Canada. Her current research focuses on women offenders, dynamic security and Aboriginal corrections.

Grant Burkitt is senior social worker in the Community Integration Program at the Victorian Institute of Forensic Mental Health. His research has concentrated on dual-diagnosis in forensic mental health and mental health recovery, as well as care coordination in secure psychiatric settings.

Andrew Carroll is consultant psychiatrist at the Victorian Institute for Forensic Mental Health and Senior Lecturer in Forensic Psychiatry at the Centre for Behavioural Science, Swinburne University, Australia. He is Chair of Advanced Training in Forensic Psychiatry. He has published in the fields of forensic psychiatric rehabilitation, clinical decision-making and violence risk assessment.

Emma Collins is a clinical and forensic psychologist working in community treatment of sex offenders, and has worked in both the United Kingdom and

Australia and in juvenile offender and correctional settings. She provides training and professional development services to the psychology profession and is an adjunct lecturer in forensic psychology.

Ian Cummins is senior lecturer in social work in the School of Nursing, Midwifery and Social Work at Salford University, Manchester, England. His international research is concerned with mental health issues across the Criminal Justice System with a particular focus on police contact and the impact of the increased use of imprisonment.

Margaret Cutajar is a psychologist at the Centre for Forensic Behavioural Science, Victorian Institute of Forensic Mental Health. Her research examines the sequelae of childhood sexual abuse – adult offending, rates of self-harm and the development of significant mental illness – all connected to the childhood experiences, the vulnerability from which predisposes to future victimisation.

Pamela Forrester is a researcher with the Addictions Research Centre, Correctional Service of Canada. Her background is in the field of community mental health, working as a mental health social worker. Her research interests include Foetal Alcohol Spectrum Disorder in offender populations, offender reintegration and Aboriginal corrections.

Ronald D. Francis is Professor Emeritus in the College of Law and Justice at Victoria University, Melbourne. He is a forensic psychologist with particular interests in court procedures, and has published widely in the fields of criminology and psychology.

Paul Michael Garrett works at the National University of Ireland, Galway. He has editorial roles with *Critical Social Policy*, the *European Journal of Social Work* and *Journal of Progressive Human Services*. His research has focused on how the introduction of Anti-Social Behaviour Orders has drawn children and young people into criminality, and re-shaped misdemeanours as offending behaviours.

Anna Gupta is a senior lecturer in social work at Royal Holloway University of London. Her practice background in social work and child protection and as a Children's Guardian in London's family courts has informed her research interests on decision-making for children involved in care proceedings and social work with black and minority ethnic children and families.

William Holt is senior forensic specialist for the Philadelphia Office of Mental Health, with appointments to youth and probation and forensic mental health services and is President of the National Organisation of Forensic Social Workers. He is Director of Behavioural Health Services for Horizon House, and Adjunct Professor, Drexel University and St Joseph's University Behavioural Criminology Program.

Sheila Howitt is a clinical lecturer in forensic psychiatry at the University of Edinburgh. She works in high and medium secure forensic settings and also delivers weekly psychiatric clinics at a Scottish prison. Her research interests lie in prisoner mental health.

Daniel Kinston is a social worker at the Victorian Institute of Forensic Mental Health with a background in inpatient psychiatric work. His research focuses on the development of community support to enable successful discharge of forensic patients back to the community. Integral to this he has developed with colleagues the Forensic Housing Needs Assessment.

Gloria Kirwan is an assistant professor in the School of Social Work and Social Policy at Trinity College Dublin and is Director of the BSS (Social Work) degree programme. Her research concentres on mental health social work and mental health service delivery.

Christopher Lennings is a clinical and forensic psychologist working with children and adolescents affected by substance abuse and involved with the juvenile justice system. He holds an adjunct post at the Charles Sturt University, Australia, in the Faculty for Policing and Law Enforcement. His research concentrates on adjustment problems in adolescence and juvenile delinquency, risk assessment in areas of substance abuse, violence and sexual violence, child protection and the interface of psychology and the law.

Ronan McLoughlin is a social worker with the Victorian Institute for Forensic Mental Health, working within the prison setting and across the rehabilitation, acute and sub-acute units with both male and female patients. His research interests are care coordination and the interface between community and custodial care and the housing needs for forensic patients.

Flora I. Matheson is a medical sociologist at the Centre for Research on Inner City Health, St. Michael's Hospital, Toronto, Canada. She works on improvements in women's health, mental health and treatment for addiction; she is concerned to improve the Canadian correctional system to ensure offenders have access to treatment for mental illness and drug and alcohol addiction.

Rima Nasr is a forensic psychologist, working with the assessment and treatment of both victims and offenders (younger and older adult offenders) presenting with forensic and other mental health concerns. She has worked in both correctional and community-based settings with violent and sexual offenders and in assessment and treatment of individuals with trauma-related mental health issues.

James Ogloff is the Foundation Professor of Clinical Forensic Psychology at Swinburne University, Australia, and Director of Psychological Services at the Victorian Institute of Forensic Mental Health. He is trained as a psychologist and lawyer, and is a Fellow of the Canadian, American and Australian psychological societies. His research addresses violence risk prediction, psychopathy and jury decision-making, and long-term outcomes for children who have been sexually abused.

Maryam Omari is Associate Professor, Edith Cowan University, Western Australia, with academic leadership positions in the MBA and Graduate Studies, International and Human Resource Management courses. Her research has examined quality of work-life issues, workplace bullying and cross cultural management.

Julie Ann Pooley is Associate Professor, Faculty of Engineering, Health and Science at Edith Cowan University, Western Australia, teaching in both undergraduate and postgraduate psychology programs.

Jelena Popovic is Deputy Chief Magistrate, Magistrates' Court of Victoria, Australia. Her legal and professional interests have concentrated on indigenous peoples, and how cultural and linguistic background, drug abuse, disability, mental health and homelessness issues impact on defendants in the criminal justice system; she has pursued study of 'meaningful' sentencing of low-level offenders.

Michael Savic is a research fellow in the Treatment and Systems team at Turning Point. He is an adjunct lecturer at the Eastern Health Clinical School, Monash University, Australia. He has a particular research interest in addiction treatment and the role of social and environmental factors in alcohol and drug use and addiction.

Katie Seidler is a clinical and forensic psychologist, involved in the treatment of both juvenile and adult offenders, with particular experience specialising in sexual and violent offenders. She has also had experience in the area of treatment of the mentally ill, child and family and community mental health clients.

Rosemary Sheehan is Associate Professor in the Department of Social Work, Monash University, Australia. Her published research has looked at child welfare and the law, mental health and judicial and corrections responses to offenders, with particular reference to women offenders. Her recent research developed a specialist list project in the Children's Court of Victoria to hear matters involving child sexual abuse; she recently completed a major study of women exiting prison.

Stuart Thomas is Professor of Forensic Mental Health in the Faculty of Social Sciences at the University of Wollongong in New South Wales. He holds an Adjunct appointment at the Centre for Forensic Behavioural Science, Swinburne University, Australia. His research portfolio concentrates on the policing of vulnerable populations, outcome measurement and mental health stigma.

Lindsay Thomson is Professor of Forensic Psychiatry at the University of Edinburgh, Scotland. Her research interests include outcomes in mentally disordered offenders; risk assessment and management of harm to others; the impact of legislative change; and service design for mentally disordered offenders. She works extensively with health, social and criminal justice services on educational programmes in forensic mental health in collaboration with the Universities of Edinburgh, Glasgow Caledonian and Stirling.

Chris Trotter is a Professor in the Department of Social Work, Monash University and is the Director of the Monash Criminal Justice Research Consortium, Victoria, Australia. He has published widely on effective work with offenders. He has a worldwide reputation for his work on pro-social modelling and has assisted correctional agencies around the world to implement pro-social modelling practices.

Preface and acknowledgements

Cross-national interest in contemporary understandings of forensic policy and practice led to the international conference 'Working within the forensic paradigm: Developing effective responses across the health, helping and legal professions' hosted by the Centre for Behavioural Science at Monash University, Australia, at the Monash Centre in Prato, Italy, 12–14 September, 2011. Speakers and delegates addressed how responses to risk and offending behaviours are increasingly shaping legal systems, with particular emphasis on control and surveillance. Conference delegates confirmed the challenges around balancing individual and community interests in determining effective responses to rehabilitation and recovery for vulnerable people within the forensic domain. It was emphasised that mental health, welfare and justice systems must work collaboratively to determine appropriate policy and service responses to individuals increasingly located on the social margins.

The idea for the book arose out of this conference, convened by Rosemary Sheehan and James Ogloff. Research presented suggested law enforcement must better accommodate strategies that more effectively address the complex social issues which intersect with forensic concerns. Better alliances between criminal justice and mental health systems, and with human rights might award important attention to social inclusion, helping to counter contemporary focus on risk management and general wariness about community-based treatment. The challenge for service providers is to remain solution-focused at a time when 'law and order' is the preferred political narrative. It was agreed more needed to be known about the needs of individuals in the forensic domain and what are effective approaches to their supervision, support and treatment. Authors who contributed to this book challenge policy-makers and service systems to attend to community provision for such individuals and resist popular calls for more punitive responses to all offenders, the mentally ill included. The range of authors from Australia, Canada, UK and USA all argue that such a lens be applied if systems are to be successful at addressing the disadvantage and risk associated with mental illness and offending behaviour.

The book is made possible by the generous support of Routledge, whose interest in criminology encourages the kind of research and debate found in this book. Our thanks go to Tom Sutton and Heidi Lee at Routledge for their assistance in bringing this book to fruition. We thank also those who contributed to the writing of the book, providing a unique cross-national perspective on making a difference for individuals located in the forensic domain.

Rosemary Sheehan and James Ogloff

Introducing the forensic domain

Rosemary Sheehan and James Ogloff

The rapid growth of concern about risk and safety, the widening of the criminal justice net, de-institutionalisation in the fields of mental health and intellectual disability, the new emphasis in child welfare on surveillance and containment, all sit alongside a general community concern about those who are seen as exhibiting anti-social behaviour. It is individuals who come to the attention of mental health, welfare and justice systems who are very often the focus of such concern. This book offers contemporary understandings of forensic policy and practice from the range of practitioners working with people within the forensic arena. It canvasses ideas about risk and offending behaviours together with what are effective responses to rehabilitation and recovery. It also explores the intersection between mental health, welfare and justice systems and the role of law in the forensic paradigm, as well as notions about care, control and cure and how to balance individual and community interests.

Those working in law, social welfare and health are regularly confronted by decisions about disorder, risk and capacity, and when treatment and intervention are compulsory. However, fragile families and high-risk communities – challenged by poverty, substance abuse, high unemployment and rising incarceration rates – increasingly propel individuals into the mental health system. The contributors to this book are drawn from the practitioners, policy contributors, advocates and researchers in mental health, welfare, law, criminology, policing and health. Negligible attention has been paid to forensic policy and practice; this book offers cross-national attention to how mental health, welfare and justice systems intersect, who they affect, and how practitioners structure effective responses for vulnerable people within the forensic domain. The book offers an international focus on policy, practice and emerging challenges when working with involuntary clients. Such international interest is significant, given the globalised nature of concern about risk, surveillance and safety, and marginal groups. Governments are seeking appropriate responses to deal with and effectively manage these concerns, and the promotion of appropriate control with social inclusion strategies through community-based programmes.

The book concentrates on a comprehensive analysis of the intersection between the forensic paradigm and work across the law, mental health and helping professions. Particular attention is given to practice frameworks and exploring what are effective responses to individuals within the forensic domain, attending not only to community attitudes but also to how individual consumers of these services are viewed and treated. Key research in this context is also presented, with debate about how it influences the principles that inform the development of policies on which to build expertise in working with individuals whose actions bring them to forensic attention.

The first five chapters form Part I of the book, examining contemporary policy and paradigmatic underpinnings of the forensic domain. These chapters identify the specialist field of forensic practice and cross-discipline contributions to working with individuals whose offending and its consequences draws them into mental health and legal systems. The chapters look also at the practice challenges in this domain, where legal process shapes the work context, and at the tension between legal and welfare obligations. The authors examine philosophies and practices surrounding risk management, increasingly the preferred ideology and service response of public services not only for people with mental illness but also in child protection, disability and youth offending, for example. Chapter 1 by Rosemary Sheehan (Australia) notes how law and work in human services are increasingly conjoined as mental health policy focuses on practitioners' decisions about disorder, risk and capacity when deciding on the nature of treatment for community service users and at what point this treatment is compulsory. We have observed that an increasing number of people receiving mental health services are also involved in the legal system, and forensic practice is extending beyond the criminal justice and mental health systems to contexts like child protection, drug and alcohol services, family violence programmes and sexual assault centres – specialist fields of practice built on central knowledge of psychological disorder and criminal behaviour, and legal process.

In Chapter 2, Andrew Carroll (Australia) argues that greater attention be given to how we 'manage risk' to identify the implications of this direction for future policy and service delivery. He reminds that the dynamic between service user, society and services needs more holistic understanding to balance out the pull between risk containment versus risk-taking, and the value conflicts embedded in how best to respond to mental illness and offending behaviour.

Chapter 3 by Chris Trotter (Australia) discusses the shortcomings of risk-based approaches to criminal justice work. Assumptions that high risk offenders warrant most criminal justice interventions are challenged, suggesting that desistance models and client-centred approaches provide a more comprehensive response to the range of offenders, and ultimately greater breadth to risk assessment and predicting recidivism. Chapter 4 by Gloria Kirwan (Ireland) outlines how a lack of shared agreement about what constitutes risk management fragments and undermines service delivery. By placing high expectations on expert systems like risk management and risk prediction, less attention is given to seeking positive outcomes for service users, and to enhancing knowledge about 'what works' in situations of identified or documented risk. Chapter 5 by Katie Seidler, Emma Collins, Rima Nasr and Chris Lennings (Australia) extends debate about risk assessment by exploring how containment and surveillance policies for sex offenders challenge human rights and rehabilitative approaches. They present a case study of a community-based sex offender program and use it to highlight the structural and professional demands around the development of such a programme, and the legal and professional accountabilities and ethical and professional challenges encountered when working within a forensic environment.

Chapter 6 by Paul Michael Garrett (Ireland) commences the five chapters that form Part II of the book which look at practical aspects of forensic responses within a community context, combining notions of care, control and community. The chapter begins by challenging the centrality of incarceration in offending responses. The 'new punitiveness' of neoliberalism influences how offending is constructed and extended across 'welfare', which is increasingly influenced by penal discourses. Chapter 7 by Jelena Popovic (Australia) extends this debate by examining the contribution of therapeutic jurisprudence to target 'at risk' individuals and address the factors that propel them into the criminal justice system. She proposes that solution-focused justice more effectively reduces offending and makes communities safer. These approaches make economic sense by addressing presenting issues in the community rather than in jail. She challenges the view that this is being 'soft on crime' and points out that incarcerating offenders as the singular response to offending does little to address presenting issues around offending behaviour. Chapter 8 by Grant Burkitt, Daniel Kinston and Ronan McLoughlin (Australia) explores expanded notions of 'home' in the community and experiences of community connection and inclusion for forensic patients leaving the 'community of custodial care'. They also examine the links between housing, community placement, the impact of community supervision and the often-felt loss of the community of custodial care. They debate contemporary understandings of social inclusion as well as what are the systemic barriers to transitioning individuals from care and forensic rehabilitation to the community.

Chapter 9 by Stuart Thomas (Australia) considers how the legal system processes young people, with particular reference to police encounters with young people. As a group, a bleak picture is painted of their behaviour and interactions with police and the justice system. This contributes to 'tough' policing, to combat an ever-increasing community fear for safety. The chapter explores the complex interface between police and vulnerable young people, and the importance of discretionary powers to moderate decision-making around a young person's entry to, or diversion from, the criminal justice system. Chapter 10 by James Ogloff and Margaret Cutajar (Australia) concludes Part II of the book by giving particular attention to the relationship between childhood sexual victimisation and later offending, which may lead the individual into a forensic setting. Less is known about the possible relationship between child sexual abuse and the development of subsequent offending behaviour by victims. This chapter gives specific attention to interventions which may reduce the progression towards offending and sexual offending among child sexual abuse victims.

Part III of the book is introduced by Anna Gupta's (England) Chapter 11 which commences the dialogue on justice, welfare and mental health. What influences decision-making processes in relation to the compulsory removal of children by the state from their birth families is examined, so too is how the legislative construct of 'significant harm' shapes these decisions. Interpretations of 'harm' in a diverse and unequal society and the influence of wider socio-political factors are also examined. Implications for policy and practice that both protect and promote their human rights are also canvassed, and these have particular resonance for individuals within a forensic context. Chapter 12 by Ian Cummins (England) highlights how such human rights are challenged by the experience of mental illness. He notes the increased marginalisation of the mentally ill, often living in a fragmented, dislocated world of bedsits, housing projects, day centres or increasingly prisons and the criminal justice system. This isolation has an impact on mental health status and poverty, and also on policing, particularly the assessment of mental health issues in the custody setting. Cummins examines research into how police officers responded to individuals detained because of concerns about their mental health and their need for forensic assessment. He concludes by noting the competing discourses of welfare of the individual and the wider considerations of the criminal justice system, and the ways in which custody can act as a key decision-making point within the system.

Ronald Francis (Australia) illustrates in Chapter 13 the frequency with which courts deal with mental health issues. He outlines the use of special 'mental health' courts that have been set up to deal with mental health concerns as they intersect with offending. The use of diversionary programmes and mediation processes offers significant alternatives to customary legal penalties. Peta Barry *et al.* (Australia) extend the discussion of vulnerability in Chapter 14 by examining what sustains staff working in offender rehabilitation, what is their level of vulnerability and how they develop resilience. Typically attention is given to offenders, their custody, care, control, rehabilitation, and restoration to victims. Given that workers bear the responsibility of offender rehabilitation, cure, care and control, more needs to be known about how workers in forensic settings process working with offenders and manage vulnerability.

William Holt and Jacqueline Blatt (USA) commence Part IV, which canvasses rehabilitation and recovery. Their Chapter 15 examines the intersections between substance abuse, mental illness and trauma, and how these contribute to homelessness with its enormous personal and societal costs. The criminal justice system fails to respond effectively to individuals with homelessness and addiction disabilities. This chapter presents a specialised homelessness initiative which was part of a broader 'recovery-focused systems transformation process' in Philadelphia, USA. This approach emphasised collaborative partnerships to enhance 'recovery' and build recovery capital for individuals with addiction disabilities. Chapter 16 by Sheila Howitt and Lindsay Thomson (Scotland) attends also to the prison setting examining the extent to which mental disorder plays a part in entry into the criminal justice process or results from it. They argue the need for greater integration of criminal justice and mental health services to improve understanding of each individual and the options to manage their rehabilitation. They look closely at models of mental health care in prisons, what are levels of need and what are 'ideal' services, and how to manage high-risk offenders. Flora Matheson, Amanda Brazil and Pamela Forrester (Canada) in Chapter 17 address the transition from prison to community with particular reference to women. Their chapter presents a framework for understanding the conditions that 'ready' a woman for her transition to the community, emphasising that the process of community reintegration involves preparation on multiple dimensions, of social, behavioural and cognitive factors. They present their study of women offenders with substance abuse problems who described what conditions either facilitated or hindered their ability to reintegrate into society after incarceration. What is also explored is the interplay of addictions and past trauma with reintegration readiness. David Best and Michael Savic (Australia) in Chapter 18 focus also on addiction and the relationship between long-term addiction and significant mental health problems. They note that significant forensic history is a barrier to addiction recovery and debate offending desistance/rehabilitation models that offer mechanisms for addressing substance use and offending from a developmental recovery perspective. Chapter 19 is the final chapter, by James Ogloff and Rosemary Sheehan. They explore how the themes developed in the book balancing legal, cultural and human rights with the forensic paradigm, and how these signal both what are effective responses and what are directions needing to be pursued for work with the individuals who are the focus of this book.

While individuals whose actions bring them to forensic attention constitute a relatively small sub-group of mental health and offender systems, they are significantly over-represented in the criminal justice system and may be responsible for serious acts. Although small in number they create great community anxiety about their capacity for community inclusion and reintegration. The past two decades have seen a significant shift in what is given forensic attention, and a shift in focus from responses that focus mostly on 'containment' of an individual to rehabilitation and social inclusion. For those whose mental illness intersects with criminal offending, there has been an increase in the forensic inpatient population across the Australian states and territories (Boyd-Caine and Chappell 2005; NSW Mental Health Review Tribunal 2011; Queensland Mental Health Review Tribunal 2009). While it is not clear why this might be so, there appears to be internationally a general increase in mental health morbidity and in traffic between prison and forensic hospitals for treatment (Boyd-Caine and Chappell 2005; Callahan and Silver 1998; Forensicare 2005). The growth of individuals coming to forensic attention gives impetus to enhancing our understanding of the legal, clinical and social factors that surround management and interventions in this domain, and the importance of promoting rehabilitation and holistic responses rather than "labelling patients as 'dangerous' or 'not dangerous'" (Green and Baglioni 1998, 845). We hope that this book, by adding to the growing literature on forensic practice, contributes to and encourages ongoing discussion and debate.

References

Boyd-Caine T. and Chappell D. 2005. "The forensic patient population in New South Wales". *Current Issues in Criminal Justice* 17(1): 5–29.

Callahan L. A. and Silver E. 1998. "Factors associated with the conditional release of persons acquitted by reason of insanity: A decision tree approach". *Law and Human Behavior* 22(2): 147–163.

Forensicare: see The Victorian Institute of Forensic Mental Health.

Green B. and Baglioni A. J., Jr. 1998. "Length of stay, leave and re-offending by patients from a Queensland security patients hospital". *Australian and New Zealand Journal of Psychiatry* 32(6): 839–847.

NSW Mental Health Review Tribunal. 2011. *Annual Report 2010–11*. Sydney: NSW Mental Health Review Tribunal.

Queensland Mental Health Review Tribunal. 2009. *Annual Report 2008–09*. Brisbane: Queensland Mental Health Review Tribunal.

The Victorian Institute of Forensic Mental Health (Forensicare). 2005. *Forensic Mental Health: Working with offenders with a serious mental illness – submission to Senate Select Committee on Mental Health.* Melbourne: The Victorian Institute of Forensic Mental Health.

Part I
The forensic domain

1 Practising in the forensic context

A cross-disciplinary perspective through the social work lens

Rosemary Sheehan

1.1 Introduction

An increasing number of people who are seeking mental health services are also involved in the legal system, whether it is because the nature of their illness invokes involuntary care or because their mental health and offending behaviours are interrelated. The law and work in the human services are increasingly conjoined as mental health policy focuses on practitioners' decisions about disorder, risk and capacity when deciding on the nature of treatment for community service users and at what point this treatment is compulsory. The key issues of detention and civil liberty are grounded in the emerging context of forensic practice, shaping work not only in the criminal justice and youth justice systems but also in mental health, child protection, drug and alcohol services, family violence programmes and sexual assault centres. This chapter examines the specialist field of forensic practice and the cross-discipline contributions to working with individuals whose offending and its consequences draws them into both the mental health and legal systems, with specific examples coming from Australian and international literature. The social work contribution is the lens through which this chapter profiles such discipline contributions. The chapter looks also at the practice challenges in this domain, the tension between legal and welfare obligations, the central place of knowledge of psychological disorder and criminal behaviour, and working in environments where legal process shapes the work context.

1.2 The specialist field of forensic practice

Practising in the forensic context is a specialist endeavour both because of the legal requirements with which treating professionals must comply and the legal parameters affecting client problems. Barker and Branson (2000) present forensic work as a highly specialised practice that is very court-oriented, and whose assessments are focused on assisting courts with their decisions in both criminal and civil matters. A range of disciplines provides treatment and services to individuals within the forensic context: nurses, psychologists, occupational therapists, psychiatrists and social workers, among others, recognising the range of environmental and interpersonal influences that contribute to mental health and criminal offending matters.

The shift from mental health care in institutions into the community has increased the need for professionals to understand the nexus between individual and community. Brownell and Roberts (2002, 2) suggest this cannot be merely explained as individual pathology, but reflects the pressured and contested life contexts of many individuals and families. Fragile families and high-risk communities are challenged by poverty, substance abuse, high unemployment and rising incarceration rates, which increasingly propel individuals into the mental health and criminal justice systems. The disciplines noted above feature in the range of systems and services responding to individuals in the mental health and criminal justice systems, with demand for assistance from community corrections, juvenile justice and child protection. This is occurring in a context in which there are increasing pressures from governments and funding agencies to medicalise mental health problems – with primary emphasis on fitting the individual into diagnostic categories – despite increased knowledge of the importance of social and personal factors to the maintenance of mental health and individual functioning.

Green *et al.* (2005, 145) describe forensic work as the application of professional practice (and they refer to social work as the specific example) in any nonvoluntary system, which includes mental health and child protection systems. Certainly, such professional practice in contemporary mental health and child protection is almost as legally intensive a practice as that in the criminal justice and corrections systems, given the range of legislation that regulates professional interventions with clients and their families. This is consistent with the US National Organisation of Forensic Social Work's (NOFSW) view of forensic social work as "practice related to legal issues and litigation, both criminal and civil" (NOFSW 2013, 1). Green *et al.* (2005, 146–147) explored Australian social workers' understandings of forensic social work by conducting focus groups with practitioners who had professional experience in forensic settings (health, justice and community settings). Specialism brings with it particular recognition of skills and knowledge, and the practitioners in the study believed this could improve perception of their role by courts and justice personnel and properly acknowledge their expertise in this complex work environment (Green *et al.* 2005, 150). As societal demands increase around prediction of risk (to determine if someone should be detained, monitored or kept in prison), avoidance of adverse circumstances (for example, child deaths), and assessing compensation (for example, victim impact), the demand for professionals with such expertise will increase. Brownell and Roberts (2002, 9) argue that the forensic social work role is equally well placed to respond to public health crises such as responses to HIV/AIDS as well as to legal initiatives such as the specialised drug and domestic violence courts, which in the US include social workers as key personnel. What characterises forensic social work, they argue, is its key understanding of systems – intrapsychic, interpersonal, familial and societal – as well as its expertise in case management. Reflecting the case in Australia (Sheehan

2012), Brownell and Roberts (2002, 9) highlight this key role of social workers: "Social workers also link prisoners with special needs to child welfare, substance abuse and mental health systems".

1.3 The social work contribution

Forensic social work has been in existence since the beginning of the profession. However, it is often 'seen' to be practised by a small number, and thus there are no unified forensic social worker practice standards (Madden 2000; Munson 2011), despite laws and associated policies, procedures and guidelines underpinning all practice. Indeed, social work education places emphasis on generic skill training – such as developing interpersonal skills – which is applicable to any welfare setting, including the legal system. Forensic specialisation is then developed though practice, guided by supervision, core social work skills and associated values and ethics (respect, social justice and professional integrity, for example) (Madden 2003).

Brownell and Roberts (2002, 3) recognise the origins of forensic social work in the US as residing in "policies, practice and social work roles with juvenile and adult offenders and victims of crime". Social work in the nineteenth and early twentieth centuries in the US was very much identified with attending to the needs of the poor and disadvantaged, people on the margins, and was strongly associated with work in prisons and with juvenile delinquency (Munson 2011). The current view of forensic social work continues in these same practice domains. The growth in demand for social work assistance from community corrections, juvenile justice and child protection recognises what Rogers and Pilgrim (2010, 8) comment on as a shift in viewing criminality in terms of "inherited disposition or bad conduct" to an "increasing interest in environmental or psychological explanations for law breaking", although Stinson *et al.* (2008, 8) caution that governments and society are more and more seeking "biological explanations for human behaviour" with less attention given to environmental and interpersonal influences. Howe (1994, 526) reminds that forensic work, with its focus on care and control, "is good at regulating society's marginal and undisciplined members". Thus, Madden (2000, 4) suggests social work needs to be "a strong voice in hostile environments ... to influence the legal system in order to improve its decisions for clients and practitioners", and to preserve the inherent dignity of the individual and their right to self-determination, albeit in the forensic context often in restricted circumstances. Balancing the rights of the individual and the community is regularly debated because of the latter's concern for community safety and a view that mental disorder and criminality are connected; with social workers regularly needing to challenge such generalisations and persuade community agencies and individuals to understand risk and precautions in a more nuanced way (Meadows *et al.* 2007). Taylor and Swain (2009, 321) remind, however, that this focus on risk and its assessment can turn attention away from a focus on recovery, with attention to self-determination and empowerment, through undue emphasis on control and protection.

Green *et al.* (2005, 142–143) argue that the social work perspective differs from that of other professions because it takes a holistic approach to each client, viewing them as a person within a social context shaped by systemic, family and environmental influences; social work views the whole person not solely as a person with a particular "diagnosis, offence or sentence" (p. 149). This approach is less familiar in Australia, where forensic social work concentrates more on understanding that part of human behaviour and motivation which intersects with offending behaviours, as evidenced in mental health, child welfare, family violence, addiction and criminal activity. The very focused definition of special-isation presented by Barker and Branson (2000) causes Howe (1994, 524) concern; it is his view that legislation and policies can fragment social work's underpinnings – or indeed the human interest focus of all involved disciplines – by shaping different kinds of practice to suits fields such as mental health, child welfare and working with adult offenders.

As previously stated, Green *et al.* (2005, 146–147), in their Australian study, conducted focus groups with practitioners who had professional experience in forensic settings. The participant social workers said they drew from their generic skills, especially system awareness, and adapted these to the needs of the justice system and focused on assessment and report writing. The participant social workers further specified that forensic work differed in terms of its inves-tigative nature, its legal scrutiny and the crucial nature of decisions that may involve involuntary treatment and deprivation of liberty. In addition, this differ-ence is also associated with the notion of power in forensic work, both the legal system's power to direct consequences for clients and its power to direct how social workers interact with their clients (Green *et al.* 2005, 148).

Sheehan (2012) extended the study undertaken by Green *et al.* (2005) by focusing on the cohort of social workers working in designated forensic social work roles in the Victorian Institute of Forensic Mental Health (Forensicare), in Australia. The social workers employed at Forensicare worked in both secure and community settings: in the secure psychiatric hospital, either in acute or con-tinuing care units or community rehabilitation units; in the community integra-tion teams; or providing a service to individuals in prison or about to be released from prison. The study participants described their practice as distinct and dis-tinctive from social work in other fields, working with involuntary clients (as in the forensic service) about whom there is increasing regulation and social control – exerted both on clients and those who care for them. Community attitudes to forensic clients have seen less concern paid to human rights and more to contain-ment and punishment for what is perceived as anti-social behaviour. One parti-cipant noted:

(Social workers) have sensitivity to family issues. The hospital says this is the treatment plan, and the family member will say 'but' and the social worker makes sure they're heard. For example, with family leave, when family not ready to have patient home. The social worker avoids potential disaster, so (we are) really advocating for family too. The social worker will get information from family members. Sees the family as expert. And family might just be the dog.

(SW 12) (Sheehan 2012, 423)

The social workers echoed the findings of Brownell and Roberts (2002, 2) that social work practice in the forensic setting must negotiate 'corrections' policies and mindset, and that the dominance of legal requirements challenged their work. The Forensicare social workers highlighted challenges from the medical context of the service and the preference for clinical approaches to assess individual functioning. They expressed concern that the major focus on mental health issues could sideline the family concerns an individual might have, and social workers had to ensure attention was given to understanding individuals' connections to their external world, to their families and the circumstances that have led them into the mental health and offending systems (Sheehan 2012).

What characterised practice in these settings was social workers' ability to apply the problem-solving methods they are trained to use (Faller *et al.* 2009); this was evident in the way study participants spoke about the range of assessments they prepared for the courts, for care planning and for rehabilitation and release, and the outreach efforts and interagency links they developed to support clients in the community. These study participants, and this would apply to other practitioners in the forensic context, conveyed a sophisticated understanding of the legal and mental health complexities of their practice domain, and were clear about their professional responsibilities and obligations in the justice system (Sheehan 2012).

1.4 The practice domains of forensic work

Madden (2000, 3–4) argues that "if the social work profession is to be in control of its future, it must become committed to the role of exerting influence on the legal system though education, advocacy and proactive policy development". Thus, knowledge of the laws plays an important role in this. Madden (2000) advocates for forensic social workers to have an understanding of the law at the philosophical, systemic and operational level.

The justice frameworks – such as retributive and distributive justice – represent philosophies underpinning the Australian legal system; such philosophies are also reflected in the legal systems of any western jurisdiction. These frameworks are often contradictory in nature and thus can undermine ethical practice (Taylor and Swain 2009). Professionals in the forensic setting work within a retributive justice framework. The key principle behind this framework is that "offenders should be punished for crimes they have committed" (Hudson 2013, 28). This framework seeks to protect the innocent and aims to ensure that the punishment reflects the crime and deters future offending (Hudson 2013; Taylor and Swain 2009). In Australia, under the Victorian Government's Sentencing Act 1991, sanctions for a criminal offence range in severity from suspended sentences, to community correction orders, to imprisonment. The increase in Victoria's prison population over the past decade, despite the overall crime rate decreasing, suggests that imprisonment is the sanction usually imposed (Ritchie 2013). Furthermore, amendments to this Act in 2011 and mid-2013 have limited court powers to impose a suspended sentence (Victorian Government Department of Justice 2013; Sentencing Amendment (Abolition of Suspended Sentences and Other Matters) Act 2013 (Vic); Sentencing Further Amendment Act 2011 (Vic)). The removal of this power has further exacerbated Victoria's already overcrowded prison system (Pearson 2012) and has practice implications for a wide variety of professionals, including forensic social workers. For example, current practice within correctional settings is already associated with high workloads with limited staff, lack of continuity of care for prisoners, insufficient communication between professionals and prisons and safety concerns (Australian Institute of Health and Welfare 2013; Nurse *et al.* 2003).

It is argued, however, that retributive justice often fails to consider the social context of crime as well as the human costs involved, prescribing to the view that individual pathology is the cause of offending (Taylor and Swain 2009). Research suggests that offending often occurs within vulnerable psychosocial contexts, including: economic disadvantage and unemployment, unstable or inadequate housing and homelessness, low educational attainment, health and mental health issues, substance abuse issues, histories of victimisation and abuse, as well as limited supportive networks and dysfunctional adult relationships (Australian Institute of Health and Welfare 2013; Baksheev *et al.* 2010; Butler *et al.* 2005; Loucks 2004; Tye and Mullen 2006).

While these psychosocial vulnerabilities do not excuse offending they do provide an important context. Women are more likely to engage in offending, such as fraud and shoplifting, to provide for their children within a context of economic disadvantage or to escape risky lifestyles such as prostitution or male violence (Berry *et al.* 2009; Moe and Ferraro 2006; Ferraro and Moe 2003); whereas men often engage in crime though peers (Victorian Government Department of Justice 2005). Furthermore, the impact of imprisonment extends beyond the offender and their victim/s. Approximately half of all prisoners are parents, with imprisoned mothers more likely to be sole parents prior to their incarceration (Dawson *et al.* 2012; Glaze and Maruschak 2008). Research has indicated that imprisonment of a parent can have physical, financial, social, psychological and cognitive costs for families, especially children (Flynn 2013; Murray *et al.* 2012; Aaron and Dallaire 2009; Woodward 2003).

In line with international data, mental illness represents a significant issue for the criminal justice system as the rates of mental illness within Australia's prisons are higher than those found within the general community (Australian Bureau of Statistics 2008; Tye and Mullen 2006; Butler *et al.* 2005; Fazel and Danesh 2002). This disproportionate figure is also found in those who are arrested and those who appear before the courts (Ogloff *et al.* 2013; Richardson and McSherry 2010). In addition, female prisoners are more likely to experience mental health issues than their male counterparts (Ogloff and Tye 2007; Tye and

Mullen 2006; Butler *et al.* 2005). Female prisoners are more likely to experience higher levels of psychological distress upon entry into prison, more likely to be accessing treatment such as medication and more likely to have a history of self-harm (Australian Institute of Health and Welfare 2013; Baksheev *et al.* 2010; Glaze and Maruschak 2008; Butler *et al.* 2005). However, these figures do not necessarily imply that a causal relationship exists between mental illness and offending, only that mental illness and offending are linked in some way (Andrews and Bonta 2010; Bonta *et al.* 1998). Instead, it suggests that mental illness represents a significant practice concern at each key component of the criminal justice system – at arrest, sentencing, imprisonment and release.

Over the past few decades, the issue of mental illness within the criminal justice system has been addressed in a number of different ways. At arrest, this includes understanding current policing responses (Ogloff *et al.* 2013), the development of crisis intervention teams and police partnerships with welfare professions (Sinha 2012; Cooper *et al.* 2008; Young *et al.* 2008; Teller *et al.* 2006; Garrett 2004; Patterson 2004) as well as jail mental health screening tools (Steadman *et al.* 2005). At sentencing, this includes the development of problem solving courts, such as mental health courts and associated diversion programmes (Richardson and McSherry 2010). During imprisonment, this includes the provision of mental health services within prisons and forensic psychiatric hospitals (Forensicare 2013; Hanley and Ross 2013), and finally, upon release, this involves referral to community-based services including community forensic mental health services (Brett *et al.* 2007).

Of interest, mental health courts (MHC) and associated diversion programmes are a recent development within Australia (Richardson and McSherry 2010; Almquist and Dodd 2009) and, as an outcome, MHC operate in the states of Victoria, South Australia and Tasmania (Lim and Day 2013). Mental health courts have been operating in the US and Canada since the 1990s (Schneider 2010). These courts are designed with a treatment-orientated and problem-solving approach to responding to offenders with mental health needs, with the underlying assumption that "the law can be used as a therapeutic agent" (Lim and Day 2013, 37). However, the traditional goals of the retributive justice framework – such as punishment, deterrence and protection – still apply (Lim and Day 2013). In examining the effectiveness of MHC in a US south-eastern county, Moore and Hiday (2006) used a non-equivalent comparison group design to compare offenders in the MHC to offenders in traditional courts. The authors found that participation in MHC reduced recidivism when compared to traditional court participants; the MHC group re-arrest rate was half that of the traditional court group (Moore and Hiday 2006). Building upon this, Hiday and Ray (2010) found that participation in MHC can reduce recidivism and this effect was evident up to two years post-court participation and completion. However, discussions by Lim and Day (2013) and Richardson and McSherry (2010) highlight a number of issues within current MHC literature. These issues include no accepted criteria of what constitutes a MHC and the associated roles of workers. Therefore, the MHC differs between legal systems and jurisdictions. Despite these limitations, the

MHC represents one important way in which the criminal justice system is responding to the mental health needs of offenders.

1.5 Practice challenges

Practitioners working within forensic settings face a number of issues, relating to individual and systemic factors. The prevailing ideology of retributive justice which informs the legal and criminal justice systems places great emphasis on security and surveillance often at the cost of rehabilitation (Mazza 2008). Working within the forensic system can thus be a significant challenge for workers whose values, principles and training, can be in direct opposition to the operations of the forensic setting (Mazza 2008), and practice within this setting will involve a great deal of worker patience and flexibility. Braye and Preston-Shoot (2006) highlighted difficulties for social workers working within the adversarial court system, where an emphasis on the quality of evidence and advocacy can set aside the importance of social welfare. Butters and Vaughan-Eden (2011) acknowledged that there is a duality, and often incompatibility, between the forensic and therapeutic roles. It is difficult to build a therapeutic alliance with a client as ethical considerations – such as informed consent, self-determination, and confidentiality – can have little meaning for court-mandated clients as well as those going through the court setting (Butters and Vaughan-Eden 2011; Odiah 2004). Moreover, the law, with its focus on legal procedure and tactics, can have potentially harmful implications for clients, implications which may not be considered by legal professionals when their goal is to win the dispute (Butters and Vaughan-Eden 2011; Braye and Preston-Shoot 2006; Madden and Wayne 2003). Madden and Wayne (2003) highlight the importance for human service workers in the forensic setting to emphasise the need for psychosocial-sensitive practice, most particularly around legal hearings and decisions.

Social workers practise in a pressured and harsh policy environment (Brownell and Roberts 2002, 2). Central to social work practice is the aim of social support for individuals and families who come to social work attention. This is challenged when working with involuntary clients (as in mental health), about whom there is increasing regulation and social control – exerted both on clients and those who care for them. What characterises practice in these settings is social work's ability to adjust to the constraints of courts and involuntary care settings and continue to advocate for clients. Yet the hardening of community attitudes to those on the margins has seen less concern paid to human rights and more to zero tolerance of what is perceived as anti-social behaviour. Forming of working relationships with clients is a significant practice challenge; the need for mindfulness of boundaries and personal safety when working with a wide variety of clients marks social work in this context as very different from working, for example, in a hospital. What may also be significant is the physical context in which work with clients from mental health and justice systems occurs.

These practice challenges are evident when examining the discharge of individuals from secure facilities. The Australian Institute of Health and Welfare

(2013, 146) notes that "discharge planning for prisoners is logistically difficult"; there is uncertainty around release and poor prison–community connections (Australian Institute of Health and Welfare 2013; Wolff *et al.* 2013), both of which are especially the case for forensic patients, and despite knowledge suggesting that the reintegration period represents a significant challenge for individuals after release due to their complex and often multiple health and wellbeing needs (Baillargeon *et al.* 2010; Baldry *et al.* 2006; Holtfreter *et al.* 2004). The provision of coordinated and effective links between prison and community-based services are especially important given that the psychosocial vulnerabilities an individual experienced prior to their incarceration are rarely solved during incarceration (Trotter 2013; Wolff *et al.* 2013). Such problems are especially played out for those whose mental health problems relate to intellectual disability (Hayes *et al.* 2007; Schofield *et al.* 2006), or individuals who are older and leaving the facility after an extended time. There are particular concerns for those who have family members, perhaps also children, and dealing with how to manage interpersonal relationships. It is important to acknowledge that substance abuse remains a major concern with individuals in the forensic context, either associated with their entry to the forensic setting or managing substances after release. Clearly, sound knowledge around disability within the criminal justice system is important for policy and service response.

Older individuals in the forensic setting, that is those aged 50 years and over, represent another concern, given that in 2012, 12 per cent of Australia's prisoners were aged 50 years and older, and the numbers of aging prisoners are likely to continue to increase, due to changes in prosecution and sentencing laws. Older prisoners are also more likely to be convicted of offences, such as sex offences and homicide, which attract longer sentences (Baidawi *et al.* 2011). They are prisoners who have a greater number of needs, compared to their younger counterparts, given chronic health problems, reduced mobility and cognitive decline. There are several international examples of prisons accommodating older prisoners, such as the specialised prisons in the US and Germany designed to accommodate older prisoners with chronic or terminal illness or special needs units within US and Australian prisons for older adults (Baidawi *et al.* 2011). In addition, older prisoners will also have greater resettlement issues due to their health, institutionalisation and isolation (Baidawi *et al.* 2011; Dawes 2009; Higgins and Severson 2009; Snyder *et al.* 2009). Clearly, the forensic setting plays an important role in meeting these needs through specialised case management and discharge planning.

There are additional challenges when dealing with women in the forensic setting. Female prisoners make up approximately 7 per cent of Australia's total prison population (Australian Bureau of Statistics 2013), and constitute 15 per cent of those in Victoria's secure forensic setting (Victorian Government Department of Justice 2013). Developing systemic interventions and treatment responses that are gender-responsive is advocated by the Victorian Government's (2005) Better Pathways Policy, Scotland's *A Better Way* (Scottish Government 2002) and the UK Corston Report (Corston 2007). However, resources to target a small number of women in the forensic setting remain problematic. Linked to this, but not exclusively the domain of women in the secure setting, is responding to children whose parents are involved in the criminal justice system (Cummins *et al.* 2012; Scott 2009). Forensic settings are essentially adult systems, and are challenged to 'see' children (Scott 2009; Odyssey Institute of Studies 2004; Nieto 2002). Scott (2009) suggests that children are relatively invisible within adult organisations, and there are often negligible protocols and resources to respond to these children. Flynn (2013) found that these adult settings featured what was described as 'displaced responsibility', whereby the adult settings often felt that others had the responsibility for children. As an outcome of such research (Nieto 2002, for example), the US state of California amended their penal code in 2006 to encourage the development of child-focused law enforcement guidelines, policies and training for when parents and/or guardians are arrested (Puddlefoot and Foster 2007).

It is clear the assumptions and frameworks that underpin the legal system present practitioners working in the forensic setting with professionally challenging issues, which they navigate with knowledge of the legal system and informed by their practice frameworks, recognising that they are working with individuals with heightened vulnerability (Butters and Vaughan-Eden 2011).

1.6 Navigating legal and welfare obligations

Green *et al.* (2005, 147) outline some of the complexities and difficulties of working in a non-voluntary system, most often with non-voluntary clients – as is often the case in the mental health and criminal justice systems. They identify as key practice challenges the priority given to knowledge of legal issues and systems, rather than the provision of welfare services,. Fundamental to this is the need for workers to understand both their professional responsibilities and the obligations of the justice system. There is a primary focus on assessment and treatment, supported by knowledge and understanding of psychological disorder, criminal behaviour and family systems. Within this context, it can be challenging to ensure there are links made between the individual and their wider experience, rather than a sole focus on their medical condition or offending behaviour. Green *et al.* (2005, 151) note that, when law enforcement is involved, this challenges welfare values and practices, and the challenge for practitioners is to draw what is needed from the legal process but maintain a focus on advocacy for the best outcomes for individuals.

Practice within the legal system involves the interplay between legal knowledge, knowledge of individual functioning, skills and values, ethics and human rights. This brings with it concerns about the re-framing of welfare practice and principles. Howe (1994, 529) is concerned about the interrelation of law and human service work, and a shift from understanding individual concerns as "essentially a medico-social problem", to "a socio-legal problem, where legal expertise takes pre-eminence". He identifies a shift from a focus on improving an individual's welfare though rehabilitation to protection for the community by identifying potentially dangerous people. He describes a shift from treatment as the main enterprise to that of surveillance, investigation, emphasis on containment and regulation and the collection and assessment of evidence (Braye and Preston-Shoot 2006). Work with the individual when situated in a legal context becomes thus less valued for its concern for the human condition and framed more as a task-orientated practice, regulated by procedures and lists of competencies. The challenge for professionals in the forensic setting is to combine advocacy with therapeutic intervention, which Brownell and Roberts (2002, 11) describe as evident in such work within specialised courts introduced in the US in recent years. The influence of therapeutic jurisprudence on the criminal justice system has seen the introduction of knowledge about human behaviour into legal responses about decisions on what sanctions ought to be applied to individuals before the courts. Judges increasingly rely on health and welfare professionals to assist them with this decision-making, and refer individuals to treatment programmes to address offending rather than simply sending them to prison. This has been especially evident in juvenile justice and MHC, both in Australia and in the US.

Central to work in the forensic context is the interdisciplinary team comprising the range of professions noted at the beginning of this chapter. Whilst the aim of all members is to treat and ameliorate the individual's condition, working in such teams can also represent a practice challenge due to differences between professional roles, perspectives, skills, knowledge, ethics and governing laws (Braye and Preston-Shoot 2006). Walsh (2012) examined the effectiveness of social worker–lawyer partnerships in community legal services in Brisbane, Australia, finding that such partnerships could be challenged by the organisational focus on the legal outcome. Where there was recognition and accommodation of each other's professional roles such partnerships were more effective. So too is the case in the forensic context where legal and medical needs can overtake other professionals' aims for the individual, and the need for a broader understanding of the psychosocial factors associated with the individual's situation. Challenges will also emerge from differing professional views about what interventions and practice models are effective for the individual in the forensic context, and the extent to which these can and should be mediated by the justice specific demands (Munson 2011). This can be complex, within a corrections system that involves secure hospital, jail and community clinics, and the need to apply a range of interventions to different populations.

Perhaps one of the greatest challenges in navigating legal and welfare obligations is the tension between individual and community interests, which is fundamental to forensic social work, where the individual is removed from the community to contain their risk of offending and to provide protection for the community (Green *et al.* 2005, 147). Howe (1994) presents *care, control* and *cure* as the three traditional cornerstones of social work and they are equally applicable to forensic work, with its focus on care and control, and the regulation of society's members.

As an outcome, forensic professionals must navigate the forensic context using core skills, with a sound understanding of the law at the philosophical, systemic and operational levels (Brownell and Roberts 2002; Madden 2000). Appropriate navigation is also dependent on use of professional values and ethics as well as mindfulness of the individual and systemic challenges encountered within the forensic context (Sheehan 2012).

1.7 Conclusion

Despite the use of social work as a lens through which this chapter viewed forensic practice, all forensic professionals, such as nurses, psychologists, occupational therapists, and psychiatrists for example, seek to preserve the inherent dignity of the individual and their right to self-determination, albeit in the forensic context often in restricted circumstances. As Stevenson (2003, 24) acknowledged, "each of us is more than the worst thing that we've ever done". Considerable changes in policies and approaches to criminal justice have divided debate between emphasis on support for reform and rehabilitation and a correctional philosophy that turns on individual responsibility. This philosophy has a significant impact on the forensic context when the legal system appears to give primacy to punitive responses rather than to therapeutic interventions. The forensic disciplines must continue to advocate for integrated responses and a continuum of options for intervention which both promote individual change and social inclusion, demonstrating to the community that this is ultimately more effective than mere incarceration.

References

Aaron L. and Dallaire D. H. 2009. "Parental incarceration and multiple risk experiences: effects on family dynamics and children's delinquency". *Journal of Youth and Adolescence* 39(12): 1471–1484.

Almquist L. and Dodd E. 2009. *Mental health courts: A guide to research-informed policy and practice.* Council of State Governments Justice Centre, New York. www.bja.gov/Publications/CSG_MHC_Research.pdf.

Andrews D. A. and Bonta J. 2010. *The Psychology of Criminal Conduct*, 5th edn. New Providence, NJ: Matthew Bender and Company.

Australian Bureau of Statistics. 2008. *National survey of mental health and wellbeing: Summary of results 2007.* www.abs.gov.au/ausstats/abs@.nsf/mf/4326.0.

Australian Bureau of Statistics. 2013. *Prisoners in Australia: 2012 reissue.* www.ausstats. abs.gov.au/ausstats/subscriber.nsf/0/24B61FAA213E5470CA257B3C000DCF8A/$Fil e/45170_2012reissue.pdf.

Australian Institute of Health and Welfare. 2013. *The health of Australia's prisoners 2012.* www.aihw.gov.au/publication-detail/?id=60129543948.

Baidawi S., Turner S., Trotter C., Browning C., Collier P., O'Connor D. and Sheehan R. 2011. *Older prisoners: A challenge for Australian corrections.* Australian Institute of Criminology. www.aic.gov.au/publications/current%20series/tandi/421–440/tandi426. html.

Baillargeon J., Hoge S. and Penn J. V. 2010. "Addressing the challenge of community reentry among released inmates with serious mental illness". *American Journal of Community Psychology* 46(3–4): 361–375.

Baksheev G., Thomas S. and Ogloff J. 2010. "Psychiatric disorders and unmet needs in Australian police cells". *Australian and New Zealand Journal of Psychiatry* 44(11): 1043–1051.

Baldry E., McDonnell D., Maplestone P. and Peeters M. 2006. "Ex-Prisoners, homelessness and the State in Australia". *Australian and New Zealand Journal of Criminology* 39(1): 20–33.

Barker R. L. and Branson D. M. 2000. *Forensic social work: Legal aspects of professional practice,* 2nd. edn. New York: Haworth Press.

Berry M., Johnson T., Severson M. and Postmus J. L. 2009. "Wives and mothers at risk: The role of marital and maternal status in criminal activity and incarceration". *Families in Society: The Journal of Contemporary Social Services* 90(3): 293–300.

Bonta J., Law M. and Hanson K. 1998. "The prediction of criminal and violent recidivism among mentally disordered offenders: A meta-analysis". *Psychological Bulletin* 123(2): 123–142.

Braye S. and Preston-Shoot M. 2006. "The role of law in welfare reform: Critical perspectives on the relationship between law and social work practice". *International Journal of Social Welfare* 15(1): 19–26.

Brett A., Carroll A., Green B., Mals P., Beswick S., Rodriguez M., Dunlop D. and Gagliardi C. 2007. "Treatment and security outside the wall: Diverse approaches to common challenges in community forensic mental health". *International Journal of Forensic Mental Health* 6(1): 87–99.

Brownell P. and Roberts A. R. 2002. "A century of social work in criminal justice and correctional settings". *Journal of Offender Rehabilitation* 35(2): 1–17.

Butler T., Allnutt S., Cain D., Owens D. and Muller C. 2005. "Mental disorder in the New South Wales prisoner population". *Australian and New Zealand Journal of Psychiatry* 39(5): 407–413.

Butters R. and Vaughan-Eden V. 2011. "The ethics of practicing forensic social work". *Journal of Forensic Social Work* 1(1): 61–72.

Cooper L., Anaf J. and Bowden M. 2008. "Can social workers and police be partners when dealing with bikie-gang related domestic violence and sexual assault?". *European Journal of Social Work* 11(3): 295–311.

Corston J. 2007. *The Corston report: A report by Baroness Jean Corston of a review of women with particular vulnerabilities in the criminal justice system – The need for a distinct, radically different, visibly-led, strategic, proportionate, holistic, women-centred, integrated approach.* Home Office, United Kingdom. www.justice.gov.uk/publications/docs/corston-report-march-2007.pdf.

Cummins P., Scott D. and Scales D. 2012. *Report of the Protecting Victoria's Vulnerable Children Inquiry.* Department of Premier and Cabinet, Melbourne, Vic. www.childprotectioninquiry.vic.gov.au/report-pvvc-inquiry.html.

Dawes J. 2009. "Ageing prisoners: Issues for social work". *Australian Social Work* 62(2): 258–271.

Dawson A., Jackson D. and Nyamathi A. 2012. "Children of incarcerated parents: Insights to addressing a growing public health concern in Australia". *Children and Youth Services Review* 34(12): 2433–2441.

Faller K., Grabarek M. and Vandervort F. 2009. "Child welfare workers go to court: The impact of race, gender and education on the comfort with legal issues". *Children and Youth Services Review* 31(9): 972–977.

Fazel S. and Danesh J. 2002. "Serious mental disorder in 23,000 prisoners: A systematic review of 62 surveys". *The Lancet* 359(9306): 545–550.

Ferraro K. and Moe A. 2003. "Mothering, crime, and incarceration". *Journal of Contemporary Ethnography* 32(1): 9–40.

Flynn C. 2013. "Mothers facing imprisonment: Arranging care for their adolescent children". *Women and Criminal Justice* 23(1): 43–62.

Forensicare 2013. *Victorian Institute of Forensic Mental Health: Report of operations 2012–2013.* www.forensicare.vic.gov.au/assets/pubs/Annual%20Report%202012–2013.pdf.

Garrett P. M. 2004. "Talking child protection: The police and social workers 'working together'". *Journal of Social Work* 4(1): 77–97.

Glaze L. and Maruschak L. 2008. *Parents in prison and their minor children.* Bureau of Justice Statistics, United States of America. www.bjs.gov/index.cfm?ty=pbdetail&iid=823.

Green G., Thorpe J. and Traupmann M. 2005. "The sprawling thicket: Knowledge and specialisation in forensic social work". *Australian Social Work* 58(2): 142–153.

Hanley N. and Ross S. 2013. "Forensic mental health in Australia: Charting the gaps". *Current Issues in Criminal Justice* 24(3): 341.

Hayes S., Shackell P., Mottram P. and Lancaster R. 2007. "The prevalence of intellectual disability in a major UK prison". *British Journal of Learning Disabilities* 35(3): 162–167.

Hiday P. and Ray B. 2010. "Arrests two years after exiting a well-established mental health court". *Psychiatric Services* 61(5): 463–468.

Higgins D. and Severson M. 2009. "Community reentry and older adult offenders: Redefining social work roles". *Journal of Gerontological Social Work* 52(8): 784–802.

Holtfreter K., Reisig M. and Morash M. 2004. "Poverty, state capital, and recidivism among women offenders". *Criminology & Public Policy* 3(2): 185–208.

Howe D. 1994. "Modernity, postmodernity and social work". *British Journal of Social Work* 24: 513–532.

Hudson B. 2013. *Justice in the risk society: Challenging and re-affirming justice in late modernity.* SAGE Publications, London. www.eblib.com.au/.

Lim L. and Day A. 2013. "Mental health diversion courts: Some directions for further development". *Psychiatry, Psychology and Law* 20(1): 36–45.

Loucks N. 2004. "Women in prison". In G. McIvor (ed.) *Women who offend: Research highlights 44.* London: Jessica Kingsley Publishers, 143–158.

Madden R. G. 2000. "Legal content in social work education: Preparing students for interprofessional practice". *Journal of Teaching in Social Work* 20(1): 3–17.

Madden R. G. 2003. *Essential law for social workers.* New York: Columbia University Press.

Madden R. and Wayne R. 2003. "Social work and the law: A therapeutic jurisprudence perspective". *Social Work* 48(3): 338–347.

Mazza C. 2008. "Within these walls: The effects of environment on social work practice in prisons". *Practice* 20(4): 251–264.

Meadows G., Singh B. and Grigg M. (eds) 2007. *Mental health in Australia: Collaborative community practice*, 2nd edn. Melbourne, Victoria: Oxford University Press.

Moe A. and Ferraro K. 2006. "Criminalized mothers". *Women and Therapy* 29(3–4): 135–164.

Moore M. E. and Hiday V. 2006. "Mental health court outcomes: A comparison of re-arrest and re-arrest severity between mental health court and traditional court participants". *Law and Human Behavior* 30(6): 659–674.

Munson C. 2011. "Forensic social work practice standards: Definition and specification". *Journal of Forensic Social Work* 1(1): 37–60.

Murray J., Farrington D. P. and Sekol I. 2012. "Children's antisocial behaviour, mental health, drug use and educational performance after parental incarceration: A systematic review and meta-analysis". *Psychological Bulletin* 138(2): 175–210.

National Organization of Forensic Social Work. 2013. *Forensic social work*. http://nofsw. org/?page_id=10.

Nieto M. 2002. *In danger of falling through the cracks: Children of arrested parents.* California Research Bureau, California. www.library.ca.gov/crb/02/09/02–009.pdf.

Nurse J., Woodcock P. and Ormsby J. 2003. "Influence of environmental factors on mental health within prisons: focus group study". *British Medical Journal* 327 (7413): 480.

Odiah C. 2004. "Impact of the adversary system on forensic social work practices: Threat to therapeutic alliance and fiduciary relation". *Journal of Forensic Psychology Practice* 4: 3–33.

Odyssey Institute of Studies. 2004. *The Nobody's Clients Project: Identifying and addressing the needs of children with substance dependent parents.* Odyssey House, Victoria. www.odyssey.org.au/images/files/kif/Nobody%27s%20Clients%20-%20Full %20report.pdf.

Ogloff J. and Tye C. 2007. "Responding to mental health needs of women offenders". In R. Sheehan, G. McIvor and C. Trotter (eds) *What works with women offenders.* Devon, UK: Willan Publishing, 142–181.

Ogloff J., Thomas S., Luebbers S., Baksheev G., Elliott I., Godfredson J., Kesic D., Short T., Martin T., Warren L., Clough J., Mullen P., Wilkins C., Dickinson A., Sargent L., Perez E., Ballek D. and Moore E. 2013. "Policing services with mentally ill people: Developing greater understanding and best practice". *Australian Psychologist* 48(1): 57–68.

Patterson G. 2004. "Police–social work crisis teams: Practice and research implications". *Stress, Trauma, and Crisis* 7(2): 93–104.

Pearson D. 2012. *Victorian Auditor-General: Prison capacity planning 2012.* www.audit. vic.gov.au/reports_and_publications/latest_reports/2012–13/20121128-prisons.aspx.

Puddlefoot G. and Foster L. 2007. *Keeping children safe when their parents are arrested: Local approaches that work.* California Research Bureau, California. www.library. ca.gov/crb/07/07–006.pdf.

Richardson E. and McSherry B. 2010. "Diversion down under: Programs for offenders with mental illnesses in Australia". *International Journal of Law and Psychiatry* 33(4): 249–257.

Ritchie, D. 2013. *Victoria's prison population 2002 to 2012*, Sentencing Advisory Council, Victoria. https://sentencingcouncil.vic.gov.au/content/publications/victorias-prison-population-2002–2012.

Rogers A. and Pilgrim D. 2010. *A sociology of mental health and illness.* Maidenhead, Surrey, UK: Open University Press.

Schneider, R. D. 2010. "Mental health courts and diversion programs: A global survey." *International Journal of Law and Psychiatry,* 33(4): 201–206.

Schofield P., Butler T., Hollis S., Smith N., Lee S. and Kelso W. 2006. "Traumatic brain injury among Australian prisoners: Rates, recurrence and sequelae". *Brain Injury* 20(5): 499–506.

Scott D. 2009. "Think child, think family: How adult specialist services can support children at risk of abuse and neglect". *Family matters* 81: 37–41.

Scottish Government. 2002. *A better way: The report of the ministerial group on women's offending.* www.scotland.gov.uk/Resource/Doc/158858/0043144.pdf.

Sentencing Act 1991(Victoria). Melbourne: Victorian Government Printer.

Sentencing Amendment (Abolition of Suspended Sentences and Other Matters) Act 2013 (Victoria). Melbourne: Victorian Government Printer.

Sentencing Further Amendment Act 2011 (Victoria). Melbourne: Victorian Government Printer.

Sheehan R. 2012. "Forensic social work: A distinctive framework for intervention". *Social Work in Mental Health* 10(5): 409–425.

Sinha R. 2012. "Social work in police stations: Challenges for front line practice in India". *Practice* 24(2): 91–104.

Snyder C., van Wormer K., Chadha J. and Jaggers J. 2009. "Older adult inmates: The challenge for social work". *Social Work* 54(2): 117–124.

Steadman H., Scott J., Osher F., Agnese T and Robbins P. C. 2005. "Validation of the brief jail mental health screen". *Psychiatric Services* 56(7): 816–822.

Stevenson B. 2003. "Crime, punishment and executions in the twenty-first century". *Proceedings of the American Philosophical Society* 147(1): 24–29.

Stinson J., Sales B. and Becker J. 2008. *Sex Offending: Causal Theories to Inform Research, Prevention and Treatment.* Washington DC: American Psychological Association.

Taylor A. and Swain P. 2009. "Social work practice in the justice system". In M. Connolly and L. Harms (eds) *Social work: Contexts and practice*, 2nd edn. South Melbourne: Oxford University Press, 319–333.

Teller J., Munetz M., Gil K. and Ritter C. 2006. "Crisis intervention team training for police officers responding to mental disturbance calls". *Psychiatric Services* 57(2): 232–237.

Trotter C. 2013. "Reduced recidivism through probation supervision: What we know and don't know from four decades of research". *Federal Probation* 77(3): 43–48.

Tye C. and Mullen P. 2006. "Mental disorders in female prisoners". *Australian and New Zealand Journal of Psychiatry* 40(3): 266–271.

Victorian Government Department of Justice. 2005. *Better pathways: An integrated response to women's offending and re-offending: A four-year strategy to address the increase in women's imprisonment in Victoria 2005–2009.* https://assets.justice.vic. gov.au/corrections/resources/ca8d074b-6949–4a2a-9870-f9614a821ef7/better_pathways_integrated_response_womens_offending_reoffending_policy%2bdocument.pdf.

Victorian Government Department of Justice. 2013. *Annual report 2012–13.* www. justice.vic.gov.au/utility/annual+reports/annual+report+2012–13.

Walsh T. 2012. "Lawyers and social workers working together: Ethic of care and feminist legal practice in community law". *Griffith Law Review* 21(3): 752–771.

Wolff N., Frueh B., Huening J., Shi J., Epperson M., Morgan R. and Fisher W. 2013. "Practice informs the next generation of behavioural health and criminal justice interventions". *International Journal of Law and Psychiatry* 36(1): 1–10.

Woodward R. 2003. *Families of prisoners: Literature review on issues and difficulties.* SSRN Scholarly Paper, Social Science Research Network, Rochester, NY. http:// papers.ssrn.com/abstract=1729033.

Young A. T., Fuller J. and Riley B. 2008. "On-scene mental health counselling provided through police departments". *Journal of Mental Health Counselling* 30(4): 345–361.

2 Implementing the risk paradigm in forensic mental health

Evidence and values

Andrew Carroll

2.1 Introduction

An emphasis on the notion of 'risk' in sociopolitical discourse has been a dominant trend throughout the developed world in recent decades (Breakwell 2007), influencing both public expectations and professional responsibilities in all spheres of public life. It is both unsurprising and appropriate that health care has not been immune to this trend: expectations around risk regulation or 'governance' have escalated in the wake of various high profile scandals (Department of Health 2002; Eastley 2013). In mental health specifically, increasing expectations around risk management have had a number of drivers: the move towards community-based care in the late twentieth century; high profile enquiries into homicides committed by patients under mental health services in the UK (Sheppard 1995); and contemporary empirical evidence that, contrary to earlier assertions, severe mental illness is indeed a statistically significant risk factor for the commission of serious violence (Mullen 1997; Douglas *et al.* 2009; Fazel *et al.* 2009). This trend, and the consequent expectations placed on mental health services, has generated understandable concerns about both unrealistic expectations being placed on psychiatrists (Holmes 2013) and the insidious erosion of traditional medical ethics that prioritise care of the individual patient over possible protection of society (Adshead 2014).

Not surprisingly, expectations around risk management for *forensic* mental health services are especially high: such services provide treatment to 'mentally disordered offenders' – persons suffering with severe mental illness (and, in some jurisdictions, severe personality disorder) with a history of serious (generally violent and/or sexual) offending – with the eventual aim of facilitating their safe reintegration into 'mainstream' society. The key question that clinicians working in such services are faced with is starkly summarised in the title of a monograph from the 1990s by the sociologist Herschel Prins: "Will they do it again?" (1999).

This chapter will focus on the dilemmas posed by this challenge for forensic mental health services, particularly the dilemmas posed by the implementation of graduated 'community leave' programmes from high-secure institutions. The emphasis will be on hospital-based secure services, although many of the issues also pertain to community- and prison-based mental health services delivered to mentally disordered offenders.

2.2 Violence risk assessment: the evidence and its limits

The key question of "will they do it again?" has now been systematically addressed by a range of studies involving both forensic and general psychiatric patients (Fazel *et al.* 2012). Such studies conclude that structured, empirically guided assessments as to the likelihood of future violent behaviour have a higher level of predictive accuracy than assessments that rely on unstructured, pure 'clinical judgement' (Douglas and Skeem 2005; Buchanan *et al.* 2012; Fazel *et al.* 2012). Although some have strongly promulgated the use of structured approaches as a means of answering the *predictive* question of whether a given individual will reoffend (Quinsey *et al.* 1998), contemporary practice, at least in the UK, Canada and Australasia, has instead emphasised the potential utility of such approaches in structuring *treatment* programmes and tailoring care plans to individuals' needs (Douglas *et al.* 2013). A parallel literature has demonstrated that rehabilitative interventions for offenders can bring about significant reductions in likelihood of future recidivism, provided that empirically guided treatment targets ('criminogenic needs') are chosen (Andrews and Bonta 2003). The key question has therefore to some extent shifted from "will they do it again?" to "how can we assist them not to do it again?". Notwithstanding this, for mentally disordered offenders at least, the requirement for 'predictive' assessments remains at certain key points in their rehabilitative pathway – most overtly when discharge or graduated access back into the community is being considered.

The limits to the evidence base around violence risk assessment have now been comprehensively articulated in the literature: its inevitably imperfect predictive accuracy, resulting in understandable concerns about false positives and false negatives (Large 2009); its inapplicability to the rarest and most severe outcomes (such as homicide) (Szmukler 2001); the ethical and empirical difficulties of applying group evidence to specific individuals – articulated by leading proponents of structured professional judgment approaches to risk assessment (Hart *et al.* 2007). In addition, the practical implementation of violence risk assessment into day to day clinical care, although widely advocated (English Department of Health 2007), so far has a relatively limited evidence base (Barry-Walsh *et al.* 2009; Troquete *et al.* 2013).

A more fundamental challenge however is that even an 'ideal' risk assessment tool could only tell us about *likelihood* of future adverse outcomes such as violence. Risk magnitude can be conceptually defined as the product of likelihood *and* impact (or *consequences*) of a particular adverse outcome of concern. Whereas likelihood can readily be operationalised and quantified, the notion of 'consequences' is not so readily finessed: it is a value-laden construct and the perceived magnitude of any given risk outcome will therefore vary between different people. For example, Mossman (2006) carried out a small study examining the thresholds at which different people (university students) would balance the trade-off between unnecessary commitment of a non-violent person versus potentially releasing a person who goes on to be seriously violent: he found that people disagreed with each other to a degree that exceeded five orders of magnitude when examined statistically. He concluded (2006, 574): "The five orders-of-magnitude span of responses that we obtained suggested that, even in a fairly homogeneous group of persons, there was no social agreement on the right balance of correct and incorrect decisions about future violence"; in a later paper (Mossman 2013) he developed the argument that quantifying predictive validity is only part of the challenge: "justifying choices or clinical practices requires a contextual investigation of outcomes, a process that takes us *beyond simply knowing global indices of accuracy*" (italics added).

In part, such differences in the perceived importance of relative values in the 'trade-off' between false positives and false negatives will be determined by the role of the person doing the valuing within a given system: managers will be concerned about consequences of adverse outcomes to service reputation (Undrill 2007); politicians about criticism in the media; the public about 'community safety'; patients about potential impact on their future progress; and clinicians (it is to be hoped) about therapeutic impact on patients under their care as well as (understandably) the impact on their own professional standing and reputation.

2.3 Competing values in forensic mental health risk management

The inevitable conclusion that violence risk assessment and management, whether in forensic mental health or more generally, cannot simply be distilled to a debate about the scientific evidence is consistent with what the psychiatrist-philosopher Bill Fulford has called the "two feet principle" (Fulford *et al.* 2012). In brief, he argues that in psychiatry, and indeed in all branches of medicine, challenging dilemmas *always* require consideration of both the evidence base *and* the values base. The role of professionals and the services they make up is therefore to attempt to achieve optimal outcomes in a way that is cognisant of the various competing values as well as the contemporary empirical evidence base. Although this point was made when the evidence-based medicine movement first took hold (Sackett *et al.* 1992), the role of values has in practice tended to be relegated to secondary importance compared to technical aspects such as the finer details of meta-analytic data.

The range of competing values at play in the management of mentally disordered offenders can be usefully considered at three distinct interfaces:

- the patient and the service
- the service and society
- the patient and society.

Key considerations at each of these boundaries will now be considered. Then we consider how the relevant values come in to play in an everyday but complex risk management decision for forensic mental health services: determining the appropriateness or otherwise of permitting patients access beyond the confines of high secure hospitals and into the wider community on progressively graduated therapeutic 'community leave' programmes.

2.4 Patients and services: mutual expectations

Mental health policy throughout the developed world, including that pertaining to forensic services (Mann *et al.* 2014), is increasingly influenced by the tenets of the 'Recovery approach' (Skuse 2012). The Recovery approach does not comprise a tightly prescriptive set of rules but is rather "a set of ideas and principles derived from the experiences of people with mental health problems" (Boardman and Shepherd 2012). The various ideas comprising Recovery have been usefully distilled (Leamy *et al.* 2011) into five key themes:

- connectedness
- hope
- identity
- meaning
- empowerment.

The theme of 'empowerment' is perhaps superordinate to the others. In tandem with the Recovery movement, and its emphasis on realigning the *power balance* between patients and professionals, is an increasing contemporary emphasis on the notion of human rights: the United Nations Convention on the Rights of Persons with Disabilities (UN 2006) sets out as its first guiding principle "respect for inherent dignity, individual autonomy including the freedom to make one's own choices...".

The 'Secure Recovery' movement (Drennan *et al.* 2012) involves patients subject to the quotidian strictures of secure forensic services legitimately expecting a greater level of empowerment and autonomy than that traditionally afforded to them (Dempsey and Davey 2011) and staking a claim to such human rights. The precise meaning of Recovery for forensic patients is still in the relatively early stages of being worked out (Dorkins and Adshead 2011; Drennan and Alred 2012; Mann *et al.* 2014). One common theme, however, is that a Recovery approach to forensic rehabilitation will need to go *beyond* simply remedying criminogenic needs and include a greater emphasis on working with the narratives of patients, in such a way that facilitates both healthy independence (Jamieson *et al.* 2006; Jamieson 2006) and a 'meaningful life' involving social inclusion (Bouman *et al.* 2009).

A parallel legitimate expectation of patients, although less commonly articulated, is that they are provided with evidence-based interventions that are likely to facilitate progress. Interestingly, there is now emerging evidence that Recovery-based collaborative approaches to risk assessment and management may have some merit in this regard (Skeem *et al.* 2013) and that an emphasis on relational elements of care, when implemented in an informed fashion, may be the key to reducing long-term risk. Recovery can arguably be seen as "the foundation for change, including changing risk behaviour" (Barker 2012, 27). There are, of course, risks in a naïvely implemented version of this: many forensic patients will simply decline to collaborate with such a process; the general Recovery approach emphasis on strengths rather than deficits may paradoxically retard progress by resulting in inadequate attention being paid to those very deficits that have resulted in offending behaviour (Drennan *et al.* 2012). A balanced 'dual focus' on both risk and protective factors, whereby security and treatment are viewed as mutually enabling rather than 'dichotomous goals' is likely to be key to successful implementation of the Recovery agenda within forensic services (Simpson and Penney 2011).

The Recovery value of empowerment, mandating that patients will be granted their *rights* to a more powerful voice in their treatment, even within secure services, realistically must be balanced by an equal emphasis on the *responsibilities* of patients. There is great potential for long-term risk reduction benefits in a service model that genuinely commits to both values:

> a solution to the ongoing tension between public safety and the needs of the individual patient could come from recognition that the greatest public protection occurs when individuals take responsibility for managing their own risk…. Acceptance of patients' rights and responsibilities is at the heart of the recovery approach and could enhance risk management if understood and supported by the wider criminal justice system.
>
> (Carr and Havers 2012, 127).

There remains much work to be done, however, to determine exactly what this means in practice: as Simpson and Penney (2011, 304–305) point out, "the recovery movement is … largely silent on how to reconcile patient autonomy and accountability".

At the clinical level, the dialectic expectations between patient and service play out as specific 'tasks' for each party that are (ideally) made overt and documented in care plans, generally predicated on the setting and achieving of various 'goals'. Psychological research into goal-setting has established a useful distinction between 'promotion-focused' goals that aim to maximise gains versus 'prevention-focused' goals that aim to minimise losses (Halvorson and Higgins 2014). In the Recovery literature, Slade (2009) has articulated a similar (although subtly different) dichotomy between 'Recovery' and 'treatment' goals:

> Recovery goals: the individual's dreams and aspirations … based on what the person actively wants, rather than what the person wants to avoid.
>
> (2009, 160)

> Treatment goals: arise from the societal requirements and professional obligations imposed on mental health services to constrain and control

behaviour and improve health. These goals will normally be about minimising the impact of an illness and avoiding bad things happening, such as relapse, hospitalisation, harmful risk, etc. The resulting actions will often be doing-to tasks undertaken by staff. Treatment goals and associated actions provide the basis of defensible practice, and are important and necessary.

(2009, 160).

Forensic work must include an emphasis on the prevention-focused goal of avoiding future reoffending; ideally, this goal is 'owned' by both the patient and the service and hence has both 'treatment' and 'Recovery' aspects. Achieving a balance between promotion-focused and prevention-focused goals and their associated values is central to the service–patient relationship in forensic rehabilitation. It is inevitable that at times there is tension between these two sets of goals: a healthy interface between service and patient will work with this dynamic tension, acknowledging and working through points of conflict as they arise.

2.5 Society and services: mutual expectations

Forensic mental health services are expensive (Joint Commissioning Panel for Mental Health 2013): taxpayers understandably have robust expectations of such services. As well as the delivery of an acceptable standard of therapeutic care, media coverage and political discourse around this area suggest that the prime value placed by society upon forensic mental health services is that of public protection. Unfortunately, in this area, the rare but inevitable adverse outcomes involving forensic patients will inevitably be perceived to be due to a failure in assessment or management. The margin of error tolerated by societies with respect to decisions around discharge and community leave is considerably lower when there is a history of serious offending: it is understandable that decision-making bodies seek a much higher level of certainty around risk assessments when there is such a history (Carroll *et al.* 2004).

It is a given that humane and effective rehabilitation of mentally disordered offenders is unlikely ever to be a vote winner. Resourcing for this endeavour is generally recognised to be inadequate throughout the English-speaking world, with an increasing number of criminal offenders with serious mental illness being dealt with by means of imprisonment rather than secure hospital care (Butler *et al.* 2006). Worse, even when severe mental illness has been recognised by the courts to have negated criminal responsibility, some jurisdictions still lack the facilities for long-term diversion into hospital treatment – an egregious example of a broader trend whereby the great majority of mentally disordered offenders never make it into hospital-based rehabilitative care. Unfortunately, not only is prison "the worst place to treat the mentally ill" (Gilligan 2013) but there is good evidence that, following release from prison into the community, those with severe mental illness have a disproportionate burden of unmet needs in terms of mental (and indeed physical) health care (Harty *et al.* 2003; Kinner 2006).

If, therefore, the public and politicians have an expectation that mental health services help to deliver effective public protection, including the safe reintegration back into society of those with mental disorder who have committed serious crimes, then there exists a reciprocal obligation that populist agendas do not mean that resources for therapeutic rather than punitive approaches are lacking.

As well as advocacy for resources, however, services could usefully promote what might be termed a 'grown-up' discussion about risk. Discourses around risk events related to forensic mental health services, such as absconded patients or reoffending, are often fairly primitive in nature with public and media quick to assume that even very rare adverse outcomes are *ipso facto* evidence of inadequate or negligent care (McMahon and Dowsley 2009). This assumption, and the related false hope of risk-free services, must be repeatedly challenged. It has been demonstrated that much of the risk involved in returning mentally disordered offenders to the community is predicated on social factors rather than psychiatric symptoms in the narrow sense (Mullen 2006; Adshead 2014); clinicians could therefore usefully assert that risk management is a correspondingly broad responsibility, involving multiple domains beyond the clinical. A recent attempt in the UK to inject some honesty into the emotive debate around child protection (Easton 2013), to clarify for the public both the impossibility of guaranteeing safety for all and the nexus between funding and risk management, provides an inspiring example of a welfare service professional engaging the public in an honest and transparent way.

2.6 Patients and society: mutual expectations

Diversion into hospital-based rehabilitative environments and away from punitive prison dispositions following a serious offence, whether by means of 'hospital orders' or criminal defence based on mental illness, may be conceived as a social contractual exercise between patient and society. The standard sentencing aims of deterrence and retribution are appropriately set aside, but the aims of rehabilitation and public protection remain; the reciprocal demand, however, is that subsequent progress beyond secure hospital care is contingent on the patient adequately engaging with rehabilitative work designed to mitigate long-term likelihood of reoffending.

The extent to which amelioration of risk factors beyond those of active symptoms of mental illness ought to be determinative with respect to release is a matter for debate: consistent with European legal proclamations,[1] ongoing detention on the basis of perceived risk per se is criticized by some (Adshead 2014). In practice, however, it is difficult to envisage public acceptance of a model that permits release into the community after a very serious violent crime that is purely aligned with symptomatic recovery. Rightly or wrongly there is a societal expectation that patients will do what they can to optimise their chances of both clinical recovery *and* of desisting from further offending by engaging in broad-based rehabilitative programmes addressing 'criminogenic needs' beyond active psychiatric symptoms alone.

For their part, patients generally seek a pathway back into society beyond the walls of the secure institution. This aligns with the Recovery value of 'social inclusion'. The unfortunate role of stigma and social *exclusion* of course is not specific to forensic patients but is likely to be particularly relevant for them. Exclusion from services and employment remains a particular challenge for this group (Mezey and Eastman 2009), something which makes the creation of a 'meaningful life' and subsequent desistance from offending especially challenging. Unfortunately, the cultural stereotype of the dangerous psychiatric patient, fomenting fear and exclusion, remains prevalent in Western culture: remarkably, for the Halloween festival in 2013 (celebrated on 31 October each year), a major British supermarket released a 'mental patient' costume complete with bloodied meat cleaver – only withdrawn from the shelves after a gratifyingly loud social media outcry.[2]

As with any contract, therefore, obligations exist for both parties: the ultimate rehabilitative goal of successful community reintegration is contingent on both 'rehabilitative work' by the patient and a willingness to 'include' on the part of society. The latter will be manifest not only by policies and attitudes of employers, housing agencies and general health services but also by broader sociocultural norms. If clinicians fail to challenge norms that equate mental disorder with notions of evil and incorrigibility, or fail to promulgate the very real possibility of successful reintegration, then the rehabilitative task for their patients will continue to be more onerous than it needs to be.

2.7 Dissensus: a possible way forward

The dialectics between the competing values at the boundaries between patient, service and society have been with us in one form or another for centuries and are not likely to be resolved any time soon. Indeed the very notion of a 'final solution' to such discourses, as the history of the twentieth century suggests, may not be an especially desirable outcome. Where competing and legitimate values are at stake, Fulford *et al.* (2012) suggest that *consensus* as such may not always be achievable. However, in practice decisions *do* have to be made and these generally end up favouring one set of values over another. Fulford *et al.* (2012) have developed the notion of *dissensus* to describe a model whereby even when one set of values has trumped another, this is not a final, once and for all, trumping, but is contingent on the complex set of variables involved in each specific scenario and is hence revisable. This model recognises that such decision-making is never easy and that this very difficulty is a sign that thoughtful professional work is taking place.

To demonstrate how the dissensus model might operate in practice when such competing priorities are in play, let us now consider decision-making regarding therapeutic off-campus leave for forensic patients in secure care. Although these decisions are logically influenced by structured violence risk assessments of the kind discussed above, they are also influenced by concerns about absconding risk (a rare, and hence essentially impossible to predict, outcome) and, appropriately, by the range of values discussed in the foregoing section. Such programmes, although not subject to a great deal of empirical outcomes research, have great intuitive appeal to clinicians, with apparent benefits including the amelioration of the toxic effects of institutional life, maintenance of crucial daily living skills, and the facilitation of a slow and gradual restoration of healthy independence (Jamieson *et al.* 2006) in such a way that minimises the likelihood of relapse by imposing overly abrupt increments in levels of stress. Allowing patients to leave the confines of secure care and to journey into the community, whether with or without escorting staff, is controversial. Its rationale is poorly understood by the general public. The inevitable, if rare, adverse outcomes of absconding and/or reoffending will generally generate intense media and political scrutiny. Where such patients have seriously offended when out on leave, treating psychiatrists' careers have been threatened.[3]

The dilemma around when and if to permit off-campus leave to a particular patient at a particular time (which is dealt with by a range of decision-making persons and bodies, depending on the jurisdiction and legislative framework involved) pits the 'promotion-focused' goal of long-term therapeutic growth and social reintegration against the 'prevention-focused' goal of minimising short-term risks of harm to the public or to service reputation. Clinical experience and some research (Hilterman *et al.* 2011) suggest that negative outcomes such as absconding or reoffending on off-campus leave are rare. However, such negative outcomes tend to be 'concrete': highly visible and heavily publicised, with negative impacts on the standing of the service (and consequently perhaps for other patients under its care). The *benefits* of community programmes are conversely relatively hidden and 'abstract': multiple successful leaves and incremental rehabilitative improvement in patients leading to successful community reintegration does not make for a vote-winning news item of interest. If such outcomes receive any publicity it is only by means of aggregated research, likely to be read only by those with a direct interest in the field.

The key message is not that the granting of off-campus leave is always the 'correct' decision, rather that decisions around such leave sit within a complex matrix of competing values amongst a range of stakeholders. There exists a dynamic tension between competing values at each of the patient/service/society interfaces, and in any given case the strengths and weaknesses of each value may subtly vary. A dissensus approach recognises the need for balance and the need for case-based application of relevant values rather than simplistic formulaic responses. That said, as therapeutic clinicians, of course our general default position must be tilted towards emphasising values relevant to the promotional end of the spectrum (Duffy 2008; Parsons 2008): the point is that non-clinical values are also at play here and are not without legitimacy.

There is a range of other contentious areas where forensic mental health professionals could usefully apply a dissensus-based approach, considering the balance of promotional versus preventative values. The treatment of sex offenders, at least in Australia, has in recent years focused heavily on the preventative, with resourcing becoming heavily biased towards prolonged incarceration and

Table 2.1 Key variables for service, society and patient relating to the decision to grant off-campus leave

	Allowing off-campus leave for rehab	Not granting leave
Focus	Longer term: proactive to achieve a distant good (independence and safe discharge)	Shorter term: reactive to avoid an imminent harm
Values	Dignity; personal growth autonomy	Life preservation; Risk minimisation
Public perception	Can be counterintuitive *Why allow a killer to be on the loose?*	'Common sense' 'Secure' patients need security
Goal (anticipated benefits)	Enhance strengths Promotional	Reduce short-term risk of harm to public Preventative
Anticipated possible negative outcomes	Concrete; highly visible and publicised if patient absconds or involved in harmful behaviour – individual outcomes	Abstract; often invisible – if publicised at all, buried in aggregated research publications unlikely to gain a wide audience
Service: benefits	Evidence-based rehabilitative care	Reduced anxiety
Service: costs	Possibility of adverse reputational damage	Suboptimal treatment
Society: benefits (relatively 'silent')	Eventual discharge of rehabilitated service user	Not exposed to potential risk
Society: costs	Exposed to potential risk	Costs of ongoing expensive detention
Service user: benefits	Effective community reintegration	Limited, unless restrictions are carefully applied and limited
Service user: costs	Challenges capacity for accepting independence	Demoralisation and institutionalisation
Society: costs	Exposed to potential risk	Costs of ongoing expensive detention
Patient: benefits	Effective community reintegration	Minimal
Patient: costs	Minimal	Demoralisation and institutionalisation

incapacitation and with scant consideration for the promotional aspect of coherent treatment packages (Sullivan *et al.* 2005). The complexities of managing suicide risk within the prison context throw up another example of this dialectic: while professionals engaged in this task readily recognise both the impossibility of a risk free system and the inevitability (even desirability) of clinician discomfort (Bell 1999), post hoc inquiries inevitably emphasise the deficiencies in prevention, which in hindsight appear all too obvious.[4] The granting of parole to prisoners with a history of violence offers a third example: a recent report in the Australian State of Victoria (Callinan 2013) has resulted in a major shift away from the promotional values of safe and gradual reintegration with supports, towards preventative incapacitation by simply serving out a sentence – privileging short-term risk reduction and political expediency over longer-term public safety benefits.

2.8 Conclusion

Although relevant empirical research is crucial in determining the shape of future service delivery in forensic mental health, it is a fallacy to think that evidence alone will resolve the key debates within the field. There is a wide range of values at play in forensic mental health, many of which go well beyond simple clinical discourse. It will be incumbent upon clinicians in the field to engage with both politicians and the public in a 'grown up' discourse around these value-laden issues. A 'dissensus' approach that acknowledges the variety of values at play and seeks to engage and educate the public in respect of our core dilemmas holds some promise.

Notes

1 *Winterwerp* v. *The Netherlands* [10979] ECHR 6301/73.
2 www.glosswatch.com/2013/09/26/so-why-did-asda-think-a-mental-patient-halloween-costume-would-be-okay.
3 *Mezey* v. *South West London & St. George's Mental Health NHS Trust* [2010] EWCA Civ 293.
4 See for example Inquest into the death of Adam Sasha Omerovic [2014], available on the Coroners Court of Victoria website.

References

Adshead G. 2014. "Three faces of justice: Competing ethical paradigms in forensic psychiatry". *Legal and Criminological Psychology* 19: 1–12.
Andrews, D. A. and Bonta J. 2003. *The psychology of criminal conduct.* Cincinnati, OH: Anderson Publishing Co.
Barker R. 2012. "Recovery and Risk". In *Secure Recovery.* G. Drennan and D. Alred. Abingdon, Oxon: Routledge, 23–40.
Barry-Walsh J., Daffern M., Duncan S. and Ogloff J. 2009. "The prediction of imminent aggression in patients with mental illness and/or intellectual disability using the Dynamic Appraisal of Situational Aggression instrument". *Australasian Psychiatry* 17(6): 493–496.

Bell D. 1999. "Ethical issues in the prevention of suicide in prison". *Australian and New Zealand Journal of Psychiatry* 33: 723–728.

Boardman J. and Shepherd G. 2012. "Implementing recovery in mental health services". *International Psychiatry* 9(1): 6–8.

Bouman Y. H. A., Schene A. H. and De Ruiter C. 2009. "Subjective well-being and recidivism in forensic psychiatric outpatients". *International Journal of Forensic Mental Health Services* 8: 225–234.

Breakwell, G. M. 2007. *The Psychology of Risk.* Cambridge: Cambridge University Press.

Buchanan, A., Binder R., Norko M. and Swartz, M. 2012. "Resource Document on Psychiatric Violence Risk Assessment". *American Journal of Psychiatry* (ata supplement) 169(3): 1–10.

Butler T., Andrews G., Allnutt S., Sakashita C., Smith N.E. and Basson J. 2006. "Mental disorders in Australian prisoners: a comparison with a community sample". *Australian and New Zealand Journal of Psychiatry* 40(3): 272–276.

Callinan I. 2013. *Review of the Parole System in Victoria.* Melbourne, Victoria: Department of Justice.

Carr S. and Havers S. 2012. "Harnessing hearts and minds for change". In G. Drennan and D. Alred. *Secure Recovery.* Abingdon, Oxon: Routledge 115–129.

Carroll A., Lyall M. and Forrester A. 2004. "Clinical Hopes and Public Fears in Forensic Psychiatry". *Journal of Forensic Psychiatry and Psychology* 15(3): 407–425.

Dempsey J. and Davey I. 2011. "Lighting the match: consumer participation at Forensicare". *newparadigm* Autumn: 16–19.

Department of Health. 2002. *Learning from Bristol: The Department of Health's Response to the Report of the Public Inquiry into Children's Heart Surgery at the Bristol Royal Infirmary 1984–1995* (Cm. 5363) London: The Stationery Office.

Department of Health. 2007. *Best Practice in Managing Risk.* London: The Stationery Office.

Dorkins E. and Adshead G. 2011. "Working with offenders: challenges to the recovery agenda". *Advances in Psychiatric Treatment* 17: 178–187.

Douglas K. and Skeem J. L. 2005. "Violence risk assessment: Getting specific about being dynamic". *Psychology, Public Policy and Law* 11(3): 347–383.

Douglas K., Guy L. S. and Hart S. D. 2009. "Psychosis as a Risk Factor for Violence to Others: A Meta-Analysis". *Psychological Bulletin* 135(5): 679–706.

Douglas K. S., Hart S. D., Webster C. D. and Belfrage H. 2013. *HCR-20: Assessing Risk for Violence, Version 3.* Lutz, Florida: PAR.

Drennan G. and Alred D. 2012. "Recovery in forensic mental health settings: from alienation to integration". In G. Drennan and D. Alred. *Secure Recovery.* Abingdon, Oxon: Routledge, 1–22.

Drennan G., Law K. and Alred D. 2012. "Recovery in the forensic organisation". In G. Drennan and D. Alred. *Secure Recovery.* Abingdon, Oxon: Routledge, 55–72.

Duffy D. 2008. "Therapeutic Risk and Care Planning in Mental Health". In A. Hall, M. Wren and S. Kirby. *Care Planning in Mental Health.* Oxford: Blackwell Publishing, 37–47.

Eastley, T. 2013 "Dr Jayant Patel case leaves legacy of change in health". www.abc.net.au/am/content/2013/s3892392.htm.

Easton M. 2013. "Keanu Williams: Are the children of Birmingham safe tonight?" Retrieved 3 October 2013, from www.bbc.co.uk/news/.

Fazel S., Singh J. P., Doll H. and Grann M. 2012. "Use of risk assessment instruments to predict violence and antisocial behaviour in 73 samples involving 24,827 people: systematic review and meta-analysis". *British Medical Journal* 345: e4692.

Fazel S., Gulati G., Linsell L., Geddes J. R. and Grann M. 2009. "Schizophrenia and violence: systematic review and meta-analysis". *PLoS Medicine* 6(8): e1000120.

Fulford K. W. M., Peile E. and Carroll H. 2012. *Essential Values-Based Practice: Clinical Stories linking Science with People.* Cambridge: Cambridge University Press.

Gilligan J. 2013. *The evolution of forensic psychiatry.* Conference paper: Royal Australian and New Zealand College of Psychiatrists Faculty of Forensic Psychiatry Annual Conference. 18 July 2013, Darwin, Australia.

Halvorson H. G. and Higgins E. T. 2014. *Focus: Use Different Ways of Seeing the World for Success and Influence.* New York: Plume Books.

Hart S. D., Michie C. and Cooke D. J. 2007. "Precision of actuarial risk assessment instruments: Evaluating the 'margins of error' of group v. individual predictions of violence". *British Journal of Psychiatry* 190 (May): s60–s65.

Harty M., Tighe J., Leese M., Parrott J. and Thornicroft G. 2003. "Inverse care law for mentally ill prisoners: unmet needs in forensic mental health services". *Journal of Forensic Psychiatry and Psychology* 14(3): 600–614.

Hilterman E. L. B., Philipse M. W. G. and de Graff N. D. 2011. "Assessment of offending during leave: development of the Leave Risk Assessment in a sample of Dutch forensic psychiatric patients". *International Journal of Forensic Mental Health* 10: 233–243.

Holmes A. 2013. "Is risk assessment the new clinical model in public mental health?" *Australasian Psychiatry* 21(6): 541–544.

Jamieson E., Taylor P. J. and Gibson B. 2006. "From pathological dependence to healthy independent living: An emergent grounded theory of facilitating independent living". *The Grounded Theory Review* 6: 79–107.

Joint Commissioning Panel for Mental Health. 2013. *Guidance for Commissioners for Forensic Mental Health Services.* London: JCPMH.

Kinner S. A. 2006. "Continuity of health impairment and substance misuse among adult prisoners in Queensland, Australia". *International Journal of Prisoner Health* 2(2): 101–113.

Large M. 2009. "Dangerousness and risk assessment (letter)". Australasian Psychiatry 17(4): 336.

Leamy M., Bird V., Le Boutillier C., Williams J. and Slade M. 2011. "Conceptual framework for personal recovery in mental health: systematic review and narrative synthesis". *British Journal of Psychiatry* 199(6): 445–452.

Mann B., Matias E. and Allen J. 2014. "Recovery in forensic services: facing the challenge". *Advances in Psychiatric Treatment* 20: 125–131.

McMahon, S. and Dowsley A. 2009. "Killers, rapists and other criminally insane patients walking streets of Melbourne". *Herald Sun* Victoria, 6 November, 2009.

Mezey G. and Eastman N. 2009. "Choice and social inclusion in forensic psychiatry: acknowledging mixed messages and double think". *Journal of Forensic Psychiatry and Psychology* 20(4): 503–507.

Mossman, D. 2006. "Critique of Pure Risk Assessment or, Kant Meets Tarasoff". *University of Cincinnati Law Review* 75: 523–609.

Mossman, D. 2013. "Evaluating Risk Assessments Using Receiver Operating Characteristic Analysis: Rationale, Advantages, Insights, and Limitations". *Behavioral Sciences and the Law* 31: 23–39.

Mullen P. 1997. "A reassessment of the link between mental disorder and violent behaviour, and its implications for clinical practice". *Australian and New Zealand Journal of Psychiatry* 31: 3–11.

Mullen P. 2006. "Schizophrenia and violence: from correlations to preventative strategies". *Advances in Psychiatric Treatment* 12 (July): 239–248.

Parsons C. 2008. "The dignity of risk: Challenges in moving on". *Australian Nursing Journal* 15: 28.

Prins H. 1999. *Will they do it again?* London: Routledge.

Quinsey V. L., Harris G. T., Rice M. E. and Cormier C. A. 1998. *Violent Offenders: appraising and managing risk*. Washington, DC: American Psychological Association.

Sackett D. L., Haynes R. B., Tugwell P. and Guyatt G. H. 1992. *Clinical Epidemiology: A Basic Science for Clinical Medicine*. Boston: Little Brown and Co.

Sheppard D. 1995. *Learning the Lessons*. London: The Zito Trust.

Simpson A. I. F. and Penney S. R. 2011. "The recovery paradigm in forensic mental health services". *Criminal Behaviour and Mental Health* 21: 299–306.

Skeem J. L., Manchak S. M., Lidz C. W. and Mulvey E. P. 2013. "The Utility of Patients' Self-Perceptions of Violence Risk: Consider Asking the Person Who May Know Best". *Psychiatric Services* 64: 410–415.

Skuse D. 2012. "Recovery". *International Psychiatry* 9(1): 3.

Slade M. 2009. *100 ways to support recovery: a guide for mental health professionals*. London: Rethink.

Sullivan D. H., Mullen P. E. and Pathe M. T. 2005. "Legislation in Victoria on sexual offenders: issues for health professionals". *Medical Journal of Australia* 183(6): 318–320.

Szmukler, G. 2001. "The mathematics of risk assessment for serious violence". *Psychiatric Bulletin* 25(9): 359.

Troquete N. A., van den Brink R. H., Beintema H., Mulder T., van Os T. W., Schoevers R. A. and Wiersma D. 2013. "Risk assessment and shared care planning in out-patient forensic psychiatry: cluster randomised controlled trial". *British Journal of Psychiatry* 202(5): 365–371.

United Nations. 2006. "Convention on the Rights of Persons with Disabilities". www.un.org/disabilities/convention/conventionfull.shtml.

Undrill G. (2007). "The risks of risk assessment". *Advances in Psychiatric Treatment* 13: 291–297.

3   Beyond the risk paradigm

Maintaining the place of the client in criminal justice interventions

Chris Trotter

3.1 Introduction

This chapter provides a brief definition of the risk paradigm and the way it has influenced practice in the field of corrections. It questions some of the assumptions underlying risk-based approaches to criminal justice work, in particular that high risk offenders benefit more from intensive supervision and that low risk offenders are unlikely to benefit, that risk assessment profiles effectively predict risk of further offending and that risk assessment tools can help to determine the most appropriate offender needs or problems to be targeted during supervision. The chapter then considers some other criticisms of risk assessment and risk driven interventions including that they may create further disadvantage, and may lead to interventions that are worker directed rather than worker–client collaborations. Alternative approaches to risk driven assessment and interventions are then considered, including desistance models, the good lives model and a collaborative problem-solving model.

3.2 What is the risk paradigm?

What is the risk paradigm in criminal justice? Paul O'Mahony (2009) refers to a risk factors prevention paradigm which he suggests is currently the predominant discourse in youth justice and has been for the past 15 years. He defines this paradigm as involving an epidemiological approach to research and practice in youth justice which is based on the findings of studies of statistical correlations of various factors relating to offending and re-offending. Haines and Case (2008, 5) refer to the risk factors prevention paradigm as involving the identification of "key risk factors that increase the probability of offending and lead to the conclusion that criminality can be prevented by implementing measures designed to counteract them".

For the purposes of this chapter the risk paradigm is taken to refer to the central role of risk assessment and risk-driven interventions in work undertaken predominantly with offenders under community supervision. This includes adult and youth probation or other community corrections orders including parole. In particular the risk paradigm is informed by risk-related studies which identify correlates of offending such as age of first offence, previous criminal history, negative peer group associations, poor school performance, lack of family support or illegal drug use. These correlates are then incorporated into risk assessment tools which can be used to identify the level of risk of particular offenders. The levels of risk – commonly low, medium and high – are then used to allocate levels of supervision. The particular risk factors identified through the use of the risk assessment tool, for example illegal drug use, may then become the priority for supervision and for treatment. Following the completion of their risk assessment, offenders may receive one to one supervision which targets their criminogenic needs and/or may be required to participate in specialist programmes, to deal with those needs – for example, anger management groups, drug treatment programmes and various cognitive behavioural programmes.

Risk assessments may take place at the beginning of an offender's order and may be repeated on a regular basis, perhaps every three or six months, after the first risk assessment. The aim is for the risk score to progressively reduce as the offender is involved in risk-based supervision and treatment programmes.

Risk assessments and risk scores may also be used to inform parole boards and courts about the level of risk an offender poses to the community, in other words the likelihood that an offender will re-offend. Corrections workers often use actuarial risk assessment tools to determine risk levels and to help determine a plan for the offender, which is communicated to courts and parole boards. The risk assessment may be taken into account by courts and parole boards in determining the type of sentence given to an offender; high-risk offenders may receive harsher penalties.

The assessment of risk is prevalent in corrections departments, particularly community corrections departments, in most Western countries including the UK, USA, Canada and Australia. A number of actuarial risk assessment tools have been developed for general offender populations but also for specific populations, including for example sex offenders, offenders with psychiatric diagnoses or serious violent offenders. Risk assessment tools have also been developed to predict other types of behaviours such as violence in prison.

One of the most popular general risk assessment tools has been developed over many years by Andrews and Bonta (2010) largely with Canadian samples and is known as the Level of Supervision Inventory. It has various versions and forms including a youth version and is currently used in many probation services in Canada, the USA, the UK and Australia (Andrews and Bonta 2010). It contains a checklist of items including criminal history, education, employment, finances, family, accommodation, leisure, companions, alcohol and drug use, emotional issues and attitudes. Each of the items is broken down into sub-items, such as age at first offence, dissatisfaction with marital situation, or criminal acquaintances. A risk score is then derived with offenders classified as high-, medium- or low-risk depending on their score.

In gathering information to complete the risk assessment profile, the worker interviews the client and also collects information from other sources. For example, a probation officer may have information on file such as a police report and prior offences. The probation officer may also talk to an offender's parents or partner as part of the assessment process. In addition, they may talk to previous probation officers or other welfare professionals who have been involved with the probationer.

Risk assessment has gained wide acceptance in the field of criminal justice. Haines and Case (2008) argue that it has been embraced with much enthusiasm by policy makers and researchers because it appears to provide a theoretical and research base to corrections supervision and interventions and it is easy to understand for administrators and policy makers. It has met an important need in the context of community concern about crime.

3.3 The arguments for and against risk assessment

The core arguments in favour of the use of risk assessment profiles are: *first*, high risk offenders are likely to benefit from intensive supervision (in terms of reduced recidivism) whereas low risk offenders are unlikely to benefit and may even be harmed by intensive supervision, therefore levels of supervision should be adjusted according to risk levels; *second*, risk assessment profiles or tools can predict risk of further offending with considerable accuracy and more effectively than clinical or professional assessments; and *third*, risk assessment tools can help to determine the most appropriate offender needs or problems to be targeted during supervision. Let us look at each of these arguments.

High-risk offenders benefit from supervision; however, low-risk offenders do not benefit

A number of reviews of the studies on this issue have found that high risk offenders generally benefit from supervision more than low risk offenders and that low risk offenders tend to show minimal benefits (e.g. Bonta and Andrews 2010; Gaes and Bales 2011; Lowenkamp *et al.* 2006). Trotter (2013), on the other hand, in a review of studies in community supervision, found that in most of the studies medium-risk offenders benefitted more from high quality supervision than either high-risk or low-risk offenders. This review examined studies that considered the impact of supervision which was characterised by the use of effective practice skills including collaborative worker/client relationships, role clarification, pro-social modelling, problem solving and cognitive behavioural techniques. In only one of the seven studies reviewed was the impact of supervision greatest with high-risk offenders. In the other studies it was either greatest with medium-risk offenders or in some cases it was effective with all offenders under supervision regardless of their risk levels.

One of the complicating factors, therefore, in assessing the impact of supervision for offenders with different levels of risk is that the nature of supervision varies. It may be that supervision of a general nature or supervision that is not based on effective practice principles is best targeted towards high-risk offenders but that good quality supervision benefits offenders regardless of their risk levels. Two studies undertaken, one with adult offenders (Trotter 1996) and the second with young offenders under community supervision (Trotter 2012) found that offenders clearly benefitted from evidence-based supervision regardless of their levels of risk. The evidence-based supervision in each study was characterised by workers who displayed skills of role clarification, pro-social modelling and problem solving. There is some evidence, therefore, for the hypothesis that good quality supervision based on evidence-based principles is good for everyone but that supervision characterised by lack of adherence to evidence-based principles may be harmful for low-risk offenders. This view is supported by Trotter's (2012) youth justice study which found that low risk offenders, assessed using the Youth Level of Supervision/Case Management Inventory (YLS-CMI), had low levels of recidivism when supervised by workers with good skills but had high rates of recidivism when supervised by workers with poor skills. It does seem that the argument therefore that high-risk offenders benefit most from supervision may be difficult to sustain once the nature of supervision is taken into account.

The effectiveness of risk assessment predicting further offending

The second key argument in support of the risk paradigm is that actuarial risk assessment profiles can effectively predict re-offending rates of offenders placed on corrections orders and they can do this more effectively than assessments based on the professional or clinical judgements of corrections workers. This includes the use of profiles such as the Level of Service Inventory – Revised (LSIR) and the Youth Level of Service/Case Management Inventory (YLS-CMI), Asset – Young Offenders Assessment Profile and numerous other tools to predict recidivism among general groups of offenders. There are also numerous adaptations of the profiles to predict recidivism among specific groups, including for example offenders with intellectual disability, women, sex offenders, violent offenders and others (Baker et al. 2011; Fitzgerald et al. 2011).

The research does support the view that risk assessment profiles generally do predict risk more effectively than assessments by corrections workers using clinical or professional judgement. In fact there is evidence that workers overestimate their ability to predict risk through their professional judgement (Childs et al. 2014).

There are a number of examples, however, where in practice the actuarial risk assessment profiles are not completed accurately by staff and as a result they lose much of their predictive capacity. An Australian study (Ching et al. 2011) found that correlations between recidivism and the LSIR were often quite weak and in the range of 0.13 to 0.35 depending on the measure used. Correlations were even lower at 0.11 to 0.13 in a sample in Colorado in the USA (Dowdy et al. 2002). In a study undertaken in Australia with an early version of the Level of Supervision inventory the correlation was only 0.215 with any further offence and 0.312 for imprisonment. Slightly higher correlations with re-offending were found when the only measure used was the number of prior convictions. In this case the correlations were 0.279 and 0.313 respectively (Trotter 1995). In other words, the risk assessment profiles in these studies predicted no better than simply using an easily accessible measure such as prior convictions. The imprecision of risk assessment profiles was also highlighted in a study by Hart and Cook (2013, 81) using a violence risk assessment profile in a forensic mental health setting. They concluded that "without major advances in our understanding of the causes of violence, ARAIs (actuarial risk assessment inventories) cannot be used to estimate the specific probability or absolute likelihood of future violence with any reasonable degree of precision or certainty".

It seems therefore that while the LSIR and other profiles may be effective methods of measuring risk, their effectiveness is dependent on the profile being completed accurately, which in practice it may not. This perhaps relates to the generally variable acceptance of risk assessment tools by corrections workers. Baker *et al.* (2011) point to a number of studies which found that while workers sometimes find that risk assessment tools allowed for greater consistency, quality and defensibility they also often found them too time-consuming, de-skilling and that they add little to the decision-making process,

Risk profiles can help to determine the most appropriate offender needs or problems to be targeted during supervision

It is argued that risk assessment profiles can help to identify the criminogenic needs of offenders; in other words needs, problems or issues which are related to the person's offending. It is argued that addressing the needs which are related to offending will in turn lead to a reduction in those needs and this will in turn lead to reduced re-offending. Bonta and Andrews (2010) found that, based on a meta-analysis, interventions targeted towards criminogenic needs were related to a 19 per cent reduction in recidivism, whereas when they were targeted towards non-criminogenic needs they were related to a very slight increase in recidivism. They suggest that the major criminogenic needs include anti-social personality, pro-criminal attitudes, social supports for crime, substance abuse, family and marital relationships, school/work and lack of pro-social recreational activities. It is argued that where these factors are related to offending in individuals they should be targeted in supervision. Non-criminogenic needs include self-esteem, mental illness, anxiety and physical health and should not be targeted in supervision.

On the other hand there is a strong argument which derives from the general counselling literature that collaborative approaches which work from the client's perspective are most effective in changing behaviour (e.g. Hepworth *et al.* 2010). It can be argued that there is little point in focusing supervision on criminogenic needs if the client does not acknowledge that they have those needs. For example if a client does not believe that they have a drug problem, a peer group problem or a family problem then there is little point in focusing on those issues.

In Trotter's (2013) review of articles on effective probation supervision, most of the studies referred to the use of problem-solving techniques which were used to address criminogenic needs. The definitions of problem solving were reasonably consistent across the studies. The definitions involved identifying offence-related problems (e.g., family issues, school/work, drugs), setting goals to address the problems, and then developing strategies to address the goals. There was, however, variation in the way problem solving was undertaken, particularly in terms of the extent to which the problems to be worked on and the goals that are set were developed by the clients, the worker or the two in collaboration. Trotter (1996; 2012) emphasises, for example, working with client definitions of problems. Robinson *et al.* (2011) suggest that the most important aspect of the skill is allowing the client to articulate the problem and the potential solution. Taxman (2007) refers to working with one criminogenic need and at the same time working with an interest of the client in order to motivate the client to commit to the change process. Bonta *et al.* (2011), on the other hand, emphasise working with criminogenic needs that are identified through a risk assessment undertaken by the worker.

It seems that problem-solving is an effective method of addressing criminogenic needs. However, there remains some doubt about the extent to which problem-solving should be a collaborative process that involves working on offence-related issues as the client defines them or whether it should involve working on criminogenic needs that emerge from a risk assessment undertaken by the worker. An excessive focus by workers on identifying risk may effectively leave the client out of the supervision process.

3.4 Other criticisms of the risk assessment paradigm

Risk assessment penalises disadvantage and is therefore unfair

Arguments are posed relating to risk assessment and human rights. To take the LSIR again as an example: the LSIR, like other actuarial profiles focuses on a number of domains including education and employment, financial, family and marital, accommodation, leisure, companions, drug use, emotional and personal and attitudes. The offender's profile in each of these domains contributes to the overall risk score. This means that if an offender is unemployed, has financial problems, little or no family support, and is homeless, then they will score higher on the risk profile. Consistent with the risk principle, the offender should then be offered higher levels of supervision (Bonta and Andrews 2010) and it is argued this will lead to lower levels of re-offending. However, in practice high-risk offenders may receive more punitive interventions as a result of being classified as high risk. In studies of youth justice (Trotter 2012; Trotter and Evans 2012) the youth justice workers made more use of evidence-based practice skills with low- and medium-risk offenders and less use of the skills with high-risk offenders. It was clear that the high-risk offenders received higher levels of contact. However, this contact was characterised by more compliance-based supervision.

Moreover, information about risk levels may be provided to courts or parole boards and that information may influence the likelihood of release on parole or the severity of sentence imposed by courts. In practice, therefore, offenders may receive higher levels of punishment because they are socially disadvantaged. Low levels of education, poor work history, homelessness, poverty and absence of family support may well lead to greater likelihood of imprisonment than for a person who has committed a similar offence but does not suffer social disadvantage to the same extent. While risk assessment profiles do not include items such as race or intellectual disability, they do include many variables over which offenders have little control and which are essentially measures of social disadvantage – as such it might be argued that they contravene basic human rights. Kemshall (2008, 23) refers to the "blame-laden language of risk" which sees unemployment, for example, as "not a product of economic conditions but a product of the skill deficit".

The validation of risk assessment tools may be compromised by the nature of interventions

As discussed above, risk assessment tools such as the LSI have been developed by correlating variables in the characteristics of offenders, such as pro-criminal attitudes or employment, with re-offending rates. For the most part, these profiles have been developed using samples of offenders on probation or under another type of supervision. One of the variables in the likelihood of re-offending is the nature of supervision received by the offenders with the potential for evidence- based supervision to influence the likelihood of re-offending by as much as 50 per cent. In other words, the nature of supervision is as influential in predicting re-offending as the offender's prior offending or employment status. To take this argument to its logical conclusion, an effective assessment of the likelihood of further offending needs to take into account the nature of supervision to be offered; yet in most cases this cannot be estimated because of the individualistic nature of worker practices. Even if it could be estimated, it might lead to the somewhat ludicrous situation of similar offenders receiving different risk assessments based not on their needs but on the skills of their workers. This is a complex argument. However, it seems that predicting recidivism is complicated by the unpredictability of the effectiveness of subsequent supervision or other interventions.

Risk assessment tools may not be relevant for some minority groups

Risk assessment profiles have generally been developed with large groups of probationers and it has been argued that the principles which emerge may not be applicable to minority groups. For example, some risk profiles, while developed largely with male or mixed populations, have shown some predictability with women (Eisenbarth *et al.* 2012). On the other hand, it is argued that the variables included in risk assessment tools have been developed with male samples and in many cases are not applicable to women. For example, in a study in the USA of more than 300 women offenders Severson *et al.* (2007) found that their needs were often not identified through the standard risk assessment measures and that they often had other emotional needs and practical needs such as child care. Davidson (2011) argues that while the LSIR is relatively effective in predicting re-offending for women it ignores issues relating to past victimisation and trauma, which are important to women's rehabilitation. It is also argued that women's greater propensity to seek treatment for mental illness, drug use and past victimisation may lead to these issues being highlighted in the assessment and lead them to be over classified as high-risk.

3.5 Maintaining the place of the client in supervision

A number of authors have argued for alternative approaches to the risk paradigm in criminal justice interventions, approaches which place more focus on collaboration with offenders and greater focus on strengths rather than risks. There is not space here to go into these approaches in any detail. However, some brief descriptions of three approaches are offered: desistance, good lives and pro-social modelling.

Desistance

The concept of desistance is increasingly referred to in the criminal justice literature (see for example Maruna and LeBel 2010; McIvor *et al.* 2004; McNeill 2006). It refers to the study of people who desist from crime rather than the study of those who commit crime. The study of desistance is concerned with the factors which are associated with the progress away from criminal lifestyles such as natural maturation with age, the development of meaningful personal relationships, the gaining of work and money, and developing a self-concept which is non-criminal and pro-social. To put it very simply, the most common pathway to a crime-free lifestyle involves turning 30 years of age, and gaining a steady job and a regular partner. While the concept of desistance does not include a practical intervention model, those who work within the desistance paradigm are concerned to help offenders work towards their life goals and help them develop meaning in their life through means other than criminal activity.

Good lives model

The desistance concept has parallels with the good lives model developed by Ward and colleagues (e.g. Ward 2010; Purvis *et al.* 2014). The model was developed with sex offenders but the authors argue that it is relevant to other groups of offenders. They argue that offenders change as they acquire goods consistent with a good life. In helping offenders to change it is important that their progress towards happy, fulfilling lives is facilitated. It is argued that assisting individuals to acquire goods through non-offending methods will lead to a reduction in offending. It is based on the view that human beings seek to achieve certain goals in life and that criminal behaviours occur when they are unable to achieve those goals through non-criminal means. Rather than focus on risks, workers working from the good lives model focus on helping offenders to achieve their goals and focus on their strengths rather than their criminogenic risk factors.

Pro-social modelling

Both the desistance model and the good live model have much in common with an approach to work with offenders known as pro-social modelling (Trotter 2006, 2012; Trotter and Evans 2012). It includes three key components, role clarification, pro-social modelling and re-inforcement and collaborative problem solving.

The model can incorporate risk assessment tools with a collaborative problem-solving approach. It has been used in both adult corrections and youth justice and has proved to be effective in reducing recidivism rates by between 20 and 50 per cent when compared to the recidivism rates achieved through usual supervision.

The first step in the model involves helping the offender to understand the nature and purpose of the supervision, including the dual social control and helping role. The next step involves working with the client to identify issues which the client would like to work on as part of the welfare aspect of the supervision. Often this will need to be integrated with the risk assessment process.

There are several ways in which risk assessment may be undertaken. It might involve briefly identifying key variables such as prior offences, drug use, age or age of first offence, or it might involve a more detailed assessment based on an assessment tool such as the LSIR. Brief assessments have been found to predict re-offending with some accuracy (e.g. Trotter 1995). However, in many cases organisations use more detailed assessment tools.

If workers are expected to work through a risk assessment tool such as the LSI-R, this can be done in a manner consistent with collaborative problem solving. As the worker goes through the risk assessment items such as family, employment, associates, drug use or attitudes, the worker can ask the client if these are issues or problems which they would like to address as part of supervision. The worker can also encourage the client to identify issues which the worker believes may be related to the offending behaviour; the criminogenic needs. The issues to be worked on should, however, be chosen by the client, consistent with the research referred to earlier which suggest that interventions will be more effective if the client identifies the problems and goals to be addressed in the intervention (Trotter 2006; 2012). The worker can then work through the problem-solving process with the client identifying goals and setting strategies to achieve them. This method effectively integrates the risk assessment with collaborative problem solving.

The third step in the model involves identifying and reinforcing pro-social comments and actions displayed by the client. This involves for example using praise, file notes, appointment frequency or other strategies to encourage the client when they express pro-social sentiments such as victim empathy, seeking employment, using fewer drugs or associating with non-criminal peers. The worker should also model these values particularly in terms of being reliable and consistent. Using this method, the worker can also encourage the client to identify issues which seem to be related to offending but about which the offender may be in denial. The worker can reinforce any acknowledgement, for example that drug use has been unhelpful to the client. Through this method the worker can help the offender to address offence-related issues but do this through a strengths-based approach. The offender can be encouraged to collaborate in the supervision process rather than the worker identifying criminogenic needs and then expecting the client to work on them.

3.6 Conclusion

This chapter has questioned some of the assumptions underlying risk-based approaches to criminal justice work, in particular that high-risk offenders benefit more from intensive supervision and that low-risk offenders are unlikely to benefit, that risk assessment profiles effectively predict risk of further offending and that risk assessment tools can help to determine the most appropriate offender needs or problems to be targeted during supervision. The chapter has also considered some other criticisms of risk assessment and risk-driven interventions, including that they may further disadvantage disadvantaged offenders, and that they may lead to interventions which are worker-directed rather than worker/client collaborations. Alternative approaches to risk-driven assessment and interventions have been considered including desistance models, the good lives model and a collaborative problem-solving model.

References

Andrews D. A. and Bonta J. 2010. *The Psychology of Criminal Conduct.* Cincinnati, USA: Anderson Publishing.

Baker K., Kelly G. and Wilkinson B. 2011. *Assessment in Youth Justice.* Bristol, UK: The Policy Press.

Bonta J., Bourgon G., Rugge T., Scott T.-L., Yessine A. K., Gutierrez L. and Li J. 2011. "Community supervision: An experimental demonstration of training probation officers in evidence-based practice". *Criminal Justice and Behavior* 38(11): 1127–1148.

Childs K., Frick P. J., Ryals J. S., Lingonblad A. and Villio M. J. 2014. "A Comparison of Empirically Based and Structured Professional Judgment Estimation of Risk Using the Structured Assessment of Violence Risk in Youth". *Youth Violence and Juvenile Justice* 12(1): 40–57.

Ching-I., Hsu Caputi P. and Byrne M. K. 2010. "The level of service inventory-revised (LSI-R) and Australian offenders: factor structure, sensitivity, and specificity". *Criminal Justice and Behavior* 38(6): 600–618.

Davidson J. 2011. "Managing Risk in the Community: How gender matters". In R. Sheehan, G. McIvor and C. Trotter (2011) *Working with women offenders in the community.* Cullompton, Devon: Willan, 216–240.

Dowdy E. R., Lacy M. G. and Prabha Unnithan N. 2002. "Correctional prediction and the Level of Supervision Inventory". *Journal of Criminal Justice* 30(1): 29–39.

Eisenbarth H., Osterheider M., Nedopil N. and Stadtland C. 2012. "Recidivism in Female Offenders: PCL-R Lifestyle Factor and VRAG Show Predictive Validity in a German Sample". *Behavioral Sciences and the Law* 30(5): 575–584.

Fitzgerald S., Gray N. S., Taylor J. and Snowden R. J. 2011. "Risk factors for recidivism in offenders with intellectual disabilities". *Psychology, Crime and Law* 17(1): 43–58.

Gaes G. and Bales W. 2011. "Deconstructing the risk principle: Addressing some remaining questions". *Criminology and Public Policy* 10(4): 979–985.

Haines K. and Case S. 2008. "The Rhetoric and Reality of the 'Risk Factor Prevention Paradigm' Approach to Preventing and Reducing Youth Offending". *Youth Justice* (8) 5–20.

Hart S. and Cooke D. 2013. "Another look at the (im-)precision of individual risk estimates made using actuarial risk assessment instruments". *Behavioral Sciences and the Law* 31(1): 81–102.

Hepworth D. H., Rooney R. R., Dewberry Rooney G., Strom-Gottfried K. and Larson J. A. 2010. *Direct Social Work Practice*, 8th edn. Pacific Grove, California: Brooks Cole.

Kemshall H. 2008. "Risks, rights and justice: Understanding and responding to youth risk". *Youth Justice* 8: 21–37.

Lowenkamp C., Latessa E. and Holsinger A. M. 2006. "The risk principle in action: What have we learned from 13,676 offenders and 97 correctional programs?" *Crime and Delinquency* 52(1): 77–93.

Maruna S. and LeBel T. 2010. "The desistance paradigm in correctional practice: from programs to lives". In F. McNeill, P. Raynor and C. Trotter *Offender Supervision: New Directions in Theory and Practice.* Cullompton, Devon: Willan.

McIvor G., Jamieson J. and Murray C. 2004. "Desistance From crime: Is it different for women and girls?" In S. Maruna and R. Immarigeon (eds) *After Crime and Punishment: Pathways to Offender Reintegration.* Cullompton, Devon: Willan.

McNeill F. 2006. "A desistance paradigm for offender management". *Criminology and Criminal Justice* 6(1): 39–52.

O'Mahony P. 2009. "Risk Factors Prevention Paradigm and the Causes of Youth Crime: A Deceptively Useful Analysis?". *Youth Justice* 9: 99–114.

Purvis M., Ward T. and Shaw S. 2014. *Applying the Good Lives Model to the Case Management of Sexual Offenders: A Practical Guide for Probation Officers, Parole Officers, and Case Workers.* Brandon, VT: Safer Society Press.

Robinson C., VanBenschoten S., Alexander M. and Lowenkamp C. 2011. "A random (almost) study of staff training aimed at reducing re-arrest: Reducing recidivism through intentional design". *Federal Probation* 75(2): 57–63.

Severson M., Berry M. and Postmus J. 2007. "Risk and Needs: factors that predict women's incarceration and inform service planning". In R. Sheehan, G. McIvor and C. Trotter *What works with women offenders.* Cullompton, Devon: Willan, 61–90.

Taxman F. 2007. "The role of community supervision in addressing re-entry from jails". Paper prepared for Urban Institute, John Jay College and Montgomery County, Maryland's Department of Corrections and Rehabilitation Re-entry Roundtable on Re-entry from Jails.

Trotter C. 1995. *The Supervision of Offenders: What Works? First and Second Reports to the Criminology Research Council.* Department of Social Work, Monash University, and Department of Justice, Victoria.

Trotter C. 1996. "The impact of different supervision practices in community corrections". *Australian and New Zealand Journal of Criminology* 29(1): 29–46.

Trotter C. 2006. *Working with Involuntary Clients.* Sydney: Allen and Unwin.

Trotter C. 2012. "Effective Supervision of Young Offenders". *Trends and Issues in Criminal Justice*, 448.

Trotter C. 2013. "Reducing recidivism through probation supervision: What we know and don't know from four decades of research". *Federal Probation* 77(2): 43–48.

Trotter C. and Evans P. 2012. "Analysis of Supervision Skills in Juvenile Justice". *Australian and New Zealand Journal of Criminology* 45(2): 255–273.

Ward T. 2010. "The good lives model of offender rehabilitation". In F. McNeill, P. Raynor and C. Trotter (eds) *Offender Supervision: New directions in theory, research and practice.* Devon, UK: Willan, 41–64.

4   Risk management

Gloria Kirwan

4.1 Introduction

Acknowledging the entwined relationship that exists between risk assessment and risk management, this chapter sets out to focus predominantly on the latter, and to explore how it is theorised, operationalised and problematised within forensic practice. It is often the view that no real dividing line exists between risk assessment and risk management and that to separate them is to create a false boundary where none actually exists. This chapter offers no objection to this view but instead aims to place a spotlight on the phenomenon of risk management; it argues that as a topic risk management tends to be blended into discussions of risk assessment and somehow overlooked for sufficient consideration as an identifiable, if not fully distinct, entity in itself. As a consequence, risk management receives less focused attention in the research literature than its counterpart, risk assessment, (Nolan and Quinn 2012, 177; Koubel and Yardley 2012, 79) and quite often the terminology is used interchangeably to the point that such focused attention as there is on *risk management*, as distinct from *risk assessment*, becomes invisible.

This chapter aims to draw together current perspectives and highlight key debates on the issue of risk management in order to assist awareness of this less-illuminated side of the risk assessment/risk management coin. To this end, the chapter explores how different writers interpret risk management and the opposing configurations that can be applied. The wider literature is used to identify the processes that drive or shape success in risk management strategies as well as the factors that can act as impediments to effective risk management practices. Working with risk leads practitioners into the territory of certainty and uncertainty and this chapter also considers the implications of both in terms of service delivery and professional education.

4.2 The rhetoric of the risk imperative

Risk can be understood as the likelihood of either positive or negative outcomes. Titterton (1999, 220) explains risk as a calculation of future benefits or harms. However, for the purposes of this chapter, the discussion of risk management is focused specifically on the narrower interpretation of risk, which understands it to mean potential hazards or dangers and risk management as the interventions and the strategies which aim to deal with those identified hazards or dangers. Across many domains, the ideas of Beck (1992; 1997) and Giddens (1993; 1998) have influenced our understanding of developments within late modernity which have brought a societal focus on this form of risk. Beck's (1992) depiction of the 'risk society' exposes the relationship between ideas of danger and of control whereby the greater the societal awareness of danger(s), the greater the impetus to control it. Giddens' (1993) concept of 'risk culture' describes how the risk society has adopted the view that risk can be controlled or eliminated by the application of procedural safeguards and scientifically informed interventions. While Rose (1998, 180) disputes the existence of the risk society as a homogenous entity, he acknowledges that the focus on risk in certain areas of life, such as the mental health services, is in response to the shared desire to bring "uncertainty under control".

As outlined in more detail in earlier chapters, risk as a concept, including its assessment and management, has moved into central position as a key focus of forensic practice. Writing about healthcare systems in general, Godin (2006, 1) comments: "'Risk assessment' and 'risk management' have become insistent imperatives, which shape a diverse range of health care." This imperative is nowhere more clear-cut than in forensic services which of themselves have become one of the main societal systems for dealing with risk, particularly any risk which is posed (or perceived to be posed) by people positioned at the intersection between criminal justice and mental health service systems. To complement their knowledge base, forensic professionals have used legislation as a means by which they can legitimately exercise risk interventions designed to prevent or eliminate danger where it is identified. Within this socio-political context, resources are allocated to support the work of protective systems, including law enforcement and forensic services. The growth of expertise as well as the resourcing of and investment in expert systems and the monitoring of the effectiveness of these systems have been labelled by Prins (1999, 7) as the "risk industry".

As actors in the risk industry, forensic practitioners find themselves performing something of a high wire act in terms of delivering services in the best interests of their clients while at the same time being charged with ensuring the exigency of a risk-free society. The weight of public reaction when danger is not contained inexorably contributes to risk-focused decision-making and interventions by some practitioners. In light of the thrust towards risk elimination now pervasive in the risk society, the focus on risk in forensic practice is dominated by a concern with risk assessment which is seen as the key means by which accurate risk prediction can be made. Leaving aside for the moment the debate on whether or not it is ever possible to contain or control all hazards or dangers with any degree of certainty, this chapter argues that such a strong focus on risk assessment detracts attention from the management of risk and leaves many relevant issues unexplored and under-researched. It is the factors that surround how

risk management decisions are made and, in particular, how they are implemented (as opposed to how risks are identified or determined in the first place)
that is the precise focus of this chapter. ✓

4.3 The juxtaposition of risk assessment and risk management

It is helpful at this point to make a clear distinction between risk assessment and
risk management. Thompson and Thompson (2008) describe risk assessment as:

> A process of identifying the risks involved in a particular situation, considering
> how likely it is that a particular untoward event will occur (abuse, self-harm or
> suicide, for example) and their likely or possible impact if they do occur.
>
> (2008, 207)

They contrast this with risk management, which they view not as an assessment
exercise but as the planning phase and related actions which are taken on foot of
the risk assessment. Similarly, Carson and Bain (2008) distinguish between risk
assessment (the identification of likely harm) and risk management (the actions
that follow the risk assessment): "Risk assessment provides the setting, and key
information, for risk management to focus on" (2008, 145).

Carson and Bain (2008, 146) refer to the work of Heilbrun (1997) who, in differentiating between risk assessment and risk management, argued for recognition
of the important contribution of risk management to service delivery. Adopting
the same perspective, Titterton (2005) believes risk management, as distinct
from risk assessment, has received less attention in the broader literature and is
often overlooked as a logical and important response to the risk assessment. He
says this leaves "an unbalanced approach where insufficient attention is paid to
the management of risk" (Titterton 2005, 88).
　Titterton (2005, 88) also draws from Reed (1997) on the need to achieve a
better balance between risk assessment and risk management in the interest of
improved service delivery: "Risk assessment alone is not enough; it must be
accompanied by a risk management plan which includes review procedures"
(1997, 5). It is important also not to over-simplify the complexities of progressing from the stage of risk assessment into the phase of risk management (Nilsson
et al. 2009). Even to suggest that risk assessment and risk management stand
alone as two distinct phases is to mislead. It is more useful to see them as
entwined, interactive but distinctive parts of a total action, which has as its aim
the delivery of a service where hazards or dangers are part of the narrative that
has led to professional involvement. Vitacco *et al.* (2009) make the point that
risk assessment and management approaches need to take into account both the
static factors and the dynamic features of individual situations if they are to be
effective but that this is a complex task for any professional, involving as it does
the balancing of hazards and safety.

Writing on the experience of working with young people detained in secure units, Biven (2002) offers a descriptive insight into the multiple factors which can present in the individual profiles of service users, often including both current issues such as behavioural problems and historical issues such as childhood abuse or neglect. The breadth and depth of empirical knowledge required to respond adequately to this wide spectrum of factors is not achievable by one singular discipline. Hence the importance commonly attached to multi-professional input.

Furthermore, to portray increased attention to risk management as a solution that will of itself resolve all risk is to raise expectations that may often be unachievable. Depicting risk management as a means to removing all risk is to simplify a process which is intrinsically complex. As Ryan posits: "There can never be a risk free environment or situation. To talk of risk management in terms of risk removal is unhelpful and raises expectations" (1996, 93). Bernstein (1998, 229) expounds on the essential futility of trying to remove all risk and refers to Keynes' (1937) concept of 'uncertain knowledge' and the impossibility of precisely calculating all outcomes in life, particularly those involving human agency in a future context. Developing this view, Hall (2014) suggests that dealing with uncertainty is a core concept in professional work and he calls for a heightened focus on the pedagogy of uncertainty in professional education.

If it is not always possible to eradicate danger and predict outcomes, what then should be the focus of risk management and what its stated objective? The literature reveals the conceptualisation of risk management as a deeply contested space wherein the push for certainty and risk removal competes with attempts to incorporate acknowledgement for the enduring uncertainty of human behaviour. The following section sets out the two main opposing views on risk management and from there considers how these viewpoints influence the approaches adopted by professionals who encounter risk in their work within forensic or other services.

4.4 Dialectical conceptualisations of risk management

Interpreting the aim of risk management seems straightforward at first glance in the context of the risk society and the accompanying imperative to eliminate danger. However, two main perspectives identified in the literature on professional responses to risk offer contrasting interpretations of the purpose of professional risk management.

By taking on the task of managing risk, forensic practitioners are charged with a somewhat double-edged sword. On the one hand, they carry professional responsibilities to individual clients and people closely connected to those clients, such as families and carers. On its own, this set of responsibilities contains multiple ethical and therapeutic issues. However, alongside the clinical focus, forensic practitioners also occupy a societal position which carries with it the imperative to protect society from dangers posed by human behaviour. Individual forensic practitioners can vary in the extent to which they are consciously aware of this dual set of responsibilities inherent in their role. However, given the potentially contentious nature of such a position, it is helpful for practitioners to identify some theoretical signposts both to inform and interpret their professional approach to risk management.

In the main, the theoretical perspectives of risk management available to practitioners fall into two main, but dialectically positioned, categories: risk elimination (sometimes referred to as risk minimisation) and risk-taking. Titterton (2005) helps us to contrast these two polarisations of risk management. Risk minimisation he places alongside surveillance and control; risk-taking he positions with ideas of client empowerment and participation. As part of the risk management debate, he believes further attention is required to be paid to the limits versus the potential of both conceptualisations of risk management.

Almost a decade earlier, Davis (1996) elaborated these two distinct perspectives within which risk can be understood and managed. In the framework she outlined, the risk minimisation model focuses on identifying serious risk and the mobilisation of interventions necessary to reduce or eliminate the identified dangers or hazards. In this light, risk management represents a set of specialised practices operating within a risk perspective that ultimately aims to control or remove risk and danger posed by individuals in society. "In effect, the risk minimization approach locates risk in a deficient and potentially dangerous minority of individuals who need to be identified, registered and managed by medication and surveillance" (1996, 113). The risk elimination paradigm draws on scientifically based procedures and tools to predict, identify, calculate and, when necessary, remove dangers in the social landscape. In a world perceived to be unsafe, its main aim is to deliver reassurance that dangers or hazards can be contained; the science of risk calculation and removal is the foundation on which this whole perspective rests.

In contrast, Davis depicts the risk-taking approach in professional practice as rooted in an empowerment paradigm. It privileges self-agency above protective practice when on balance the anticipated benefits of promoting the autonomy of the client appear to outweigh the possible but not definite negative consequences. Although risk-taking can incorporate the use of checklists, procedural guidelines and other tools of probability calculation, it incorporates an ideological shift which embraces a value-informed approach to risk management that is aligned with client-centred practice and client self-determination perspectives. Davis (1996) draws on service user research to help us see that risk comes in many forms and that the responses to it often flow directly from whatever perspective is driving the intervention:

> When people using mental health services are asked about the elements which contribute to hazard and risk in their own lives they are likely to point to the part that poverty, poor housing, unemployment, crime, stigma and social exclusion play ... a perspective which contrasts sharply with the diagnostically and service-driven perspectives of many mental health practitioners.
>
> (1996, 115)

From this viewpoint, the unique circumstances of the service user must be taken into account and the individual understood as part of a wider system. In the assessment and management phases, predictive checklists and other means of calculating probability are useful, but interpreting the behaviour of the service user in the context of their lived reality is also regarded as vital (Stalker 2014, 214).

It is clear, therefore, that the risk-taking framework can accommodate ideas of uncertainty (in which the professional accepts they cannot predict everything), but Koubel (2012) explains this does not render the risk management task any easier. For example, Heyman and Davies (2006) highlight the complex decision-making processes that can enter service delivery when practitioners seek to find a balance between autonomy of service users and general issues of safety. Horton (2006) explores a similar point in her discussion of the challenges for practitioners in managing risk while simultaneously promoting independence in the care of older adults. Adopting the risk-taking paradigm will confront practitioners with the challenges of uncertainty at both theoretical and practice levels. Manthorpe (2007), for example, makes the distinction between reasonable and excessive risk-taking strategies and suggests that the implementation of a risk-taking approach to risk management may require the establishment of additional procedural safeguards thus leading to increased risk-related bureaucracy: "The notion of reasonable risk taking may actually require further protocols in order to discern the reasonable from the excessive … [and] prove problematic due to the administrative burden of an increasingly formalized risk bureaucracy" (2007, 237–238). It is fair to say that neither risk elimination nor risk-taking is easily achieved in the reality of practice settings. It also appears that service providers are not permanently locked into one perspective or another. Kirwan (2010) found that service providers gravitate towards one risk management framework or the other depending on the case-related factors which they encounter. In this study, practitioners favoured risk minimisation interventions in situations where they identified an immediate threat to life or physical safety. For example, in case studies involving the presentation of acute psychotic symptoms the research participants favoured risk-minimization interventions. In case examples where the dangers were viewed as less acute or critical, but where a degree of risk was present nonetheless, the research participants displayed greater openness to considering risk-taking approaches. It emerged clearly in this study that the service providers were concerned to engage with the multiple levels of need and risk that they identified in the case vignettes they were asked to consider and they drew flexibly in their proposed responses from both risk elimination and risk-taking paradigms of risk management. Nolan and Quinn (2012, 181) report similar findings in their study where their participants interpreted the need to match the risk management approach with the needs of the individual service user rather than simply adopt 'a uniform approach' in all cases.

It is clear then that the implementation of a risk management strategy or set of practices, although complicated in itself, will also be influenced by many context-specific factors. The next section considers additional factors that can impact, positively or negatively, on the delivery of risk management services.

4.5 Risk management in practice

While forensic risk management practice can be located in a societal and expert-system context, the day to day reality for practitioners is that their work is also carried out within an organisational culture and is shaped by the individual inputs of the various professionals involved in the actual risk management task. Therefore, as a set of activities that follow the outcome, or provisional outcome, of risk assessment, risk management is a culturally bounded and socially constructed action. Organisational cultures and societal influences can be powerful forces, but the awareness of risk, the interpretations of risk assessments and the wider skills base that the network of service providers carry into any individual case also all play a part in shaping the quality of the risk management strategy. Moreover, there are many tensions which may arise in the implementation of a risk management plan. Differences may emerge within the professional network regarding how best to balance risk versus gain, autonomy versus protection and the safety of others versus the freedom of the individual service user.

The broader literature reflects awareness of and a general concurrence with the view that no one professional, acting alone, can adequately respond to the complex issues and general uncertainties that arise in cases involving risk, particularly in the context of forensic services. The dominant discourse within the literature suggests that in situations of acute risk, practitioners with different professional expertise need to come together to make decisions, formulate responses and deliver appropriate interventions (Johnson 2009) and that multidisciplinary responses are better resourced to address the needs of individual service users adequately (Maschi and Killian 2011, 27).

Under the aegis of this type of multidisciplinary intervention, there is a societal expectation that professionals will manage risk, or more precisely that they will eliminate it or at least contain it. The role of the professional thus becomes one of managing complexity and the public places trust in the expertise of professionals to carry out this role on behalf of society (Alaszewski and Brown 2007), particularly in cases of serious risks that may arise in the forensic context. However, in reality, there are many factors that affect the overall success of any multidisciplinary risk management strategy in forensic practice. Many of these factors are also present in other systems that deal with risk such as child protection services and services for older people, and the literature on risk in a range of contexts is therefore useful for this discussion.

The first set of factors that influences the outcome of risk management interventions returns us to the risk assessment/risk management loop as without a careful assessment, risk management rests on less than solid foundations. Taylor and White (2001) point to the fundamental expectation that the actions of professionals will flow from an informed and considered position, based on the facts of any given situation and with reference to their disciplinary knowledge and skills. They indicate that when serious incidents occur, any shortfall or perceived shortfall of rigorous assessment by service providers leaves them open to criticism for making: "bad decisions based on gut feelings or common sense rather than objective, dispassionate ones based on careful appraisal of the evidence and recourse to broader, research-based generalizations about problems and effective solutions" (2001, 40). For professionals, utilising a scientific evidence base as the scaffold of their practice provides them with the advantage of being able to reasonably justify or explain their professional judgements and actions. Broadhurst *et al.* (2010), for example, favour evidence-based practice for the objectivity and clarity it brings to decision-making. However, Taylor and White (2001, 39) argue that scientifically informed service delivery is not straightforward where risk is a central issue. Likewise, Rogers (2000, 595) refers to "the perils and pitfalls regarding any uncritical acceptance of risk assessment". Schön's distinction (1991, 42), echoed later by Thompson (2000, 107), between the "high, hard ground ... of research-based theory and technique" versus the "swampy lowland where situations are confusing 'messes' incapable of technical solution" captures the inherent disjuncture which sometimes exists in trying to apply knowledge or theory in any particular case. In the field of child protection, a number of past studies suggest that service providers, on occasion, apply knowledge in an unsystematic way (Munro 1999). In later research on child protection services, Buckley (2000, 261) also found that the social workers in her study "rarely theorised in an informed and explicit manner". She strongly advocates for professional education to better equip service providers with the ability to apply theory to what she describes as the "political and value-laden context of daily work" (2000, 261). Although these studies were not specifically referring to practice in the forensic context, it is argued here that similar tensions can arise in forensic practice between the appeal of neatly applied scientific theory versus the challenges of applying it to the complicated realities of individual situations.

The difficulties for forensic practitioners in theorising their practice are compounded by the lack of agreement within the research literature on predictors of violence/danger/risk or on how best to balance any identified hazards against identified signs of safety. For example, Gunstone (2003) refers to "the Grey Areas" or factors which may or may not contribute to overall outcomes for service users, including issues such as self-neglect and non-compliance with treatments. Taylor and White (2001) advise social workers to reflexively analyse the evidence base and the practice wisdom they incorporate into decision-making and in similar vein forensic practitioners need to be critically judicious regarding their use of professional knowledge and expertise. However, Heyman (2010a; 2010b) helps us understand the expansiveness of risk management which he suggests involves risk managers in activities such as "categorizing, valuing, uncertain expecting, and time-framing" (2010a, 34) and from this perspective it is clear that integrating theory with risk management practice is a very complicated task.

It is widely accepted that multidisciplinary input can enhance service provision to clients and Thompson (1995, 78) encourages service providers involved in multidisciplinary work to support each other and to acknowledge and appreciate each other's roles and pressures. However, the wider literature also acknowledges the problems that can arise due to lack of understanding across disciplines about each other's levels of expertise or the nature of what each can deliver. Barnes *et al.* (2000, 565) note the potential for difficulty in multidisciplinary collaboration arising from paradigm clashes related to "different models of mental health, conflicting value systems, divergent approaches to care and treatment, and distinct organizational cultures". There exists, it seems, a tension across a range of service systems and between disciplines regarding the validity of different currencies of knowledge. Such misunderstandings can lead to problems of communication and collaboration including breaches of trust or respect between professions or organisations (Hornby and Atkins 2000; Horwath 1999) or failure to locate and communicate with the relevant people who can help contribute to the risk management strategy. For example, this could include failing to call a case conference (Stanley and Manthorpe 2001) which can leave individual practitioners carrying more responsibility for the welfare or safety of a client than their role or level of expertise can support. Maddock (2014, 13) illuminates how failures of communication impede what he describes as "patient-centred collaborative practice". It is clear that the implication of these factors for professional risk management is that it is carried out in a bumpy terrain of competing paradigms and different perspectives. Walton (1999) suggests: "Practice by the main professional groups within the mental health system is underpinned by different, often competing but broadly legitimated, theories of mental health, distress and help ... these disciplines [cannot] be spliced together unproblematically..." (1999, 379). Clashing perspectives, misunderstandings and failure to find common theoretical ground, while troublesome, can also directly contribute to failures in systems of care and in responses to identified risks. Johnson (2009, 165) captures this point succinctly by stating that "those differences of perception often serve to impede the workforce, rather than inform it". If we are to develop improved risk management responses, we need deeper insight, informed by further research, into the processes, knowledge sources and any other factors that influence how practitioners can best work together to deliver successful risk management services.

A different phenomenon which also influences the quality of risk management service delivery is highlighted by Brown *et al.* (2000) which they refer to as "creeping genericism" (a term first introduced by Patmore and Weaver (1991)). It describes situations in multi-professional contexts where roles become overly blurred and the different disciplines involved in a case believe they can do any of the tasks that are required, somehow forgetting the distinctive features of the individual disciplines' knowledge bases. Consequently, Brown *et al.* (2000) argue service users can be deprived of the benefit of specialist skills and knowledge. In contrast, Williams (2002, 120) identifies what he refers to as "competent boundary spanners", that is, professionals who achieve successful levels of cross-disciplinary collaboration without the loss of their own professional identity or focus.

Poor comprehension of the distinctive theoretical and philosophical foundations of different disciplines can lead to tensions in the delivery of multidisciplinary services. Reflecting on findings from child abuse inquiries in the aftermath of serious failures to protect vulnerable children, Horgan (1996) identifies obstacles to multi-professional collaboration which include differences in values, practices and professional ethos "arising from a range of social, cultural and historical processes" (1996, 4). A different limitation is noted by Stevenson (1989) who cautions against investing high expectations into multidisciplinary service systems. She references Packman and Randall's (1989) point that the issues that arise in risk-laden cases are not always amenable or responsive to professional intervention and that even the best multidisciplinary collaboration can fail to resolve intractable or unsolvable risks. In their view, cross-disciplinary collaboration of itself, despite the many arguments in its favour, offers "no panacea or magic power" (1989, 104).

From a completely different stance, Richards and Horder (1999) lament the absence of debate on the merits of multidisciplinary collaboration, except for Pinker (1990) whom they report as stating that "partnership is humbug" and a "waste of time". Simic (1995, 137) believes that 'collaboration' and 'partnership' are "buzzwords of the nineties" which carry overly optimistic blanket expectations of what a multidisciplinary network can offer in all situations. Other writers, too, have highlighted potential weak spots in multidisciplinary intervention. For example, Buckley (2002) reminds us of Blyth and Milner's (1990) concern about collaborative partnerships potentially becoming too comfortable or even collusive. Imber-Black (1988) highlights the problems that can arise for service users when too many service providers become involved in their care, including being overburdened with appointments and possibly receiving conflicting advice and guidance.

Yet, despite these reservations, multidisciplinary approaches carry considerable advantages in terms of delivering risk management interventions. The literature notes the repeated calls from many inquiry reports (Bailey 2012; Howlett 1996; Rose 1996; Ryan 1996) for greater multi-professional collaboration. Many of these reports consistently highlight and strongly condemn failures of communication and cooperation in the professional network.

However, despite the importance attached to it, multidisciplinary and/or cross-agency collaboration is fraught with difficulties which at times serve to diminish its potential. Suter et al. (2009, 48) found effective communication and shared understanding of each other's roles as the two most valued competencies which practitioners believed underpinned effective collaboration. However, Williams (2002) makes the point that the essential ingredients of a successful professional network, including the necessary practitioner skills and abilities, may not always be present. At a micro level, relationship factors arising in the professional network, for example, may influence the success or otherwise of multidisciplinary approaches. These may involve relationship issues between disciplines or within disciplines such as role competition, role confusion or hierarchical power struggles (Suter et al. 2009; Buckley 2002; Hornby and Atkins 2000; Scott 1997; Abramson and Mizrahi 1994, 1996; Grunbaum and Gammeltoft 1993; Reder et al. 1993). A number of writers trace difficulties in multidisciplinary collaboration to the different educational traditions of the various disciplines which can give rise to conflicting perspectives on individual cases (Hall 2005; Secker and Hill 2001; Hornby and Atkins 2000; Buckley 1999; Birchall 1995). For example, based on a case study of a multidisciplinary mental health team, Maddock (2014) revealed that team members were incorporating diverse and at times contradictory models of mental illness, drawn from their educational backgrounds, into their attempts at joint work. The ethical imperatives of the various professions and differences in professional values may also put a strain on multidisciplinary collaboration (Bailey 2012, 12; Horgan 1996) and the different processes of professional education may not prepare practitioners well in terms of how best to collaborate effectively with other disciplines (Hall 2005; Freeth 2001). A common example of how these different traditions can influence practice arises in terms of the varying judgements by practitioners on how best and when to share case-sensitive information or concerns appropriately with other professionals and agencies.

Apart from the multidisciplinary issues that can deplete the effectiveness of risk management interventions, at a wider level, organisations themselves may also contribute to promoting or limiting the possibility for effective collaboration (Adams 2012, 59). Scott (1997, 73) points to the "significance of organizational culture, structure, mandate and imperatives" and how these influence the success or failure of professional collaboration. For over two decades, the literature has highlighted a range of organisational factors that can impede multidisciplinary service delivery including agency morale, unclear hierarchies of accountability, dysfunctional group or management processes, high staff turnover and unfilled vacancies or lack of resources (Bailey 2012; Buckley 2002; Reder *et al.* 1993).

When two or more organisations need to work together, an even wider range of factors can also influence the outcome of risk management work including differences in organisational philosophy, culture or ethos (Morrison 2002; Ferguson 2001; Barnes *et al.* 2000; Scott 1997; Reder *et al.* 1993), different rotas and hours of work which impede communication between service providers located in different agencies (Buckley 2002; Reder *et al.* 1993) and lack of co-terminosity, which may confuse communication and understanding between service providers (Exworthy and Peckham 1999). Collaboration can suffer when protocols do not exist between agencies or practitioners fail to implement them (Buckley 2002) or when there is inadequate sharing of information between agencies (Stanley and Manthorpe 2001). Heyman (2010a, 33–34) raises the issue of risk ownership, a concept he links with ideas of corporate governance and accountability. He makes the point that in a service system the risk owner may not necessarily be the frontline worker but someone further up the hierarchical chain of command who holds responsibility for the services delivered by a particular team or agency. As Heyman (2010a) points out this can lead to tension when those on the frontline feel they carry out the direct work but do not hold the mandate to make decisions.

At the macro level, Glover-Thomas (2011), echoing a similar point by Perkins and Repper (1998, 44), highlights the tensions which can arise for practitioners in fulfilling their risk management mandate while simultaneously protecting the rights of service users. This illuminates the sometimes contradictory demands on practitioners, where on the one hand they are required to control the risk-related behaviour of service users while at the same time they are ethically bound to respect the views, wishes and autonomy of the same individuals. The views of service users, once a silent topic in the forensic arena, are now gaining increased research attention, not only in forensic services but also in the wider health and mental health systems (Crossley 2006). There is also a growing literature on the benefits of incorporating service user consultation, participation and feedback into how health services of all kinds are evaluated and how outcomes are measured (Tait and Lester 2005; Simpson and House 2002). Stewart *et al.* (2012), for example, offer an interesting discussion on both the possibilities as well as the limitations of incorporating service user views into the evaluation of a group treatment programme in a forensic setting.

4.6 Conclusions

In contemporary society, risk, in the form of danger or hazard, is unwanted and the expectation is that professionals will act to control it. To deal with dangerous or potentially dangerous human behaviour, a risk industry has been constructed, staffed by certain expert disciplines, guided by legislation and protocols and supported by investment allocated through the various systems of governance. In this social context, high expectations are placed on professionals to predict, manage and deal with serious dangers or hazards posed by individuals and no system is more clearly imprinted with this mandate than forensic services. But this rhetoric is too simplistic for the realities of forensic practice and exposes professionals to criticism and blame when they are found to fail in their role as guardians of safety on behalf of society (Mullen 2000, 307). When systems of care, such as the forensic system, fail to expunge risk, then public trust in the value of expertise is shaken and anger and blame can swiftly follow.

It is not surprising then to find that in professional education, including those disciplines most often represented in forensic services, considerable emphasis is placed on learning about the calculation of certainty, or the science of risk prediction and measurement. However, it is clear that the practice of risk management depends on many factors and involves the application of a complex set of knowledge and skills which must be supported by effective multidisciplinary collaboration. Hall (2005, 191) calls for greater use to be made of the opportunities at university level to promote enhanced interdisciplinary understanding of the distinct roles, values and knowledge of the different professions. Furthermore, despite the promotion of risk elimination as the dominant discourse within professional training, a counter-discourse is gaining ground which expresses doubt regarding the wisdom of offering blanket clinical assurances that all dangerous behaviour can be eradicated. Referring to professional education in general, but making a point which fits well with this discussion, Hall (2014) proposes that increased attention needs to be paid to teaching about uncertainty across a wide range of professional disciplines so that service providers can better understand how it impacts on their practice and the outcomes they achieve.

Whichever position one favours in terms of the preferred knowledge base and focus of education, there can be little doubt that service providers engaged in risk management will benefit from reflexive consideration of the theories, knowledge and perspectives which influence their practice. To work with risk without reflective insight into the underlying beliefs that shape practice leaves the practitioner with an under-developed theoretical foundation to inform their practice. It is also clear that the conceptualisations of risk management adopted by practitioners are interwoven with the way services are delivered. To assist the smooth delivery of multidisciplinary care, it is helpful for practitioners to identify the conceptual frameworks they employ in their work as well as those employed by other disciplines in the professional network because unrecognised or unacknowledged differences can lead to breakdown and fragmentation of the overall professional response to individual service users. Poor coordination and weak collaboration within the professional network can leave service users with compounded problems with which they must live and somehow try to survive.

Greater attention needs to be paid not only to the ways in which the early stage education of professional disciplines theorises risk and risk management but also what messages it conveys regarding the role that collaboration within the professional network plays in delivering effective service responses in cases involving risk. The classroom offers a useful environment where different theoretical perspectives on risk and its management can be outlined, explored and deconstructed and where the merits of both evidence-based interventions and reflective practice can be considered. Professional education is also the incubator for how professional disciplines view each other and it is a forum in which awareness building and appreciation of the roles of other disciplines can be properly established.

Bailey (2012, 81) captures the essential connection between successful risk management and how services are organised when she says that "effective interdisciplinary working is necessary to underpin risk assessment, prediction and management". Achieving this end involves a challenging journey through a maze of competing paradigms, negotiated relationships and the complexities of human life and we need educational systems in place which prepare professionals with the awareness and skills to undertake risk management work in the real-world context. In tandem with an enriched educational curriculum on the issue of risk, increased research activity is also needed so that we can critically interrogate current forms of risk management practices and discover how services can work better towards positive outcomes for all concerned.

References

Abramson J. S. and Mizrahi T. 1994. "Examining social work/physician collaboration: An application of grounded theory methods". In C. Kohler Riessman (ed.) *Qualitative Studies in Social Work Research*. London: Sage 28–48.

Abramson J. S. and Mizrahi T. 1996. "When social workers and physicians collaborate: Positive and negative interdisciplinary experiences". *Social Work* 41(3): 270–281.

Adams A. 2012. "Rights, risks and responsibilities in an age of uncertainty". In G. Koubel and H. Bungay (eds) *Rights, Risks and Responsibilities: Interprofessional Working in Health and Social Care* . Hampshire, UK: Palgrave Macmillan 43–62.

Alaszewski A. and Brown P. 2007. "Risk, uncertainty and knowledge". *Health, Risk and Society* 9(1): 1–10.

Bailey D. 2012. *Interdisciplinary working in mental health.* London: Palgrave Macmillan.

Barnes D., Carpenter J. and Dickinson C. 2000. "Interprofessional education for community mental health: attitudes to community care and professional stereotypes". *Social Work Education* 19(6): 565–583.

Beck U. 1992. *Risk Society: Towards a new modernity.* London: Sage.

Beck U. 1997. "A risky business". *London School of Economics Magazine* 10, 15–16. Referenced in H. Prins 1999. *Will they do it again? Risk Assessment and management in criminal justice and psychiatry.* London: Routledge.

Bernstein P. L. 1998. *Against the Gods: The remarkable story of risk.* New York: John Wiley and Sons.

Birchall E. with Hallett C. 1995. *Working Together in Child Protection.* London: HMSO.

Biven B. M. 2002. "Freedom and Authority: a conceptual focus in work with violent adolescents". *Southern African Journal of Child and Adolescent Mental Health* 14(1): 37–49.

Blyth E. and Milner J. 1990. "The process of inter-agency work". In the Violence Against Children Study Group (ed.) *Taking Child Abuse Seriously.* London: Routledge. 194–211. Referenced in H. Buckley 2002. *Child Protection and Welfare: Innovations and Interventions.* Dublin: Institute of Public Administration.

Broadhurst K., Hall C., Wastell D., White S. and Pithouse A. 2010. "Risk, instrumentalism and the humane project in social work: identifying the informal logics of risk management in children's statutory services". *British Journal of Social Work* 40(4): 1046–1064.

Brown B., Crawford P. and Darongkamas J. 2000. "Blurred roles and permeable boundaries: the experience of multidisciplinary working in community mental health". *Health and Social Care in the Community* 8(6): 425–435.

Buckley H. 1999. "Child protection: Conflicting legal and medical perspectives". *The Medico-Legal Journal of Ireland* 5(1): 18–22.

Buckley H. 2000. "Child protection: an unreflective practice". *Social Work Education* 19(3): 253–263.

Buckley H. 2002. *Child Protection and Welfare: Innovations and Interventions.* Dublin: Institute of Public Administration.

Carson D. and Bain A. 2008. *Professional risk and working with people. Decision-making in health, social care and criminal justice.* London: Jessica Kingsley Publishers.

Crossley N. 2006. *Contesting Psychiatry: Social movement in mental health.* London: Routledge.

Davis A. 1996. "Risk work and mental health". In H. Kemshall and J. Pritchard (eds) *Good Practice in Risk Assessment and Risk Management.* London: Jessica Kingsley Publishers 109–120.

Exworthy M. and Peckham S. 1999. "Collaboration between health and social care: Coterminosity in the 'New NHS'" *Health and Social Care in the Community* 7(3): 225–232.

Ferguson H. 2001. "Promoting child protection, welfare and healing: the case for developing best practice". *Child and Family Social Work* 6: 1–12.

Freeth D. 2001. "Sustaining interprofessional collaboration". *Journal of Interprofessional Care* 15(1): 37–46.

Giddens A. 1993. *Sociology*. 2nd edn. Oxford: Blackwell Publishers.

Giddens A. 1998. *The Third Way: The renewal of social democracy*. Cambridge: Polity Press.

Glover-Thomas N. 2011. "The age of risk: Risk perception and determination following the Mental Health Act 2007". *Medical Law Review* 19(4): 581–605.

Godin P. 2006. "Introduction". In P. Godin (ed.) *Risk and Nursing Practice*. Hampshire: Palgrave Macmillan 1–23.

Grunbaum L. and Gammeltoft M. 1993. "Young children of schizophrenic mothers: difficulties of intervention". *American Journal of Orthopsychiatry* 63(1): 16–27.

Gunstone S. 2003. "Risk assessment and management of patients who self-neglect: a 'grey area' for mental health workers". *Journal of Psychiatric and Mental Health Nursing* 10: 287–296.

Hall B. 2014. " 'How do you know?' The threshold concept, multidisciplinary approaches and the age of uncertainty". In C. O'Mahony, A. Buchanan, M. O'Rourke and B. Higgs (eds) *Threshold Concepts: From Personal Practice to Communities of Practice*. Cork, Ireland: NAIRTL 94–98.

Hall P. 2005. "Interprofessional teamwork: Professional cultures as barriers". *Journal of Interprofessional Care* Supplement 1, May 2005: 188–196.

Heilbrun K. 1997. "Prediction vs management models relevant to risk assessment: the importance of legal decision-making context". *Law and Human Behaviour* 21: 91–106. Referenced in D. Carson and A. Bain, 2008. *Health, Social Care and Criminal Justice*. London: Jessica Kingsley Publishers.

Heyman B. 2010a. "The concept of risk". In B. Heyman, M. Shaw, A. Alaszewski and M. Titterton (eds) *Risk, safety, and clinical practice: Health care through the lens of risk*. Oxford: Oxford University Press 15–35.

Heyman B. 2010b. "The social construction of health risks". In B. Heyman, M. Shaw, A. Alaszewski and M. Titterton (eds) *Risk, safety, and clinical practice: Health care through the lens of risk*. Oxford: Oxford University Press 37–58.

Heyman B. and Davies J. 2006. "The tension between autonomy and safety in nursing adults with learning difficulties". In P. Godin (ed.) *Risk and Nursing Practice*. Hampshire, UK: Palgrave Macmillan 135–149.

Horgan D. 1996. "Interprofessional Co-operation: Team work and child protection". *Irish Social Worker* 14(1): 4–6.

Hornby S. and Atkins J. 2000. *Collaborative Care: Interprofessional, Interagency and Interpersonal*. Oxford: Blackwell Science.

Horton K. 2006. "Balancing risk and independence in nursing older adults". In P. Godin (ed.) *Risk and Nursing Practice*. Hampshire, UK: Palgrave Macmillan.

Horwath J. 1999. "Inter-agency practice in suspected cases of Munchausen Syndrome by Proxy (Fictitious Illness by Proxy): dilemmas for professionals". *Child and Family Social Work* 4(2): 109–118.

Howlett M. 1996. "Community care homicide inquiries and risk assessment". In H. Kemshall and J. Pritchard (eds) *Good Practice in Risk Assessment and Management*. London: Jessica Kingsley Publishers.

Imber-Black E. 1988. *Families and larger systems: A family therapist's guide through the labyrinth*. London: The Guildford Press.

Johnson K. 2009. "Safeguarding children and mental health practice: Experiencing the field". In L. Hughes and H. Owen (eds) *Good Practice in Safeguarding Children:*

working effectively in child protection. London: Jessica Kingsley Publishers 163–180.

Keynes J. M. 1937. "The General Theory". *Quarterly Journal of Economics* L1: 209–233. Referenced in P. L. Bernstein 1998. *Against the Gods: The Remarkable Story of Risk.* New York: John Wiley & Sons.

Kirwan G. 2010. *Risk management and parental mental illness: An exploratory study of service providers' views.* Unpublished thesis. Trinity College, Dublin, Ireland.

Koubel G. 2012. "Critical reflections on balancing rights, risks and responsibilities". In G. Koubel and H. Bungay (eds) *Rights, risks and responsibilities: Interprofessional working in health and social care* 195–212. Hampshire, UK: Palgrave Macmillan.

Koubel G. and Yardley C. 2012. "Managing Risk in a Complex Society". In G. Koubel and H. Bungay (eds) *Rights, risks and responsibilities: Interprofessional working in health and social care.* 65–84. Hampshire, UK: Palgrave Macmillan.

Maddock A. 2014. "Consensus or contention: an exploration of multidisciplinary team functioning in an Irish mental health context". *European Journal of Social Work.* www.tandfonline.com/doi/abs/10.1080/13691457.2014.885884#.Ux3kiIUw9mY.

Manthorpe J. 2007. "Managing risk in social care in the United Kingdom". *Health, Risk and Society* 9(3): 237–239.

Maschi T. and Killian M. L. 2011. "The evolution of forensic social work in the United States: Implications for 21st century practice". *Journal of Forensic Social Work* 1: 8–36.

Morrison T. 2002. "Child Protection Work: Impacts, Models and Strategies". *Soileir* 4(1): 3–7.

Mullen P. E. 2000. "Forensic Mental Health". *British Journal of Psychiatry* 174: 307–311.

Munro E. 1999. "Common errors of reasoning in child protection work". *Child Abuse and Neglect* 23(8): 745–758.

Nilsson T., Munthe C., Gustavson C., Forsman A. and Anckarsäter H. 2009. "The precarious practice of forensic psychiatric risk assessments". *International Journal of Law and Psychiatry* 32: 400–407.

Nolan D. and Quinn N. 2012. "The context of risk management in mental health social work practice". *Social Work in Action* 24 (3): 175–188.

Packman J. and Randall J. 1989. "Decisions about children at risk". In P. Sills (ed.) *Child Abuse: Challenges for Policy and Practice.* Community Care and London Boroughs Training Committee. Referenced in O. Stevenson (ed.) 1989. *Child Abuse: Professional practice and public policy.* Hertfordshire, UK: Harvester Wheatsheaf.

Patmore C. and Weaver T. 1991. *Community Mental Health Teams: Lessons for planners and managers.* London: Good Practices in Mental Health.

Perkins R. and Repper J. 1998. *Dilemmas in Community Mental Health Practice: Choice or Control?* Abingdon, Oxon: Radcliffe Medical Press.

Pinker R. 1990. *Social Work in an Enterprise Society.* London: Routledge. Referenced in G. Richards and W. Horder 1999. "Mental health training: the process of collaboration". *Social Work Education* 18(4): 449–458.

Prins H. 1999. *Will they do it again? Risk assessment and management in criminal justice and psychiatry.* London: Routledge.

Reder P., Duncan S. and Gray M. 1993. *Beyond Blame: Child Abuse tragedies revisited.* London: Routledge.

Reed J. 1997. "Risk assessment and clinical risk management: the lessons from recent inquiries". *British Journal of Psychiatry* 170(32): 4–7. Referenced in M. Titterton

2005. *Risk and Risk Taking in Health and Social Welfare*. London: Jessica Kingsley Publishers.

Richards G. and Horder W. 1999. "Mental health training: the process of collaboration". *Social Work Education* 18(4): 449–458.

Rogers R. 2000. "The uncritical acceptance of risk assessment in forensic practice". *Law and Human Behavior* 24(5): 595–605.

Rose N. 1996. "Psychiatry as a political science: advanced liberalism and the administration of risk". *History of the Human Services* 9(2): 1–23.

Rose N. 1998. "Governing risky individuals: The role of psychiatry in new regimes of control". *Psychiatry, Psychology and Law* 5(2): 177–195.

Ryan T. 1996. "Risk management and people with mental health problems". In H. Kemshall and J. Pritchard (eds) *Good Practice in Risk Assessment and Risk Management* 93–108. London: Jessica Kingsley Publishers.

Schön, D. A. 1991. *The Reflective Practitioner. How professionals think in action.* Aldershot, UK: Ashgate Publishing Ltd.

Scott D. 1997. "Inter-agency conflict: an ethnographic study". *Child and Family Social Work* 2: 73–80.

Secker J. and Hill K. 2001. "Broadening the partnerships: experiences of working across community agencies". *Journal of Interprofessional Care* 15(4): 341–350.

Simic P. 1995. "Book reviews: Collaborative Care. Interprofessional, Interagency and Interpersonal by Sally Hornby". *Health and Social Care in the Community* 3: 137–138.

Simpson E. L. and House A. O. 2002. "Involving users in the delivery and evaluation of mental health services: systematic review". *British Medical Journal* 325: 1265–1269.

Stalker K. 2014. "Managing risk and uncertainty in social work: A literature review". *Journal of Social Work* 3(2): 211–233.

Stanley N. and Manthorpe J. 2001. "Reading mental health inquiries: Messages for social work". *Journal of Social Work* 1(1): 77–99.

Stevenson O. 1989. (ed.) *Child Abuse: Professional practice and public policy.* Hertfordshire, UK: Harvester Wheatsheaf.

Stewart S., Oldfield A. and Braham L. 2012. "The violent offender treatment programme: service user consultation and evaluation". *The British Journal of Forensic Practice* 14(2): 138–149.

Suter E., Arndt J., Arthur N., Parboosingh J., Taylor E. and Deutschlander S. 2009. "Role understanding and effective communication as core competencies for collaborative practice". *Journal of Interprofessional Care* 23(1): 41–51.

Tait L. and Lester H. 2005. "Encouraging user involvement in mental health services". *Advances in Psychiatric Treatment* 11: 168–175.

Taylor C. and White S. 2001. "Knowledge, truth and reflexivity: The problem of judgement in social work". *Journal of Social Work* 1(1): 37–59.

Thompson N. 1995. *Age and Dignity: working with older people*. Aldershot, UK: Arena.

Thompson N. 2000. *Theory and Practice in Human Services.* Oxford: Oxford University Press.

Thompson N. and Thompson S. 2008. *The Social Work Companion.* Hampshire, UK: Palgrave Macmillan.

Titterton M. 1999. "Training professionals in risk assessment and risk management: What does the research tell us?" In P. Parsloe (ed.) *Risk Assessment in Social Care and Social Work* 217–247. London: Jessica Kingsley Publishers.

Titterton M. 2005. *Risk and Risk Taking in Health and Social Welfare*. London: Jessica Kingsley Publishers.

Vitacco M. J., Caldwell M., Ryba N. L., Malesky A. and Kurus S. J. 2009. "Assessing risk in adolescent sexual offenders: Recommendations for clinical practice". *Behavioural Sciences and the Law* 27: 929–940.

Walton P. 1999. "Social work and mental health: refocusing the training agenda for ASWs". *Social Work Education* 18(4): 375–388.

Williams P. 2002. "The competent boundary spanner". *Public Administration* 80(1): 103–124.

5   Sexual offending

Katie Seidler, Emma Collins, Rima Nasr and Chris Lennings

5.1 Introduction

Sexual offending has gained increasing attention in recent decades and, as a result, there has been a proliferation of treatment opportunities for offenders; associated with which there are burgeoning research initiatives into this treatment offering the clinical community far greater knowledge about 'what works' with offenders (e.g. Andrews and Bonta 2007; Gendreau and Goggin 1996). There has also been a solid push for 'get tough on crime' initiatives and being perhaps the most publicly unpalatable of criminals, sex offenders have borne the brunt of such sentiments. The 'tough on (sex) crime' agenda has brought about a range of harsh and restrictive sentencing and management sanctions for sex offenders, which have been instituted under the guise of community protection (Birgden 2007; Centre for Sex Offender Management 2008; Gendreau *et al.* 2000a).

The current state of knowledge is unarguably clear that, while incarceration serves as both punishment for offenders and protection for the community, it does not work as a deterrent for future offending, nor does it have any therapeutic effect in addressing criminogenic needs (Andrews and Bonta 2007; Byrne and Taxman 2006; Smith *et al.* 2002). Moreover, recent research has suggested that as many as one third of offenders who are incarcerated do not find jail an adverse experience (Crank and Brezina 2013).

5.2 Sex offender management

Research has established that structured correctional therapeutic programming can reduce recidivism by both statistically and socially significant amounts, provided that such treatment is based on the risk, needs and responsivity principles (Andrews and Bonta 2007; Hudson *et al.* 2002). Within the sex offender field, treatment based on these principles has been well researched and the message is generally that offence-focused treatment can have a significant impact on re-offence rates (e.g. Gendreau and Goggin 1996; Hanson *et al.* 2002).

The base rates for sexual offending are relatively low, at about 14 per cent over 10 years (Hanson and Morton-Bourgon 2005; Helmus *et al.* 2009), which is considerably lower than for most other offence types. Without information on base rates or without education about the dynamics of sexual offending, and within the current media and political climate, members of the community have developed a distorted and inherently unhelpful view of sex offenders as being dangerous and untreatable (Centre for Sex Offender Management 2000). This perspective has informed recent legislative initiates for the post-custodial management of sex offenders that focus on individual-level change; these include a priority on individual control and detention, rather than community-based initiatives that see change and responsibility for offending occurring on a wider scale (Byrne and Taxman 2006). Further, the control initiatives driven by recent policies are generally punitive and are not couched in therapeutic jurisprudence principles that might motivate offenders to take responsibility and address their offending behaviour (see also Ogloff and Doyle 2009).

The effect of these legislative initiatives has been to allow for the indefinite and/or extended detention or supervision of sex offenders who are deemed dangerous, as well as the registration of sex offenders in the community, often for many years after the expiration of their legal sentences. This means that sex offenders are staying in custody longer, they are being watched in the community more closely and they are forced to conform to strict policing and regulatory guidelines (Parent and Barnett 2004; Petrunik 2002). It is arguable as to whether such restrictive practices have increased community safety (Vess 2009; Watson and Vess 2008).

Recent legislative and policy initiatives have been the subject of increasing debate and research and there is to date no evidence that these so-called 'intermediate sanctions' have any demonstrable effect on recidivism (e.g. Gendreau *et al.* 2000a, 2000b). It has been argued that, rather than decreasing risk, such measures actually place offenders under increased stress and pressure, thereby serving potentially to increase the risk of re-offence (Petrunik 2002; Wilson *et al.* 2007b). As such, the current climate relating to sex offenders may be having the opposite effect to that intended with respect to community protection.

5.2.1 Community treatment

A significant number of sex offenders will not serve custodial sentences for their offending and will be managed in the community. Therefore, the community represents an important site for the provision of sex offender-specific intervention that has only been recently recognised in the literature (e.g. Losel 2010).

Group-based treatment is popular within the forensic domain, with offenders who participate in such intervention demonstrating improvements in institutional adjustment, interpersonal skills and self-esteem, as well as reduced anger and anxiety levels (Morgan and Flora 2002). Further, even with the significant attrition rates in forensic group programmes, those that adhere to the Risk, Needs and Responsivity (RNR) principles espoused by Andrews and Bonta (2007) and also target dynamic risk factors produce notable reductions in recidivism (Collins *et al.* 2009; Olver *et al.* 2011), which is the ultimate measure of effectiveness in forensic psychology.

In light of the argument for holistic treatment for sexual offenders, it is quite surprising that there is limited research on community-based interventions as compared with the vast array of information available regarding the efficacy of institutional offence-specific programming or therapeutic communities. Some may argue that this makes common sense, in that most offenders who remain in the community are ostensibly lower risk and, according to the RNR model, their treatment needs would accordingly be low, although recent research suggests that this group still needs approximately 100 hours of offence-specific treatment (Wakeling *et al.* 2012). Furthermore, there is an argument that interventions need to be targeted towards moderate and higher risk offenders who are more likely to reoffend (Hanson *et al.* 2009), and such a viewpoint is fully supported by the authors. The observation that most high-risk offenders eventually leave jail and move into the community, where situational and opportunity risk factors are high, belies the argument that treatment needs for offenders in the community are low, especially when one considers the waiting lists for treatment in jail that mean not all incarcerated offenders will receive offence focused treatment. It is also the case that there are offenders who are given community-based orders who could be at higher risk than determined by their assessed risk rating (e.g. by virtue of the index offence perhaps representing an onset in sexual offending), and hence require some form of specific intervention related to their offending. Finally, community-based programmes may also access offenders at nominally moderate levels of risk but for whom, so far, offending has not been disclosed. Therefore, having appropriate interventions available in the community remains an important priority.

5.2.2 Group-based interventions

Research has suggested that there are a number of important gains for sex offenders who participate in group treatment. These include positive changes in identity (Collins and Nee 2010), understanding of offence-related concepts (Collins *et al.* 2010) and empathy (Wakeling *et al.* 2005). Further, the provision of social support through group treatment cannot be overstated for this client group (Frost *et al.* 2009). This is not surprising when one considers the established link between intimacy deficits, emotional loneliness and sexual offending behaviour (e.g. Marshall 1993; Seidman *et al.* 1994).

Allam and Browne (1998) suggest that treatment gains for sex offenders who have participated in group-based treatment can be between 36 and 69 per cent (see also Friendship *et al.* 2003), although other research has been less encouraging (e.g., Hanson *et al.* 2004; Losel and Schmuker 2005). However, this does not change the fact that the treatment of sex offenders is an important initiative that continues to be carried out in forensic settings in the interests of community safety and child protection. That being said, however, waiting lists are typically long and resources few in the community, which means many offenders go untreated. Further, where treatment is available, there are unique challenges that make intervention with sex offenders in the community difficult.

5.2.3 Resource challenges

The first challenge to the successful management of sex offenders in the community is that there is often a tenuous balance for clinicians in being able to recognise and manage the rights of all parties invested in the care and protection of children in relation to sexual abuse. This challenge occurs in the context of an overarching model of community protection with sex offenders that prioritises surveillance and control in order to protect victims (Birgden 2007; Centre for Sex Offender Management 2000; Kemshall and Wood 2007). The difficulty with this model is that it has limited effectiveness in preventing acts of sexual abuse (Gendreau *et al.* 2000a, 2000b), while at the same time creating additional challenges in managing sex offenders within the complex rubric of multiple systems and services that may include stakeholders and where communication is limited but should be prioritised with the purpose of ensuring victim safety.

As a result of recent policy and management initiatives, sex offenders in the community are required to work closely with agencies like community corrections, the Police, child protection services and the local Registration Law monitors. However, conventionally, there is little communication between these various arms of offender management in the community, often compromising the efficacy of treatment and offender responsiveness to change.

The literature suggests that offenders who experience a supportive treatment team and environment have a more positive experience of intervention and change (e.g. Collins *et al.* 2010; Frost *et al.* 2009; Wakeling *et al.* 2005). For example, the success of Circles of Support initiatives in various jurisdictions goes some way to highlighting the usefulness of a cooperative and supportive approach with offenders (Wilson *et al.* 2007a, 2007b, 2007c). This ideal, however, is very difficult to achieve in most community settings.

Unfortunately, stand-alone community-based treatment programs for sexual offenders are rare and typically hard to resource, at least in Australia. Resourcing community-based options is a major challenge within most countries. Many offenders have to undertake significant travel to source such programming (Sloas *et al.* 2012) and this is a reality that is experienced by the authors who run a private practice that offers group-based treatment for sexual offenders in Sydney (New South Wales). Such stand-alone programs remain important in that they are able to service participants with emerging sexual behaviours who attend on a voluntary basis often prior to being convicted of any crime. To this end, it is important that community treatment is readily available irrespective of whether a person has offended sexually (Brown 2005).

It is crucially important for any community programming to undertake rigorous evaluation in order to determine the success of any treatment undertaken. Sex offender research has advocated 'gold standard' evaluations such as the California Sex Offender Treatment and Evaluation Project (Marques *et al.* 2005), which came with unforeseen problems due to random allocation of higher risk participants in the comparison group. Reconviction data, a distal outcome measure (e.g. recidivism or institutional conduct as described by Jung and Gulayets 2011), is suggested as the best outcome measure but proximal factors are most closely aligned to treatment change (e.g. empathy, motivation, responsibility taking etc.). The reliance on distal factors for community treatment evaluation, such as recidivism, is considered problematic if it is the primary source of evaluating treatment efficacy. Typically official recidivism figures will underestimate actual recidivism. Given the low base rate of sexual re-offending, this can lead to a higher potential for false positive errors (Hanson and Morton-Bourgon 2005; Conroy and Murrie 2007).

There has been a long-standing argument for supplemental assessment of treatment effectiveness (e.g. Marques *et al.* 1994). The use of proximal factors has the added benefit of immediate measure (post-treatment) and gives valuable information about individual change versus general programme effectiveness (Barbaree 1997). Proximal factors can be measured through questionnaire data or through in-programme task assessment, for example. Perhaps most importantly, assessment of proximal factors allows clinicians to gather information about within-treatment change (Collins *et al.* 2009; Jung and Gulayets 2011), which will inform evidence-based practice and the refinement of programming in this field.

5.2.4 Effectiveness of community-based interventions

There is scant research available on community-based treatments for sexual offenders and a brief review of known studies updated from an earlier review of the literature (Collins *et al.* 2009) is reported below. The list is not exhaustive, in that it does not include programmes specific to intellectually disabled sex offenders or adolescents. Nonetheless, it highlights a change in treatment evaluation in recent years, where reliance on reconviction data has been replaced with a review of clinical treatment factors and questionnaire data. Some may argue that such an approach weakens evaluation integrity but the reality of following up offenders in the community for more than five years (the average time for follow-up to compensate for low base rate of offending) is hard to achieve, particularly considering high attrition rates based purely on factors like mobility. The problem of attrition loss reinforces the need for inter-agency collaboration in monitoring and working with sexual offenders so as to retain an ability to track community-based participants in the long term. This is especially difficult for those who provide intervention outside the criminal justice system.

Despite the methodological issues, research conducted to date has allowed for greater information on community treatment efficacy than has been previously available. See Table 5.1 for an overview of community-based treatment evaluations published.

Table 5.1 demonstrates consistency with the established base rate of sexual re-offending based on risk ratings (Hanson and Morton-Bourgon 2005), although it is noted that most of the earlier studies did not speak to the risk level of the participant prior to beginning the group. Given the base rate for re-offending will vary by risk level, it would have been advantageous to have available the risk ratings of the participants so as to allow comparison of different groups moderated by risk. Hence, considering what is known, treatment is assessed to be effective for the vast majority of offenders based in the community and a demonstrable change in criminogenic needs established. Further, if treatment undertaken is matched in length with risk and treatment needs (Wakeling *et al.* 2012) as opposed to giving a

Table 5.1 Community sex offender treatment outcome studies

Author	Date	Sample size	Programme information	Risk ratings	Follow-up length and method	Outcomes
Marshall and Barbaree (Canada)	1988; 1991	68 Tx[1] completers, 58 did not complete	Limited information, mixed CBT. Appears incorporated deniers content	Not discussed	1 to 11 years	Tx completers = 13.2% recidivism Tx uncompleted = 34.5%
Bingham and Turner (USA)	1995	N=202	Mixed CBT Tx programme run for 44 weeks	Not discussed	5 year follow-up	4 participants referred to programme reoffended
Procter (UK)	1996	54 Tx matched with 54 supervision only			5 year evaluation	3/54 offended in the Tx group, 9/54 in the control group, but not significant due to small sample size
Lee et al. (Victoria, Australia)	1996	Data available on 35 of 58 participants	35-week CBT programme	Not discussed, only referred to prior sexual offending and paraphilias	1 year	8.1%. No comparison group.
Lambie and Stewart (NZ)	2003	175 in 3 groups. 79 complete Tx, 5 fail Tx and 91 still in Tx. Compared to 181 probation only	Three Tx groups, programs varied between 12, 18 months and two years. Individual and family components, largely CBT and psycho-educative content	Not directly discussed	5 years	5.2% recidivism for Tx completers; 8.1% for overall sample

	Year	Sample	Programme	Risk assessment	Follow-up	Findings
Bates et al. (UK)	2004	183 offenders, no control	CBT. Length not discussed	Use of static element of Risk Matrix 2000	4 years – 1995 to 1999	5.5% reconviction rate after four years ($n=110$) 4=very high; 2=high; 3=medium; 1=low risk
Mandeville-Norden, Beech and Hayes (UK)	2008	341	3 programmes that run between 50 and 190 hours weekly. Targets core CBT areas with sex offenders and relapse prevention (RP)	Assessed using Risk Matrix 2000: 48.6%=low; 31.7%=med; 15.9%=high; 3.8% very high risk	2002 to 2007 using pre-and post-questionnaire data	Clinically significant change in questionnaire data across all risk rating groups. Participants also reported changes in offending attitudes and socio-emotional functioning
Jung and Gulayets (Canada)	2011	47/91	20-week CBT and RP program	Not discussed	Immediate (post-treatment)	Changes in personal responsibility and internalisation. No change in empathy and cognitive distortion, all assessed via pre- and post-questionnaire
Butler et al. (Sydney, Australia)	2012	88 Tx completers; 120 used as comparison group	2–3 year programme for intrafamilial offenders based on CBT, narrative and insight oriented	Static-99: 60–69% of both samples scored at 0 risk	1987 to 2000	6.8% Tx completers reoffended; 12.8% comparison group reoffended
Beech, Mandeville-Norden and Goodwill (UK)	2012	413 offenders	Core offence-specific programme and RP. Approx 100 for low risk and 200 for higher risk offenders	57% low treatment needs; 32% medium need; 10% high need	2 to 4 years	44/51 offenders who recidivated committed a sexual offence (12%)

continued

Table 5.1 continued

Author	Date	Sample size	Programme information	Risk ratings	Follow-up length and method	Outcomes
Harkins *et al.* (UK)	2012	643/777 20 qualitative interviews	36 hour programme based initially on RP issues and later Better Lives (based on Good Lives Model)	1.9 mean score on Risk Matrix 2000 (overall medium rating score)	Unclear – under 5 years and included historical data. Largely focused on recent attendees, hence immediate post-treatment review	Not discussed. Self-report of Tx gains reviewed only, and discussed positively
Swinburne *et al.* (USA)	2012	744; 170=evaluation group	Not discussed	Static-99	30-year follow-up[2]	13% sexual recidivism; 20% any criminal recidivism
Percosky *et al.* (South Texas)	2013	34	2–5 year core treatment group. Therapeutic content not directly discussed.	Not discussed	Unclear – analysis of PAI data	Treatment efficacy not directly discussed. Instead reviewed PAI scores (BOR scale) in predicting treatment non-compliance.

Notes
1 Tx=treatment
2 Incorporates data from two earlier studies – see Dwyer and Anderson 1985 and Dwyer and Myers 1990.

high dose of treatment to a generally low risk sexual offender, this should go some way to reducing recidivism risk for those offenders who remain in the community.

5.3 Views of offenders on community management strategies

Offenders are living their lives in the community while engaging in treatment and this means that they will interact with people who may place them at risk. The common way this occurs is by offenders coming into contact with children in their extended family or social networks. It is important to balance the risks offenders may pose to those in their lives with their need to live an independent and fulfilling life, as has been highlighted so poignantly by the Good Lives model (Ward 2002; Ward and Brown 2004). This raises ethical issues that are difficult to balance in the community where the safety of potential victims needs to be balanced with providing offenders with the opportunities they need to practise the skills they learn in treatment in 'real life' settings.

5.3.1 The child protection register

Recent qualitative research with a sample of sex offenders being managed by the Child Protection Register in New South Wales (Seidler 2010) sought to examine offenders' lived experience of the Register and, in particular, whether this was an initiative that was useful in terms of managing risk. The Register is managed by the NSW Police Service and entails known sex offenders being 'registered' on a centralised database, whereby they are under obligation to inform the authorities of salient personal information with the failure to do so carrying legal implications that may result in re-incarceration.

This research highlighted that although offenders understood that theoretically the purpose of the Register was to protect the community, in a practical sense it offered little benefit to the community or to offenders, other than assisting police in targeting known offenders if another crime was committed. Subsequent community-based research (see Bollinger *et al.* 2012) confirmed the naïvety with which the community sees the Register and similar initiatives, which they believe assist in child protection in tangible terms by controlling offenders.

Offenders indicated that their experience of the Register served to create further acrimony in their relationships with police, making them less likely to be compliant and disclosing and driving them further 'underground', potentially also increasing the likelihood that sex offenders will have contact with one another as other relationships are limited and discouraged by authorities. This is potentially dangerous as encouraging secrecy and facilitating isolation are 'critical elements' in sexual offending behaviour (Wilson *et al.* 2007b).

Participants recognised how many procedures necessary for basic living were made more difficult for them as a function of the Register and the public hysteria surrounding this. This results in further marginalisation and stigmatisation, whereby many offenders find it difficult to secure employment, social support or stability in accommodation (Byrne and Taxman 2006; Parent and Barnett 2004) which are crucial factors in successful community reintegration. Further, offenders experience the Register and its requirements as highly stressful and distressing, which clearly relates to a number of dynamic risk factors that have been demonstrated to contribute to risk of sexual recidivism (Andrews and Bonta 2007; Boer *et al.* 1997). This is antithetical to the intended impact of the Register and counterintuitive to members of the general public in terms of how they understand community sex offender management (Bollinger *et al.* 2012; Centre for Sex Offender Management 2008).

While the Register may deter some offenders from reoffending (Birgden 2007; Centre for Sex Offender Management 2008), it does not provide offenders with any tangible means of reducing or managing risks, which ultimately comes down to individual motivation and responsibility. Specifically, the Register, as with other such community-based management strategies, does not speak to issues of loneliness, social isolation, sexual deviancy, unstructured personal routine, substance abuse etc. that have been reliably demonstrated to be associated with acute risk of sexual abuse (e.g. Boer *et al.* 1997; Marshall 1993; Seidman *et al.* 1994). Hence, the Register does not speak to either risk management or risk assessment, thereby making its relationship with community protection tenuous.

In sum, it is our contention that, while there are some benefits of accountability associated with recent initiatives with sex offenders, the recent community-based sex offender management initiatives that have followed are ostensibly law enforcement tools (Wilson *et al.* 2007b) that have no demonstrable effect on reoffending (Byrne and Taxman 2006) and, therefore, no tangible impact on community safety, despite the community's belief to the contrary. Moreover, the current system is not meeting the needs of offenders, especially with respect to accessing treatment and facilitating the establishment of positive and prosocial routines within the community (Wilson 2007c). To this end, the subordination of treatment alternatives and individual autonomy to the greater demands of community safety and retribution or punitive sanctions is not supported (Birgden 2007) and treatment should be considered a crime-control strategy (e.g. Bryne and Taxman 2006), rather than a luxury for offenders.

5.4 Conclusion

It is argued that the best approach to community management of sex offenders is one whereby there is a continuity of care between the prison system and the community, such that offenders can access available and effective treatment, as well as being managed and contained in such a way that they are being held responsible and accountable to the community, at the same time as being supported and encouraged to develop meaningful, appropriate and positive prosocial routines. Management, supervision and intervention should also be tailored according to risk (Andrews and Bonta 2007), rather than offering all offenders a blanket approach, such as that which the Register offers.

Offenders will need to be prepared for their release to the community after prison and this should be done in a structured fashion (e.g. Parent and Barnett

2004). Ideally, this would involve a comprehensive process of relapse prevention planning that includes consideration of the various aspects of life that contribute to a meaningful, satisfying and prosocial existence (e.g. Ward and Brown 2004), such as employment, recreation, social support and accommodation.

A continuity of care model prioritises interagency cooperation and communication. To this end, sexual abuse needs to be seen as a community problem or public health issue that requires multiple sites of service, intervention and support. At a minimum, mental health and criminal justice services will need to liaise closely. Unfortunately, professionals working outside the correctional system often share pejorative community attitudes towards sex offenders, making sensible dialogue between professionals who may be managing differing aspects of the offender's care, or integration with family members, difficult. A range of services is implicated in sex offender management, including the education system, community services and social welfare agencies. It is only through a coordinated approach that we as a community will make a meaningful contribution to child protection in relation to sexual abuse.

References

Allam J. M. and Browne, K. D. 1998. "Evaluating community-based treatment programmes for men who sexually abuse children". *Child Abuse Review* 7: 13–29.

Andrews D. A. and Bonta, J. 2007. *The Psychology of Criminal Conduct*. Ohio: Anderson Publishing.

Barbaree H. 1997. "Evaluating treatment efficacy with sexual offenders: The insensitivity of recidivism studies to treatment effects". *Sexual Abuse: A Journal of Research and Treatment* 9: 111–128.

Bates A., Falshaw L., Corbett C., Patel V. and Friendship C. 2004. "A follow-up study of sex offenders treated by Thames Valley Sex Offender Groupwork Programme, 1995–1999". *Journal of Sexual Aggression* 10: 29–38.

Beech A. R., Mandeville-Norton R. and Goodwill A. 2012. "Comparing recidivism rates of treatment responders/nonresponders in a sample of 413 child molesters who had completed community-based sex offender treatment in the United Kingdom". *International Journal of Offender Therapy and Comparative Criminology* 56(1): 29–49.

Bingham J. E. and Turner B. W. 1995. "Treatment of sexual offenders in an outpatient community-based program". *Psychological Report* 76: 1195–1200.

Birgden A. 2007. "Serious Sex Offenders Monitoring Act 2005 (Vic): A therapeutic jurisprudence analysis". *Psychiatry, Psychology and Law* 14(1): 78–95.

Boer D. R., Hart S. D., Kropp R. P. and Webster C. D. 1997. *Sexual Violence Risk 20*. Florida: Psychological Assessment Resources.

Bollinger J., Seidler K. and Kemp R. 2012. "Who thinks what about child protection: Community perceptions and awareness of child protection strategies and their effectiveness for reducing sexual reoffending". *Sexual Abuse in Australia and New Zealand* 4(1): 33–40.

Brown S. 2005. *Treating sex offenders: An introduction to sex offender treatment programmes*. Devon, UK: Willan Publishing.

Butler L., Goodman-Delahunty J. and Lulham R. 2012. "Effectiveness of pre-trial community-based diversion in reducing reoffending by adult intrafamilial child sex offenders". *Criminal Justice and Behavior* 39(4): 493–513.

Byrne J. M. and Taxman F. S. 2006. "Crime control strategies and community change – Reframing the surveillance vs treatment debate". *Federal Probation* 70(1): 3–12.

Centre for Sex Offender Management. 2000. *Public opinion and the criminal justice system: Building support for sex offender management programmes.* Silver Spring, MD: Centre for Effective Public Policy.

Centre for Sex Offender Management 2008. *Legislative trends in sex offender management.* Silver Spring, MD: Centre for Effective Public Policy.

Collins S. and Nee C. 2010. "Factors influencing the process of change in sex offender interventions: Therapists' experiences and perceptions". *Journal of Sexual Aggression* 16(3): 311–331.

Collins E., Peters L. and Lennings C. 2009. "Community intervention with sex offenders? Do dynamic risk factors change with treatment?" *Sexual Abuse in Australia and New Zealand* 1(2): 87–96.

Collins E., Brown J. and Lennings C. 2010. "Qualitative review of community treatment with sex offenders: perspective of the offender and the expert". *Psychiatry, Psychology and Law* 17(2): 290–303.

Conroy M. A. and Murrie D. C. 2007. *Forensic assessment of violence risk.* Hoboken, NJ: John Wiley.

Crank B. R. and Brezina T. 2013. "Prison will either make ya or break ya: Punishment, deterrence and the criminal life style". *Deviant Behaviour* 34: 782–802.

Dwyer S. M. and Amberson J. I. 1985. "Sex offender treatment program: a follow-up study". *American Journal of Social Psychiatry* 5: 56–60.

Dwyer S. M. and Myers S. 1990. "Sex offender treatment: a six-month to ten-year follow-up study". *Annals of Sex Research* 3: 305–318.

Friendship C., Mann R. E. and Beech A. R. 2003. "Evaluation of a national prison-based treatment program for sexual offenders in England and Wales". *Journal of Interpersonal Violence* 18(7): 744–759.

Frost A., Ware J. and Boer D. P. 2009. "An integrated groupwork methodology for working with sex offenders". *Journal of Sexual Aggression* 15(1): 21–38.

Gendreau P. and Goggin C. 1996. "Principles of effective correctional programming". *Forum on Corrections Research* 8(3). Correctional Service of Canada.

Gendreau P., Goggin C. and Smith P. 2000b. "Cumulating knowledge: How meta-analysis can serve the needs of correctional clinicians and policy makers". In L. L. Motiuk and R. C. Serin (eds) *Compendium 2000 on Effective Correctional Programming*, www.csc-scc.gc.ca/text/rsrch/compendium/2000/index-eng.shtml.

Gendreau P., Goggin C., Cullen F. T. and Andrews D. A. 2000a. "The effects of community sanctions and incarceration on recidivism". In L. L. Motiuk and R. C. Serin (eds) *Compendium 2000 on Effective Correctional Programming*. www.csc-scc.gc.ca/text/rsrch/compendium/2000/index-eng.shtml.

Hanson R. K. and Morton-Bourgon K. E. 2005. "The characteristics of persistent sexual offenders: A meta-analysis of recidivism studies". *Journal of Consulting and Clinical Psychology* 73(6): 1154–1163.

Hanson R. K., Broom I. and Stephenson M. 2004. "Evaluating community sex offender treatment programs: A 12-year follow-up of 724 offenders". *Canadian Journal of Behavioural Science* 36(2): 87–96.

Hanson R. K., Bourgon G., Helmus L. and Hodgson S. 2009. "The principles of effective correctional treatment also apply to sexual offenders: A meta-analysis". *Criminal Justice and Behavior* 36: 865–891.

Hanson R. K., Gordon A., Harris A. J. R., Marques J. K., Murphy W., Quinsey V. L. and

Seto M. C. 2002. "First report of the collaborative outcome data project on the effectiveness of psychological treatment for sex offenders". *Sexual Abuse: A Journal of Research and Treatment* 14(2): 169–194.

Harkins L., Flak V. E., Beech A. R. and Woodhams J. 2012. "Evaluation of a community-based sex offender treatment program using a good lives model approach". *Sexual Abuse: A Journal of Research and Treatment* 24(6): 519–543.

Helmus L., Hanson R. K. and Thornton D. 2009. "Reporting Static-99 in light of new research on recidivism norms". *The Forum* 21 (1), Winter 2009: 38–45.

Hudson S. M., Wales D. S., Bakker L. and Ward T. 2002. "Dynamic risk factors: The Kia Marama evaluation". *Sexual Abuse: A Journal of Research and Treatment* 14(2): 103–119.

Jung S. and Gulayets M. 2011. "Using clinical variables to evaluate treatment effectiveness in programmes for sexual offenders". *Journal of Sexual Aggression* 17(2): 166–180.

Kemshall H. and Wood J. 2007. "Beyond public protection: An examination of community protection and public health approaches to high-risk offenders". *Journal of Criminology and Criminal Justice* 7(3): 203–222.

Lambie I. D. and Stewart M. W. 2003. *Community solutions for the community's problem: an outcome evaluation of three New Zealand community child sex offender treatment programmes.* Wellington: New Zealand Department of Corrections.

Lee J. K. P., Proeve M. J., Lancaster M. and Jackson H. J. 1996. "An evaluation and 1-year follow-up study of a community-based treatment for sex offenders". *Australian Psychologist* 31: 147–152.

Lösel F. 2010. *What works in offender rehabilitation. A global perspective.* Paper presented at the 12th Annual Conference of the International Corrections and Prisons Association.

Lösel F. and Schmucker M. 2005. "The effectiveness of treatment for sexual offenders: A comprehensive meta-analysis". *Journal of Experimental Criminology* 1: 117–146.

Mandeville-Norden R., Beech A. R. and Hayes E. 2008. "Examining the effectiveness of a UK community-based sexual offender treatment programme for child abusers". *Psychology, Crime & Law* 14(6): 493–512.

Marques J. K., Day D. M., Nelson C. and West M. A. 1994. "Effects of cognitive-behavioural treatment goals and recidivism among child molesters". *Behavior, Research and Therapy* 32: 577–588.

Marques J. K., Wiederanders M., Day D. M., Nelson C. and Van-Ommeren A. 2005. "Effects of a relapse prevention program on sexual recidivism: Final results from California's Sex Offender Treatment and Evaluation Project (SOTEP)". *Sexual Abuse: A Journal of Research and Treatment* 17: 79–107.

Marshall W. L. 1993. "The role of attachments, intimacy, and loneliness in the aetiology and maintenance of sexual offending". *Sexual and Marital Therapy* 8(2): 109–121.

Marshall W. L. and Barbaree H. E. 1988. "The long-term evaluation of a behavioural treatment program for child molesters". *Behaviour Research and Therapy* 26: 499–511.

Morgan R. D. and Flora D. B. 2002. "Group psychotherapy with incarcerated offenders: A research synthesis". *Group Dynamics: Theory, Research and Practice* 6(3): 203–218.

Ogloff J. R. P. and Doyle D. J. 2009. "A clarion call: Caution and humility must be the theme when assessing risk for sexual violence under post-sentence laws". *Sexual Abuse in Australia and New Zealand* 1(2): 59–69.

Olver M., Stockdale K. C. and Wormith J. S. 2011. "A meta-analysis of predictors of offender treatment attrition and its relationship to recidivism". *Journal of Consulting and Clinical Psychology* 79(1): 6–21.

Parent D. G. and Barnett L. 2004. "Improving offender success and public safety through system reform: The transition from prison to community initiative". *Federal Probation* 68(2): 25–30.

Percosky A. B., Boccaccini M. T. Bitting B. S., Brian S. and Hamilton P. M. 2013. "Personality Assessment Inventory scores as predictors of treatment compliance and misconduct among sex offenders participating in community-based treatment". *Journal of Forensic Psychology Practice* 13(3): 192–203.

Petrunik M. G. 2002. "Managing unacceptable risk: Sex offenders, community response, and social policy in the United States and Canada". *International Journal of Offender Therapy and Comparative Criminology* 46: 483–511.

Procter E. 1996. "A five year outcome evaluation of a community-based treatment programme for convicted sexual offenders run by the probation service". *Journal of Sexual Aggression* 2: 3–16.

Seidler K. 2010. "Community management of sex offenders: Stigma versus support". *Sexual Abuse in Australia and New Zealand* 2(2): 67–77.

Seidman B. T., Marshall W. L., Hudson S. M. and Robertson P. J. 1994. "An examination of intimacy and loneliness in sex offenders". *Journal of Interpersonal Violence* 9(4): 518–534.

Sloas L. B., Steele P. D. and Hare T. S. 2012. "Geographical access to treatment for sex offenders under community supervision in Kentucky". *Journal of Sexual Aggression* 18(3): 294–310.

Smith P., Goggin C. and Gendreau P. 2002. *The effects of prison sentences and intermediate sanctions on recidivism: General effects and individual differences*. Research Report, Solicitor General Canada.

Swinburne R. R. E., Miner M. H., Poulin D., Dwyer M. S. and Berg D. 2012. "Predicting re-offense for community-based sexual offenders: an analysis of 30 years of data". Sexual Abuse: *Journal of Research and Treatment* 24(5): 501–514.

Vess J. 2009. "Extended supervision or civil commitment for managing the risk of sexual offenders: Public safety and individual rights". *Sexual Abuse in Australia and New Zealand* 1(2): 70–78.

Wakeling H. C., Mann R. E. and Carter A. J. 2012. "Do low-risk sexual offenders need treatment?" *Howard Journal of Criminal Justice* 51(3): 286–299.

Wakeling H. C., Webster S. D. and Mann R. E. 2005. "Sexual offenders' treatment experience: A qualitative and quantitative investigation". *Journal of Sexual Aggression* 11(2): 171–186.

Ward, T. 2002. "Good Lives and the Rehabilitation of Offenders: Promises and Problems". *Aggression and Violent Behaviour* 7(5): 513–528.

Ward T. and Brown M. 2004. "The Good Lives Model and conceptual issues in offender rehabilitation". *Psychology, Crime and Law* 10(3): 243–257.

Watson T. and Vess J. 2008. "Short term reoffending by child victim sex offenders in New Zealand: A comparison with those with and without extended supervision". *Sexual Abuse in Australia and New Zealand: An Interdisciplinary Journal* 1(1): 44–52.

Wilson R. J., Cortoni F. and Vermani M. 2007a. "Circles of support and accountability: A national replication of outcome findings". *Research Report, #R-185*, Correctional Service of Canada.

Wilson R. J., Picheca J. E. and Prinzo M. 2007c. "Evaluating the effectiveness of professionally-facilitated volunteerism in the community-based management of high-risk sexual offenders: Part one – effects on participants and stakeholders". *The Howard Journal* 46(3): 289–302.

Wilson R. J., McWhinnie A., Picheca J. E. Prinzo M. and Cortoni F. 2007b. "Circles of support and accountability: Engaging community volunteers in the management of high-risk sexual offenders". *The Howard Journal* 46(1): 1–15.

Part II

Care, control and community

6 Neoliberalism and 'welfare' in the shadow of the prison

Paul Michael Garrett

6.1 Introduction

Customer Charter: Rules of Conduct

We aim to give a quality service to our customers. To help to do this, please treat our staff, our other customers and our public offices with respect. In particular please obey the following rules:

1   Do not act in any way that disrupts others and interferes with their use of the office.
2   Do not harass any staff or members of the public by using abusive, racist, obscene or threatening language.
3   Do not use violence, threaten violence to staff or members of the public. If you do we will report you to the Gardai [police].
4   Do not intentionally damage or steal the Department's property.
5   Do not smoke in the Department's offices.
6   Do not drink alcohol or take illegal drugs while in our offices.
7   Do not leave personal property unattended while using our offices.
8   If one of our staff has already dealt with you, please do not loiter.

Please use our public offices in a responsible and considerate way by observing these rules.

How are we to interpret these words from a poster taped on the wall of a dull and down-at-heel Department of Social Protection office – colloquially the 'dole' – in the Republic of Ireland? What work is the poster performing? What kind of social relations is it signalling and seeking to reaffirm? Clearly, the vocabulary used is saturated in contempt for those visiting the office. Although jarringly informed by the lexicon of the 'new public management' (customer, charter, quality), it conveys the notion that benefit claimants are an unpredictable mass of wayward, troublesome characters. They are seemingly volatile others who are likely to be animalistic, foul and vulgar, prone to racist behaviour, violent outbursts and drug use. Although, they are in 'our' public building they are presented as *prisoners* in need of vigilant attention, constant supervision and monitoring.

In examining the conjoined unfolding of policy and practices in relation to prisons and 'welfare', this chapter draws on Loïc Wacquant's (2009a) *Punishing the Poor*. He refers to it as part of a 'sort of trilogy' (Wacquant 2009a, 315): the first book is *Urban Outcasts* (Wacquant, 2008) and the final part *Deadly Symbiosis* (Wacquant 2009b). Each book's focus is on his seeking to "unravel the tangled triangular connections between class restructuring, ethnoracial division, and state crafting in the era of neoliberal ascendancy" (Wacquant 2009a, 315). For this French thinker, the "penalisation of public aid extends even to its material setting and ambiance" and so the "physical resemblance of the post-reform welfare office to a correctional institution is striking" (Wacquant 2009a, 102). What is more, visitors to such locations are now frequently positioned as "abnormal, truncated, suspect beings who threaten the moral order and whom the state must therefore place under harsh tutelage" (Wacquant 2009a, 81).

Deploying a single analytical frame, Wacquant highlights how "precarious fractions of the urban proletariat" are now subject to the "programmatic convergence and practical interlock" of workfare and the prison system (Wacquant 2009a, xx). After sketching in the main elements of his argument and identifying some of its potential weaknesses, the chapter concludes by maintaining the relevance of Wacquant's contribution for social workers engaging with the forensic paradigm.

6.2 Punishing the poor: neoliberal penality

> Tens of thousands of inmates in gaols across California have gone on hunger strike to protest solitary confinement and other conditions that they say amount to torture ... mounting what was thought to be the biggest protest of its kind in California history.
>
> > ("Thousands go on hunger strike in California's jails",
> > Rory Carroll, *Guardian*, 11 July 2013)

> Thousands of benefits cheats are being snared by lie detector system.... More than a third of claimants in some areas are being exposed as making fraudulent claims after being ... tested by the technology ... councils ... are estimated to have saved millions since 2007 alone.
>
> > ("Lie detector tests trap fraudsters claiming hundreds of thousands in
> > housing benefit" Andrew Levy, *Daily Mail*, 22 January 2009)

These two 'new stories', one related to prisons in California and other from the UK's The Daily Mail, breathlessly reporting on a voice recognition technology software being used to detect 'benefit cheats' appear largely unrelated. The former can be perceived as connected solely to penal affairs within the inflated US prison system; the latter may be viewed as solely of significance to those interested in social policy developments pertaining to the contemporary governance of 'welfare'. In what follows, however, it will be suggested that it is important for social workers to examine developments in these seemingly separate domains through the same lens. In 2001, Wacquant observed that the penal apparatus in the "post-Keynesian era of employment":

> serves to discipline the fractions of the working class that buck at the new, precarious service jobs; it neutralises and warehouses its most disruptive elements, or those considered superfluous with regard to the transformations of the demand for labour; and it reaffirms the authority of the state in the limited domain that is henceforth assigned to it.
>
> (2001, 405)

Indeed, one of Wacquant's chief assertions is that those intent on analysing the evolution of 'welfare' within neoliberalism fail to take into account incarceration. For example, the "irruption" of the penal state in America has gone "virtually unnoticed" by those academics focusing on the "crisis of the welfare state" (Wacquant 2009a, xiii). Key definers of neoliberalism on the political left have furnished defectiveness analyses because of this lacuna. David Harvey's (2005) respected contributions on the rise of neoliberalism is, therefore, "woefully incomplete" because he has "barely a few passing mentions of the prison and not a line on workfare" (Wacquant 2009a, 309).

Wacquant's prime focus is the US which, he maintains, can be viewed as the "Living Laboratory of the Neoliberal Future" (Wacquant 2009a). In this context, it is vital that we "construe the prison as a core political institution, instead of a mere technical implement for enforcing the law and handling of criminals" (Wacquant 2009a, xviii). He emphasises the sheer "grandeur" of the penal state in the US and reveals how the growth in prison numbers is approximately coterminous with the rise of neoliberalism. After 1973, the confined population "doubled in ten years and quadrupled in twenty" (Wacquant 2009a, 114). If it were "a city, the carceral system of the United States would be the fourth-largest metropolis, behind Chicago" (Wacquant 2009a, 114). Wacquant is also particularly attentive to how imprisonment and welfare are racialised (Wacquant 2009a).

Wacquant's theoretical 'architecture' seeks to establish an "empirical and analytical rapprochement between social policy and penal policy" (Wacquant 2009a, 14). These two domains continue to be examined separately, in isolation from each other, by social scientists as well as by those who wish to reform them, "whereas in reality they already function in tandem" (Wacquant 2009a, 13). Following on from this analysis, he proposes "first, that we construe the prison as a core political institution ... and, second, that we recognise that 'workfare' and 'prisonfare' are two integral components of the Leviathan" (Wacquant 2009a, xviii). He not only provides an account of the growth in prison numbers, he also endeavours to "link the modifications of social policies to those of penal policies so as to decipher the *double regulation* to which the post-industrial proletariat is now subjected through the joint agency of the assistantial and penitential sectors of the state" (Wacquant 2009a, xviii, original emphasis).

Welfare provision and criminal justice are "animated by the same punitive and paternalist philosophy that stresses the 'individual responsibility' of the 'client'" (Wacquant 2009a, 16). Consequently, there is a need to leave behind traditional frames focused on 'prisons' or 'welfare' in order to adopt a more "expansive approach, encompassing in a single grasp the totality of actions whereby the state purports to mould, classify and control the populations deemed deviant, dependent and dangerous living in its territory" (Wacquant 2009a, 16). It is important, therefore, to try to interpret and respond to how the state and its associated bureaucratic fields, in the US and the European Union, are aiming to manage and regulate problem populations, or 'castaway categories', during a period of neoliberalism (Wacquant 2009a, 4). According to Wacquant (2009a, xxi) there are at least "three main strategies to treat the conditions and conducts" perceived as "undesirable, offensive or threatening": socialisation, medicalisation and – the "invisibilisation" of "social problems" – penalisation.

Wacquant's discussion on the US Personal Responsibility and Work Opportunity Reconciliation Act of 1996 (PRWORA) is illuminating. This federal law, which altered the way in which cash assistance was made available, is important and influential beyond the US because of how it set out, with its "vast web of 'disentitlement strategies'" (Wacquant 2009a, 91) to restrict financial help. Equally significantly, and reflected in the Orwellian titling of the legislation, is how its introduction and operationalisation has aimed to marinate 'welfare' in stigma. The Act marked the "conversion of the right to 'welfare' into the obligation of 'workfare' designed to dramatize and enforce the work ethic at the bottom of the employment ladder" (Wacquant 2009a, 43). Moreover, Wacquant observes that the doctrinal ambiance of this 'reform' fostered a "programmatic convergence with penal policy" (Wacquant 2009a, 79).

It is no longer possible to analyse the "implementation of welfare policy at ground level without taking into account the overlapping operations of the penal institution" (Wacquant 2009a, 99). Welfare offices are now borrowing the:

> stock-in-trade techniques of the correctional institutions … a constant close-up monitoring, strict spatial assignments and time constraints, intensive record-keeping and case management, periodic interrogation and reporting, and a rigid system of graduated sanctions for failing to perform properly.
>
> (Wacquant 2009a, 101–102).

Such practices are undergirded by a:

> paternalist conception of the role of the state in respect to the poor, according to which the conduct of disposed and dependent citizens must be closely supervised and, whenever necessary, corrected through rigorous protocols of surveillance, deterrence and sanction, very much like those routinely applied to offenders under criminal justice supervision.
>
> (Wacquant 2009a, 59–60)

In this context, the "new punitive organization of welfare programs operates in the manner of a labor parole program designed to push its 'beneficiaries' into the subpoverty jobs that have proliferated after the discarding of the Fordist-Keynesian compromise" (Wacquant 2009a, 43).

Particular targeted groups, such as 'poor single mothers', are positioned not "as citizens participating in a community of equals, but as subjects saddled with abridged rights and expanded obligations until such time as they have demonstrated full commitment to the values of work and family by their reformed conduct" (Wacquant 2009a, 98). For Wacquant, gender is significant in that the "social silhouette" of recipients of Temporary Assistance for Needy Families, administered and paid under PRWORA, "turns out to be a near exact-replica of the profile of jail inmates save for gender inversion" (Wacquant 2009a,98).

Some of Wacquant's critics, as we shall see, have argued that he overemphasises the rupture which has taken place with past practices in terms of how problem populations are confined, managed and regulated. However, alert to this criticism, he argues that the key difference today is the reach and capacity of the state which is now "endowed with budgetary, human and technological resources without equivalent in history" (Wacquant 2009a, 28). At the end of the nineteenth century it "sufficed for an individual to change his name and move to a different city or region and melt into the surrounding landscape for the authorities to lose track of him" (Wacqaunt 2009a, 28). Operating "increasingly through the networks woven by its impressive apparatus", the state now possesses the infrastructural and surveillant power able "to penetrate the population under its aegis and rule over their behaviours" (Wacqaunt 2009a, 28; see also Nellis 2005).

For Wacquant, if we are to regard the welfare state as existing, beyond the boundaries of 'prisonfare', it is better to identify it as merely 'a *charitable state'* which is limited, fragmentary and informed "by a moralistic and moralizing concept of poverty as a product of the individual failings of the poor" (Wacqaunt 2009a, 42, emphasis added). Within this paradigmatic perspective, the "guiding principle of public action in this domain is not solidarity but *compassion*: its goal is not to reinforce social bonds, and still less to reduce inequalities, but at best to relieve the most glaring destitution and to demonstrate society's moral sympathy for its deprived yet deserving members" (Wacquant 2009a, 42).

As Nicola Lacey (2010, 780) argues, "it is especially important to identify and reflect on the weak points in Wacquant's analysis – not least as a basis for building productively on his insights". In what follows, therefore, the focus will be on some of the criticisms which his provocative contribution on prisons and welfare has generated. This, in itself, is a rich and diverse body of work which is derived from, for example, special issues and symposia in a number of academic journals. Six criticisms of Wacquant will be dwelt on relating to: his theorisation of the state; definitional and methodological ambiguity; the fact that the US may be exceptional and unrepresentative of more widespread international trends; insufficient historical dimension to his analysis; inattentiveness to other forms of detention emerging beyond the walls of prisons; lack of acknowledgement of resistance to neoliberal penality.

6.3 Criticisms of the 'neoliberal penality' perspective

Misreading the state

A first cluster of interrelated problems exists with Wacquant's theorisation of the state. There is little indication, for example, of whom, or what, is driving the punitiveness process and what benefits or advantages may be accrued (see also Nelken 2010). He notes, if the "notion of dominant class is invoked … it is only as a stenographic designation pointing to the balance of patterned struggles over the remaking of the state going on within the field of power" (Wacqaunt 2009a, 29). Similarly, Wacqaunt (2009a, xx) dismisses the very idea that the penalization of poverty is a deliberate 'plan'. Rather it is the outcome of:

> struggles involving myriad agents and institutions … I forcefully reject the 'functionalism of the worst case' which casts all historical developments as the work of an omniscient strategist or as automatically beneficial to some abstract machinery of domination and exploitation that would 'reproduce' itself no matter what.
>
> (Wacqaunt 2009a, xx)

Such comments make it seem as if the evolution of this punitive upsurge is a consequence of rather arbitrary mechanisms and processes and fails to address questions about the forces that stand to gain from the growth of prisons. More specifically, he does not appear to accept that a particular class – the 'dominant' class – may have differential access to the levers of power and be better able to prompt changes to suit its own class interests.

Although Wacquant's encourages us to look at prisons and 'welfare' through the same analytical optic, he offers no insights into the possible movement of personnel across the two fields. This lacuna has led Jones (2010, 401) to maintain that "Wacquant's project is not completed, and some aspects of it have yet to be started": that is to say, investigating the state apparatus requires a more detailed ethnographic approach following not only individuals targeted for prison or 'welfare' interventions, but also the employment routes of state personnel involved in the combined fields.

Wacquant posits that the state has a 'left hand' and 'right hand'. The former is perceived as 'female' and the role it fulfils is mostly protective and nurturing: institutionally it is embodied by the spending ministries which fulfil social functions and cater for social services, health etc. The 'right' hand is depicted as 'masculine', steering the financial institutions and being responsible for order and control. However, the two 'hands' – on occasions referred to as 'arms' – analysis remains unconvincing (see also Gelsthorpe 2010; Bumiller 2013). This conceptualisation "casts the Keynesian welfare state in inappropriately rosy glow" (Mayer 2010, 97) and implies that the interventions of the 'left hand' are unambiguously benign. Specifically in relation to social work and related spheres, it fails to address adequately abuses which take place in care settings

(Wardhaugh and Wilding 1993). In short, the 'left hand of the state' can also be a punishing hand. Similarly, the so-called 'left hand' has, both historically and in a more contemporary context, performed a key ideological role, serving to delineate the 'deserving' from the 'undeserving' poor (Chunn and Gavigan 2004).

Another gap in Wacquant's analysis relates to the measures employed by the state in the post credit crunch era and, indeed, since the inception of the war on terror and the preoccupation with security. Wacquant argues, for example, that "the state stridently reasserts its responsibility, potency and efficiency in the narrow register of crime management at the very moment when it proclaims and organizes its own impotence on the economic front" (Wacqaunt, 2009a, xviii). However, in both the US and Europe, governments have clearly exhibited potency in decisively intervening to bail out the banks. Furthermore, even before the global economic turmoil, 'big government' had returned in the form of a new "military and intelligence expansion, new surveillance and security systems, propaganda policies' harnessed to the leading trope of the 'war on terror'" (Nederveen Pieterse 2004, 124).

Definitional and methodological ambiguity

A second set of criticisms levelled at Wacquant's perspective concern its definitional and methodological ambiguity. One commentator has observed that his more recent work is delivered with "maximum rhetorical force" but at the "cost of analytic clarity" (Lacey 2010, 783). Jones (2010, 394) is "uncomfortable with the extent of his macro-generalisations" and maintains that a range of questions may serve to complicate Wacquant's perspective: for example, low prison rates might also be an "index of an especially punitive social order"; alternatively low rates might mask the fact that, beyond the walls of the prison, other forms social control and detention are proliferating. Although not directly engaging with Wacquant's work, O'Sullivan and O'Donnell (2007) refer to a *decline* in coercive confinement within the Republic of Ireland. Their perspective takes into account the manifest rise in prison numbers, but situates this escalation alongside the diminution in the numbers confined within places of semi-confinement, constraint and restriction. Hence, for them, what is required is a more nuanced approach which – while computing the rise in prison numbers – also brings into vision other locations of coercive confinements such as psychiatric hospitals, homes for 'unmarried mothers' and various residential institutions for children placed by the courts. Similarly, focusing on the US, Harcourt (2010) has drawn attention to the fall in the number of those detained in institutions for the mentally ill.

US exceptionalism

Wacquant points to overall and emerging trajectories in the US and EU and perhaps fails to consider adequately the distinctiveness of specific jurisdictions. Furthermore, some detractors deem his emphasis on the US to be rather misleading in that trends there may be somewhat at odds with more widespread international developments (Mayer 2010; Nelken 2010). Wacquant's "story of creeping global 'neoliberalism' risks projecting a story which is, essentially, an American one onto the whole planet" (Lacey 2010, 787). Thus, as Newburn (2010, 346) reminds us, "when discussing purportedly globalising trends, we remember that in some respects attention to the 'local' becomes *more* rather than less important" (original emphasis).

Some countries have not, it is maintained, opted for high rates of imprisonment and a punitive approach to law-and-order issues; Jones (2010), for example, has identified seemingly more lenient approaches in Italy. Responding to Wacquant by examining the situation in Greece, Cheliotis and Xenakis (2010, 67) have pointed to the "danger of occidentalist presumptions" if theoretical frameworks based on "Western experiences of capitalist development are problematically applied to states of the semi-periphery, given their very different social and economic trajectories". More fundamentally, Wacquant "underestimates the difficulties of concepts 'travelling', and the obstacles to bringing criminal justice practices into line with those elsewhere" (Nelken 2010, 337). Thus, Lacey (2010, 781) has argued that different states act in different ways. In Western Europe, for example, other culturally embedded approaches are comparatively resilient and are still able to challenge neoliberal penality. Nellis (2005), for example, has referred to the continuing relevance of an embattled "humanistic-rehabilitative discourse" and the rise of a "mangerialist–surveillant" discourse which imports concepts and practices from the commercial and corporate sectors.

Related to this line of criticism, other writers have focused on Wacquant's insufficiently nuanced portrayal of developments even within the US. Even here "the 'workfare' to 'prisonfare' nexus is working differently in different parts of the country" (Lacey 2010, 783). All too often, "the USA is discussed as if it were uniform in its approach to crime and punishment rather than a federalised system encompassing diverse arrangements and practices". (Newburn 2010, 346). However,

> huge variation can be seen if we return to state-level changes.... In this regard, it is interesting to note that since 1999 four states – Kansas, Michigan, New Jersey and New York – have reduced their prison populations by between 5 and 20 per cent.
>
> (Newburn 2010, 348)

Lack of a historical dimension

A further criticism levelled at Wacquant charges that his perspective fails to embrace an adequate historical dimension (Jones 2010). If the "primary impulse of 'neoliberalism' ... is the move to the targeted exclusion of marginalized groups, 'neoliberal' punishment has been around in Britain for centuries" (Lacey 2010, 784); for Jones (2010, 398), the Poor Law was, in fact, "Penal State Mark 1". Indeed, "mechanisms for the selective demonization and exclusion of targeted low-status 'outsiders' have a depressingly long history" with the "infamous distinction between the 'deserving' and 'undeserving' poor echoing down through the arrangements of the welfare state, even in its supposed golden age" (Lacey 2010, 783; see also Hancock and Mooney 2012, 210). This form of historically informed critique also leads Piven (2010) to dwell on the detectable continuities and parallels between how the poor are regulated and policed under both Fordist and neoliberal capitalism in the US: what was "new in the 1996 reform was not work enforcement so much as its administrative reinvigoration" (Piven 2010, 113).

The growth of other forms of detention

Yet another critique of Wacquant points to the insufficient attention paid to other forms of detention emerging beyond the walls of prisons. The "new punitiveness" (Pratt *et al.* 2005), so central to neoliberalism's mode of social regulation, is reflected in locations beyond the prison and this dimension could be more thoroughly investigated by Wacquant. Such developments relate to the tendency to locate particular sections of the population (those regarded as ambiguously 'troublesome' and ambiguously 'out of place') within enclosures which may not in the ordinary sense of the word be prisons but which remain zones of varying degrees of confinement, monitoring and supervision (see also Butler 2004). What is more, there is the connected aspiration to use technology for surveillance purposes to track the troublesome in the community (see also Nellis 2005). Related to the emergence of quasi-prisons and other types of enclosure and supervision, it is now possible to detect a "whole variety of paralegal forms of confinement ... including pre-emptive or preventive detention prior to a crime being committed" (Rose 2000, 335). These are targeted at, for example, potential paedophiles and potential terrorists – "monstrous individuals", the "incorrigibly anti-social" and others representatives of a "new human kind" (Rose 2000, 333).

Such forms of neoliberal penality can also be analytically conjoined to a series of not entirely dissimilar transformations relating to detention and detainees which are becoming more and more central in the context of national security and the safeguarding of borders. Although Wacquant fails to embrace it in his analysis, there are stark "continuities between domestic prison practices and the detention of migrants, asylum seekers and enemy combatants" (Martin and Mitchelson 2009, 460). In 2008, it was reported that the Correction Corporation of America had announced "plans to build a 3,000-bed 'megaprison' in San Diego, California, which if built would be the largest immigrant detention center in the United States" (Lawston and Escobar 2010, 1). During the following year, in the US alone, "approximately 380,000 people spent time in the vast and continuously expanding migrant detention system" (Mountz *et al.* 2012, 2). The UK, along with a number of other countries, has expanded its use of migrant detention. Indeed, the evolution of such practices, particularly as they relate to racialisation, has given rise to the evolution of a whole new academic field of study: 'detention studies' (Mountz *et al.* 2012, 2).

Failing to recognise resistance

Finally, a number of Wacquant's critics have referred to his failure to mention forces opposing 'neoliberal penality' in its various guises (Jones 2010; Newburn 2010). These include international bodies such as the United Nations Committee Against Torture and the European Committee for the Prevention of Torture and Inhuman or Degrading Treatment or Punishment. Within civil society, in a number of countries, groups and individuals also coalesce around counter hegemonic penal policies. In Ireland, for example, a coalition of reformers has prompted the announcement that a notorious prison for children is to be gradually closed (Office of the Inspector of Prisons 2012).

6.4 Concluding remarks

Despite these targeted criticisms, Wacquant's work on neoliberal penality can help practitioners involved in forensic networks to situate the contemporary patterning of 'welfare' within a more embracing explanatory framework. While mostly concerned with developments in the US, his analysis can inflect our critical understanding of developments in Europe. For example, in the UK the prison population grew by approximately 40 per cent during the period of New Labour governments (1997–2010). Taking into account the already mentioned criticisms of O'Sullivan and O'Donnell (2007), Wacquant's analysis can also be utilized to comprehend developments within the Republic of Ireland. The prison population there has been steadily rising over recent decades. Indeed, the rate of imprisonment – the number of prisoners per 100,000 – has risen rapidly over the past four decades: from "25.2 per 100,000 in 1970 to 36.1 in 1980, and from 60.1 in 1990 to 80.4 in 2000. In December 2011, the rate was 95.8" (Jesuit Centre for Faith and Justice 2012, 6). What is more, and illustrating the concerns of those now focusing on 'detention studies', a so-called Direct Provision System (DPS) has been introduced to provide temporary accommodation for asylum seekers. In December 2010, an estimated 2,778 of the 6,107 people living in DPS centres had been there for more than 36 months and more than 1,200 had been there for between 24 and 36 months (United Nations General Assembly 2011, 21).

In both the UK and Ireland, 'welfare' is increasingly infused by the discursive ambiance of the penal regime and this is likely to impact on social workers' involvement with a range of client groups. As Wacquant's analysis suggests, the "'clients' of both assistantial and penitential sectors of the state fall under the same principled suspicion: they are considered morally deficient unless they periodically provide visible proof to the contrary" (Wacquant 2009a, 15). This was certainly apparent in the terms of New Labour's approach to "jobseekers" in the UK, which endeavoured to extend the surveillance of claimants begun during the period of British government of both Prime Ministers Thatcher (1979–1990) and Major (1990–1997). More pervasively, the discursive presentation of "welfare reform" under both New Labour and the Conservative/

Liberal Democrat administrations has tended to gel with Wacqaunt's perspective. For example, the independent report published by the UK Department for Work and Pensions in late 2008 – in setting out a vision for "a radically reformed welfare system between now and 2015" – frequently referred to some benefit recipients, "found to be playing the system", as "repeat *offenders*" (Gregg 2008, 74, emphasis added). This encroaching "criminalisation" is also reflected in the voice risk analysis technology, referred to earlier in the discussion, which tests whether housing benefit claimants are providing false information.

In October 2013 Joan Burton, the Irish Minister for Social Protection, proposed that officers from *An Garda Síochána* [the police] might begin to set up checkpoints in estates and on roads early in the morning to randomly interrogate people about their employment status. Many, she suspected, were likely to be going off to work, not declaring earnings and going on to fraudulently claim benefits. This idea not only reflects the demise of a more benign social democratic vision within the Irish Labour Party, it also illuminates encompassing economic and social politics being pursued by the current government. Such trends may also be detectable in terms of how the clients of social workers are, in some instances, also treated as a "problem population whose civic probity is by definition suspect" (Wacquant 2009a, 98). An example of this embryonic trend, attesting to the US influence on EU policy making, is the intensified surveillance to be targeted at parents suspected of misusing alcohol:

> For the past six months the Family Drug and Alcohol Court in London has been piloting a scheme using alcohol-monitoring bracelets in child protection cases where parental alcohol addiction was a concern. The trial is the first of its kind in the UK, but the bracelets are widely used in the US. They measure alcohol level in water vapour on the surface of the skin. The measurements are recorded automatically every 30 minutes. Supporters of the device say they can be used to help parents prove their sobriety and resist the temptation to drink.
>
> (BBC News, 22 March 2013)

Developments such as this should prompt concerns among a social work profession which asserts principles of human rights and social justice are "fundamental" (Hare 2004). In this context, a better theoretical understanding of the evolution of the prison and 'welfare' might aid our efforts to confront and resist policies and practices targeted at those described and contained as 'castaway categories'.

References

BBC News. 2013. "Are ankle tags the answer for tackling parents with drink problems?", 22 March. Report by Chris Vallance. www.bbc.co.uk/news/uk-21882189.

Bumiller K. 2013. "Incarceration, welfare state and market nexus: the increasing significance of gender in the prison system". In M. Seagrave and B. Carlton (eds) *Women*

Exiting Prison: Critical essays on gender, post-release support and survival. Abingdon, Oxon: Routledge.

Butler J. 2004. *Precarious Life.* London: Verso.

Cheliotis L. K. and Xenakis S. 2010. "What's neoliberalism got to do with it? Towards a political economy of punishment in Greece". *Criminology and Criminal Justice* 10(4): 353–373.

Chunn D. E. and Gavigan S. A. M. 2004. "Welfare law, welfare fraud, and the moral regulation of the 'never deserving' poor". *Social and Legal Studies* 13(2): 219–243.

Gelsthorpe L. 2010. "Women, crime and control". *Criminology and Criminal Justice* 10(4): 375–386.

Gregg P. 2008. *Realising Potential: A vision for personalised conditionality and support.* London: UK Department for Work and Pensions.

Hancock L. and Mooney G. 2012. "Beyond the penal state: advanced marginality, social policy and anti-welfarism". In P. Squires and J. Lea (eds) *Criminalisation and advanced marginality: Critically exploring the work of Loïc Wacquant.* Bristol: Policy Press.

Harcourt B. E. 2010. "Neoliberal penality: A brief genealogy". *Theoretical Criminology* 14(1): 74–92.

Hare I. 2004. "Defining social work for the 21st century: The international federation of social workers' revised definition of social work". *International Social Work* 47(3): 407–427.

Harvey D. 2005. *A Brief History of Neoliberalism.* Oxford: Oxford University.

Jesuit Centre for Faith and Justice. 2012. *The Irish Prison System: Visions, values, reality.* Dublin: Jesuit Centre for Faith and Justice. www.jcfj.ie/images/stories/jcfj_prison_paper_with_cover.pdf.

Jones M. 2010. "Impedimenta state: Anatomies of neoliberal penality". *Criminology and Criminal Justice* 10(4): 393–404.

Lacey N. 2010. "Differentiating among penal states". *The British Journal of Sociology* 61(4): 778–795.

Lawston J. M. and Escobar M. 2010. "Policing, detention, deportation, and resistance: Situating immigrant justice and carcerality in the 21st Century". *Social Justice* 36(2): 1–7.

Martin L. L. and Mitchelson M. L. 2009. "Geographies of detention and imprisonment: Interrogating spatial practices of confinement, discipline, law and state power". *Geography Compass* 3(1): 459–477.

Mayer M. 2010. "Punishing the poor: Some questions on Wacquant's theorizing the neoliberal state". *Theoretical Criminology* 14 (1): 93–103.

Mountz A., Coddington K., Catania R. T. and Loyd J. M. 2012. "Conceptualizing detention: Mobility, containment, bordering, and exclusion". *Progress in Human Geography* 37(4): 522–541.

Nederveen Pieterse J. 2004. "Neoliberal Empire". *Theory, Culture and Society* 21(3): 119–140.

Nelken D. 2010. "Denouncing the penal state". *Criminology and Criminal Justice* 10(4): 331–340.

Nellis M. 2005. "Electronic monitoring, satellite tracking, and the new punitiveness in England and Wales". In J. Pratt, D. Brown, M. Brown, S. Hallsworth and W. Morrison (eds) *The New Punitiveness: Trends, theories and perspectives.* Devon, England: Willan.

Newburn T. 2010. "Diffusion, differentiation and resistance in comparative penality". *Criminology and Criminal Justice* 10(4): 341–352.

Office of the Inspector of Prisons. 2012. *Report of an Inspection of St. Patrick's Institution by the Inspector of Prisons Judge Michael Reilly.* Nenagh: Office of the Inspector of Prisons, Ireland.

O'Sullivan E. and O'Donnell I. 2007. "Coercive confinement in the Republic of Ireland: The waning of the culture of control". *Punishment and Society* 9(1): 27–48.

Piven F. F. 2010. "A response to Wacquant". *Theoretical Criminology* 14(1): 111–116.

Pratt J., Brown D., Brown M., Hallsworth S. and Morrison W. (eds). 2005. "Introduction". In J. Pratt, D. Brown, M. Brown, S. Hallsworth and W. Morrison (eds) *The New Punitiveness: Trends, theories and perspectives.* Devon, England: Willan.

Rose N. 2000. "Government and Control". *British Journal of Criminology* 40: 321–339.

United Nations General Assembly. 2011. *Report on the independent expert on the question of human rights and extreme poverty – Mission to Ireland, Magdalena Sepúlveda Carmona,* 17 May (A/HRC/17/34/Add.2). http://daccess-dds-ny.un.org/doc/UNDOC/GEN/G11/132/17/PDF/G1113217.pdf?OpenElement.

Wacquant L. 2001. "The penalisation of poverty and the rise of Neo-Liberalism". *European Journal on Criminal Policy and Research* 9: 401–412.

Wacquant L. 2008. *Urban Outcasts.* Cambridge, England: Polity Press.

Wacquant L. 2009a. *Punishing the poor: The neoliberal government of social insecurity.* Durham, NC: Duke University Press.

Wacquant L. 2009b. *Deadly Symbiosis.* Cambridge, England: Polity Press.

Wardhaugh J. and Wilding P. 1993. "Towards an explanation of the corruption of care". *Critical Social Policy* 13(1): 4–32.

7 Solution-focused justice in the time of 'law and order'

Jelena Popovic

7.1 Introduction

As the principles of therapeutic jurisprudence gain momentum, so too do calls for harsher penalties and tougher approaches to criminal behaviour. Solution focused justice is not only consistent with crime reduction strategies, it actually enhances them. This chapter examines how these approaches are not 'soft on crime'; rather, what is required of the participants is often far more onerous than a traditional penalty. Specialist courts and programmes address the causes of criminal behaviour to reduce reoffending and make communities safer. This chapter also looks at the economic sense in addressing the presenting issues in the community, rather than through incarceration.

Specialist courts and programmes involve the application of specific and individualised therapeutic jurisprudence principles and interventions within the legal system for a range of offenders before the courts where specific factors or co-morbidities directly affect their entry into the criminal justice system. These courts include Aboriginal Courts, Community Courts, Drug Courts, Mental Health Courts, and various pre-sentence court support programmes, for example. Such problem-solving court approaches aim to address the causes of the criminal behaviour, with a view to reducing a person's offending behaviour and its impact on the community. From a 'justice reinvestment' perspective, it makes far more economic sense to address the presenting issues in the community rather than in jail.

This chapter examines the use of therapeutic jurisprudence in practical terms, and the role of solution focused judging in courts. The greater utility of problem-solving approaches and investment in specialist courts and programmes is explored against the 'tough on crime' and 'law and order' strategies favoured often by populist political agendas and the community at large.

7.2 Therapeutic jurisprudence in practice

The term 'therapeutic jurisprudence' came into usage after the work in the field by Bruce Winick and David Wexler in the early 1990s (Wexler and Winick 1991). Therapeutic jurisprudence has now become a recognised component of mainstream courts in the US, UK, Canada, Australia and New Zealand (King 2008, 155; King *et al.* 2009, 22). Therapeutic jurisprudence in practice encompasses various approaches (Popovic 2002, 121); it is a concept that involves the understanding and targeting of underlying causes of criminal offending.

Solution-focused judging

The term 'therapeutic jurisprudence' when applied in the criminal justice system means the court and the judicial officer take the opportunity to address the factors underlying the offending behaviour which brings the accused person before the court. The judicial officer uses this opportunity to bring about behaviour change in the offender, thus reducing the person's future offending, and in turn reducing the impact of their offending on the community.

In applying therapeutic jurisprudence or solution focused judging, the tenets typically applied include:

- the utilisation of the court appearance and contact with the criminal justice system as a catalyst for change;
- the use of individualised treatment methods and interventions to address offending-related behaviour;
- placing an offender in treatment participation in order to reduce recidivism and harm in the community.

The judicial officer assesses factors surrounding the alleged offending in each individual case; any prior convictions of the accused person; what issues the person before the court might present with; services available to assist their rehabilitation; and their desire to effect behaviour change. Professionals or court-based clinicians provide information to assist judicial decision-making so any decisions made about a therapeutic programme are sound.

The types of matters that come before the Magistrates' Court in Victoria (Australia) have seen significant change over the past 20 years. At that time most of the offenders coming before the courts of summary jurisdiction were involved in traffic offences, some alcohol related violence and theft matters. Few offenders came to court with substance abuse issues, mental impairment or in a state of homelessness. The breadth of matters currently dealt with by the Magistrates' Court sees offenders presenting with problems with mental illness, mental impairment, intellectual disability, acquired brain injury (of which there has been a significant increase), illegal and legal drug dependencies, alcohol dependence, foetal alcohol syndrome, homelessness, intergenerational dysfunction *et al.* and these problems often co-exist, introducing a new complexity into legal decision-making. The traditional court approach of determining guilt and imposing a sentence in accordance with sentencing law in these types of cases is outdated and an ineffective means of tackling the causes of criminal behaviour. It is self-evident that as communities change, so should the criminal justice response evolve to meet the changing needs of communities.

The practice of therapeutic jurisprudence continues to evolve, and its expression takes many forms. There is no 'one size fits all' approach. In its simplest form, the implementation of therapeutic jurisprudence principles may involve speaking directly to the accused in order to elicit a more individual response, such as a clearer articulation of remorse or an indication of the underlying cause of the offending. A key component is procedural fairness, and ensuring that it is made clear to offenders that they have a voice in the proceedings, and that they will be listened to and respected. The application of therapeutic jurisprudence may take the form of the referral of an offender to a specific programme to address either the offending, or the issue (or issues) which may have led to the offending. At its most sophisticated level, the problem-solving approach may involve the offender's participation in a 'problem-solving' court, set up to address specifically the main presenting issue causing the person to come to the attention of the police.

Warner (2014) describes how the sentencing principles of general and specific deterrence, central to court-imposed punishments, have little deterrent effect. A study by the Sentencing Advisory Council (Ritchie 2011) found that the thought of imprisonment has little general deterrent effect on offenders prior to the commission of an offence. In particular, deterrence is not a useful concept when dealing with people who are alcohol or drug affected, as their ability to think logically is grossly impaired. The prospect of imprisonment has either no effect on specific deterrence, or leads to the creation of a 'criminal learning' environment, an inappropriate way to address underlying causes of crime for both older and young offenders. This study found that "given the aims of rehabilitation and reintegration, the lack of evidence for a specific deterrent effect suggests that custodial penalties for young offenders should be used sparingly and for purposes other than for specific deterrence" (Ritchie 2011, 22).

Specialist and problem-solving courts

Specialist and problem-solving courts across the US, the UK, Canada, New Zealand and Australia, include:

- drug courts for both adults and juveniles for offenders whose offences are directly linked to the possession or sale of illicit substances or whose dependence on substances is leading to the commission of crime to fund the dependency;
- family drug courts which aim to reunify families where children have been removed from substance abusing parents (Levine 2012);
- Mental Health Courts (MHC) (Woodward 2014);
- Family Violence Courts, which aim to provide specialist intervention to reduce the incidence of intra-familial violence (for Australian and overseas examples, see Stewart 2011);
- courts for adult and juvenile indigenous offenders, for example, the Koori Courts in Victoria, Circle Sentencing Courts in NSW, Nunga Courts in

South Australia (Cannon, 2007), Maori Youth Rangatahi Courts in New Zealand, First Nations Court in Canada, Healing to Wellness Courts and Navajo Court in the US;

- homelessness courts, for example the Red Hook Community Court in New York (see: www.courtinnovation.org/project/red-hook-community-justice-center) and the California Homeless Courts (see: www.courts.ca.gov/5976.htm);
- re-entry courts which assess a prisoner's suitability to be released on parole, for example, the Harlem Parole Reentry Court at the Harlem Community Justice Center, New York (see www.courtinnovation.org/project/parole-reentry-court) (Reentry Court Solutions);
- veterans' treatment courts (Justice for Vets 2014), which assist returned members of the US military;
- youth peer courts, also known as teen courts, an example of which is the Harlem Youth Court in New York. The model in the Harlem Court utilises a number of teenage peers trained as lawyers, judges and jurors to be involved in actual cases. Positive peer pressure is exerted to change behaviour and to make young people more accountable for their offending behaviour (Center for Court Innovation, 2014);
- courts which address specific offending around 'driving under the influence' or driving after the licence to drive has been removed from a driver. Throughout the US, these are known as DWI Courts and aim to change drink driving behaviour through treatment (National Center for DWI Courts. 2014). Victoria has commenced a pilot to address drink driving behaviour through judicial monitoring for individuals sentenced to a Community Corrections Order for drink driving offences (Sentencing Act (Vic), 1991).

Additionally, there are Community Courts where cases involving offenders in the local community are determined. A material example of this in Victoria is the Neighbourhood Justice Centre (NJC), established in 2007 (Department of Justice NJC Evaluation 2010, 1), which aimed to reduce crime and improve community feeling. There has also been a growth in 'specialist' lists which address specific types of offending or a specific cohort of offenders. One example of this in Melbourne, Victoria, is the 'Tuesday Afternoon List', which provides a safe environment to address the treatment needs of street sex-workers in Melbourne (see Popovic 2005, 71).

The problem solving courts such as those mentioned above have the following key elements in common:

- matching judicial and community resources to the needs of each case;
- the formation and utilisation of partnerships with service providers and other professionals, such as victim support, police, corrections (as appropriate);
- the development of expertise for judicial officers and other team members, to enable the judicial officer to make better informed decisions.

Judicial monitoring comprises one of the main aspects of problem-solving courts, as offenders are required to reappear before the judicial officer monitoring their case, which in turn increases accountability of offenders, motivates treatment participation and results in lasting behaviour change. The combined efforts of the teams involved in these courts assist in achieving improved health outcomes, which then lead to a reduction of the seriousness and quantity of reoffending.

A significant difference between solution-focused approaches and traditional court practices is that, in a traditional court, an offender rarely engages in direct communication with the sentencing judicial officer. The communication generally takes place between the judicial officer and the accused's lawyer or advocate. The only direct communication generally occurs as the sentence is handed down, and sometimes not even at that stage. Additionally, in the sentencing process of traditional courts, victims and police officers have limited roles. As previously mentioned, offender accountability is one of the main features of specialist problem-solving courts. It is important to note that within the contexts of specialist and problem-solving courts, there is a much higher level of offender accountability.

Problem-solving courts also incorporate elements of restorative justice. Victims are encouraged to attend court and to have a voice in proceedings. Similarly, police informants are also given a voice in such proceedings. Prosecutors, especially in problem-solving courts with a 'team' approach, are given a significant role in explaining the effect of the offending behaviour on the community. When a problem-solving approach is applied in sentencing, the penalty can be structured so as to make reparation to victims. A commonly used approach is to direct that payment be made by the offender to a charity nominated by the victim. In this way, the victim is included in the sentencing process by having a voice, but is also given the opportunity to benefit a charity so that the suffering they endured is recognised in a beneficial way.

Pre-sentence programmes and specialist courts also assist with bail compliance, as bail is better supervised and police informants advised of unsatisfactory compliance. In indigenous courts, accountability is even more forcefully accentuated in that the accused is accountable to both the 'elders' sitting at the table at time of sentencing and to community members.

Any preconception that therapeutic or problem-orientated approaches are necessarily 'soft' on crime is not the reality. In addition to the emphasis on personal responsibility and accountability as mentioned above, the majority of participants in therapeutic programmes and courts voluntarily engage in court supervision – which far outweighs the penalty to which they might otherwise have been sentenced. Participants in specialist courts and programmes must voluntarily participate and informed consent is often a prerequisite. For example, section 4S(3)(c) of the Magistrates' Court Act 1989 (Vic) provides that a matter must not be referred to the Assessment and Referral Court (ARC) List unless the accused consents, and in relation to the Koori Court (the indigenous matters court), section 4F(1)(d) similarly notes that the consent of an accused is required for the Koori Court to exercise jurisdiction.

Participation in specialist courts and programs generally necessitates numerous court appearances, attendances with court-appointed case managers, inpatient admissions at treatment facilities such as drug and alcohol detoxification and residential rehabilitation clinics, and appointments with treating professionals. Treatment regimes can be quite onerous, and could be considered far more difficult than paying a fine or spending time in prison.

Further enhancement of problem-solving approaches

In Victoria, and this is replicated in other jurisdictions, individuals with mental illness coming into contact with the criminal justice system either on arrest or as prisoners are significantly over-represented. Ogloff *et al.* (2010, 871) found that in excess of 50 per cent of people taken into custody had a prior mental health treatment history, and one-sixth were registered with a psychiatric service at the time of arrest (Ogloff 2012, 5). Statistics such as these highlight the need for an improved 'whole of government' response to mentally ill offenders (Ogloff 2010), and also throw the role of MHC into sharp relief. As a consequence of Woodward's (2014) three-year study of the success of MHC in Michigan, USA, legislation has been introduced to expand these courts from a pilot operation to a mainstream option. Woodward (2014) found that, following court directed treatment, recidivism was reduced by 14 per cent.

It is important to engage with offenders as quickly as possible after apprehension, and the clinicians attached to Victoria's court support services and specialist courts find that immediate programmatic responses maximise the probability that offenders will attend programmes, and capitalise on their plight to facilitate behaviour change. It is recognised that the point of crisis is also the point of opportunity. It is recognised also that many offenders do not engage if they have to make an appointment in the future. The availability of pre-sentence support programmes to police officers at the time of apprehension would enable problem-solving to commence at the earliest opportunity, thus greatly reducing the number of offenders arrested and placed in remand facilities.

The Victoria Police previously initiated a program known as PACT (Police and Community Triage), which involved the creation and evaluation of a team of workers with skills in alcohol and other drugs, mental health and other areas (Victoria Police 2011, 49). These workers provided a single point of interface between police and the local health and community service centre. The primary objective was to develop an organisational delivery blueprint for collaborative partnerships between Victoria Police (and other emergency services) and the community services sector to address issues affecting community safety, health and well-being. This programme was a fresh direction for police and community services, and acknowledged the critical role police and other emergency services play as a point of early intervention in the community (Victoria Police 2011). It also reduced demands on police. Over the two and a half years that the programme operated (until funding ceased in 2013), it received 500 referrals from police members for people experiencing multiple and complex issues (Wellings

2013). Local services were supportive and contributed to the programme's success. Access to the programme significantly altered the manner in which police problem-solved when dealing with challenging people. An additional benefit was the enhancement of communication and collaboration between police, community and other services to achieve better outcomes for these people (Wellings 2013).

The value of these approaches has been recognised by the community sector, which has endorsed the ethos and work of therapeutic approaches, and the initiatives implemented by the courts. The Victorian Council of Social Service (VCOSS) noted that government needs to redirect 'spiralling prison costs', and invest in diversion programmes, preventative measures, rehabilitation, and support to help former prisoners from re-offending (VCOSS 2013, 1). Welfare workers also point to the need for increased drug and alcohol support, and a renewed emphasis in schools to teach students to respect each other.

7.3 'Law and order' and 'tough on crime' strategies

The move towards 'law and order' and 'tough on crime' agendas

It appears that some Australian states are out of step with the rest of the Western world in terms of embracing non-custodial alternatives to imprisonment. 'Law and order' was a significant election issue in Victoria's State election in 2010, fuelled by international riots reported by media (the so-called 'BlackBerry riots' of August 2011 in England an example of this).

In Victoria, changes to the legislation since 2011 have resulted in an unprecedented rise in prisoner numbers. These changes include the abolition of suspended sentences in the higher courts and Magistrates' Court, mandatory minimum imprisonment periods for some violent offences, and new offences relating to the breach of bail conditions. There have also been amendments to the parole regime, which reduced the number of prisoners granted parole and increased numbers of parolees whose parole is cancelled.

The Productivity Commission in Victoria has reported that spending on Victorian prisons increased from $517 million in 2008–2009 to $625 million in 2012–2013, and that the average daily prison population increased from 4,299 inmates to 5,120 (Commonwealth of Australia, Productivity Commission 2014, 8A.33). Prisoner numbers and the costs associated with increased incarceration are predicted to be even greater as the legislative changes take effect (Commonwealth of Australia, Productivity Commission 2014).

The increased incarceration rate is out of proportion to the crime statistics, which indicate that over a ten-year period there has been an overall decrease in the crime rate of 12 per cent. There was a small increase in the overall crime rate for 2012–2013 of 1.6 per cent, mainly attributable to the increase in family violence-related offending and associated with the increase in reporting and policing practices (an increase of 18.4 per cent from 2011–2012). Rape reports decreased by 3.1 per cent, robbery reports decreased by 14.2 per cent, armed robberies decreased by 9.3 per cent, and there was an overall decrease of 3 per cent in offences relating to property (Victoria Police 2013, 4–5).

Regrettably, the trend towards problem-solving approaches in courts has been reversed in some parts of Australia. In July 2012, the NSW Government ceased the operation of the Youth Drug Court on the grounds of expense (Harvey 2012). The *Sydney Morning Herald* (Sydney Morning Herald Editorial, 2012) commented as follows:

> The youth drug court is not a soft option. In the 2004 review one of the participants [said] it would have been easier just to go to jail.... An appropriately thorough review might have concluded that more needed to be spent on the program to shore up its effectiveness.

In September 2012, the Queensland Government defunded and closed the Drug Court, Murri (indigenous) Court and the Special Circumstances (mental impairment) Court. The Attorney-General and Minister for Justice, Jarrod Bleijie, stated that the courts were not cost effective (Lemmon 2012).

The Northern Territory had a pre-sentence specialist court known as the SMART Court (Substance Misuse Assessment and Referral for Treatment) for both adult and juvenile offenders who had a serious history of drug or alcohol misuse, and acknowledged guilt. Consenting participants were placed on a SMART Court order and received treatment, clinical oversight and judicial monitoring for 6 to 12 months (Northern Territory Magistrates Courts 2013). The programme was defunded and repealed in December 2012. In its place, the Northern Territory Government has enacted the Alcohol Mandatory Treatment Act 2013 (NT).

The North Liverpool Community Justice Centre in the UK, which was opened in 2002 and was based on the Midtown Community Court, has also been defunded and has now closed. It has been suggested that the number of offenders summoned to the court was too low to justify the running costs. Merseyside's Police and Crime Commissioner, Jane Kennedy, has been reported as stating that the work of the police with regard to troublesome offenders would be more difficult with the closure of the Court (BBC News Liverpool 2013).

Fortunately, Victoria has not experienced a reduction or cessation of any specialist lists with the exception of the Koori family violence support workers. The ARC List's pilot has been extended for two years pending further evaluation. A Family Drug Court is being piloted. A specialist list will be piloted at Frankston Magistrates' Court (a large outer-suburban area of Melbourne challenged by socio-economic deprivation) to address the offending behaviour of repeat drink-drivers and offenders who drive while their licence has been cancelled or suspended. The Magistrates' and Children's Courts of Victoria have found resources within existing budgets to establish sittings of the Koori Children's Court in four regional areas of Victoria (Latrobe, Shepparton, Bairnsdale and Warrnambool circuits). A Koori Court began sitting at Melbourne Magistrates' Court in August 2014. Additionally, an Aboriginal Hearing Day has been implemented in the suburban Melbourne Heidelberg Magistrates' Court. In addition to the Magistrates' Court's commitment to broadening the number of indigenous persons who can access the Koori Court, other government agencies such as the youth justice service and Aboriginal organisations such as the Victorian Aboriginal Legal Service and Aboriginal co-operatives and health service agencies are providing additional support without additional funding. The County Court's Koori Court has received funding and has commenced sitting at Melbourne as well as in one large regional area in Victoria (Gippsland).

Community perceptions, crime and sentencing

In a study of juries from 138 trials in Tasmania, Australia, more than half the jurors surveyed suggested a more lenient sentence than the trial judge imposed. After being informed of the judge's actual sentence, 90 per cent said that the judge's sentence was (very or fairly) appropriate (Davis *et al.* 2011, 25–26). Lovegrove's (2007) study asked community members in Melbourne to indicate what sentence they would have imposed in actual cases. What was found was that judges were not more lenient than the community, and there was a disparity in the range of sentences that the community members would have imposed reflecting the diversity of community views. Community member participants in the study, when deciding sentencing, took into account factors individual to the offender, not just the seriousness of the offending (Lovegrove 2007).

Gelb's 2011 survey of community members in Victoria in relation to crime sentencing and the courts demonstrated support for alternatives to imprisonment, in particular as a response to prison overcrowding and vulnerable offenders (e.g. young people, individuals with mental illness and drug dependent offenders). The study found that people who worry about being affected by crime, such as being victims of crime, are less likely to favour alternatives to imprisonment (favouring incarceration over alternative sentences) than people who do not share these concerns concerned about crime (Gelb 2011a).

A study of community views of the purposes of sentencing in Victoria looked at socio-demographic variables impacting on sentencing views. The only consistent factor influencing sentencing views was media use. The research highlights the impact and influence the media has in the formation of punitive attitudes towards crime and sentencing. It demonstrates that public concerns are based on how crime is reported in the media instead of the actual trends in crime and sentencing (Gelb 2011b).

7.4 Investing in specialist and problem-solving courts

Currently, one of the main disadvantages of problem-solving courts is that there are often programmatic limitations, mainly geography, which prevent otherwise eligible offenders participating in the courts and programmes. That is to say that not all courts or locations are serviced by problem-solving opportunities, either through a lack of resources or a lack of will. Regrettably, this eventuates in the phenomenon referred to as 'postcode justice', where access and eligibility for specialist courts and programmes is confined to specific locations. Ideally, these approaches would be mainstreamed so that they could be available to any offender who wished to avail themselves of the services and individualised approach.

Many of the specialised courts and programmes implemented in Australia have had evaluation components built into the programme design. The subsequent evaluations demonstrate reductions in rates of substance misuse, recidivism and crime; the increased accountability of offenders (Borowski 2009; Harris 2006; Department of Justice's CISP Evaluation Report 2010; Department of Justice NJC Evaluation 2010); and the enhancement and improved integration of the response to both victims and offenders. Additionally, there is a demonstrable improvement in family relationships, health outcomes, and perceptions of procedural fairness. Compliance with bail conditions and readiness to participate in community-based sentencing dispositions are also improved. Where local communities have a local justice centre, there is also an improved public confidence in the justice system.

Cost-benefit analyses

There is also a demonstrable cost saving where these problem-solving approaches are in place. For example, with respect to the Court Integrated Services Program (CISP) in Victoria, the economic benefit due to reductions in re-offending, imprisonment and breaches of court imposed orders was estimated to be AU$5.90 for every dollar spent, and AU$2.60 over a five year period, and AU$1.70 over two years (Department of Justice CISP Evaluation 2010). The report into CISP demonstrated significant improvements in the mental and physical health of participants. The Auditor-General for Victoria reported that both CISP and the NJC achieved their stated aims and that CISP demonstrably reduced re-offending (Auditor-General of Victoria 2011). The findings of the NJC evaluation found that the NJC reduced recidivism rates by 7 per cent (and double that to a drop in 14 per cent for NJC offenders comparative to offenders from other courts), and brought other tangible benefits for the community including higher rates of offenders completing Community Based Orders and undertaking community work, cost-benefit outcomes that would result in higher returns on initial investments in the NJC and facilitating "greater confidence in the justice system than at other courts" (Department of Justice NJC Evaluation 2010, 2).

Victoria's MHC, the ARC List, was initially funded as a pilot and evaluated in 2012. The aims of the List are to:

- reduce the risk of harm to the community by addressing the underlying factors that contribute to offending behaviour;
- improve the health and well-being of accused persons with a mental impairment by facilitating access to appropriate treatment and other support services;

- to increase public confidence in the criminal justice system by improving court processes and increasing options available to courts in responding to accused persons with a mental impairment; and
- to reduce the number of offenders with a mental impairment received into the prison system.

The 2012 evaluation found that the ARC List met its stated aims and the pilot was extended for a further two-year period. In November 2013, the work and contribution to the community of the ARC List was acknowledged by the Melbourne City Council by the prestigious award for 'Contribution to Community by a Corporation' (Magistrates' Court of Victoria 2013).

Justice reinvestment

Justice reinvestment has been described by the Smart Justice coalition as 'a new approach that redirects money spent on prisons to community-based initiatives which aim to address the underlying causes of crime. It promises to cut crime and save money' (Smart Justice 2012, 1). Internationally, one of the main drivers of justice reinvestment is a coalition of conservative politicians who established 'Right on Crime'. Their motto is "The Conservative Case for Reform: Fighting Crime, Prioritising Victims and Protecting Taxpayers" (Right on Crime 2010). One of the examples cited by this website is the State of Texas, where it is reported that the justice reinvestment approach taken in that state has resulted in the saving of US$2 billion in incarceration costs. It also reports a reduction of 52.9 per cent in the number of juveniles in state institutions (Right on Crime 2010). The approach taken has been to divert significantly more accused persons into supervised treatment and residential rehabilitation units through probation rather than to sentence them to imprisonment. This has necessitated additional funds being allocated to probation services, but has resulted in a significant decrease in the cost of imprisonment. It has been so successful that the State of Texas in the US has closed one prison and will close another in the medium term. Additionally, the rates of offending, reoffending and reoffending on parole dropped significantly (Right on Crime 2010).

In June 2013, the Legal and Australian Senate Constitutional Affairs References Committee published its report on the value of a justice reinvestment approach to criminal justice in Australia. The Committee made recommendations that the Commonwealth take a leading role in identifying and establishing a national approach to collecting the data necessary to implement justice reinvestment; commit to sharing justice reinvestment data and initiatives with other jurisdictions; and establish a clearing house in relation to the subject. Additionally, the Committee recommended that Australian governments recognise the importance of long term sustainable funding for programmes to reduce address the needs of marginalised (through poverty, mental-illness or aboriginality) and complex offenders, and that such funding include evaluation of the programmes (Commonwealth of Australia, Senate Legal and Constitutional Affairs References Committee 2013, 111–112).

An economic example of justice reinvestment in an Australian context is the work of the Australian National Council on Drugs (ANCD), in relation to the cost benefits, as well as other considerable benefits in terms of health and mortality, of diverting offenders into residential rehabilitation instead of imprisoning them. A report commissioned from Deloitte Access Economics by the ANCD (2013) concluded the following:

- The total financial savings associated with diversion to community residential rehabilitation compared with prison are $111,458 per offender (estimated for the year 2012–2013: Deloitte Access Economics 2013, 63).
- The costs of treatment in community residential rehabilitation services are substantially cheaper than prison. Diversion would lead to substantial savings per offender of AU$96,446 per annum (based on a cost of community residential rehabilitation treatment of AU$8,385 per offender).
- Community residential treatment is also associated with better outcomes compared with prison; lower recidivism rates and better health outcomes, with particular reference to the burden of the cost of Hepatitis C and premature mortality (Deloitte Access Economics 2013, 62) representing considerable savings in health system costs. The savings associated with these additional benefits of community residential treatment are approximately AU$15,012 per offender per year.
- In addition, treatment of indigenous offenders in the community rather than in prison is also associated with lower mortality and better health-related quality of life. In monetary terms, these non-financial benefits have been estimated at AU$92,759 per offender (Deloitte Access Economics 2013, 63).

The provision of ongoing financial support for court-based support programmes and specialist courts that strive to address the underlying issues causing offenders to commit crime help to reduce recidivism and protect the community, and fall squarely within the notion of justice reinvestment – a smarter way of reducing crime.

7.5 Conclusion

The problem-solving approaches and implementation of therapeutic jurisprudence by courts over the last two decades are complementary to the reduction of crime and recidivism rates, promotion of community safety and responsible spending of taxpayer monies. The difference between the 'tough on crime' approach and the 'problem-solving' approach is the view of the problem-solving thinkers that incarceration is not always the best mechanism by which to achieve lasting change and a safer community.

Specialist court programmes and courts are more expensive to operate than usual court lists. For example, many dozens of cases are listed in a busy court on one day. By comparison, Victoria's Koori Courts list no more than five new cases and three review cases per day. Specialist courts and programmes also require additional court and clinical staff. However, when evaluating these programmes, it is important to factor in the savings in terms of the time saved by emergency services and police, and the cost to victims. Provision for the funding of appropriate evaluation, both quantitative and qualitative, of any program is vital. Ideally, it is longitudinal evaluations that ought to be provided for.

Victorian Magistrates' Courts have undergone a change in thinking. Initially, problem-solving courts and approaches did not receive any additional budgetary component. The attitude taken by the pioneers of problem-solving courts was 'build it and they will come'. This certainly proved to the case with most of these programmes. Courts were unable to sustain the demands on services, and thus in the past ten to 15 years, the court did not commence any new programme without funding being firmly in place. However, with the downturn in the economy, and fiscal restraint exercised by government, courts in Victoria have reverted to setting up some specialist lists and courts without additional funding, in the hope that they will be able to convince the government to fund them in the future.

Ultimately, it is up to policy-makers to decide how best to invest precious community resources to reduce crime and its effect on members of the community. Consideration must be given to the provision of effective, goal oriented solutions and judicial decisions to reduce the incarceration of some of the most marginalised (through poverty, inter-generational grief and trauma, mental illness, substance abuse or mental impairment, for example) persons in our communities.

References

Auditor-General of Victoria. 2011. *Problem-Solving Approaches to Justice.* Melbourne: Victorian Government Printer. www.audit.vic.gov.au/reports_and_publications/latest_reports/2010–11/20110406_justice.aspx.

BBC News Liverpool. 2013. "Save North Liverpool Community Justice Centre call". *BBC News*, 28 August. www.bbc.com/news/uk-england-merseyside-23870847.

Borowski A. 2009. *Courtroom 7: An evaluation of the children's Koori Court of Victoria.* Melbourne: La Trobe University.

Cannon A. 2007. "Nunga Court II: Aboriginal Sentencing Conferences". *Restorative Justice Online.* www.restorativejustice.org/10fulltext/cannonandrew/view.

Center for Court Innovation, Youth Court. 2014. www.courtinnovation.org/topic/youth-court.

Commonwealth of Australia, Senate Legal and Constitutional Affairs References Committee. 2013. *Value of a justice reinvestment approach to criminal justice in Australia.* Canberra: Senate Printing Unit.

Commonwealth of Australia, Productivity Commission. 2014. *Report on Government Services (Volume C: Justice).* Canberra: Steering Committee for the Review of Government Service Provision.

Davis J., Warner K. and Bradfield R. 2011. "Interviewing the jury: three case studies from the Tasmanian jury sentencing study". In L. Bartels and K. Richards (eds) *Qualitative Criminology: Stories from the Field.* Sydney: The Federation Press.

Deloitte Access Economics. 2013. *An economic analysis for Aboriginal and Torres Strait Islander offenders.* Civic Square, Canberra: Australian National Council on Drugs.

Department of Justice Victoria. 2010. *Court Integrated Services Program: Tackling the causes of crime.* Melbourne: Department of Justice, Victoria.

Department of Justice Victoria. 2010. *Evaluating the Neighbourhood Justice Centre in Yarra 2007–2009.* Melbourne: Victorian Government Printer.

Gelb K. 2011a. *Alternatives to imprisonment: Community views in Victoria.* Melbourne: Sentencing Advisory Council.

Gelb K. 2011b. *Purposes of sentencing: Community views in Victoria.* Melbourne: Sentencing Advisory Council.

Harris M. 2006. *A Sentencing conversation: Evaluation of the Koori Courts Pilot Program October 2002 – October 2004.* Melbourne: Victorian Department of Justice, Courts and Programs Development Unit.

Harvey A. 2012. "Anger as NSW axes youth drug court". *ABC News.* www.abc.net.au/news/2012–07–03/experts-baffled-as-axe-falls-on-youth-drug-court/4108366.

Justice For Vets. 2014. *What is a Veteran's Treatment Court?* www.justiceforvets.org/what-is-a-veterans-treatment-court.

King M. 2008. "Problem-solving court judging, therapeutic jurisprudence and transformational leadership". *Journal of Judicial Administration* 17: 155–177.

King M., Freiberg A., Batagol B. and Hyams R. 2009. *Non-Adversarial Justice.* Annandale. NSW: The Federation Press.

Lemmon K. 2012. "Murri court axed to save millions". *The Queensland Times.* Annandale. www.qt.com.au/news/murri-court-is-axed-to-save-35-million-closure/1545357/.

Levine G. 2012. *A study of Family Drug Treatment Courts in the United States and the United Kingdom: Giving parents and children the best chance of reunification.* Melbourne: The Winston Churchill Memorial Trust of Australia.

Lovegrove A. 2007. "Public opinion, sentencing and lenience: An empirical study involving judges consulting the community". *Criminal Law Review* 2007: 769–781.

Magistrates' Court of Victoria 2013. *ARC List receives 2013 Melbourne Award.* www.magistratescourt.vic.gov.au/news/arc-list-receives-2013-melbourne-award.

National Center for DWI Courts. www.dwicourts.org.

Northern Territory Magistrates Courts 2013. *Specialist Courts: Smart Court.* www.nt.gov.au/justice/ntmc/specialist_courts.shtml.

Ogloff J. 2010. "The nether regions of justice: in custody and mentally ill". *The Age.* www.theage.com.au/federal-politics/society-and-culture/the-nether-regions-of-justice-in-custody-and-mentally-ill-20100530-wndx.html.

Ogloff J. 2012. "We know about the problems – What about the solutions? Policing people with mental illness". Paper presented at the 32nd Annual ANZAPPL Congress, 23 November 2012, Melbourne. www.lephcon.com.au/files/9313/5886/0191/James-Ogloff-LEPH-Nov2012.pdf.

Ogloff J., Warren L., Tye C., Blaher F. and Thomas S. 2010. "Psychiatric symptoms and histories among people detained in prison cells". *Social Psychiatry and Psychiatric Epidemiology* 46: 871–880.

Popovic J. 2002. "Judicial officers: Complementing conventional law and changing the culture of the judiciary". *Law in Context* 20(2): 121–136.

Popovic J. 2005. "Court processes and therapeutic jurisprudence: Have we thrown the baby out with the bathwater?" *Murdoch University Electronic Journal of Law* 1: 60–77.

Reentry Court Solutions. www.reentrycourtsolutions.com/category/reentr-courts/.

Right on Crime 2010. *State Initiatives: Texas.* www.rightoncrime.com/reform-in-action/state-initiatives/texas/.

Ritchie D. 2011. *Does Imprisonment Deter? A Review of the Evidence.* Melbourne: Sentencing Advisory Council.

Smart Justice 2012. *Justice reinvestment: investing in communities not prisons.* Smart Justice factsheet, Melbourne: Smart Justice.

Stewart J. 2011. "Specialist domestic violence courts: what we know now – how far have Australian Jurisdictions progressed?" *Australian Domestic & Family Violence Clearing House.* www.adfvc.unsw.edu.au/PDF%20files/Topic%20Paper%2020.pdf.

Sydney Morning Herald Editorial 9 July 2012. "Quiet death of the youth drug court". www.smh.com.au/federal-politics/editorial/quiet-death-of-the-youth-drug-court-20120708–21p7h.html.

Victorian Council of Social Service (VCOSS) 2013. *Emergency prison bed funding 'sign of crisis'.* Media release. VCOSS. Melbourne, 29 November 2013.

Victoria Police. 2011. *Annual Report 2010–11.* Melbourne: Victoria Police.

Victoria Police. 2013. *Crime Statistics 2012–13.* Melbourne: Victoria Police.

Warner K. 2014. "Panel participant: The historical bases for theories of sentencing, punishment and deterrence and the deterrent value of sentencing". Paper presented at *Sentencing: From Theory to Practice.* National Judicial College of Australia Conference. ANU College of Law and NJCA, 8–9 February, 2014.

Wellings E. 2013. Personal correspondence 17 April 2013 from Acting Sergeant Elli Wellings to Magistrate Jelena Popovic concerning PACT project close down.

Wexler D. and Winick B. 1991. *Essays in therapeutic jurisprudence.* Durham, NC: Carolina Academic Press.

Woodward D. 2014. "Mental health courts expand to treat offenders". *Grand Rapids Business Journal.* www.grbj.com/articles/79192-mental-health-courts-expand-to-treat-offenders.

8 From care to community

Leaving the 'community of custodial care' and the challenge of community transition

Grant Burkitt, Daniel Kinston and Ronan McLoughlin

8.1 Introduction

The safe and successful return to the community for those in custodial care is ultimately the overriding aim for both hospital-based and community forensic mental health services. Forensic mental health systems are tasked with the role of protecting the public while providing expert and specialist rehabilitation that seeks to allow individuals to reside in less restrictive settings and with reduced monitoring and supervision in time. In recent decades the focus of much of the research literature in this field has centred on risk assessment and recidivism with less attention being paid to how this population and the professionals involved attempt to achieve, rather than predict, sustained community integration, and much less on what consumers say about their experiences of transitioning out of custodial care environments (Coffey 2012).

While the mental health consumer community has been central in the devolution from deinstitutionalisation to community care they remain a substantially disadvantaged population, both in socioeconomic indicators and in community inclusion (Adams and Hess 2001). In the Victorian context, admissions to custodial care for forensic patients – those found not guilty for reasons of mental impairment (CMIA 1997) – are counted in years rather than months, and many forensic patients may spend decades in custodial care following offences (Ruffles 2010). Nonetheless, legislative reforms commencing in the mid-1990s have seen a positive shift towards graduated leave programmes and phased conditional community supervision that have improved trajectories for forensic patients. One significant element of such reforms has been a greater exposure and connection to non-custodial environments during admission and graduated leaves programmes that involve a mix of day and overnight leaves. Forensic patients in Victoria commonly experience varying and increasing degrees of escorted, staff attended, unescorted and overnight community access to various destinations building up over a period of years before applying to the courts for a variation to full-time living under community supervision (CMIA 1997). This process is experienced and framed in a number of ways; arguably none more poignantly than as a liminal phase where one has a foot in both camps – 'more out than in' – as neither fully residing in the community nor entirely 'in custody' as denoted by medico-legal classification.

Similarly, the discourse of forensic rehabilitation can often involve a dichotomous framing of this process where forensic patients gain access to and transition, based on a multitude of factors, from a custodial environment to a non-custodial, or community, one. Yet, the binary of 'custody and community' in forensic mental health research and practice can fail to equip clinicians and patients with a language to describe adequately the process of moving from one community to another, or indeed the interplay of multiple geographical, functional and virtual communities over time. In practice, *the* community frequently refers one-dimensionally to 'not in custody'; and, more broadly, in the health disciplines 'community' remains a poorly operationalised and understood term (Ife 2013). As such, the aim of this chapter is to introduce and explore contemporary notions of community and experiences of community transition for forensic patients leaving the 'community of custodial care'. Selected research on transitioning from custodial care environments for forensic patients is introduced and the authors examine the links between housing, community placement and impacts of community supervision as well as the often felt loss of the community of custodial care. This chapter will critique the somewhat romantic idea of accessible community resources for those in the forensic mental health system and draw on contemporary understandings of systemic barriers to transitioning from custodial care and principles of forensic rehabilitation.

8.2 Entering and residing in the community of custodial care

The transition from custodial to non-custodial care is far from straightforward and this can also be said of the reverse transition, non-custodial (community) to custodial (hospital or prison). While there is an established research interest in prison release and transition there is limited contemporary research on patient experiences of entering custodial care environments. General opinion suggests that institutionalisation was eradicated by the 1980s in Victoria (in Australia) and yet, while many facilities were decommissioned, institutions remain in some form as a component in many modern mental health systems. Indeed, Salize *et al.*'s (2008) work on international trends of mental health service users in custody and incarceration notes the term *re-institutionalisation* to refer to the increasing prevalence of mental health problems in prison populations and the evident cycle of revolving incarceration. This type of research points to a common theme of prison and correctional systems replacing hospitals in the wake of deinsitutionalisation and that the increase in those with mental health problems in custody has been significant globally in recent years.

The physical environment for forensic patients in custodial care largely remains one characterised by restricted access, isolation from wider society and the ever present monitoring of daily activities and interactions. In Goffman's *Asylums* 'total institutions' were defined as places of "residence and work where a large number of like-situated individuals, cut off from the wider society for an appreciable period of time, together [led] an enclosed, formally administered round of life" (Goffman 1961, 11). Goffman also notes a process of 'mortification', where patients are stripped of their social roles and identities. Martin (1955) observed that patients then adopt the official or staff view of themselves and in custodial care are required to accept the social and cultural norms of the 'patient role'. Non-acceptance of the patient role can place major barriers in transition and progress and forensic systems have historically required patients to be 'well institutionalised' – "implying that the patient 'has ceased to rebel against, or to question the fitness of, his [*sic*] position in a mental hospital; he has made a more or less total surrender to the institution life" (Martin 1955, 1188).

In the process of admission, forensic patients are in some form rejected, isolated and experience a 'social death': they have arguably acquired a distorted identity that is both reinforced and countered in the process of custodial care and one that is bound not only by medico-legal constructs but also in the structural and systemic operations of custodial care (Adshead 2012). The development of this identity is one that occurs over a number of years yet, importantly, as a medico-legal construct has only a temporary quality rather than an enduring role or identity.

The work of Johnson and Rhodes (2007) on conceptual developments in institutionalisation shows the contemporary research interest in this area. While encompassing a range of care settings and theoretical and empirical studies, and a number of independent and dependent variables, this review notes several constructs that positively correlate to the development of institutional syndromes.

Their model is comprised of five constructs: four contributing factors (i) individual vulnerability, (ii) the conditions of institutional settings, (iii) resident perceptions of the institutional environment, and (iv) time in care; and the fifth, the outcome, the syndrome of institutionalism:

> *Individual vulnerability:* very young or very old age, poor physical health, compromised cognitive functioning, psychiatric illness, lack of a strong social network, poor coping skills, lack of mobility, and low self-efficacy. We should note, however, that even without identified deficits, all people have basic human needs that leave them vulnerable to extreme environments. Wirt (1999) suggests, "the restrictive environment of institutional settings coupled with oppressive staff [are] capable of producing institutionalism in almost any person regardless of diagnosis, predispositions, or personality".

> *Characteristics of the environment:* confiscation/control of personal belongings, size (resident capacity), isolated location, low staff to resident ratio, authoritarian or disempowered and inadequately trained staff, rigidity of routine, drab or standardized physical environment, lack of stimulation, enforced idleness, lack of choice and control, lack of privacy, lack of program or unit designated for long-term residents and absence of meaningful relationships.

Resident perceptions of environment and time: lack of input into the placement decision, acceptance of patient or inmate label, feelings of isolation, loss of control and sense of purpose, expectation of lengthy or permanent stay.

(Johnston and Rhodes 2007, 227)

Following this model, features and characteristics within each construct are additive or cumulative. A patient may have multiple vulnerabilities and an environment may have some but not all of the characteristics listed; and contributing factors may have a multiplicative and magnifying effect. This is then exacerbated by the actual length of time spent in the custodial care, as well as the resident's perception of prolonged hospitalisation and little or no hope of community transition (Johnston and Rhodes 2007).

In Coffey's (2013) work on time-relevant discourse in accounts of conditionally discharged forensic patients, regularities included timed phases for achieving discretionary permission for greater liberty from services and discontinuities indicated mismatches between hospital and community time. Notably, benchmarking by patients against those who are perceived as progressing smoothly through the system was common and discharged patients in the study implicated the passing of time since past behaviours, custodial care and offending as an important resource in claiming ordinary identities.

Johnston and Rhodes conclude that institutionalism and institutional syndromes can be measured by the manifestation of their symptoms: "apathy, lethargy, passivity, and the muting of self-initiative; compliance and submissiveness; dependence on institutional structure and contingencies; social withdrawal and isolation; an internalization of the norms of custodial culture; and a diminished sense of self-worth and personal value" (2007, 228). This presents a complicated challenge in forensic mental health in distinguishing symptomology, personality traits and course of illness as contributing factors; this may be the case for many reasons but a noted factor is that professional practices are subject to similar manifestations in custodial care and can often occur insidiously given time. Heuristic and attribution biases can affect team decision-making and the individuation of behaviour causes can emanate as much from organisational, as from relational and structural influences.

Notably, institutional syndromes and the desire to stay in hospital or custodial care may be distinct phenomena and may interact or manifest amid changing circumstances and events over the trajectory of custodial care (Wing and Brown 1970). Nonetheless, the shifts in environment or physical structures and individual vulnerabilities, including illness management and clinical risk factors, during custodial care are significant factors in eventual community transition. For many the resources, relationships and structures of custodial care present a more favourable setting than anywhere else – it is here that we turn our attention to what some perceive as a stark and challenging prospect, life beyond custodial care.

8.3 What do you mean by community?

Social inclusion and community participation are terms that feature in many health and community programme objectives as well as operational and government policy. As noted, defining what is meant by 'community' is a challenging task and in using the term it is often necessary to provide a definition specific to a context. Despite definitions being highly problematic, community is understood as a form of social organisation, one that is distinct from macro-level societal processes and structures. The conceptual treatment of community in practice traditions such as community development and community work and is commonly couched with reference to broader social, political and ecological contexts. Despite the robust emphasis on the politics of risk assessment and management, links between social, political and ecological contexts and community transition are frequently deficient in the understandings of community found in forensic mental health and criminal justice research (Hudson 2003).

Ife's (2013) characteristics of a community are noted below and are understood to be interrelated and overlapping:

- *Human Scale* – as a counter to large, impersonalised and centralised structures; so that community-level interactions are at a scale that can be readily accessed and controlled by individuals.
- *Identity and belonging* – belonging to a community gives one a sense of identity; concept of membership stems from this and how one views one's place in the world.
- *Obligations* – being a member of a community involves some level of active participation and is not passively experienced.
- *Gemeinschaft* – relates to structures and relationships; a community will enable its members to interact with each other in a variety of roles in less differentiated and categorical ways.
- *Culture* – this enables the valuing, production and expression of a local community, which allows members to become active producers of that culture rather than passive consumers.

(Ife 2013, 111–115)

Of particular note in Ife's work is the distinction between geographical and functional communities, and to an extent the virtual community, as well as the critical question of whether notions of community and its resources are geographically based. This distinction centres on whether a community is defined more by locality than on some common element providing a sense of identity.

Ife (2013) stresses that because of its subjective nature it is unhelpful to think of community as 'existing' or to operationalise community in such a way that we can measure it. Community is seen as dynamic and evolving and that enduring reconstruction is in fact a feature inherent to its organisation, structure and processes. The task for forensic patients, as with all who access communities, is therefore as much an exercise in engaging in collectively constructing communities and negotiating one's membership over time; for the forensic patient this refers to something that is distinct from the locality, boundaries and roles that have stemmed, at least in part, from prolonged custodial care. This task is manifold given the potential for stigma, isolation and disclosure issues relating to offence history, mental illness, long-term hospitalisation and, importantly, social dislocation.

Compounding this is the common expectation that intensive input from multiple service providers will permeate to successful integration of personal and peer networks. Community integration as an aim and strategy for management of forensic patients can be seen to have a fundamental weakness in the assumption of an entity – 'the community' – where care and support services are enacted for the individual within a localised cluster of largely pro-social non-professional relationships and groups. Gray *et al.*'s (2003) contribution to this aspect of community supervision and conditional discharge is noteworthy. They observe a retreat from the 'social' in modern Western societies, and moreover a retreat from approaching risk as something to be shared between members of a society. Correspondingly, where contemporary social organisation entails less localised collective action there is an increased reliance on centrally funded and centrally controlled state mechanisms to control risk.

Everingham's (2001) work notes the use of community in Australia government policy back to the Whitlam era where the replacement of 'state' with 'community' fostered perceptions of government resources as community resources. This framing harnessed the affective value of community to promote the thrust of public investment (Darcy 1999). The contemporary Australian neoliberal environment is much changed. Community is framed now as distinct from government and the replacement of government provision with community solutions in the new discourse of health and welfare (Mowat *et al.* 2005).

The re-emergence of the 'community' in the public policy frameworks corresponds with the fading promise of neomanagerialism and economic rationalism (Adams and Hess 2001). In public mental health systems the tension between providing holistic care and providing core clinical business is an ever-present one with funding imperatives at the centre of the debate. Forensic mental health services, while historically less affected by outcome and activities based funding models, are encountering like issues and in many ways face a more difficult challenge in attempting to interface with communities, many of which are unwilling to induct this population or are simply unaware of the issues.

8.4 Accessing and transitioning to non-custodial communities

As noted, clinicians in custodial care invariably seek to work with forensic patients in transitioning at some point. The transition from custodial to non-custodial care can be seen as the gateway to a more independent life and the accordant rehabilitation jails are largely preparatory and occur prior to discharge. There are a number of historical studies that show forensic patients and others in custodial care prefer the community in 'institutions' over other settings, are resistant to transition or experience problematic community tenure resulting in readmission or revocation of community supervision orders.

Goldman noted that a sizeable segment of the population in mental hospitals was found to have "no substantial interest in ever returning to the community" (Goldman 1965, 322). Weinstein (1998) reviewed 38 quantitative studies of patient attitudes towards mental hospital and found that favourable attitudes predominated in 79 per cent of participants across studies. Rosenblatt and Mayer (1974) observed that patients with a greater number of previous hospital admissions were more likely to return to the hospital, independent of the severity of their illness. Drake and Wallach (1992) found a preference for residing in custodial care was associated with past hospital admissions, symptoms of psychosis and severity of drug abuse. Rosenheck and Neale (1998) point out that community deficits are as much an influence as custodial ones when exploring the difficulties in transitioning from custodial care. Patients may often feel secure, supported and safe in custodial care and, for better or worse, there are often fewer supports readily available and accessible when in non-custodial communities. However, this is not universally the case and opposite or ambivalent views certainly exist and for a number of reasons.

Community-based forensic mental services are an established component of forensic mental health services internationally, and integrated community forensic models feature in service provision as well as regional and catchment level forensic expertise being available to mainstream community mental health services (Mohan and Fahy 2006; Brett *et al.* 2007). As in non-forensic services, case management and consultation is a component of service provision and is perhaps a requirement in directly addressing a major criticism of deinstitutionalisation – that consumers face a large, diverse, fragmented and uncoordinated system of services that they frequently experience difficulty in negotiating. Conceptual models underpinning case management have their origins in social work case work and draw on theory and research indicating that a patient's social network, in conjunction with a network of services, could help people with chronic mental illness adapt to community living (Tessler and Goldman 1982). Gustafsson *et al.* (2011) found that having a social network (people that could support the consumer both socially and if issues arose), an occupation (not limited to paid employment, but more routines and structure that could occupy their time in the community in what the consumer considered a meaningful way), secure housing (affordable, stable accommodation that offered support up to the level that individual consumers required) and financial self-management were important areas in successful community transitions. Their work also found that good collaboration between stakeholders, significantly prior to the point of discharge to non-custodial care, ensured that there was a greater chance of success.

This notwithstanding, community follow-up as part of conditional release for forensic patients is often both more intensive and more prolonged than for typical general mental health patients. This may have an advantage for services developing greater partnerships in facilitating transitions from custodial to non-custodial but it has the potential disadvantage of developing connections in a prescribed localised area rather than maintaining or re-establishing previous connections. There is also the expectation or necessity that patients engage in the established groups/programmes or community activities in proximity to custodial care facilities given leave restrictions or interagency agreements. These elements of a patient's rehabilitation can have significant impacts on eventual discharge location and geographically determined engagement with community-based forensic mental health services. This can be extended further to note that housing needs to be genuinely accepted as the vital component in community care and that a housing orientation enhances the quality of community care (Boschel *et al.* 1999; Bostock *et al.* 2004).

Jones (2009) and Melnychuk *et al.* (2009) provide two examples of research into discharge locations for forensic patients. Jones (2009) surmised that the tendency of discharging patients to the local area might reflect forensic mental services favouring local placements for ease of ongoing supervision. Findings in his study in Norfolk, UK, showed that patients lived considerably closer to the community forensic mental health service on discharge than they had on admission; that patients were discharged disproportionately to localities immediately surrounding the clinic and that longer admissions are strongly associated with change of address on discharge. As with the development of institutional syndromes, the length of admission can be a determining factor in discharge location.

Melnychuk *et al.* (2009) adopted a similar geospatial research design and investigated the impact of neighbourhood and community factors on the reintegration of forensic patients leaving custodial care in British Columbia, Canada. Residential locations, return to hospital rates and unsuccessful community placement (resulting in revocation of community-based orders) was tracked over time and locations collectively mapped. Findings suggested that patients who were released to certain socially disorganised neighbourhoods, characterised by low income, high unemployment, poor educational achievement and concentrated rental accommodation, returned to custodial care at a higher frequency. The authors in both studies point to the proximity and mitigation of related destabilising features as having significant influence on the long-term success or failure of discharge and that decisions around discharge location are typically controlled by service providers.

The impact of this for forensic patients is that there is likely to be a higher concentration of forensic patients using local mainstream service networks, and in many cases peer and personal networks for those under community supervision may be populated predominantly by other forensic patients. Disruptions of social and family support are closely linked to this and in a number of cases family members are the victims of the index offence. There are patients who refuse to or cannot return to their area of origin because of notoriety, family or community opposition. What can be observed here is the potential for fixed pathways for community transition, pathways that entail pre-established interagency links between custodial and non-custodial and forensic and non-forensic community-based services but are significantly limited in geographical and sociocultural choice for individuals.

Ultimately, the forensic patient population is a unique service user group that has received little attention in housing policy or evidenced-based matched housing research (Shaw *et al.* 2001). Forensic patients who are not assessed as requiring clinical residential programme support in order to transition out of custodial care are now competing for community resources with other groups. Eligibility criteria can be exclusionary and long-stay forensic patients are rarely assessed as 'at risk' for homelessness. Implications for custodial care practices may commence with early completion of housing and community placement assessments as well as early screening for homelessness, broader service system eligibility, needs for long-term supported placement and patient preferences in discharge and step-down locations.

Ultimately, such considerations raise the question of what housing-related support services for forensic patients will look like in future unless a research agenda is adopted. These research efforts need to show effectiveness of community transition models, why they are needed, how best to organise them in conjunction with clinical service provision and community supervision. The work of Quinley (2010) and Sweeney and Rani (2013) helps prompt a rethinking of how housing stock and support roles are commissioned and provides an argument for further integration for forensic mental health services and housing support, but not necessarily merely by bringing housing support services into the forensic fold. Notably, reference is made by Quinley (2010) to the research finding and policy belief that generic and forensic specialist models are equally effective. Ashton and Capgemini (2009) note here that both models appear to be needed within the context of local and regional level systems.

The considerations of community transition and integration of forensic mental health and supported housing services align to an emerging issue of the current service configuration and service development in this field. The operations of custodial care settings involve continuity of care in the form of attached forensic community-based services and reliance on or at least interface with community resources for rehabilitation efforts in ways that are distinct from traditional state run service provision. One of the fundamental principles of forensic rehabilitation applicable here is that forensic patients should receive mainstream integrated services wherever possible. Ideally, this should occur within a rubric of integrated care pathways that acknowledge and cater to the impacts of prolonged custodial care. In an era of devolving health and welfare systems where discrete eligibility, high risk and complex needs are often determinants for accessing services, the social context and accessibility of a localised community has implications beyond risk management and an individual's capacity for community supervision.

8.5 Conclusion

Broad social structures and the potential for media scrutiny can impact greatly on forensic mental health services in custodial care settings and under community supervision. However, transitioning out of custodial care or between communities largely occurs at the level of community. Issues of access and stigma from within health and welfare systems and disconnection from local geographic and functional communities are potentially more commonly experienced and most challenging during points of transition for forensic patients. Centralised custodial care environments and state-wide/regional service structures can contribute to removing patients from their area of origin and from opportunities for accessing service providers outside the forensic mental health service system. The language and conceptual understanding of community and its roles in successful community transition should be given greater emphasis in the research agenda in this field. A focus on the peer and personal networks of forensic patients, geospatial assessment in community placement outcomes and the inclusion of non-forensic service providers in models of integrated forensic rehabilitation may provide avenues for further enhancing community transitions. We conclude that the role of forensic mental health services must remain broader than core clinical and supervisory tasks if we are to work effectively with those in the forensic mental health system.

References

Adams D. and Hess M. 2001. "Community in public policy: fad or foundation?". *Australian Journal of Public Administration* 60(2): 255–281.

Adshead G. 2012. "'Mirror Mirror' Parallel process in forensic institutions". In J. Adlam, A. Aiyegbusi, P. Kleinot, A. Motz and C. Scanlon (eds) *The therapeutic milieu under fire: Security and insecurity in forensic mental health*. Forensic Focus Series. London: Jessica Kingsley Publishers.

Ashton T. and Capgemini C. 2009. *Research into the financial benefits of the Supporting People programme*. London: Department for Communities and Local Government.

Bochel C., Bochel H. and Page D. 1999. "Housing: the foundation of community care?" *Health and Social Care in the Community* 7: 492–501.

Bostock L., Gleeson B., McPherson A. and Pang L. 2004. "Contested housing landscapes? Social inclusion, deinstitutionalisation and housing policy in Australia". *Australian Journal of Social Issues* 39(1): 42–62.

Brett A., Carroll A., Green R., Mals P., Beswick S., Rodriguez M., Dunlop D. and Gagliardi C. 2007. "Treatment and security outside the wall: Diverse approaches to common challenges in community forensic mental health". *International Journal of Forensic Mental Health* 6(1): 87–99.

Coffey M. 2012. "Negotiating identity transition when leaving forensic hospitals". *Health* 16(5): 489–506.

Coffey M. 2013. "Time and its uses in accounts of conditional discharge in forensic psychiatry". *Social Health and Illness* 35(8): 1181–1195.

Crimes (Mental Impairment and Unfitness to be Tried) Act 1997 (VIC) (Austl).

Darcy M. 1999. "The discourse of 'community' and the reinvention of social housing policy in Australia". *Urban Studies* 36(1): 13.

Drake R. E. and Wallach M. A. 1992. "Mental patients' attraction to the hospital: Correlates of living preference". *Community Mental Health Journal* 28: 5–13.

Everingham C. 2001. "Reconstituting community: Social justice, social order and the politics of community". *Australian Journal of Social Issues* 36(2): 105.

Goffman E. 1961. *Asylums: Essays on the social situation of mental patients and other inmates*. Garden City, NY: Anchor Books.

Goldman A. R. 1965. "Wanting to leave or stay in a mental hospital: Incidence and correlates". *Journal of Clinical Psychology* 21: 317–322.

Gray N., Laing J. and Noaks L. 2003. *Criminal justice, mental health and the politics of risk*. London: Cavendish Publishing

Gustafsson E., Holm M. and Flensner, G. 2011. "Rehabilitation between institutional and non-institutional forensic psychiatric care: important influences on the transition process". *Journal of Psychiatric and Mental Health Nursing* 19: 729–737.

Hudson, B. 2003. *Understanding Justice: An introduction to ideas, perspectives and controversies in modern penal theory*, 2nd edn. Buckingham, UK: Open University Press.

Ife J. 2013. *Community development in an uncertain world: vision, analysis and practice*. Port Melbourne, Australia: Cambridge University Press.

Jones C. 2009. "Community Residence on discharge from a medium secure unit: Where have all the patients gone?" *The Journal of Forensic Psychiatry and Psychology* 20(2): 225–238.

Johnson M. M. and Rhodes R. 2007. "Institutionalization: A theory of human behaviour and the social environment". *Advances in Social Work* 8(1): 219–235.

Martin D. V. 1955. "Institutionalization". *Lancet* 2: 1188–1190.

Melnychuk R., Verdun-Jones S. and Brink J. 2009. "Geographic Risk Management: A spatial study of mentally disordered offenders discharged from forensic psychiatric care". *International Journal of Forensic Mental Health* 8(3): 148–168.

Mohan R. and Fahy T. 2006. "Is there a need for community forensic mental health services?" *Journal of Forensic Psychiatry and Psychology* 17: 365–371.

Mowat P., Holley P. and Lau G. 2005. "Enhancing community participation for consumers of a mental health service through partnerships". www.engagingcommunities2005. org/abstracts/Mowat-Peter-final.pdf.

Quinley L. 2010. "Housing-related support and the needs of mentally disordered offenders". *Housing, Care and Support* 13(2): 14–19.

Rosenblatt A. and Mayer J. E. 1974. "The recidivism of mental patients: A review of past studies". *American Journal of Orthopsychiatry* 44: 697–704.

Rosenheck R. A. and Neale M. S. 1998. "Cost-effectiveness of intensive psychiatric community care for high users of inpatient services". *Archives of General Psychiatry* 55(5): 459–466.

Ruffles J. 2010. *The management of forensic patients in Victoria: The more things change, the more they remain the same*. Unpublished thesis, Monash University.

Salize H., Schanda H. and Dressing H. 2008. "From the hospital into the community and back again – A trend towards re-institutionalisation in mental health care?" *International Review of Psychiatry* 20(6): 527–534.

Shaw J., Appleby L., Amos T. and McDonnell R. 2001. "Mental disorder and clinical care in people convicted of homicide: a national clinical survey". *British Medical Journal* 318: 1240–1244.

Sweeney S. and Rani S. 2013. "Housing preferences of Irish forensic mental health service users on moving into the community". *Journal of Forensic Nursing* 9(4): 235–242.

Tessler R. and Goldman H. 1982. *The chronically mentally ill: assessing community support programs*. Cambridge, Mass: Ballinger.

Weinstein L. B. 1998. "The Eden Alternative: A new paradigm for nursing homes". *Activities, Adaption and Aging* 22(4): 1–8.

Wing J. K. and Brown G. W. 1970. *Institutionalism and schizophrenia: A comparative study of three mental hospitals, 1960–1968*. London: Cambridge University Press.

Wirt G. L. 1999. "Causes of institutionalism: Patient and staff perspectives". *Issues in Mental Health Nursing* 20: 259–274.

9 Policing young people

Stuart Thomas

9.1 Introduction

One of the biggest contemporary challenges for the police relates to their encounters with youth. Young people are vilified in the mass media and substantially feared by local communities (Constantinou *et al.* 2008). Crime statistics internationally suggest that youth predominates in rates of criminal offending, suggesting a significant burden on the criminal justice system and consequently, in the first instance, on the police. This chapter seeks to elucidate the challenges and potential complexities of police contacts with young people in the community. It reviews what is known about the nature and extent of police contact with this group, and considers the central importance of police discretion and perceptions of legitimacy, as well as stigma, in the often delicate balance between community interests and public safety.

9.2 Media representations of young people

Mass media representations of crime generate a level of fear among community members that is all too commonly disproportionate to the level of risk actually posed to an individual living in that community (Kitzinger and Reilly 1997). This is particularly the case with respect to media depictions of young people, who are typically vilified, castigated and demonised by the mass media and therefore to be feared and avoided at all costs, despite these oft quoted 'facts' being at odds with the available evidence (e.g. Flood-Page *et al.* 2000). The media are the main source of information that members of the general public use (along with personal experience and recollections of discussions had with friends/acquaintances) to form opinions about a particular topic; they also provide a forum to express public opinion on certain issues (Collins *et al.* 2006). The portrayal of young people is this manner can therefore be highly problematic. Contemporary media reports paint a portrait of increasingly violent groups of youth engaging in acts of violence for thrill-seeking reasons (Ching *et al.* 2012), even though the evidence suggests that this type of violence is actually uncommon (Ching *et al.* 2013). The media portrayal creates a sense of 'otherness' which instils a sense of fear among members of the community who will then equate a heightened risk to their personal safety to any and all situations involving young people (Slovic *et al.* 1982, 467), thus creating what Cohen (1972) termed a 'moral panic'. A cursory glance at official crime statistics supports, and thus reinforces, these media representations and sense of panic.

9.3 Crime statistics

Australian crime statistics consistently suggest that in excess of one in five of those who are arrested and/or processed by police for criminal offences are young males (aged between 18 and 24 years old). For example, statistics released by Victoria Police in September 2012 state that 29,687 juvenile offenders (aged 10–17 years old) were processed in 2011–2012; meanwhile NSW police crime statistics show that violent crimes by juveniles have risen by 18.1 per cent between 2001 and 2011 (BOCSAR 2012). A recent Australian Institute of Health and Welfare report (AIHW 2011) reported that, from the June quarter 2007 to the June quarter 2011, the number of young offenders detained in Australia increased by 12 per cent, with the largest majority being detained in NSW and Victoria. Similar crime rates are evident internationally (e.g. Armstrong 2004). Rates of offending among young people are therefore, unquestionably, a significant problem; furthermore, they are consistently higher for young offenders as compared to adult offenders, with 40 per cent of young offenders reoffending within 12 months and a further 15 to 20 per cent within two years (DHS 2001; Holmes 2012).

Of note, young people's contacts with the criminal justice system are not limited to offending; a recent report by the Australian Bureau of Statistics highlighted that youth under 20 years old make up about 30 per cent of all reported victimisation experiences of physical assault (ABS 2011). In fact, international crime statistics suggest that young people are more likely to be victims rather than perpetrators of crime (Armstrong 2004; Crawford 2009). Furthermore, the very fact that they are 'official crime statistics' means that they only represent those offences for which the individual(s) involved have been formally processed (whether that be arrested, charged or convicted for an offence). Consequently, official offending statistics, while superficially compelling to the naïve reader, are limited and should be interpreted with caution as they in no way reflect the true nature and extent of police involvement with members of the community.

The available evidence does tell us that there are certain 'high-risk' groups of young people who account for the overwhelming majority of those found in the justice system. For example, there is significant evidence of the over-representation of mental disorders amongst young people in the juvenile justice system (e.g. Chitsabesan *et al.* 2006). On an individual level, studies into youth violence suggest strong correlations between the perpetration of violence and antisocial peers and childhood depression, as well as prior exposure to domestic violence (Ferguson *et al.* 2009). Additionally, high levels of anger and behavioural inhibition (Vermeersch *et al.* 2013) and, more broadly, weak social bonds

with the community have also been documented among young offender populations (Mazerolle *et al.* 2000). Young indigenous Australian people appear to be
particularly disadvantaged by the current supervision and support systems
(AIHW 2013), as do those who experience mental illness and those who do not
have fixed or stable housing (e.g. Gardiner 2013). An Australian Institute of
Criminology report published in 2010 found that the over-representation of indigenous youth in the criminal justice system was due to very different patterns of
diversion between indigenous and non-indigenous youth, with indigenous youth
being far more likely to appear in court (Allard *et al.* 2010). This is despite evidence suggesting that the use of cautioning and conferencing processes is associated with better outcomes by circumventing the potentially deleterious
criminogenic effects associated with other more formal contacts with the justice
system (Bernberg and Krohn 2003).

Despite these somewhat persuasive facts and statistics, we still do not fully
understand why certain groups of young people continue to be over-represented
in police contacts; we do, however, know that they continue to fall between the
gaps of our health and welfare services and hence ultimately end up in our criminal justice system. We also know that these young people all too commonly have
complex patterns of mental health, education and social welfare needs. The very
fact that these kinds of issues are commonly found in our justice system indicates that these needs are clearly not being catered for adequately (Cocozza and
Skowyra 2000; Chitsabesan *et al.* 2006). Collectively though, this points to substantial limitations with, and the ongoing failing of, the current justice–health–
welfare nexus.

9.4 How and why do young people come into contact with police?

The goals of any police–citizen interaction from a police perspective are based
around obtaining information, establishing behavioural order, obtaining respect
from the citizen, and achieving an appropriate resolution of the situation (Sykes
and Brent 1980). However, this will not necessarily be consistent with the goals
of the citizen, especially if they are a 'suspect' of an alleged offence that has
occurred. Alpert and Dunham (2004, 180) argue that when either party comes to
the realisation that their goals in relation to the police–citizen encounter are not
being met, any degree of reciprocity in the relationship breaks down and those
involved necessarily revert to pursuing their own interests (such as running
away, becoming aggressive, or using force). Notably here, while early theories
perceived police behaviour as being dictated by four different static categories of
behaviour (Black 1976), Schulenberg (2010) found that police commonly resort
to using more than one type of law, and to varying degrees to resolve encounters, especially when it comes to contacts with young people (2010, 117). Force
is actually rarely used in police–citizen encounters (Strong 2009), and even more
rarely with young people; when it is required, officers' use of force is likely to
come under extreme scrutiny (Bronitt and Gani 2012, 155–156). This in itself

suggests that police are most commonly using other methods to resolve their encounters and fulfil their policing functions.

Somewhat surprisingly, therefore, very little is actually known about the true nature and extent of police contact with young people, or indeed those depicted as being 'high-risk' encounters, such as those between police and young people who are experiencing mental illness. Recent Australian research has shown that police contact with people (regardless of age) with mental illness is commonplace and that it occurs in a wide variety of different contexts (e.g. as a suspect/perpetrator, victim or person in need of assistance) (Godfredson *et al.* 2011). Similarly, contacts between police and members of the public are commonplace and diverse in nature, to the extent that the traditional role of 'catching the crooks and locking them up' is only part of a much broader 'helping' function. Indeed, some scholars have argued that the recent advent of problem-orientated policing has made the police more accessible than ever before to the community. As well as contributing to a modest decrease in crime (Weisburd *et al.* 2008), this change in policing focus has had the knock-on effect of changing the very nature of the police role to embrace more of a social welfare element (e.g. Goldstein 1979), with their increased visibility and engagement with communities bringing them into contact with a wider array of risk, need and vulnerability (Thomas 2013).

These fundamental changes in policing orientation were also influenced by the realisation of the need for community-based policing where 'good' relationships between police and the community are a necessary prerequisite for a productive and mutually beneficial relationship. The social context of the community has been found to be important, especially in relation to the levels of social/economic disadvantage, indices of population density and the proportion of young people residing in the area (Sozer and Merlo 2013). Indeed youth have been the target of much of the police efforts in this 'good public–police' relationship building exercise over recent years (Hinds 2007; Stewart *et al.* 2014). Similarly, however, the police's continued purposeful targeting of antisocial behaviour, arguably in order to visibly address public anxieties (Crawford 2007) and thus promote/maintain perceptions of police legitimacy, commonly has the reverse effect of antagonising young people. A big part of the problem is the very subjective nature of what actually constitutes 'antisocial behaviour' and at what point and on what basis police need to intervene. Crawford (2009, 29) argues that young people are still in the process of "evolving competencies and forging identities"; as such the potential for detrimental experiences associated with what the young people perceive to be overly or unnecessarily intrusive interventions by the police should be of real concern.

Other contemporaneous evidence suggests that, quite apart from dealing with these subjective perceptions of troublesome behaviour of youth, homelessness and domestic violence are particularly prevalent concerns for police in the context of their encounters with young people in the community (Gardiner 2013). Other recent research has further suggested that missing person reports include a significant proportion of young people, their rate being some three times higher than that of adults (Henderson *et al.* 2000). A significant proportion of these are young people who go missing from/do not return to institutions or services where they are housed. Anecdotally, while many of these young people can go 'missing' on a regular basis and may not represent an 'urgent risk' from the perspective of staff/responsible carers in terms of personal safety or safety to others, the very fact that they are procedurally reported as 'missing' necessitates a police response which can be time consuming and burdensome on police resources. Police decision-making around these sometimes sensitive issues is therefore of paramount importance.

9.5 Discretionary powers

Police decision-making, i.e. determining when and how to intervene (Roberg *et al.* 2000), is framed around their unique powers which are set out under the relevant criminal legislation in each jurisdiction and their powers of apprehension under provisions of mental health legislation. The police also have important discretionary powers (i.e. the decision not to invoke formal social control even when the circumstances allow it) that are less visible and, as such, consequently not as well understood (Bronitt and Stenning 2011; Goldstein 1960). Watson *et al.* (2005) point to the central importance of these powers, surmising that it is these powers which ultimately determine a person's access to the criminal justice or mental health systems, and therefore whether the person receives treatment or, alternatively, is otherwise faced with a criminal justice system that is "ill-prepared to meet their needs" (2005, 199). As mentioned above, the impact of these decisions on the pathways of young people into, through, or around our criminal justice system cannot be emphasised enough (Allard *et al.* 2010; Bernberg and Krohn 2003).

So, in many ways, the gap in our understanding around police discretion is not whether police should have discretionary powers, but on what basis such judgements should be made. The core importance of understanding police discretion is that police can be more uniformly informed about the appropriate use of these powers (Wortley 2003) and bolster public perceptions of their procedural fairness (Mazerolle *et al.* 2013; Murphy 2009). Alpert and Dunham (2004) propose a framework for understanding both this and police decision-making around the need to use force that they call "authority maintenance theory". This approach conceptualises encounters from an interpersonal perspective and starts from the position that authority plays an integral part of a police–citizen encounter, and that ultimately police are most concerned with maintaining their authority over citizens in the encounter to resolve it. In the context of this power dynamic, Alpert and Dunham (2004, 173–176) argue that there is an inherent expectation that the citizen will defer to the demands/requests of the police officer, so when the citizen does not respond in an expected manner, other non-verbal gestures and behaviours may be perceived in an exaggerated way and lead to an escalation of the encounter and necessitate the use of force. This appears particularly problematic when police encounter individuals they perceive to be experiencing mental illness (Kesic *et al.* 2013) and for dealing with young people whose presenting antisocial behaviours (e.g. congregating in groups in public spaces and engaging in 'bravado', or related group-based activities) may be cause for concern. Therefore, the particular importance of the fair and distributive use of police discretionary powers around when and in what circumstances to use them plays a significant role in the effectiveness of youth–police relations. Stewart *et al.* (2014) suggest that this is the case because, for many young people, the police will be the only 'formal' contact the person has with the justice system.

9.6 Police legitimacy

Public opinion about the police (in particular, but also the broader criminal justice system), and support for these processes, are considered to be significant and necessary precursors to the degree to which members of the public accept police authority in regard to rules, decisions and actions; ultimately, Tyler (2006, 26) argues that this determines whether people are law abiding or not. The legitimacy of the police, i.e. trust in the police and the obligation to obey police commands (Sargeant *et al.* 2013, 73), is therefore considered to be a core component in relation to public opinion and crime control (Kochel 2012). What shapes the perception, maintenance and any changes to this concept of 'legitimacy' are therefore people's experiences, whether first-hand through their own encounters with police, or second-hand through hearing of other people's experiences. Murphy and Cherney (2010) point out that this tension can be further complicated in police encounters with ethnic minority groups where they may have had negative experiences with authorities in their countries of origin, or perhaps consider some laws illegitimate. This is therefore arguably one of the key points at the public–police interface where police actions, and the relative acceptability of these both individually and collectively, shape people's perceptions of police and contribute to the nature of their engagement and encounters with them.

The core challenge for police, therefore, is to try to balance the oft-times competing community interests with relationship building and trust with the young people who are increasingly being focused on. Ouellette (2006) suggests that increasing the likelihood that young people will experience positive outcomes from their interactions with police, and also that they gain a more positive view of the police as a result of this, are key to the improvement of their encounters with the police. However, this is perhaps easier said than done and, in fact, directly at odds with the practicalities of resolving encounters and with the available evidence about the means of police resolution of encounters with certain groups of young people. For example, Terrill and Mastrofski (2002) found that police resorted to using more coercive measures with disadvantaged and younger people, irrespective of their behaviour during an encounter (2002, 243). Terrill and Mastrofski go on to argue that this lack of proportionality in the treatment of these individuals has the distinct potential to undermine the young peoples' perceptions of police legitimacy and thus impact deleteriously on the (already tenuous) relationship between police and young people. Therefore, understanding some of the reasons why this lack of proportionality in behaviour/response may come about becomes pertinent.

9.7 Attitudes and stigma and social distance

A number of social science scholars have explored the influences of attitudes on behaviour, including those of the police. For example, LaMotte *et al.* (2010) suggest that one of the key factors that needs to be targeted to reduce the likelihood that police interactions with young people lead to arrest is changing the attitudes of police towards young people. However, the research around attitudes and behaviour remains equivocal, with some arguing that attitudes impact on decision-making behaviours while others suggest that this is not the case (Glasman and Albarracin 2006; Wallace *et al.* 2005). For example, differences in police officers' attitudes towards mental illness are highly idiosyncratic and found to be unrelated to experience (Cooper *et al.* 2004; Cotton 2004).

A related concept of potential influence here is that of stigma. Link and Phelan (2001, 367) define stigma in relation to the co-occurring elements of labelling, stereotyping, separation, status loss and discrimination in the context of a power situation. Stigma, with respect to the perceived dangers associated with encounters with young people, can therefore be seen as being akin to what Jorm and Oh (2009) refer to as the perceived need for social distance and is associated with being a marker for a number of adverse experiences including isolation, social exclusion and blame (Byrne 2000). It is important to note here that the police, being members of the general community, are not immune to populist positions and stereotypical images; as such, the potential role and influence of the media cannot be overestimated here. The same is true with respect to police officers' prior experiences and their impact on opinion and future decision making. Social stigma is something that is hard to change because it is systemic (Kidd 2007). Even though the media are considered to be a necessary means to challenge and replace the current dominant stereotypes (Byrne 2000), it still remains unlikely you will read many 'good news' stories about police encounters with disadvantaged young people which serve to challenge these longstanding misrepresentations.

9.8 Summary

To summarise, there remains a significant gap in our understanding with respect to police decision-making around their encounters with young people. While it is clear that the police do face complex and, at times, dangerous challenges when dealing with young people, a continued lack of transparency in the process and consistency of their courses of action contribute to the continuation of a confused rhetoric around whose community interests are actually being served. This knowledge gap, in terms of both the frequency and the nature of contact with young people, is vitally important because filling it would significantly support police being able to demonstrate impartiality in any given situation, or indeed provide evidence to the contrary. This information is arguably additionally important due to the police's public accountability function, and also additionally informative when dealing with situations that involve marginalised or other public interest groups where the current multi-agency service responses continue to fall short.

If the police were better equipped with tangible and effective referral options to channel young people into a broader suite of health, social and welfare services this may help to encourage more opportunities for the police to use their discretionary powers. A feedback loop, in terms of what happens to those young people diverted away from formal justice options, would arguably greatly support the uptake and use of such options by police officers as it would serve to provide practical examples to them about the effectiveness of diversionary practices and thus provide more positive experiences for the police as well as for the young people.

References

Allard T., Stewart A., Chrzanowski A., Ogilvie J., Birks D. and Little S. 2010. "Police diversion of young offenders and indigenous over-representation". *Trends and Issues in Crime and Criminal Justice* No. 390. Canberra: Australian Institute of Criminology.

Alpert G. P. and Dunham R. G. 2004. *Understanding police use of force: Officers, suspects and reciprocity.* Cambridge, UK: Cambridge University Press.

Armstrong D. 2004. "A risky business? Research, policy, governmentality and youth offending". *Youth Justice* 4: 100–116.

Australian Bureau of Statistics. 2011. *In Focus: Crime and Justice Statistics*, September 2011. www.abs.gov.au/ausstats/abs@.nsf/Lookup/4524.0Chapter500September%202011.

Australian Institute of Health and Welfare. 2011. *Juvenile detention population in Australia 2011.* Canberra: AIHW.

Australian Institute of Health and Welfare. 2013. *Young people aged 10–14 in the youth justice system in 2011–12.* Canberra: AIHW.

Bernberg J. G. and Krohn M. D. 2003. "Labelling, life chances and adult crime: The direct and indirect effects of official intervention in adolescence on crime in early adulthood". *Criminology* 41: 1287–1318.

Black D. J. 1976. *The behavior of law.* New York: Academic Press.

BOSCAR 2012. *Is juvenile crime increasing?* NSW Bureau of Crime Statistics and Research. NSW Government. 26 April 2012. www.bocsar.nsw.gov.au/lawlink/bocsar/ll_bocsar.nsf/pages/bocsar_fastfact_03.

Bronitt S. and Stenning P. 2011. "Understanding discretion in modern policing". *Criminal Law Journal* 35(6): 319–332.

Bronitt S. and Gani M. 2012. "Regulating reasonable force: Policing in the shadows of the law". In S. Bronitt, M. Gani and S. Hufnagel (eds) *Shooting to kill. Socio-legal perspectives on the use of lethal force.* Oñati International Series in Law and Society. Oregon: Hart Publishing.

Byrne P. 2000. "Stigma of mental illness and ways of diminishing it". *Advances in Psychiatric Treatment* 6: 65–72.

Ching H., Daffern M. and Thomas S. 2012. "Appetitive violence: A new phenomenon?" *Psychiatry, Psychology and Law* 19(5): 745–763.

Ching H., Daffern M. and Thomas S. 2013. "A comparison of contemporary and traditional classification schemes used to categorise youth violence". *The Journal of Forensic Psychiatry and Psychology* 24: 658–674.

Chitsabesan P., Kroll L., Bailey S., Kenning C., Sneider S., MacDonald W. and Theodosiou L. 2006. "Mental health needs of young offenders in custody and in the community". *British Journal of Psychiatry* 188: 534–540.

Cocozza J. J. and Skowyra K. R. 2000. "Youth with mental health disorders: Issues and emerging responses". *Juvenile Justice* 7: 3–13.

Cohen S. 1972. *Folk devils and moral panics: The creation of the Mods and Rockers.* London: MacGibbon Kee.

Collins P. A., Abelson J., Pyman H. and Lavis J. N. 2006. "Are we expecting too much from print media?" *Social Science and Medicine* 63: 89–102.

Constantinou M., Pilipenko P. and Karekla M. 2008. "Violence and crime by youngsters: 'Little terrorism' or partly a myth in the making?" *PsyCRITIQUES* 53(12): DOI:10.1037/a0011379.

Cooper V. G., McLearen A. L. and Zapf P. A. 2004. "Dispositional decisions with the mentally ill: Police perceptions and characteristics". *Police Quarterly* 7: 295–310.

Cotton D. 2004. "The attitudes of Canadian police officers toward the mentally ill". *International Journal of Law and Psychiatry* 27: 135–146.

Crawford A. 2007. "Reassurance policing: Feeling is believing". In A. Henry and D. J. Smith (eds) *Transformations of Policing*. Aldershot, UK: Ashgate, 143–168.

Crawford A. 2009. "Criminalising sociability through anti-social behavior legislation: Dispersal powers, young people and the police". *Youth Justice* 9: 5–26.

Department of Human Services. 2001. *Recidivism Among Victorian Juvenile Justice Clients 1997–2001.* Melbourne: Victorian Government Department of Human Services.

Ferguson C. J., San Miguel C. and Hartley R. D. 2009. "A multivariate analysis of youth violence and aggression: The influence of family, peers, depression and media violence". *The Journal of Pediatrics* 155(6): 904–908.

Flood-Page C., Campbell S., Harrington V. and Miller J. 2000. *Youth crime: Findings from the 1998–99 youth lifestyles survey.* Home Office Research Study 209. London: Home Office.

Gardiner B. 2013. "Casting a watchful eye over Stonnington". *Victoria Police Association Journal* 79(2): 16–20.

Glasman L. R. and Albarracin D. 2006. "Forming attitudes that predict future behavior: A meta-analysis of the attitude–behavior relation". *Psychological Bulletin* 132: 778–822.

Godfredson J., Thomas S., Ogloff J. and Luebbers S. 2011. "Police perceptions of their encounters with individuals experiencing mental illness: A Victorian study". *Australian and New Zealand Journal of Psychiatry* 44: 180–195.

Goldstein H. 1979. "Improving policing: A problem-oriented approach". *Crime and Delinquency* 25(2): 236–258. DOI: 10.1177/001112877902500207.

Goldstein J. 1960. *Police discretion not to invoke the criminal process: Low visibility decisions in the administration of justice.* Yale Law School Faculty Scholarship Series. Paper 2426. http://digitalcommons.law.yale.edu/fss_papers/2426.

Henderson M., Henderson P. and Kiernan C. 2000. "Missing persons: Incidence, issues and impacts." *Trends and Issues in Crime and Criminal Justice* No. 144. Canberra: Australian Institute of Criminology.

Hinds L. 2007. "Building police–youth relationships: The importance of procedural justice". *Youth Justice* 7: 195–209.

Holmes J. 2012. *Re-offenders in New South Wales.* Crime and Justice Statistics, BOSCAR, New South Wales.

Jorm A. F. and Oh E. 2009. "Desire for social distance from people with mental disorders: A review". *Australian and New Zealand Journal of Psychiatry* 43: 183–200.

Kesic D., Thomas S. and Ogloff J. 2013. "Mental disorders in incidents of police use of nonfatal force". *Social Psychiatry and Psychiatric Epidemiology* 48: 225–232. DOI: 10.1007/s00127–012–0543–4.

Kidd S. A. 2007. "Youth homelessness and social stigma". *Journal of Youth and Adolescence* 36: 291–299.

Kitzinger J. and Reilly J. 1997. "The rise and fall of risk reporting: Media coverage of human genetics research, 'false memory syndrome' and mad cow disease". *European Journal of Communication* 12: 319–350.

Kochel T. R. 2012. "Can police legitimacy promote collective efficacy?" *Justice Quarterly* 29: 384–419.

LaMotte V., Ouellette K., Sanderson J., Anderson S. A., Kosutic I., Griggs J. and Garcia M. 2010. "Effective police interactions with youth: A program evaluation". *Police Quarterly* 13: 161–179.

Link B. G. and Phelan J. C. 2001. "Conceptualising stigma". *Annual Review of Sociology* 27: 363–385.

Mazerolle P., Burton Jr. J. S., Cullen F. T., Evans T. D. and Payne G. L. 2000. "Strain, anger and delinquent adaptations: Specifying general strain theory". *Journal of Criminal Justice* 28(2): 89–101.

Mazerolle L., Bennett S., Davies J., Sargeant E. and Manning M. 2013. "Procedural justice and police legitimacy: A systematic review of the research evidence". *Journal of Experimental Criminology* 9(3): 245–274.

Murphy K. 2009. "Public satisfaction with police: The importance of procedural justice and police performance in police–citizen encounters". *Australian and New Zealand Journal of Criminology* 42(2): 159–178.

Murphy K. and Cherney A. 2010. "Understanding minority group willingness to cooperate with police: Taking another look at legitimacy research". Working Paper 15. Melbourne, Victoria: Alfred Deakin Research Institute.

Ouellette K. 2006. *Effective police interactions with youth: Instructor guide.* Hartford, Conn: Connecticut Juvenile Justice Advisory Committee.

Roberg R. R., Crank J. and Kuykendall J. 2000. *Police and Society*, 2nd edn. Los Angeles: Roxbury Publishing.

Sargeant E., Wickes R. and Mazerolle L. 2013. "Policing community problems: Exploring the role of formal social control in shaping collective efficacy". *Australian and New Zealand Journal of Criminology* 46: 70–87.

Schulenberg J. L. 2010. "Patterns in police decision-making with youth: An application of Black's theory of law". *Crime, Law and Social Change* 53: 109–129.

Slovic P., Fischhoff B. and Lichenstein S. 1982. "Facts versus fears: Understanding perceived risk". In D. Kahneman, P. Slovic and A. Tversky (eds) *Judgment under uncertainty: Heuristics and biases.* New York: Cambridge University Press, 463–492.

Sozer M. A. and Merlo A. V. 2013. "The impact of community policing on crime rates: Does the effect of community policing differ in large and small enforcement agencies?" *Police Practice and Research* 14: 506–521.

Stewart D. M., Morris R. G. and Weir H. 2014. "Youth perceptions of the police: Identifying trajectories". *Youth Violence and Juvenile Justice* 12: 22–39.

Strong M. 2009. *Review of the use of force by and against Victorian police.* Melbourne: Office of Police Integrity.

Sykes R. and Brent E. 1980. "The regulation of interaction by policing: A systems view of policing". *Criminology* 18: 182–197.

Terrill W. and Mastrofski S. D. 2002. "Situational and officer-based determinants of police coercion". *Justice Quarterly* 19: 215–248.

Thomas S. 2013. "Core requirements of a best practice model for police encounters involving people experiencing mental illness". In D. Chappell (ed.) *Policing and the mentally ill: International perspectives.* New York: CRC Press, 121–136.

Tyler T. R. 2006. *Why people obey the law.* Princeton, NJ: Princeton University Press.

Vermeersch H., T'Sjoen G., Kaufman M. and Van Houtte M. 2013. "Social science theories on adolescent risk taking: The relevance of behavioural inhibition and activation". *Youth and Society* 45: 27–53.

Wallace D. S., Paulson R. M., Lord C. G. and Bond C. F. 2005. "Which behaviors do attitudes predict? Meta-analyzing the effects of social pressure and perceived difficulty". *Review of General Psychology* 9: 214–227.

Watson A., Ottati V., Lurigio A. and Heyrman M. 2005. "Stigma and the police". In P. Corrigan (ed.) *On the stigma of mental illness: practical strategies for research and social change.* Washington: American Psychological Association, 197–217.

Weisburd D., Telep C., Hinkle J. and Eck J. 2008. *Effects of Problem-Oriented Policing on Crime and Disorder.* US Department of Justice. 2007-IJ-CX-0045.

Wortley R. K. 2003. "Measuring police attitudes towards discretion". *Criminal Justice and Behavior* 30: 538–558.

10 Child sexual abuse

Providing protection and turning away from future offending

James R. P. Ogloff and Margaret Cutajar

10.1 Introduction

One of the great plights that continues to plague society in contemporary times is the sexual abuse and victimisation of children. While it has been known for millennia that children can be the victims of sexual abuse, it has only really been since the 1980s that childhood sexual abuse (CSA) has gained much public awareness and acknowledgment. The evidence is now incontrovertible: CSA occurs in our communities at an alarming rate of up to 30 per cent for CSA of any kind, to a prevalence interval between 5 and 10 per cent for more severe forms involving penetration (Fergusson and Mullen 1999). Compelling evidence suggests that CSA is a pervasive problem associated with an array of short- and long-term deleterious outcomes, including emotional, behavioural and social dysfunctions (for reviews see Andrews *et al.* 2004; Fergusson and Mullen 1999; Gilbert *et al.* 2009; Paolucci *et al.* 2001).

The relationship between CSA and offending, particularly sexual offending, is of considerable interest in society. Questions arise regarding the extent to which CSA may contribute to the development of offending behaviour in general and sexual deviance more specifically. While some victims may follow a trajectory that leads to offending behaviours, others seem to get caught in the perpetual experience of being victimised. However, studies on the relationship between CSA, offending behaviour, and revictimisation have suffered from a lack of the empirical sophistication seen in more recent research on the relationship between CSA and psychopathology. This has left a large gap in our understanding of the fundamental epidemiological questions pertaining to how many sexually abused male and female children end up offending, and, specifically, how many commit sexual offences, or experience revictimisation.

To further understand the relative risk of offending and victimisation rates among CSA victims, it is important to compare them to people drawn from a non-abused population to determine whether CSA poses a risk factor for offending and victimisation. If indeed a significant relationship exists between CSA and offending or victimisation, the next step in empirical research is to determine factors that differentiate those within the CSA population who exhibit the deleterious outcome from those who do not. Although these are fundamental and important empirical and clinical questions, no study has adequately examined any of them to date.

In this chapter, we briefly review the literature that has investigated the extent to which children who experience CSA subsequently proceed to offending behaviour, including sexual offending. The literature to be reviewed includes both retrospective self-report studies and prospective studies. We will also consider the factors that might serve to mediate or moderate the effects of the abuse on detrimental outcomes. The chapter will also touch on the topic of the revictimisation of people who were sexually abused as children. We then report on the findings of a comprehensive programme of research we have conducted investigating the relationship between CSA and offending. Finally, we provide a discussion of the need for interventions to address this problem to perhaps reduce the risk of offending and sexual offending that follows CSA.

As we turn to a review of the literature, it is important to consider the different methodologies that have been used to determine the relationship between having been sexually abused and subsequently becoming an abuser. First, some studies have surveyed offenders, asking them to recall retrospectively whether they had been abused. Second, studies have attempted to prospectively follow people known to have been abused as children to determine how many proceed to engage in sexual offending. These studies will be summarised below.

10.2 Reported history of sexual abuse and offending

Since Curtis (1963) raised clinical concern that abused children would "become tomorrow's murders and perpetrators of crimes of violence", the intergenerational transmission of violence where abused children develop to become abusers has been one of the most commonly held beliefs in both the scholarly and popular literature (Widom 1989a and b). More specifically, a proportion of authors in the abused to abuser literature have championed the notion that the type of maltreatment experienced in childhood influences a similar method of abuse perpetrated later, with sexual abuse victims progressing to become sexual abusers (see Bagley *et al.* 1994).

Retrospective studies on convicted child sex offenders indicate up to 75 per cent report a history of CSA, with Hanson and Slater's (1988) review of 18 studies showing that 33 per cent of convicted male child sex offenders had reported experiencing any sexual contact during childhood. More broadly, a study of 100 incarcerated males found 59 per cent reported some form of CSA (Johnson *et al.* 2006). While such studies lack a comparison group to provide a base rate of reported sexual abuse in a non-offending population, these rates are higher than Fergusson and Mullen's (1999) meta-analyses of the cumulative prevalence rate of any form of CSA, which revealed that the prevalence among males who were the victims of child sexual abuse was from 10 to 20 per cent.

The obvious flaw with the hypothesis that the nature of abuse experienced in childhood is subsequently perpetrated, however, is that significantly more females than males are sexually abused, yet the majority (over 90 per cent) of child sex offenders are males (Fergusson and Mullen 1999). Moreover, retrospective studies that compare the reported CSA histories of sex offenders to offenders convicted of non-sexual offences provide an account that reported experiences of sexual abuse may not be entirely synonymous with subsequent sex offending.

Jespersen *et al.* (2009) conducted a meta-analysis of 17 studies comparing sex offenders with non-sex offenders on sexual abuse histories. All but one study reported greater odds of sex offenders reporting having been sexually abused compared to non-sex offenders. However, out of these 16 studies, only seven yielded significant odds ratios, ranging between 2.49 and 15.00, suggesting that the majority (ten) of the studies examined did not find a significant difference in reporting histories of sexual abuse between sex and non-sex offenders. Considering the findings together, Jesperson and colleagues (2009) calculated a significant weighted average odds ratio of 3.36, suggesting that sex offenders were three times more likely to report a history of sexual abuse than non-sex offenders. Furthermore, they found no difference in the retrospective reporting of sexual abuse between adult rapists and child molesters.

Others (Benoit and Kennedy 1992; Hanson and Slater 1988) have argued that the nature of the abuse experienced in childhood does not lead to the same method of offending, but rather that childhood abuse is simply associated with offending behaviour in general. This supposition is supported, in part, by the unequivocal findings that the vast majority of sex offenders have a diverse criminal offending repertoire, including non-sexual offences (Hanson and Bussiere 1998; Smallbone and Wortley 2004).

Taken together, while male prisoners in general and sex offenders in particular report a higher incidence of CSA relative to prevalence rates found in the general community, the question of whether male sex offenders have an increased rate of sexual abuse history compared to non-sex offenders has yielded mixed findings.

The majority of studies have focused on the incidence of sexual abuse among male offenders due to the over-representation of sex crimes perpetrated by males, and the commonly held view that males externalise their abuse to aggressive acts, while females internalise their abuse to psychopathological states. However, it is now recognised that a relatively small percentage of cases of sexual abuse against children is in fact committed by females (Dube *et al.* 2005; Johansson-Love and Fremouw 2006). As such, it is important to consider whether female children who are abused are more likely to proceed to sexually abuse children when compared to females who were not the victims of CSA.

According to the US Bureau of Justice Statistics, 25.5 per cent of state prison female inmates self-identified as having experienced sexual abuse prior to the age of 18 years (Harlow, 1999). In an Australian study, Nathan and Ward (2002) examined the histories of 12 female sex offenders. Three quarters of the female sex offenders reported a history of CSA. A few studies (Fromuth and Conn 1997; Kaplan and Green 1995; Mathews *et al.* 1997; Miccio-Fonseca 2000; Pothast and Allen 1994), using a variety of samples including incarcerated offenders and anonymous university students, have found that female sexual offenders reported experiencing CSA at a higher frequency than other groups, including other offending incarcerated females, male sex offenders and non-sex offending female students. ✓

Retrospective studies of the outcome of CSA

Retrospective studies involve the self-reporting of earlier experiences usually at the same time as outcome variables are measured. This common methodological approach has been criticised for at least three reasons: (1) sampling bias or representation of the population; (2) reporting bias or the veracity of recollections of past events; and (3) the cross-sectional and correlational nature of findings. Briefly, most sexual abuse and offending research involve samples drawn from offender populations, typically incarcerated male felons. These specialised, and to a large extent convenient, populations can be regarded as a biased sample of overall population groups, as the extent to which such samples represent the larger non-incarcerated offender population is unknown. It is well documented that most sexual offences go unreported, and of those that are reported, most do not proceed past the investigation stage to court (Fitzgerald 2006). As such, convicted sex offenders may not be representative of the general pool of men and women who sexually abuse children.

Second, the reliance upon unsubstantiated retrospective recall of CSA reports raises the issue of recall bias and the veracity of claims (Widom *et al.* 2004). Although strong evidence indicates that within the general population people, particularly males, tend to fail to report their past experiences of CSA (Fergusson *et al.* 2000; Hardt and Rutter 2004), the opposite effect of false positive claims of CSA among the offending population is plausible. Reporting bias is of particular concern among an offender population as external motivation to report a history of CSA in an attempt to elicit sympathy and/or receive a lenient sentence cannot be excluded (Falshaw 2005). Due to these inaccuracies, retrospective studies may potentially produce a high rate of false positive results in the association between offending and a history of CSA.

Finally, existing studies have been criticised for their reliance on cross-sectional and correlational methodologies. Such approaches do not enable researchers to determine reliably the temporal ordering of child abuse exposure in relation to outcomes (Gilbert *et al.* 2009; Widom *et al.* 2004). As such, meaningful analyses on the potential cause and effect nature between CSA and offending behaviour cannot be achieved. At best, retrospective cross-sectional studies only allude to a correlational nature of a reported history of CSA and offending behaviour.

Prospective studies of the outcome of CSA

The second approach to ascertaining information about the long-term consequences of CSA, including later offending, relies on identifying samples of people who were sexually abused in childhood and investigating, prospectively, their outcomes. These studies, arguably, offer some methodological advantages over self-reporting retrospective studies. These include establishing temporal order, causal priority, potential to control confounding variables, and avoidance of recall bias and sampling bias by the selective inclusion of participants based on outcomes (Fergusson and Mullen 1999; Gilbert *et al.* 2009). These methodological strengths overcome many of the limitations of retrospective studies; however, the longitudinal and economic requirements of prospective studies raise practical challenges that are seldom met, resulting in a very limited number of prospective studies in general and specifically in the field of CSA.

An alternative cost and time effective methodology that maintains some of the features of prospective designs involves the linkage of official records of substantiated sexual abuse to a range of contemporaneous administrative databases (e.g. police, psychiatric and coronial records). However, it is recognised that reliance on official records may still be subject to systematic biases, such as overrepresentation of severe forms of abuse and family dysfunction, affecting the representativeness of victims of CSA. Nevertheless, this approach has utility as the sequencing of events can be established and epidemiological investigations on the risks of CSA at the severe end of the spectrum can be answered with greater confidence.

Prospective studies provide a different perspective, as these designs allow for the investigation of how many victims subsequently offend (or experience the alternative outcome variable of interest), providing a more accurate picture of the association between CSA and offending. Here we consider the few studies that have attempted to examine this association, with concluding comments on the overall limitations in these studies.

Burgess *et al.* (1987) conducted an early study of 34 of 66 sexually abused children who were interviewed six to eight years after their abuse. This prospective study was largely descriptive in nature. The followed-up youth (mean age of 17 years) were divided into two groups based on the severity and duration of abuse as well as the environments from which they came. When comparing abused youth with non-abused students, the authors reported no difference in the less severe group with respect to delinquent and criminal activity. The more severe group, however, was found to be significantly more aggressive and more likely to have been in trouble with the law, with all 17 cases being arrested compared to two arrests out of 13 students in the non-abused group. Given the severity of offending (i.e. two male CSA victims had been convicted for sexual assault and two for attempted or completed homicide prior to the age of 18 years), these findings are unlikely to be generalisable to the broader group of CSA victims.

Another descriptive follow-up study by Salter and colleagues (2003) involved the UK nation-wide collection of records on 224 males who had received medical attention for sexual abuse (mean age 11 years) between the years 1980 and 1992. A nationwide search of official criminal records was performed in 1999, some seven to 19 years after the initial abuse, when the subjects were aged between 18 and 34 years. Of the 224 male victims, the majority (88 per cent) were not found to have committed a sexual offence, with seven of the 26 sexually perpetrating cases which did exist receiving an official caution or conviction for their offence. Information on 17 of these cases revealed all but one had offended against children. Within group analyses found that victims who sexually offended were more likely also to have been cautioned or convicted for other violent offences (23 per cent) than non-sex offending victims (12 per cent), and had on average committed more crimes per person overall (6.1 vs 4.2).

Siegel and Williams (2003a) retrieved information on 206 cases from one American city emergency room of sexual abuse (67 per cent involving penetration) against females aged up to 12 years who underwent forensic examination during 1973 and 1975, and matched these cases to 205 non-abused girls from the same emergency room on age, race, and date seen. Official arrest information was obtained. While the majority of cases were not found to have an official arrest record, victims were nearly two times more likely than matched controls to have been arrested as adults (20.4 per cent vs 10.7 per cent). The arrest rate for violent (9.3 per cent vs 4.4 per cent) and property (9.3 per cent vs 5.4 per cent) offences were similarly around two times greater than controls; however, these offence groups were not operationalised and it is therefore unknown whether violent offences included those of a sexual nature. The largest difference in adult offending between CSA victims and their non-abused counterparts was in arrests for drug offences, at 7.8 and 1.5 per cent respectively.

Widom and colleagues (Widom and Ames 1994; Widom and Maxfield 2001) conducted research on 908 substantiated cases of children abused between 1967 and 1971 matched to 667 non-abused cases. All subjects were followed up through a search of local, state and federal arrest records in 1988 (Widom and Ames 1994) and again in 1994 (Widom and Maxfield 2001). People in the abused group were all victimised prior to the age of 11 years and all types of child abuse were included (i.e. physical abuse, neglect and sexual abuse); sexual abuse cases represented the lowest number at 125 (13.8 per cent) cases, and predominately comprised females (84 per cent), with only 20 boys.

The majority of abused and non-abused cases had no juvenile or adult criminal record; however, a higher proportion of abused cases compared to the non-abused group were arrested as a juvenile (27 per cent vs 17 per cent) or adult (42 per cent vs 33 per cent) (Widom and Maxfield 2001). Whether these differences reached statistical significance was not reported. A higher proportion of males than females in both abused and non-abused groups was arrested for violent offences, including rape and sodomy; however, a significant difference was only established for abused females relative to their non-abused counterparts. An analysis by abuse type revealed that sexually abused victims were least likely, and physically abused most likely, to have been arrested for a violent offence; however, as Widom and Maxfield acknowledged, this result is likely to be an underrepresentation due to the low number of male CSA victims included in their study. Moreover, sexual and non-sexual violent offending was not distinguished. However, in her earlier study, Widom and Ames (1994) found 3.9 per cent of abused children compared to 0.4 per cent of controls were arrested for a violent sex crime, and this was largely attributed to the physically abused group.

Although these follow up studies offered a number of methodological strengths that overcame many of the limitations of retrospective studies to arrive at the similar conclusion that the majority of CSA victims do not go on to commit crimes, they need to be considered in light of some shortcomings. Of greatest relevance, none of these studies adequately examined the association between CSA and subsequent sexual offending. The samples were typically small, particularly for male victims. Given that the base-rate of offences (particularly sexual offences) is low, and mostly perpetrated by males, the studies have not adequately addressed the question of the relationship between CSA and offending. The victims also were still typically quite young at follow-up, thereby perhaps falling short of the peak period for being convicted for sex offences. Finally, only a limited range of offences was examined as outcomes, or offences were combined to form broad groups that did not distinguish sex crimes from other violent offences.

10.3 Factors that mediate the relationship between CSA and offending

Findings from both retrospective and prospective studies underscore the fact that not all CSA victims go on to offend. This raises important questions of why does one victim of CSA and not another develop problem behaviours, and what factors interact with CSA to mediate or moderate the subsequent expression of negative or positive outcomes. Investigating possible mechanisms underlying offending behaviour following CSA is of great relevance to establishing a framework for understanding the apparent associations and to identifying areas of target for intervention. Although a review of all the possible mechanisms that may lead to an increase in criminogenic factors (i.e. those factors that contribute to offending) is beyond the scope of this chapter, the role of abuse characteristics and mental illness will be briefly examined.

The dose-response hypothesis posits that the level or severity of abuse dictates the degree of consequences, with abuse of greater severity resulting in a greater response (i.e. negative outcome) (Fergusson and Mullen 1999). Accordingly, it would be expected that CSA involving multiple incidents of penetration by multiple perpetrators over an extended period would result in poorer outcomes than a one-off non-contact sexual abuse incident. However, empirical evidence from prospective studies has been limited and inconsistent, with some (Burgess *et al.* 1987) finding a positive association between severity of abuse and offending behaviours, while others (Salter *et al.* 2003) found no difference.

The child abuse literature is also divided on which age or developmental period at which abuse occurs exerts the greatest deleterious impact. Some theorists and researchers (Barker-Collo and Read 2003; Manly *et al.* 2001) argue that abuse which occurs when a child is younger is more detrimental since the abuse might impede the timely achievement of developmental milestones. By contrast, others (Browne and Finkelhor 1986; Kendall-Tackett *et al.* 1993; Thornberry *et al.* 2001) postulate older age at abuse is of greater detriment, arguing younger age acts as a buffer for abuse due to a young child's undeveloped cognitive abilities to comprehend the implications of being abused (Finkelhor 1995). Moreover, sexual victimisation at an older age during the psychosexually sensitive period of adolescence may have a greater impact on behavioural problems. While there is some evidence indicating older age at abuse is associated with externalising problems or delinquency in youth (Burgess *et al.* 1987; Kaplow and Widom 2007; Thornberry *et al.* 2001), whether these findings are specifically applicable to adult victims of CSA in terms of criminal behaviour is unknown.

The association between mental illness and offending has received a great deal of attention, finding high rates of mental illness among male (Ogloff 2009) and female (Ogloff and Tye 2007) offenders. Research comparing the rate and type of offending among a sample of more than 4,000 men and women with schizophrenia and a control group has revealed that the people with schizophrenia have higher rates of all types of offences (i.e. general, violent, non-violent, family violence) (Short *et al.* 2013).

There is also an over-representation of mental illness among CSA victims (see reviews by Andrews *et al.* 2004; Browne and Finkelhor 1986; Fergusson and Mullen 1999; Gilbert *et al.* 2009; Paolucci *et al.* 2001; Putnam 2003). Previous research by our group (Cutajar *et al.* 2010a; 2010b; 2010c) 43-year follow up study on a large cohort of CSA victims has provided compelling evidence that CSA is a substantial risk factor for a range of mental disorders, with victims being 3.65 times more likely than the general population to have contact with public mental health services. Mental illness in victims of CSA may increase the risk of offending; however, no study utilising prospective methodologies has yet investigated this interaction by linking these three important factors together.

10.4 Child sexual abuse and re-victimisation

In addition to questions that have been raised about the future offending of people who were sexually abused as children is the extent to which CSA victims are revictimised in some form later in life (for reviews see Classen *et al.* 2005; Noll 2005; Roodman and Clum 2001). As with many of the studies regarding CSA and later offending, these studies tend to be retrospective in nature and focus on the sexual re-victimisation of victims (especially women) drawn from samples of convenience at college or clinical sites.

Results from large community studies indicate that both males and females who report an adult experience of sexual assault, or general interpersonal violence, were more likely to report a history of CSA (Briere and Elliott 2003; Elliott *et al.* 2004). Nevertheless, retrospective studies fail to answer how many CSA victims experience subsequent re-victimisation. Again, only a few prospective studies exist to answer this, and their findings are generally limited to sexual re-victimisation of the female victim population.

An Australian study on 183 substantiated cases of CSA followed up six years later revealed 17 per cent of youth had further substantiated notifications for subsequent CSA (Swanston *et al.* 2002); however, this study lacked a comparison group, and gender differences were mentioned. An American study followed up and interviewed 74 out of 84 confirmed intra-familial female CSA victims seven years after their initial assessment, and found 20.9 per cent reported experiencing rape or sexual assault compared to 10 per cent of women in a comparison sample (Noll *et al.* 2003). Although CSA victims were twice as likely to be raped as non-abused females in the general population, this difference did not reach significance, due in part to the small sample size and relatively low base-rate of rape. However, CSA victims were significantly more likely, at 1.6 times, to experience a physical assault.

In an extension of their prospective study of 206 female CSA victims noted above, Siegel and Williams (2003b) interviewed 84 victims and 84 comparisons up to 24 years later. There were no differences between the abused and comparison groups in self-reporting of sexual assault victimisation in adolescence (28.7 per cent vs 24.1 per cent) or adulthood (48.3 per cent vs 37.9 per cent); however, this non-significant finding may be attributable to the fact that one third of women in the comparison group reported that they had been sexually abused prior to 13 years of age.

Taken together, these findings suggest about a fifth and half of female CSA victims experience sexual revictimisation in youth and adulthood, respectively; however, due to the limited and flawed prospective studies it cannot be concluded that CSA among female victims poses an increased risk factor for later sexual assault. As with studies of CSA and subsequent offending, the general and sexual re-victimisation of adult male CSA victims tends to be a neglected area that requires empirical exploration.

10.5 The Victorian CSA linkage study

Beginning in the mid to late 1990s, Mullen and colleagues (Spataro *et al.* 2004) assembled a database of children who were medically confirmed to have been sexually abused in childhood. The database was constructed from files obtained from the Victorian Institute of Forensic Medicine pertaining to children who were examined by forensic medical practitioners who were responsible for assessing the children following a report to the police that the child had been sexually abused. This database was then added to beginning in 2007 and now includes the records of 2,759 females and males who were sexually abused as children between 1964 and 1995. Although the sample is mostly comprised of female victims, there are 558 cases where the victim was a boy. A comparison group was identified from the Australian Electoral Commission that was matched to the CSA group based on gender and age.

In a programme of research, Cutajar and colleagues (Cutajar *et al.* 2010a, 2010b, 2010c) linked the CSA and comparison databases to the Victorian public mental health database and the coronial database that enabled a comparison of rates of psychopathology, un-natural death, suicides, and death by drug over-dose. More recently, Ogloff, Cutajar and Mullen have linked the databases to the criminal history database to obtain information regarding subsequent charges and convictions of offences among CSA victims and those in the comparison group (Ogloff *et al.* 2012). Finally, along with Mann, the group has also been considering the subsequent re-victimisation of CSA victims and those in the comparison group. These studies represent the largest sample of males and female CSA victims considered and followed for the longest follow-up period (up to 45 years in some cases).

With respect to psychopathology and contact with mental health services, results revealed that almost one-quarter (23.3 per cent) of CSA victims had contact with public mental health services compared to 7.7 per cent of controls (Cutajar *et al.* 2010b). The rate of contact among CSA victims was 3.65 times higher (95% CI, 3.09–4.32, $p<0.001$). It was further found that exposure to sexual abuse increased risks for the majority of outcomes including psychosis, affective anxiety, substance abuse and personality disorders. Rates of clinical disorders diagnosed in adulthood and childhood remained significantly higher among CSA cases. Older age at sexual abuse (aged 12 years and above) and those exposed to severe abuse involving penetration or multiple offenders were associated with greater risk for developing psychopathology.

Looking narrowly at psychotic disorders, Cutajar and colleagues (2010a) found that significantly more CSA victims than people in the comparison group accumulated a diagnosis of psychosis generally (2.8 per cent vs 1.4 per cent) or schizophrenia specifically (1.9 per cent vs 0.7 per cent). Those exposed to pene-trative abuse had even higher rates of psychosis (3.4 per cent) and schizophrenia (2.4 per cent). Abuse without penetration was not associated with significant increases in either psychosis or schizophrenia. As with psychopathology gener-ally, the risks were highest for those whose abuse involved penetration, who were older at the time of being abused (aged 12 years and above), and whose abuse involved more than one perpetrator. Those CSA victims who met all of these conditions had surprisingly high rates of psychosis (17.2 per cent) and schizophrenia (8.6 per cent).

Cutajar and colleagues (2010c) also considered the rate of suicide and acciden-tal fatal drug overdose (i.e. overdose deemed not to have been suicide) in CSA victims compared to age-limited national population data. The base-rate of fatal self-harm was low (21/2759 cases, 0.76 per cent); however, the rate of both suicide (18.09 times greater) and fatal drug overdose (49.22 times greater) was signifi-cantly greater when compared to the general population. Similar to the general population, CSA victims who died as a result of self-harm were predominantly aged in their 30s at the time of death. Most had contact with the public mental health system and half were recorded as being diagnosed with an anxiety disorder.

Using the same sample and methodology, Ogloff *et al.* (2012) linked the CSA database to the criminal history database maintained by the Victoria Police. Almost one-quarter ($n=652$, 23.63%) of CSA victims had a recorded offence, compared to 5.9 per cent ($n=157$, 87 males and 70 females) of people in the comparison sample. The average number of charges was significantly higher for CSA cases than the comparison group (31.59 vs 19.18) and more CSA victims ($n=114$, 4.1%) than controls ($n=14$, 0.052%) received a custodial sentence.

CSA victims were five times more likely than their peers from the general population to have been charged with an offence, and this difference remained significant for both male (4.34 times) and female (6.71) victims. CSA cases were significantly more likely to be charged with all types of offences compared to the general population. Four CSA victims (2 males and 2 females) were charged with homicide, compared to no control cases. Charges with the most marked elevation among CSA cases compared to controls were sexual offences, violent offences and breaches of orders.

All offences were significantly higher for both male and female CSA victims compared to their general population peers, although the associations were stronger for female victims, with charges for threatening violence and assault being the strongest. Sexual offences, violent offences and breaches of orders remained most strongly associated with CSA among male victims. However, when comparing male and female CSA cases, sexually abused males were significantly more likely than their abused female counterparts to have been charged with all types of offences with the exception of homicide and prostitution.

Considering sexual offending more specifically, 5 per cent (one out of 20) of male CSA cases were subsequently convicted of a sexual offence, which was significantly greater than for males in the control group, of whom only 0.6 per cent (six out of 1,000) had convictions for sexual offending. The difference was even greater when considering boys who had been victimised at age 12 years or above, where 9.2 per cent (almost one in ten) was subsequently found to have been convicted of a sexual offence. This was significantly greater than the rate for male CSA cases who were abused when under the age of 12 years (2.9 per cent). By contrast, for girls there were no significant differences in the percentage who went on to be convicted of a sexual offence, regardless of whether they were abused before or after age 12 years (0.1 per cent or one out of 1,000 cases).

When examining the effects of the sexual abuse variables of age at abuse (before and after 12 years of age), penetration, frequency of abuse (one vs multiple) and number of perpetrators (one vs multiple) upon presence of criminal history among the CSA population, older age at abuse was found to be significant. The strongest relationship yielded was for males sexually abused after the age of 12 years, being 3.33 times more likely than younger males to be subsequently charged with a sexual offence. This remained significant even when other factors, such as severity or duration of abuse, were considered.

Finally in ongoing research, the group is considering revictimisation of CSA victims. The mean number of victimisation incidents was higher for CSA cases than for the comparison group (2.94 vs 1.93). Overall, CSA victims were significantly younger than the others when they were first re-victimised (average 22.73 years versus average 27.60 years). However, there was no significant age difference between CSA victims and the general population when comparing the average age of first sexual (re)victimisation (16.79 vs 17.81 years).

CSA victims (36 per cent) were 1.14 times more likely than others (33.4 per cent) to have been victimised for any offence; however, this difference was only statistically significant for male victims. With the exception of theft and bad public behaviour, CSA cases were significantly more likely to be victimised for all types of offences compared to the general population. Male CSA cases were significantly more likely than male comparisons to have been victimised for sexual and violent offences. Female CSA cases were significantly more likely than comparison females to report victimisation for a sexual offence, threat of violence, violence and property damage. The association for sexual victimisation was stronger for male CSA cases relative to their male peers compared to females; however, female CSA cases were significantly more likely than CSA males to be sexually re-victimised. Conversely, while male CSA cases were significantly more likely to have been a victim of violence than the CSA females, the association to being a victim of violence compared to the general population was stronger for female CSA cases.

10.6 Summary and conclusions

Taken together, existing research shows convincingly that CSA victims are more likely than other people to experience a broad array of adverse outcomes over their lifespan. It is important to emphasise, however, that the majority of CSA victims did not have adverse outcomes and they did not go on to offend or become victims of crime. The resilience of children is generally quite strong and protective.

Of particular interest and focus in this chapter is the relationship between CSA victimisation and subsequent offending by the victim. As discussed, much of the previous research has relied on a retrospective self-report methodology, which has limitations. Moreover, many studies have had either no male CSA victim participants or very small numbers of them.

Overcoming many limitations of previous studies, the recent research by Ogloff and colleagues (2012) revealed that, in general, CSA victims were more likely to have some form of contact with the police for *any* matter compared to other members of the general community. Although the overwhelming majority of CSA victims (i.e. 77 per cent) did not have an official criminal record, CSA victims were almost five times more likely than others to be charged with any offence, with the strongest associations yielded for sexual and violent offences and breaches of orders. It was contact with the police for being a victim of crime, however, that accounted for a large proportion of all contacts. Nonetheless both male and female CSA victims were significantly more likely than non-abused people to be charged all types of offences, in particular violence and sexual offences.

Not only were CSA victims more likely than others to offend, they had a greater number of charges, a higher proportion of charges resulting in a guilty verdict, more custodial sentences and they continued offending to an older age. These findings suggest that offences committed by sexual abuse victims are not isolated to sexual offences or the male gender (Benoit and Kennedy 1992).

While the majority (99 per cent) of male and female victims of CSA were not charged for a sexual offence, CSA victims were almost eight times more likely to be charged with sexual offences than the general population. Moreover, as the results show, a surprisingly high percentage of male victims were subsequently convicted of a sexual offence (5 per cent of all male victims and 9.25 per cent of those aged 12 years and above at the time of their victimisation). Some other research has found no association between childhood victims of sexual abuse and future sexual offending; however, this may be due to the small sample size of CSA victims and the fact that the samples comprised mostly females (Widom 1989a and b). In a meta-analysis of factors related to recidivism in sex offenders, Hanson and Bussiere (1998) did not find a relationship between sexual abuse victimisation and subsequent sexual offending. This is of course due to the nature of the studies included in the meta-analysis, which have largely relied on self-reporting and retrospective methodology.

As expected, male CSA victims were largely responsible for the increased rate of sexual offences, in particular those boys abused at 12 years or older. Given that almost one in ten boys who were sexually abused in this age group subsequently were convicted of a sexual offence, sexual victimisation may be an important risk factor for this population (but not for females). The hallmark feature of this period is psychosexual development, whereby heightened sexual arousal may be paired with cognitive distortion/implicit theories relating to sexual relations (Ward 2000) and aberrant sexual urges which may develop and underlie sexual offending. Possible explanations for the phenomenon were not examined in this study, but should be investigated in subsequent studies.

The preliminary findings lend further support to the association between CSA and re-victimisation. With the exception of theft and bad public behaviour, CSA cases were more often a crime victim than non-abused comparisons, with highest associations found for sexual offences (5× more likely), threats of violence (4×) and violent offences (3×). On average, CSA cases reported more separate victimisation incidents than the general population; however, there was no difference in the number of separate incidents relating to sexual assault. This is the first prospective study to demonstrate that male victims of CSA were significantly more likely than males in the general population, but significantly less likely than their female abused counterparts, to be a victim of a subsequent sexual assault.

The findings of the studies showing increased levels of offending and re-victimisation in the CSA samples have a number of implications for clinical, policing and judicial practices. One clear implication is the need for therapeutic interventions targeted at adolescent male CSA victims with a focus on positive sexuality in an attempt to reduce their heightened risk of committing a sexual offence. The benefits of psychological treatment for trauma, addressing victims' mental health problems and preventing or addressing criminogenic risk factors such as low education and employment attainment, substance abuse, and negative supports, in the aftermath of sexual abuse to both male and female victims is also likely to reduce the risks of offending in general and violent offences in particular.

Legal and judicial representatives, as well as forensic mental health practitioners who may assess offenders, should take into consideration the complex interplay between history of CSA, mental illness, and offending. Offender treatment programmes in the community or custodial settings may need to be adapted to consider the role of childhood abuse in an attempt to reduce recidivism. Many now do not allow for the discussion of offenders' own sexual victimisation.

These findings have a number of implications for clinical, policing and judicial practices. Of perhaps most significant relevance is the need for therapeutic interventions targeted at victims of sexual abuse. In particular, adolescent male victims require interventions with a focus on positive sexuality in an attempt to reduce their heightened risk of committing a sexual offence. The benefits of psychological treatment for trauma, addressing victims' mental health problems and preventing or addressing criminogenic risk factors such as low education and employment attainment, substance abuse, and negative supports in the aftermath of sexual abuse to both male and female victims is also likely to reduce the risks of offending in general and violent offences in particular.

Police officers who come into contact with either male or female victims, and to a lesser extent offenders, should be cognisant of the possibility of dealing with an individual with a history of sexual abuse and the need for sensitivity and respect. Legal and judicial representatives, as well as forensic psychologists and psychiatrists who may assess offenders, should take into consideration the complex interplay between history of CSA, mental illness, offending, the unlikelihood of adhering to court appointed orders and the (un)suitability of a harsh custodial environment when considering the needs of offenders. If a non-custodial disposition is considered appropriate, assertive follow-up, supports and interventions would be necessary to prevent additional offending. It may be beneficial for receptive practices within prisons to enquire systematically about CSA histories to alert involved custodial officers to better identify relevant needs such as sexual assault counselling, help understand and manage disruptive behaviours, be sensitive to the need for protection from sexual predators, or adapt prison protocols (e.g. strip searches) to prevent further traumatisation. Offender treatment programmes in the community or custodial settings may need to be adapted to consider the role of childhood abuse in an attempt to reduce recidivism.

Finally, the rate of revictimisation among CSA victims is alarming and tragic. This is a phenomenon that is not well understood. Doubtless, being sexually victimised results in some CSA victims becoming more vulnerable to subsequent victimisation, including sexual victimisation. As such, further research and clinical attention is required in this important area.

Taken together, the information in this chapter confirms that CSA has many detrimental effects on victims. Focusing on the increased risk of offending and in particular sexual offending by male victims shows yet again how disadvantage and victimisation can contribute to the development of offending. Helping child victims not only can help meet their own needs but it can in fact prevent the victimisation of other children and crime victims more generally. As noted, the rate of revictimisaton, which is a relatively novel research question, requires considerably more clinical and research attention.

References

Andrews G., Corry J., Slade T., Issakidis C. and Swanston H. 2004. "Child sexual abuse". In M. Ezzati, A. Lopez, A. Rodgers and C. Murray (eds) *Comparative quantification of health risks* Vol. 2. Geneva, Switzerland: World Health Organization, 1850–1940.

Bagley C., Wood M. and Young L. 1994. "Victim to abuser: Mental health and behavioral sequels of child sexual abuse in a community survey of young adult males". *Child Abuse and Neglect* 18(8): 683–697.

Barker-Collo S. and Read J. 2003. "Models of response to childhood sexual abuse". *Trauma, Violence and Abuse* 4(2): 95–111.

Benoit J. L. and Kennedy W. A. 1992. "The abuse history of male adolescent sex offenders". *Journal of Interpersonal Violence* 7(4): 543–548.

Briere J. and Elliott D. 2003. "Prevalence and psychological sequelae of self-reported childhood physical and sexual abuse in a general population of men and women". *Child Abuse and Neglect* 27: 1205–1222.

Browne A. and Finkelhor D. 1986. "Impact of child sexual abuse: a review of the research". *Psychological Bulletin* 99: 66–77.

Burgess A. W., Hartman C. and McCormack A. 1987. "Abused to abuser: Antecedents of socially deviant behaviors". *American Journal of Psychiatry* 144(11): 1431–1436.

Classen C., Palesh O. and Aggarwal R. 2005. "Sexual revictimization: A review of the empirical literature". *Trauma, Violence and Abuse* 6: 103–129.

Curtis, G. 1963. "Violence breeds violence – perhaps?" *American Journal of Psychiatry* 120: 386–387.

Cutajar M., Mullen P. E., Ogloff J. R. P., Thomas S. D., Wells D. L. and Spataro J. 2010a. "Schizophrenia and other psychotic disorders in a cohort of sexually abused children". *Archives of General Psychiatry* 67: 1114–1119.

Cutajar M., Mullen P. E., Ogloff J. R. P., Thomas S. D., Wells D. L. and Spataro J. 2010b. "Psychopathology in a large cohort of sexually abused children followed up to 43 years". *Child Abuse and Neglect* 34: 813–822.

Cutajar M. C., Mullen P. E., Ogloff J. R. P., Thomas S. D., Wells D. L. and Spataro J. 2010c. "Suicide and fatal drug overdose in child sexual abuse victims: An historical cohort study". *Medical Journal of Australia* 192(4): 184–187.

Dube S., Anda R., Whitefield C., Brown D., Felitti V. and Dong M. 2005. "Long-term consequences of childhood sexual abuse by gender of victim". *American Journal of Preventative Medicine* 28(5): 430–438.

Elliott D., Mok D. and Briere J. 2004. "Adult sexual assault: Prevalence, symptomatology, and sex differences in the general population". *Journal of Traumatic Stress* 17(3): 203–211.

Falshaw L. 2005. "The link between a history of maltreatment and subsequent offending behaviour". *Probation Journal* 52: 423–434.

Fergusson D. and Mullen P. 1999. *Childhood sexual abuse. An evidence based perspective.* Thousand Oaks, Calif: Sage Publications.

Fergusson D., Horwood L. and Woodward L. 2000. "The stability of child abuse reports: A longitudinal study of the reporting behavior of young adults". *Psychological Medicine* 30: 529–544.

Finkelhor D. 1995. "The victimization of children: A developmental perspective". *American Journal of Orthopsychiatry* 65(2): 177–193.

Fitzgerald J. 2006. *The attrition of sexual offences from the New South Wales criminal justice system.* NSW Bureau of Crime Statistics and Research.

Fromuth M. and Conn V. 1997. "Hidden perpetrators. Sexual molestation in a nonclinical sample of college women". *Journal of Interpersonal Violence* 12(3): 456–465.

Gilbert R., Widom C., Browne K., Fergusson D., Webb E. and Janson S. 2009. "Burden and consequences of child maltreatment in high-income countries". *The Lancet* 373, 68–81.

Hanson R. and Bussiere M. 1998. "Predicting relapse: A meta-analysis of sexual offender recidivism studies". *Journal of Consulting and Clinical Psychology* 59: 662–669.

Hanson R. and Slater S. 1988. "Sexual victimization in the history of sexual abusers: A review". *Annals of Sex Research* 1: 485–499.

Hardt J. and Rutter M. 2004. "Validity of adult retrospective reports of adverse childhood experiences: review of the evidence". *Journal of Child Psychology and Psychiatry* 45(2): 260–273.

Harlow C. W. 1999. *Prior abuse reported by inmates and probationers* (No. 172879). Washington, DC: US Department of Justice, Bureau of Justice Statistics.

Jespersen A., Lalumiere M. and Seto M. 2009. "Sexual abuse history among adult sex offenders and non-sex offenders: A meta-analysis". *Child Abuse and Neglect* 33: 179–192.

Johansson-Love J. and Fremouw W. 2006. "A critique of the female sexual perpetrator research". *Aggression and Violent Behavior* 11: 12–26.

Johnson R., Ross M., Taylor W., Williams M., Caravajal R. and Peters R. 2006. "Prevalence of childhood sexual abuse among incarcerated males in county jail". *Child Abuse and Neglect* 30: 75–86.

Kaplan M. S. and Green A. H. 1995. "Incarcerated female sexual offenders: A comparison of sexual histories with eleven female nonsexual offenders". *Sexual Abuse: A Journal of Research and Treatment* 7(4): 287–295.

Kaplow J. and Widom C. S. 2007. "Age of onset of child maltreatment predicts long-term mental health outcomes". *Journal of Abnormal Psychology* 116(1): 176–187.

Kendall-Tackett K., Williams L. and Finkelhor D. 1993. "Impact of sexual abuse on children: A review and synthesis of recent empirical studies". *Psychological Bulletin* 113(1): 164–180.

Manly J., Kim J., Rogosch F. and Cicchetti D. 2001. "Dimensions of child maltreatment and children's adjustment: Contributions of developmental timing and subtype". *Development and Psychopathology* 13: 759–782.

Mathews R., Hunter J. and Vuz J. 1997. "Juvenile female sexual offenders: Clinical characteristics and treatment issues". *Sexual Abuse: A Journal of Research and Treatment* 9(3): 187–199.

Miccio-Fonseca L. C. 2000. "Adult and adolescent female sex offenders: Experiences compared to other female and male sex offenders". *Journal of Psychology and Human Sexuality* 11(3): 75–88.

Nathan P. and Ward T. 2002. "Female sex offenders: Clinical and demographical features". *Journal of Sexual Aggression* 8(1): 5–21.

Noll J. G. 2005. "Does childhood sexual abuse set in motion a cycle of violence against women? What we know and what we need to learn". *Journal of Interpersonal Violence* 20(4): 455–462.

Noll J. G., Horowitz L. A., Bonanno G. A., Trickett P. K. and Putnam F. W. 2003. "Revictimization and self-harm in females who experienced childhood sexual abuse. Results from a prospective study". *Journal of Interpersonal Violence* 18(12): 1252–1271.

Ogloff J. R. P. 2009. "Mental disorders among offenders in correctional settings". In M. Gelder, J. Lopez-Ibor, N. Andreasen and J. Geddes (eds) *New Oxford textbook of psychiatry*, 2nd edn. Oxford: Oxford University Press.

Ogloff J. R. P. and Tye C. 2007. "Responding to mental health needs of women offenders".

In R. Sheehan, G. McIvor and C. Trotter (eds) *What works with women offenders.* Devon, UK: Willan Publishing.

Ogloff J. R. P., Cutajar M., Mann E. and Mullen P. E. 2012. "Child sexual abuse and subsequent offending and victimisation: A 45-year follow-up study". *Trends and issues in crime and criminal justice* 440. Canberra: Australian Institute of Criminology.

Paolucci E. O., Genuis M. L. and Violato C. 2001. "A meta-analysis of the published research on the effects of child sexual abuse". *The Journal of Psychology* 135(1), 17–36.

Pothast H. and Allen C. 1994. "Masculinity and femininity in male and female perpetrators of child sexual abuse". *Child Abuse and Neglect* 18(9): 763–767.

Putnam F. 2003. "Ten-year research update review: Child sexual abuse". *Journal of American Academy of Child and Adolescent Psychiatry* 42(3): 269–278.

Roodman A. and Clum G. 2001. "Victimization rates and method variance: A meta-analysis". *Journal of Traumatic Stress* 21: 183–204.

Salter D., McMillan D., Richards M., Talbot T., Bentovim A. and Hastings R. 2003. "Development of sexually abusive behaviour in sexually victimised males: A longitudinal study". *The Lancet* 361: 471–476.

Short T., Thomas S., Mullen P. and Ogloff J. R. P. 2013. "Comparing violence in schizophrenia patients with and without comorbid substance-use disorders to community controls". *Acta Psychiatrica Scandinavica* 128(4): 306–313.

Siegel J. A. and Williams L. M. 2003a. "The relationship between child sexual abuse and female delinquency and crime: A prospective study". *Journal of Research in Crime and Delinquency* 40(1): 71–94.

Siegel J. A. and Williams L. M. 2003b. "Risk factors for sexual victimization of women". *Violence Against Women* 9(8): 902–930.

Smallbone S. and Wortley R. 2004. "Criminal diversity and paraphilic interests among adult males convicted of sexual offences against children". *International Journal of Offender Therapy and Comparative Criminology* 48(2): 175–188.

Spataro J., Mullen P., Burgess P., Wells D. and Moss S. 2004. "Impact of child sexual abuse on mental health. Prospective study in males and females". *British Journal of Psychiatry* 184: 416–421.

Swanston, H., Parkinson, P., Oates, R., O'Toole, B., Plunkett, A. and Shrimpton, S. 2002. "Further abuse of sexually abused children". *Child Abuse and Neglect* 26: 115–127.

Thornberry T. P., Ireland T. O. and Smith C. A. 2001. "The importance of timing: The varying impact of childhood and adolescent maltreatment on multiple problem outcomes". *Development and Psychopathology* 13: 957–979.

Ward T. 2000. "Sexual offenders' cognitive distortions as implicit theories". *Aggression and Violent Behavior* 5: 491–507.

Widom C. 1989a. "Does violence beget violence? A critical examination of the literature". *Psychological Bulletin* 106, 3–28.

Widom C. 1989b. "The cycle of violence". *Science* 244, 160–167.

Widom C. and Ames, M. 1994. "Criminal consequences of childhood sexual victimization". *Child Abuse and Neglect* 18: 303–318.

Widom C. S. and Maxfield M. G. 2001. "An update on the 'cycle of violence'" (No. 184894). Washington, DC: US Department of Justice, National Institute of Justice.

Widom C. S., Raphael K. G. and DuMont K. A. 2004. "The case for prospective longitudinal studies in child maltreatment research: Commentary on Dube, Williamson, Thompson, Felitti, and Anda 2004". *Child Abuse and Neglect* 28: 715–722.

Part III

Justice, welfare and mental health

11 Significant harm

The application of the law in practice with vulnerable children

Anna Gupta

11.1 Introduction

How a society responds to its most vulnerable children is central to the debate about the relationship between children, families and the state. When and how to intervene in private family life where there are concerns about child maltreatment are dilemmas with which child welfare practitioners have to continually grapple. Compulsory intervention by the state has life-long consequences and the permanent removal of a child from his or her birth family is one of the most draconian actions a state can take. Alternatively a lack of timely and appropriate responses to children at risk of abuse and neglect can result in serious harm or even the death of the child. The law, policies and practices developed reflect the historical, social and political contexts of the particular country. In England and Wales, the legal threshold for compulsory state intervention in private family life is the concept of 'significant harm', introduced over 20 years ago in the Children Act 1989. This chapter explores the value and use of the concept of significant harm. Research and practice evidence, including case law, is drawn upon to examine how the concept is being interpreted and what has influenced its application in practice in the family courts over the past two decades. While the focus of this chapter is practice in the United Kingdom, particularly England and Wales, reference is also made to other countries.

11.2 The Children Act 1989 and significant harm

The Children Act 1989, when implemented in England and Wales, was a significant piece of legislation that redrew boundaries between the state and the family. The Act was developed during the 1980s, which saw a series of high profile child abuse inquiries that were critical of both the failures to protect vulnerable children and over-zealous intervention on the part of professionals (Blom-Cooper 1988; Butler-Sloss 1988). It requires the state, in the form of local authorities, to safeguard and promote the welfare of children in their area who are in need; and so far as is consistent with that duty, to promote the upbringing of such children by their families by providing a range and level of services appropriate to those children's needs (s.17 Children Act 1989). As Brophy

(2008, 80) argues "support and investigation must usually precede statutory intervention; that is the essence of the 'social contract' and the democratic state's responsibility with regard to parents where there are concerns about child care".

The Children Act 1989 gave statutory force to the concept of significant harm by setting it as the threshold justifying compulsory intervention into family life where this is in the best interests of the child. A family court can only make a care order if the 'threshold criteria' of significant harm are met. The harm or likelihood of harm needs to be attributable to parental care 'not being what it would be reasonable to expect a parent to give to him' (s. 31(2)(b)(i) Children Act 1989). The Act sets broad criteria for significant harm and identifies three areas of concern: ill-treatment (e.g. physical, sexual or emotional abuse); the impairment of physical or mental health; and the impairment of physical, intellectual, emotional or behavioural development. An amendment included in the Adoption and Children Act 2002 added to the types of harm "impairment suffered from seeing or hearing the ill-treatment of another" (s.120), in recognition of an increased awareness of the harm caused to children living in homes where there is domestic violence. A child beyond parental control is also deemed to be at risk of significant harm.

Significant harm is the first test that has to be met before a court decides whether the making of the order is in the child's best interests. Once the threshold criteria are crossed the court must decide on the least interventionist approach necessary to promote the child's welfare. For some children, this involves remaining at home or being placed with carers within their kinship network. For others, the plan will be permanent substitute care options, such as long-term foster care or adoption. In accordance with the Human Rights Act 1998 any breach of a person's right to respect for private and family life (Article 8 of the European Convention on Human Rights (ECHR)) must be proportionate, and attention must also be paid to parents' and children's right to a fair trial (Article 6 of the ECHR). The ECHR, since its incorporation in UK domestic law in the Human Rights Act 1998, has been an important influence on decision-making about children coming into care and the balance between parents' rights, children's welfare and the role of the state (Masson 2012).

11.3   International comparisons

The legal system in England and Wales for the protection of children is based on the adversarial model, where the local authority, parents and other adult parties and children are separately legally represented. Parents, irrespective of their means, are provided with legal representation funded by the state, if a local authority issues care proceedings in relation to their child. Children are also appointed a Children's Guardian, a social worker who provides independent representation for children in care proceedings. Children's Guardians work with and instruct the solicitor appointed for the child, unless the child is capable of giving her or his own instructions to the solicitor and their views differ from the Guardian's assessment and recommendations to the court. This system is in contrast to other European countries whose court systems are more inquisitorial, and where there is less formality and less use of legal representation (Hetherington *et al.* 1997).

With regard to the thresholds for judicial intervention, in all the countries except for England studied by Hetherington *et al.* (1997), including Belgium, France, Germany, Italy and the Netherlands, there was the possibility of judicial intervention on the basis of the child's welfare alone, without the need for evidence of significant harm. The use of compulsion therefore is possible, but not necessarily desirable, earlier in the systems in countries studied other than England. Permanent separation of children from their parents, especially via adoption, is far less common in many European countries than in the UK, and there is a greater reluctance to break family ties (Selwyn and Sturgess 2000; Dumaret and Rosset 2005). Therefore the possible consequences of court proceedings are less drastic for families. As Cooper *et al.* (1995, 9) explain with reference to the French and English systems: "It is much easier for a French family than an English one to be forced to engage with the legal system, but the *consequences* are likely to be much less dramatic".

The proportion of children coming into care with parental agreement varies greatly across different countries. In England the majority of children are in care on an order of the court (73 per cent), with only 23 per cent in care with their parents' consent or because there is no one with parental responsibility (DfE 2013). In Japan and Sweden over 80 per cent of those who enter care do so under arrangements agreed with parents and/or the young people themselves (Thoburn 2000). In some European countries, including Denmark, France and Germany, placement away from home is seen as a necessary part of the family support systems, not as a last resort as it is generally seen to be in the UK (Boddy *et al.* 2009). Although the child protection and judicial systems are more similar to England and Wales, non-consensual adoption from care is rare in Australia and New Zealand (Thoburn 2000). On the other hand, in the USA, children unable to return to their birth families are placed whenever possible for adoption (Selwyn and Sturgess, 2000). Two factors that are therefore important when considering the significance of the threshold criteria are the possible long-term consequences and the issue of compulsion.

11.4 The children and families involved in care proceedings

The backgrounds, needs and circumstances of the over 10,000 children in involved in care proceedings in England each year are extremely diverse. In Brophy's (2006) review of child care proceedings, 60 per cent of the children were under the age of six years, with up to 14 per cent under 12 months old. In Masson *et al.*'s (2008) study of care proceedings, almost 60 per cent were under the age of four. This reflects concern over the vulnerability of young children, which is borne out in Brandon *et al.*'s (2010) review of serious case reviews into child deaths or serious abuse, which found that just under a half of the children were less than one year of age. The majority of children in care are from white

British backgrounds. However, some minority ethnic groups, such as children of mixed parentage and from black African or Caribbean communities, continue to be over-represented amongst the care population (Owen and Statham 2009; DfE, 2013). Masson *et al.*'s (2008) study also found that mixed parentage children were over-represented, as were children and families whose immigration status was uncertain.

Most of the families involved in care proceedings share common experiences of low income, housing difficulties and social exclusion. In Brophy's (2006) study the majority (84 per cent) of parents were dependent upon state benefits. Ward and colleagues (2010) studied infants at risk of significant harm and found few parents had supportive partners, friends or family. Neighbourhood and housing problems compounded their difficulties. In addition, most parents involved in care proceedings struggle with complex personal problems, such as mental illness, substance misuse, learning difficulties, domestic violence and chaotic lifestyle (DH 2001; Brophy 2006; Masson *et al.* 2008). In Masson *et al.*'s (2008) study, only 15 per cent of mothers were recorded as not experiencing any of these, and many experienced multiple difficulties. Information available about fathers in this study was generally far more limited than about mothers. This was felt to reflect the large number of fathers who did not have parental responsibility or were not currently living with their children (Masson *et al.* 2008), and could also be indicative of a relatively poor engagement of fathers by child welfare services (Maxwell *et al.* 2012). Brophy (2006) found that the majority of parents (61 per cent) were abused as children, 27 per cent had a physical disability and 22 per cent learning difficulties. The majority of families were known to Children's Services for some time prior to proceedings being initiated.

In terms of the types of harm, Masson *et al.* (2008, 37) found that neglect was the most common (74.9 per cent). Emotional abuse was alleged in almost two-thirds of the cases, with physical abuse in 44.6 per cent and sexual abuse in 17.4 per cent. At least two of these harms were cited in two-thirds of these cases, with neglect and emotional abuse together being the most common. Similarly Brophy *et al.*'s (2003) research found that all cases were complex; most contained more than one type of ill-treatment and several allegations and concerns resulting in failures of parenting. In Masson *et al.*'s (2008) study the majority of the cases related to actual harm, with 27 per cent being based solely on likely harm. These latter cases mainly involved young infants. In a significant majority of cases brought before the family courts in England, the threshold criteria are met (Brophy, 2006).

11.5 The interpretation of significant harm in case law

There are no absolute criteria for making an assessment of significant harm. Harwin and Madge (2010) argue that the absence of a clear operational definition of significant harm is both its strength and its weakness. It allows for professional discretion, given the complex and varied circumstances of children and families, but discretion is also vulnerable to personal values as well as external contextual factors influencing its interpretation and application in practice. When considering judicial thresholds for compulsory state intervention on the basis of harm, some countries have more explicit criteria. For example, the Canadian Children and Family Services Act 1990 lists 13 specific criteria that could lead to a child needing protective services. Unlike the Children Act 1989 in England and Wales, explicit reference is made in the Canadian law to children under 12 requiring protective services if they have committed serious offences.

Over the past two decades how significant harm should be interpreted has been subject to much judicial scrutiny and important case law judgments have resulted. A key question has been 'how significant is significant'? There is no objective criterion, but reference is made in guidance and case law to 'significant' meaning 'considerable, noteworthy or important'. In a Supreme Court judgment *Re B (A Child)* [2013] UKSC 33, Baroness Hale confirmed this dictionary definition as being helpful and reaffirmed that the threshold could not be crossed by trivial or unimportant harm. In an earlier judgment, in the case of *Re B (Children)* (FC) [2008] UKHL 35, she had explicitly addressed the significance of the consequences of judicial decisions and warned against social engineering:

> taking a child away from her family is a momentous step, not only for her, but for her whole family, and for the local authority which does so. In a totalitarian society, uniformity and conformity are valued. Hence the totalitarian state tries to separate the child from her family and mould her to its own design. Families in all their subversive variety are the breeding ground of diversity and individuality. In a free and democratic society we value diversity and individuality. Hence the family is given special protection in all the modern human rights instruments.
>
> (paragraph 20)

A similar sentiment was expressed in *Re L (Care: Threshold Criteria)* [2007] 1 FLR 2050 when Hedley J stated that:

> society must be willing to tolerate very diverse standards of parenting, including the eccentric, the barely adequate and the inconsistent ... it was not the provenance of the state to spare children all the consequences of defective parenting; the compulsive powers of the state could only be exercised when the significant harm criteria made out.
>
> (paragraph 50)

However what is considered 'noteworthy and considerable' is clearly influenced by value judgments as reflected in the case of *Re M [2009]* EWCA Civ 853. In this case the Supreme Court judges disagreed and the final judgment based on a majority view was that while the child had been physically assaulted this did not constitute significant ill-treatment as there were no physical signs. Also in this case, the witnessing of the ill-treatment of another (unrelated) child in the home was not considered to reach the threshold for significant emotional harm by the majority of the Supreme Court judges involved in the decision-making process.

In civil proceedings, such as care proceedings, the standard of proof is on the balance of probabilities, rather than the higher threshold of beyond reasonable doubt that is the test in criminal cases. There had been some confusion about the burden of proof required, especially where the allegations related to sexual abuse. However *Re B (Children)* (FC) [2008] UKHL 35 clarified the burden of proof as being "that the fact in issue more probably occurred than not". However the significant harm threshold criteria are not restricted to actual harm and decisions about facts relating to past incidents, but also include the likelihood of harm, which can be a more complex balancing exercise. In the Supreme Court case *Re B (A Child)* [2013] UKSC 33, it was reaffirmed that likelihood of significant harm means "a real possibility, a possibility that cannot be ignored having regard to the nature and gravity of the feared harm in the particular case" (paragraph 24). It was emphasised that the significance of the harm is interrelated with the likelihood of it being suffered, so the more significant the harm, the less required level of likelihood and vice versa. This was a case of possible impairment of the child's psychological and emotional development. Due to the personalities of the parents and the mother's mental health problems it was felt that they would be unable to work with professionals to promote their baby's welfare. Although with some reservation, Baroness Hale agreed with the other Supreme Court judges that the threshold criteria had been crossed, but disagreed on the adoption plan based on the requirement that 'nothing else will do', when nothing else had been tried. The harm that was feared was subtle, long term and may never happen (paragraph 223). This landmark judgment confirmed that the decision determining whether the threshold is met is a "value judgment, particularly, but not only, when the court is surveying likelihood". (paragraph 44).

11.6 Issues of inequality and difference

The Human Rights Act 1989 and the Equalities Act 2010 require that public bodies in the UK, such as local authorities and the courts, treat people fairly and do not discriminate on the grounds of race, gender, disability, religion and other characteristics. However, there are challenges posed when judgments need to be made about very diverse child-rearing practices. It can be difficult for child welfare professionals to get the balance between a culturally relativist approach which fails to protect some children, and overly punitive practice that fails to respect different, but not necessarily harmful, child rearing traditions (Bernard and Gupta 2008). A case law judgment, *Re K (Local Authority)* v. *N and Others* [2005] EWHC 2956 (Fam), highlighted the important and difficult balance of respecting cultural diversity whilst at the same time ensuring children's safety, by stating that:

> The task of the court considering threshold for the purposes of s31 of the
> 1989 Act may be to evaluate parental performance by reference to the

objective standard of the hypothetical 'reasonable' parent, but this does not mean that the court can simply ignore the underlying cultural, social or religious realities. On the contrary, the court must always be sensitive to the cultural, social and religious circumstances of the particular child and family.... We must guard against the risk of stereotyping. We must be careful to ensure that our understandable concern to protect vulnerable children (or, indeed, vulnerable young adults) does not lead us to interfere inappropriately – and if inappropriately then unjustly – with families merely because they cleave, as this family does, to mores, to cultural beliefs, more or less different from what is familiar to those who view life from a purely Euro-centric perspective.

(paragraphs 26 and 93)

Brophy *et al.*'s (2003) study of minority ethnic families' experiences of public law family court proceedings found no examples of 'single issue' cases where allegations of significant harm rested unequivocally on behaviours/attitudes viewed as culturally acceptable by a parent but which social workers argued were unacceptable within western European assessments of ill-treatment. They did, however, find that there was evidence of 'cultural conflict' between parents and professionals about issues such as when children can be left home alone or boundaries surrounding teenagers' behaviour. However these issues were not usually central to whether the threshold criteria had been met, but often formed part of a pattern in which there were other, more serious, allegations of maltreatment. This study also found that the willingness of parents, or lack of it, influences the decision about court proceedings, and some minority ethnic parents saw state intervention in parenting practices as a complete anathema, especially those recently arrived in the UK from countries with no equivalent child protection services. They also conclude that language barriers and poor interpretation services "raise some serious questions about access to justice for parents whose first language is not English" (Brophy *et al.* 2003, 139). Brophy (2008, 91) argues that whilst "there was no evidence that the 'significant harm' criteria are in need of re-assessment, there was evidence that the process could be greatly improved". She suggests that, given the complex circumstances and multiple power relationships that frame the lives of the families, an approach based on ideas of intersectionality, a dynamic not static view of culture and an analysis of power or 'space' to examine issues of racism in professional practice is necessary (Brophy 2008, 92–93).

Parents with learning difficulties are most likely to lose their children to the state, and there is some evidence that parents with learning difficulties meet a presumption of incompetence that too easily leads to their child being deemed at risk and 'reasonable care' benchmarked against the non-disabled population in the community, without the provision of compensatory services (Booth *et al.* 2005). In *Re L (Care Proceedings: Significant Harm)* [2006] EWA Civ 1282 the Court of Appeal judges noted that cases in which the concern for a child's welfare was based on the learning difficulties or intellectual deficits of the parents were among the most difficult of care cases. They stated that if a care order is to be made it could not be made simply on the basis that the parents suffered from learning difficulties and courts should not sanction the removal of children from their biological parents on the basis that substitute parents would provide greater intellectual stimulus. In times of severe budget cuts in local authorities and reductions in family support services under the current UK Government, it is likely that parents with learning difficulties will continue to be over-represented among families involved in care proceedings. Judges will be faced with very difficult 'last resort' decisions about permanent separation, when it is known that long-term support could assist parents to care for their children but is simply not going to be available.

Neglect is the most common form of harm experienced by children involved in care proceedings (Masson *et al.* 2008). However, due to the chronic nature of neglect, decision-making about timing and attribution is complex (Harwin and Madge 2010; Masson 2012). Reviews of serious case reviews into child deaths or serious harm to children have found that neglect is disproportionally represented in these cases (Brandon *et al.* 2008). The concept of significant harm contributes to the identification of many, but not all, neglected children (Harwin and Madge 2010). A number of reasons for this have been suggested. Neglect is frequently linked to poverty and social deprivation, and decision-making where families are overwhelmed by stressful circumstances rather than being intentionally neglectful can be difficult (Dickens 2007). Brandon *et al.* (2008) also identify the 'start again' syndrome. In these circumstances, knowledge of the past is put aside with a focus on the present, without adequate professional reflection about whether the capacity to care for the child has in reality changed. It is often a way of dealing not only with overwhelming amounts of information but also the feelings of helplessness generated by families, especially in long term neglect cases. The lack of a trigger event or 'catapult' may also lead to delay in bringing cases to court (Dickens 2007).

11.7 The influence of wider social, political and policy contexts

The wider social, political and policy contexts influence the lives of the children and families as well as the practice of professionals involved in care proceedings. While the vast majority of parents living in poverty do not maltreat their children, poverty clearly impacts on parenting in a number of ways and generally makes parenting harder. A number of studies have identified increased risk of physical abuse and neglect associated with poverty (Cawson *et al.* 2000; Hooper *et al.* 2007). Hooper *et al.*'s (2007) study explored the complex relationships between poverty, parenting and children's well-being in diverse social circumstances. They found that "stress, unless buffered by sufficient social support and/or mitigated by other sources of resilience, is likely to be significant in the increased risk of some forms of maltreatment among parents living in poverty" (Hooper *et al.* 2007, 105). There is evidence of increasing numbers of children and families experiencing poverty and deprivation in Britain (Ridge 2013). It has been suggested that half a million children are not adequately fed in the UK today, not as a result of negligence but due to a lack of money largely brought about by changes in the benefit system (Cooper and Dumpleton 2013). In addition, severe cuts to local authority budgets have led to many community resources, such as libraries and children's centres, being shut down with disproportionate effect on the lives of children and families living in adverse social circumstances (Ridge 2013).

Decision-making about parental culpability and 'reasonable parenting', particularly in cases of neglect, are especially complex given the severe cuts to welfare benefits, housing and family support services. For families involved in care proceedings, their problems are not presented as simply due to poverty or social deprivation; however, these issues characterise many of their lives. How the causal factors in relation to parents' and children's difficulties are understood will determine how families are responded to prior to and during court proceedings. The dominant political discourse is one of blaming poor families for their poverty and related difficulties, and there is much evidence to suggest that challenging this discourse is not a feature of many social work assessments. For example Hooper *et al.* (2007, 109) concluded that in social work with children and families "poverty has slipped out of sight". This raises questions about the rights of children and families living in poverty, especially their rights under Article 8 of the ECHR. These questions have been absent from debates about the family justice system.

The variation in the numbers of applications for care orders would indicate that the interpretation of the threshold criteria and need for compulsory state intervention is influenced by wider contextual factors. In the period from April to July 2008, applications for care orders in England and Wales fell by 25 per cent compared with the same period in the previous year (Lloyd-Jones 2008). This coincided with the implementation of the Public Law Outline by the Ministry of Justice, which required more emphasis to be given to the prevention of cases coming to court. At the end of that year, there was a dramatic and sustained increase in the numbers of care proceedings. This followed the reports and publicity surrounding the death of Peter Connolly, which was highly critical of social workers and other professionals (Gupta and Lloyd-Jones 2010). 'Moral panics' following the murder of a child by his or her parents are not new, and have led to less supportive and more risk averse, punitive approaches to child protection practice (Clapton *et al.* 2013).

In 2014 there are many changes taking place in the family justice system following the recommendations of the Family Justice Review (MoJ *et al.* 2011). The Family Justice Review (MoJ *et al.* 2011) concluded that the legal framework is robust, but that proceedings are taking too long to the detriment of children, and are too costly. Central to the reforms is the introduction of a time limit of 26 weeks when courts are considering whether a child should be taken into care for all but 'exceptional' cases. These are being implemented, alongside the promotion of adoption as the 'gold standard' for children in care. Not only is it now seen as important to "rescue children from chaotic, neglectful and abusive homes" (HM Government 2013, 22) but also it is government policy to take more children into care, to prioritize adoption as a mainstream policy option for those in care, and to speed up the process. Parton (2014, 22) argues that what has emerged is an "authoritarian neoliberal state" that is changing the nature of relationships between the state and families, particularly families from lower socio-economic backgrounds.

Interestingly, however, there have been a number of highly significant case law decisions that provide a challenge by senior members of the judiciary to the dominant political and policy discourse. In September 2013, the President of the Family Division sitting in the Court of Appeal handed down a judgment, *Re B-S (Children)* [2013] EWCA Civ. 813, which has huge and wide-ranging implications for professional practice and decision-making in public law family court proceedings. As part of this judgment, the President felt it necessary to restate key principles in relation to adoption being an extremely draconian step, one that requires the highest level of evidence, and is a last resort, when "nothing else will do" (paragraph 22). Judges are required to be "rigorous in exploring and probing local authority thinking in cases where there is any reason to suspect that resource issues may be affecting the local authority's thinking" (paragraph 29). The judgment makes it clear that if the evidence is not available an adjournment over the time limit must be directed, especially for non-consensual adoptions, in light of the gravity of the issues and potential for breaches of children's and parents' human rights. In January 2014 Mrs Justice Pauffley in her judgment, *Re NL (A Child) (Appeal: Interim Care Order: facts and Reasons)* [2014] EWHC 270 (Fam), similarly stated that "justice must never be sacrificed upon the altar of speed" (paragraph 40).

11.8 Conclusion

While there has been much debate and discussion about most aspects of the public law family justice system in England since the implementation of the Children Act 1989 over two decades ago, the concept of significant harm has largely remained unchallenged. The concept is broad enough to encompass the extremely diverse circumstances of children and families involved in care proceedings. However, the lack of a clear operational definition also allows for value judgments, subjectivity and external contextual pressures to influence the interpretation and application of the threshold criteria in practice. Decisions about when and how professionals should intervene to safeguard and promote the welfare of a child suffering or likely to suffer significant harm are extremely complex and can have life long consequences. The considerable body of case law that has developed can inform practice and decision-making in individual cases, but professionals also need to reflect critically upon and analyse the influence of their own and others values, assumptions and wider social, policy and political contexts and discourses in order to be able to practice within a human rights and social justice framework.

References

Bernard C. and Gupta A. 2008. "Black African children and the Child Protection System". *British Journal of Social Work* 38: 476–492.

Blom-Cooper L. 1988. *A Child in Trust: The report of the Panel of Inquiry into the circumstances surrounding the death of Jasmine Beckford.* London: London Borough of Brent.

Boddy J., Statham J., McQuail S., Petrie P. and Owen C. 2009. *Working at the 'edges' of care? European models of support for young people and families.* London: Institute of Education, University of London.

Booth T., Booth W. and McConnel D. 2005. "The prevalence and outcomes of care proceedings involving parents with learning difficulties in the family courts". *Journal of Applied Research in Intellectual Disabilities* 18(1): 7–17.

Brandon M., Bailey S. and Belderson P. 2010. *Building on the learning from serious case reviews: A two-year analysis of child protection database notifications 2007–2009.* London: Department for Education.

Brandon M., Belderson P., Warren C., Howe D., Gardner R., Dodsworth J. and Black J. 2008. *Analysing child deaths and serious injury through abuse and neglect: What can we learn? A biennial analysis of serious case reviews 2003–2005.* London: Department for Children, Schools and Families.

Brophy J. 2006. *Research review: Child care proceedings under the Children Act 1989.* London: Department for Constitutional Affairs.

Brophy, J. 2008. "Child maltreatment in diverse households: challenges to law, theory, and practice". *Journal of law and society* 35(1): 75–94.

Brophy J., Jhutti-Johal J. and Owen C. 2003. *Significant harm: Child protection litigation in a multi-cultural setting.* London: Department for Constitutional Affairs.

Butler-Sloss E. 1988. *Report of the Inquiry into Child Abuse in Cleveland.* London: HMSO.

Cawson P., Wattam C., Brooker S. and Kelly G. 2000. *Child maltreatment in the United Kingdom: A study of the prevalence of abuse and neglect.* London: NSPCC.

Clapton G., Cree, V. and Smith M. 2013 "Moral panics, claims-making and child protection in the UK". *British Journal of Social Work* 43(4): 803–812.

Cooper A., Hetherington R., Baistow K., Pitts J. and Spriggs A. 1995. *Positive child protection: A view from abroad.* Dorset, UK: Russell House.

Cooper N. and Dumpleton S. 2013. *Walking the breadline: The scandal of food poverty in twenty-first century Britain.* Oxford: Oxfam GB/Church Action on Poverty.

Department for Education. 2013. Children looked after in England (including adoption and care leavers) year ending 31 March 2013. SFR 36/2013. www.gov.uk/government/uploads/system/uploads/attachment_data/file/244872/SFR36_2013.pdf.

Department of Health. 2001. *Children Act Now: Messages from research.* London: The Stationery Office.

Dickens J. 2007. "Child neglect and the law: catapults, thresholds and delay". *Child Abuse Review* 16: 77–92.

Dumaret A. C. and Rosset D. J. 2005. "Adoption and child welfare protection in France". *Early Child Development and Care* 175(7–8): 661–670.

Gupta A. and Lloyd-Jones E. 2010. "The representation of children and their parents in public law proceedings since the Children Act 1989: High hopes and lost opportunities?" *Journal of Children's Services* 5(2): 64–72.

Harwin J. and Madge N. 2010. "The concept of significant harm in law and practice". *Journal of Children's Services* 5(2): 73–83.

HM Government. 2013. *Working together to safeguard children.* London: Department for Education.

Hetherington R., Cooper A., Smith P. and Wilford G. 1997. *Protecting children: Messages from Europe.* Dorset, UK: Russell House.

Hooper C., Gorin S., Cabral C. and Dyson C. 2007. *Living with hardship 24/7: The diverse experiences of families in poverty in England.* London: Frank Buttle Trust.

Lloyd-Jones E. 2008. *The forward march of children's justice halted.* Axminster, UK: Triarchy Press.

Masson J. 2012. "What are care proceedings really like?" *Adoption and Fostering* 36(1): 5–12.

Masson J. M., Pearce J. and Bader K. 2008. *Care profiling study.* London: Ministry of Justice.

Maxwell N., Scourfield J., Featherstone B., Holland S. and Tolman, R. 2012. "Engaging fathers in child welfare services: A narrative review of recent research evidence". *Child and Family Social Work* 17(2): 160–169.

Ministry of Justice. 2011. *The Family Justice Review: Final report.* London: Ministry of Justice, the Department for Education and the Welsh Assembly Government.

Owen C. and Statham J. 2009. *Disproportionality in child welfare: The prevalence of black and minority ethnic children within 'looked after' and 'children in need' populations and on child protection registers in England.* London: Department for Children, Schools and Families.

Parton N. 2014. *The politics of child protection: Contemporary developments and future directions.* Basingstoke, UK: Palgrave Macmillan.

Ridge T. 2013. "'We are all in this together'? The hidden costs of poverty, recession and austerity policies on Britain's poorest children". *Children and Society* 27(5): 406–417.

Selwyn J. and Sturgess W. 2000. *International overview of adoption: Policy and practice.* Bristol, UK: School for Policy Studies.

Thoburn J. 2000. *A comparative study of adoption.* Norwich, UK: University of East Anglia.

Ward H., Brown R., Westlake D. and Munro E. R. 2010. *Infants suffering, or likely to suffer, significant harm: A prospective longitudinal study.* Loughborough, UK: Centre for Child and Family Research.

12 Policing, custody and mental illness

Ian Cummins

12.1 Introduction

The issue of how the Criminal Justice System (CJS) should respond to the needs of people with mental health problems is a complex and challenging one. The starting point for these debates is trying to agree some consistent definition of the term 'mentally disordered offender'. The controversies regarding the possible links between mental illness and offending are considered elsewhere in this volume so will not be explored here. However, they are clearly important – do we mean offenders who commit crime because of their mental health condition or should we take a much broader approach so that the term means anyone in contact with the CJS who has recognised symptoms of a mental illness. The first group is a relatively small one and this approach makes the philosophical assumption that it is possible to establish a clear and causal link between symptoms and offending behaviour. The second group is a much larger one. This chapter will use this second approach. The interlocking relationship between mental health systems and the CJS is a well-established but often confusing one. In his inspection of the prisons in the 1780s, John Howard identified that there were too many 'lunatics' in the gaols that he inspected. He went on to observe the detrimental effects that this had on the health of the individuals.

This chapter is concerned with one key aspect of the CJS – policing. The Sainsbury's Centre (2008) study concluded that 15 per cent of police work involved a mental health issue. This figure includes dealing with people in crisis, interviewing witnesses or victims and all other matters. The media focus in this area is often on high profile cases where individuals with mental health problems commit violent offences and homicides (Cummins 2010). However, it is important to note that individuals with mental health problems are much more likely to be victims than perpetrators of crime. This chapter will explore two of the most important social policies and trends of the past 40 years: deinstitutionalisation and the shift towards more punitive approaches to social problems. These have intersected so that the CJS in general and the police in particular are often the default providers of mental health care or support to those in crisis. Whilst this chapter draws from an England and Wales perspective, similar trends are clearly visible in a number of jurisdictions across the world. Wood *et al.*'s

(2011) review of trends in the UK, Canada and the USA highlights the fact that police forces face similar issues in all these jurisdictions. Ogloff *et al.* (2013) in their review of the Australian situation note that, despite this being acknowledged as an important area of police work, there has been relatively little attention paid to it. This is certainly the case when compared to the literature exploring the experiences of people with mental health problems in prisons. In response to the difficulties in mental health services, a range of national agencies in England and Wales including the police came together to sign and issue a Mental Health Crisis Concordat (17 February 2014. www.gov.uk). This is an agreement by policy makers and leading stakeholders to tackle the issue of poor service provision in mental health services. One of the key themes in the document is the need to ensure that police cells are not used for the detention of those experiencing acute mental illness. The Concordat commits the signatories to:

> work together to improve the system of care and support so people in crisis because of a mental health condition are kept safe and helped to find the support they need – whatever the circumstances in which they first need help – and from whichever service they turn to first. We will work together, and with local organisations, to prevent crises happening whenever possible through prevention and early intervention. We will make sure we meet the needs of vulnerable people in urgent situations. We will strive to make sure that all relevant public services support someone who appears to have a mental health problem to move towards Recovery.

There is a need to shift slightly the focus of attention away from prisons – though the expansion of the use of imprisonment remains a key social issue – to the relationship between the policing and mental health services (Cummins, 2012a).

12.2 Deinstitutionalisation

'Anti-psychiatry' is a short-hand term for a 1960s group of thinkers such as R. D. Laing and Thomas Szasz who, from often quite opposing ideological viewpoints, were critical of the psychiatric establishment. Laing and Szasz represent two poles of political thought, Laing being a radical anti-establishment intellectual figure, while Szsaz was the libertarian whose views were much more in tune with the neoliberal doxa of individualism and small government. Both trained as psychiatrists but came to be very critical of the power of the therapeutic state. For Laing, psychiatry was a form of social control rather than an attempt to alleviate distress. In the spirit of the time, this control was seen to assist in the maintenance of the capitalist system. As with Marcuse (2002), Laing (1959; 1967) argued that the 'mentally ill' had almost revolutionary potential. Along with other socially marginalised groups, they could form a coalition of the disadvantaged to challenge the established order. Szasz (1974) from his radical libertarian view saw psychiatry as a means of undermining individualism. He fundamentally objected to the role that the State takes in the lives of its citizens. What both these positions have in common is a theme of anti-statism. Whatever their original purposes may have been, by the 1960s the asylums had become unsustainable. The institutions themselves were cut off, physically and metaphorically, from mainstream developments in medicine. Large institutionalised care was seen as corrosive and abusive. In the UK, the so-called Water Tower speech of 1961 by Enoch Powell (UK Minister for Health at the time) is seen as the beginning of the end for the long-stay psychiatric institution. In this speech Powell committed policy makers to reducing the number of psychiatric inpatient beds by 50 per cent, as there were now alternatives to this outdated provision. As Powell (1961) concluded, the policy would lead the closure of a number of asylums:

> They imply nothing less than the elimination of by far the greater part of this country's mental hospitals as they exist today. This is a colossal undertaking, not so much in the new physical provision which it involves, as in the sheer inertia of mind and matter which it requires to overcome. There they stand, isolated, majestic, imperious, brooded over by the gigantic water-tower and chimney combined, rising unmistakable and daunting out of the countryside – the asylums which our forefathers built with such immense solidity to express the notions of their day.
>
> (www.canehill.org.history/enochpowells – 1961 speech, 1)

From this point on, the number of inpatient beds began to decline; ironically, one of the features of the current crisis in modern mental health services is the lack of inpatient provision. The closure programme was given later impetus by the Thatcher government in Britain in the 1980s. As well as failing to meet the needs of patients, the asylums were costing too much.

The passing of the National Health Service and Community Care Act (1990) in England and Wales saw the introduction of a new system of funding of services. The Act was also committed to the idea that individuals should be supported to live in the community and enjoy as independent a life as possible. This policy did not just apply to services for people with mental health problems; it was the basis for a range of services from adults with physical disabilities to older people. It became known as 'care in the community' or 'community care'. This shorthand encapsulates the optimism of the initial service reconfiguration. Despite the fact the policy was introduced by a government essentially opposed to public service provision, there were hopes that this would lead to better quality of life outcomes for this cohort of patients, many of whom had spent a significant proportion of their adult lives in one of Goffman's (1968) 'total institutions'. Scull (2004) has described the term 'community care' as Orwellian. The policy in the mental health field, in the late 1980s and 1990s, soon unravelled. There is a fundamental irony that a policy termed 'community care' was introduced by a government led by the Prime Minister of the time (Margaret Thatcher) who did not believe that there was any such thing as society. The second wave of community care was marred by underfunding, long-standing boundary issues between health and social services and a lack of political will to support it fully. Mental health services have long been marginalised in funding and other debates. This policy was also introduced at a time of huge social, economic and political changes. Mass unemployment and the increase in the use of illicit drugs with the associated crime that this brings meant that many communities and services did not have the means to meet the needs of this vulnerable group.

The media reporting of community care in the 1990s focused almost entirely on the failings of the policy in the area of mental health. Cross (2010) has discussed the importance of the representations of the 'mad' and how these continue to be disseminated through a range of popular cultural forms. This is not to say that these forms are direct continuations of older forms. There are similarities as well as disjunctures. Modern media representations in the tabloid press, such as Britain's *Sun* newspaper with its notorious 'Bonkers Bruno Locked Up' headline, is not that far removed from Tom O'Bedlam. This was very important in the period under discussion as the tabloid reporting served to undermine the foundations of the policy. The eighteenth century image of the mad as wild, dishevelled creatures chained to the asylum walls was replaced in modern forms: the 'psycho' killer of popular cultural legend or the homeless man with his shopping cart containing all his belongings. The homeless became a feature of the urban environment and of what Bauman (2003) termed the 'new poor'. This marginalised existence alongside but not part of the new world of modern urban consumer capitalism is captured by Knowles (2000) in an ethnographic study of the daily lives of homeless people in Montreal (*Bedlam on the Streets*). This shows how homeless people negotiate the new terrain of public urban spaces. As Moon (2000) has pointed out, there is a geographical paradox at the heart of community care. A policy which seeks to overcome social and civic isolation has created a new form. The asylum was not replaced by a network of community-based mental health service provision. The new asylum is not one institution but an informal cluster of poor quality housing, shelters, drop-in centres and increasingly the prisons and the CJS (Wolff 2005; Cummins 2010).

12.3 The role of the police in modern mental health services

Policing is a complex and at times contradictory process. The media and cultural representations of policing focus on the allegedly more glamorous aspects of the work: undercover surveillance and drugs work, investigating major crimes and increasingly in film and TV the arrest of serial killers. The recent report in Britain by Lord Adebowale's Commission (2013) which examined mental health and policing confirmed the findings of the earlier Sainsbury's Centre investigation: mental health issues are, in the terms of the report, "core police business". The Commission was established to examine this issue following a series of cases of deaths in custody where the detained person had a history of mental illness. The report shows that the Metropolitan Police dealt with over 60,000 mental health related incidents in 2012. This is an average of 160 a day. The range of these contacts is highlighted by a survey carried out as part of the Adebowale Commission (2013) investigation. Metropolitan Police Service officers indicated that they had 'daily or regular' contacts as follows: victims (39 per cent), witnesses (23 per cent) and suspects (48 per cent). The survey also showed that 67 per cent of officers had encountered unusual behaviour, which they saw as being caused by illicit drugs and/or alcohol or a combination of the two. The report also concluded that individuals with mental health problems were at a particularly increased risk of being victims of crime. These risks seem significantly increased for violent offences. The report also concludes that victims who indicated that they had a mental health problem were generally dissatisfied with the service that they received from the MPS.

Deinstitutionalisation is a policy that has been followed across most of Europe, North America, Australia and New Zealand. A simple comparison between these areas is not possible because of the varying cultural, legal and social factors. However, it is clear that, in all these areas, one of the impacts of community care has been to increase the role that the police play in mental health services. Wood *et al.* (2011, 6) show that in the US context the police have become "front-line workers who often come into contact with persons with mental illnesses and must respond to their needs with *whatever tools lie at hand"* (emphasis added). Godfredson *et al.*'s study (2011) concluded that the police spend a significant amount of their working week dealing with mental health related issues. Despite this, the study noted that it is an area that even experienced officers find difficult. In particular, the police as reflected in the Adebowale review (2013) struggle to respond appropriately on an individual level to those in acute mental distress. In addition, the police officers felt that it was difficult to access support from mental health services. Delays and lack of robust community mental health services are a consistent cause of police officers' frustration in this area.

The current context of policing outlined above means that police officers need some core skills to carry out their role and ensure that vulnerable people receive appropriate care. Despite the evidence that this is a key aspect of police work, it is an area that has been neglected in police training. Pinfold *et al.*'s (2003) study indicated that police officers held a number of rather stereotypical views about people with mental health problems. These views were a reflection of the wider ones held in society. Chief among them was the idea that people with mental health problems were likely to be violent. Other work in this field, Cummins (2007), shows that officers receive little if any specific mental health training. The training tended to concentrate on the legal powers they have rather than what might be termed a more value-based approach. Police officers clearly have to deal with people in acute distress in a number of aspects of their work. For example, the role of the family liaison officer requires a range of the skills that would be transferable to mental health work. There does not appear to be a systematic approach to police training. There are over 40 police forces in England and Wales so some variations are inevitable. The difficulty here is the scope of these variations. Research by Cummins and Jones (2010) outlined the potential of a different model of training for officers. This model was based on the principles of experiential learning. Officers spent time on the wards at the local mental health unit. The course also included input from a range of staff but most importantly from service users. One of the most immediate benefits of this programme was the way that it helped break down the barriers that stigma creates. The benefits were seen later when the officers were dealing with service users in crisis situations. For example, it was clear that officers were less likely to use force in mental health emergencies following the training.

Morabito (2007) has provided a model to analyse the factors that affect police officers' decision making in this filed – in particular the decision as to whether arrest an individual. In Teplin's (1984) seminal study of police encounters, she coined the term *mercy booking* to describe the situation where officers were arresting individuals not to maintain public order but because they felt that this would ensure that the person had food and shelter – even if was in a jail. Morabito (2007, 1583) argues that police decision-making is shaped by a number of variables that she terms "horizons of context". These are outlined as follows. The *scenic* context refers to the community resources that are available. This would include community mental health services, access to hospital services or expert mental health advice. The police clearly exercise discretion and judgement but if there are limited community resources then custody becomes unfortunately a more likely option. Morabito (2007) terms the further contexts as *temporal* and *manipulative*. Here, *temporal* refers to the individual and *manipulative* to the actual incident that the police have been called to deal with. There will be some rare incidents, for example ones where a violent crime has been committed, where the police have very little alternative but to take that person into custody. Alternatively, an experienced officer dealing with a minor incident involving an individual that the local station knows well will have more scope. As Morabito (2007) concludes, the current literature exploring police decision-making may oversimplify the processes involved. The local context is vitally important: those areas with greatest mental health and social needs are almost by definition the ones with fewest community resources.

12.4 Policing, police powers and the custody setting

In England and Wales, the law provides specific powers to the police in relation to mental health issues. It also provides additional protection to people who are taken into police custody. Section 136 of the Mental Health Act (MHA 1983) allows a police officer to take a person who is in a public place and who appears to be mentally disordered to a place of safety. The MHA Code of Practice makes it clear that a police station should only be used as a place of safety in exceptional circumstances. Ideally, the person should be taken to be assessed at a hospital, and a number of hospitals in England have established so-called section 136 suites for these assessments. If someone is detained under section 136 (MHA 1983) they must be formally assessed by a psychiatrist and an Approved Mental Health Professional. There have been increasing pressures on community-based mental health services, particularly but not exclusively in the major cities. One of the results is the fact that far too many people who have mental health problems spend time in police cells.

A joint review by HM Inspectorate of Constabulary, HM Inspectorate of Prisons, the Care Quality Commission and Healthcare Inspectorate Wales in 2013 found that there were significant examples of this practice. A variety of reasons were given but the most common were: the person was drunk, violent or had a history of violence; or there were insufficient beds or staff at the health-based provision. As the report notes, once the person is taken into custody at the police station, they are treated like any other detained person. They are booked in, searched and finally locked in a cell. In 2012, the case of *MS* v. *UK* reached the European Court of Human Rights (ECHR). MS was detained under section 136 following an assault on his aunt. He was assessed as not fit for interview by medical staff called to the station by the police. There then followed a prolonged delay over attempts to transfer him to appropriate psychiatric care. This lasted so long that the 72-hour limit of section 136 was breached. The case found that there had been a breach of Article 3 which prohibits inhumane or degrading treatment and torture. The judgement was not a criticism of the initial decision to detain MS under mental health legislation. It was rather the delays in organising the provision of appropriate psychiatric care. The impact that this had manifested itself in the deterioration in MS's mental state. This case highlights the need for the police to be adequately supported by mental health services. In January 2014, ten pilot sites were announced in England and Wales where mental health nurses are to be allocated to police custody suites to assist in the assessment of detained persons suffering acute mental distress.

As noted above, the Police and Criminal Evidence Act (PACE 2004) ensures that there are additional safeguards in place when the police arrest an individual who has mental health problems. These protections are on top of the usual ones that all detained persons have, for example the right to legal advice and the taping of police interviews. The major additional protection comes in the role of the appropriate adult (AA). The role of the AA is a rather odd one. They are not advocates within the usual meaning of the term, nor are they legal representatives, and they do not enjoy legal privilege. However, they should ensure that the interview is carried out in an appropriate way, for example ensuring that there are reasonable breaks. Given the difficulties in assessing mental health problems, the busy public nature of the custody suite and the relatively short periods that officers have to book someone in, it is hardly surprising that mental health issues are often missed. McKinnon *et al.*'s study (2013) shows that there is a need for a more sophisticated screening tool in the custody setting. In this study, current procedures missed a quarter of cases of severe mental illness and moderate depression. In Ogloff *et al.*'s study (2011) over a third of detainees exhibited some psychiatric symptoms while in custody:

> More than half of police cell detainees had previously had contact with public mental health services at some point during their lives. One in three

were in treatment for mental disorders at the time of being arrested, with half treated within the public mental health system.

(Ogloff *et al.* 2011, 877)

From a public health perspective, police custody has to be viewed as a significant site for interventions. This is not to advocate the *mercy bookings* of Teplin's (1984) study but rather to recognise the level of need that exists.

The issues here are essentially the same as those in the prison environment where attempts are made to screen offenders. The identified risk factors for suicide such as alcohol or substance misuse, a history of mental illness and unemployment are much more prevalent in offenders than the wider population. Rivlin *et al.*'s (2013) study highlights the extent of these difficulties. The study interviewed 60 prisoners who had made near lethal attempts on their own lives. The experiences of this group were compared with a control group of 60 other prisoners. The study found that the majority of the prisoners who had made these serious attempts on their own lives were not identified as being 'at risk' at the time. This seems to indicate that vulnerable prisoners who were seen as being at risk were not being better supported. The most common methods used were hanging or ligatures (*n* = 40) followed by serious incidents of cutting (*n* = 12). Institutions such as prisons or psychiatric units try to design out or reduce the opportunities for self-harm and injury. However, it is clearly not possible to do this completely. Fifth-nine of these incidents took place in the prisoner's own cell. Only 12 of the prisoners were in a segregation unit at the time where there would normally be more staff. The study demonstrated that prisoners who had no educational qualifications, had been in prison previously, had been imprisoned for less than 30 days or had been in the current prison for less than 30 days were at much greater risk. The research also emphasises one of the key problems that is faced in trying to tackle this issue: identifying vulnerable prisoners. The risk factors for suicide and self-harm that wider research identifies are much more likely to be present in this cohort. Thus identifying those most at risk becomes increasingly difficult. The barriers are increased by the organisational and cultural realities of prison life. Prisons are not therapeutic environments. They are overcrowded, prisoners are frequently moved and vulnerable prisoners are at risk of bullying. In this study only 40 per cent (*n* = 24) of the cases were identified as being at risk at the time of the attempt on their own lives. As the study concludes, much more effective screening tools are required to begin to tackle this issue

The issue of the overlap between the CJS and mental health services is one that forces society to consider a number of important ethical and philosophical issues. Prins' (2010) seminal work *Offender, Deviant or Patient* considers the question of how society should respond to the individual who has mental health problems and has committed an offence. The position that is taken on these issues will determine the response; societies, on the whole, attempt to treat rather than punish the sick. However, in practice such clear divisions are not readily sustainable. Penrose (1939; 1943) grappled with these issues, putting forward the idea that there was an essentially fluid relationship between the CJS and mental health systems. Penrose was using what would be seen now as a very broad definition of mental health service provision. Penrose argued that it was possible to calculate a state of development index: the number of people in mental health facilities divided by the number of those in prison. Large and Nielessen (2009) concluded that this hypothesis holds for low and middle income countries. The study concluded that there was no such relationship in higher income countries. However, a broad range of scholarship which has examined mass incarceration has demonstrated that the CJS is now the default provider of mental health care. It is argued that it is possible to view Penrose's work as a moral argument that calls for more therapeutic approaches and interventions. One of the effects of the reduction in emphasis on rehabilitation is that more punitive sanctions have spread from the CJS to other areas; Cummins (2012b) provides a discussion of the development of mental health policy in England and Wales, emphasising that the response to the failure to provide adequately resourced mental health services in the past 20 years has been to focus on managerialist solutions – audit, surveillance and risk assessment – which culminated in the introduction of community treatment orders in England and Wales in 2008.

Seddon (2007) suggests that there is a fundamental flaw at the heart of these debates about offender versus patient. For Seddon (2007), it is impossible to create such clear distinctions between the 'mad' and the 'bad'. To do so ignores the power struggles that underpin these discourses and the rivalry between the professions of medicine and the law. The focus of our analysis should be the processes and dynamics of these relationships which create, maintain and disseminate these categories that marginalise individuals and groups (Foucault 1988). As Seddon (2007) concludes there have always been people who we would now term 'mentally ill' in the CJS. This will always be the case; the question for us to explore is how these institutions function and what are the implications of being classified as 'mentally ill'. Until relatively recently, the focus of research and policy has been on the experiences of individuals with mental health problems in the CJS. The focus of this research has been on the prison estate rather than earlier stages. Seddon (2007) identified a number of 'key decision points' in the CJS, which impact on the career of the psychiatric patient. He did not identify the police custody setting as one of them. From the Reed Report (1992) onwards, the official aim of policy in this area has been to divert, wherever possible, people with mental health problems from the CJS at the earliest opportunity. There is a body of research that looks at the impact of different models of diversion. In the past decade, there have been two key Inquiries in this field. The Bradley Review (2009) examined the experiences of people with mental health problems or learning difficulties across the CJS. One of its most important recommendations was that the National Health Service should take responsibility for the commission of healthcare across the whole of the CJS including custody. The Corston Inquiry (2007) into women in prison was established following an increase in the suicide rate amongst women prisoners –

including six suicides in one year at HMP Styal. This Inquiry highlighted the very high rates of mental health need among women in prison, many of whom had experienced sexual and domestic violence.

The main focus of research has been on offenders in prison. There has been a recent shift as the area of police contact is now being recognised as key. Teplin's (1984) study is key in demonstrating that the failings of community care were increasing police contacts. Later works such as Lamb *et al.* (2002) emphasised that these policies were combining and resulting in the criminalisation of the mentally ill. This research needs to be combined with work such as Barr (2001) which shows the impact of policies such as zero tolerance. She shows the ways that the mentally ill – cut adrift from community support – will almost inevitably be drawn into the CJS.

12.5 The custody setting

Once in the CJS, it can be very difficult to exit. In terms of the assessment of mental illness, the police patrol officer can clearly exercise discretion – and decide to use section 136 MHA (1983). The figures on the use of section 136 MHA are notoriously unreliable. It is a relatively rare option that is taken. In this final section, I will explore the research that I have undertaken examining issues in custody. The research was carried out with two police forces in the north-west of England. The three studies can be read together to give a snapshot of the processes involved here. They outline the custody officers' experiences of assessing the individual's acute mental distress. The studies also examine how the police seek additional support in this area to ensure that vulnerable people are safe but also access healthcare. The studies demonstrate the pressures that police face in these situations.

Seddon's (2007) model of 'decision points' when agencies – criminal justice, mental health or other public authorities – decide on some sort of intervention identifies a number of possible sites. These might include initial diagnosis, civil or compulsory admission to hospital or the courts using a psychiatric disposal rather than imprisonment. Seddon significantly does not include the custody setting as one of these key decision points. However, decisions by beat officers and custody officers are vital.

In the Cummins (2007) study, assessment by the custody sergeant was identified as one of the key decision points. Ten police officers working as custody sergeants across the force were interviewed. At that time, the force was divided into ten divisions each working with a slightly different configuration of community mental health provision. All the interviewees were volunteers and the interviews took place at their local stations. The interviews were not recorded but contemporaneous notes were taken. Only one of the officers was female. The group was an experienced group of officers: each had at least ten years' service. Before taking on the custody sergeant role, they had carried out a wide range of policing roles. One of the most prominent recurring themes in this set of interviews was the personal sense of responsibility that they felt in this role. This was often accompanied by a sense of professional isolation – they demonstrated little, if any, confidence, that they would be supported by senior managers if a tragedy occurred. The Police and Criminal Evidence Act PACE (2004) is the legislation in England and Wales that governs the arrest and detention of individuals. It sets out clear guidance, including timescales for reviews and limits on detention, that officers have to follow. It was clear that the management of the custody environment involving the juggling of pressures from a range of sources including the demands of PACE (2004) was one of the key generators of stress in the custody officers' working environment.

The focus of the study was on mental health issues. It was soon apparent that this was one of a number of concerns; the most common not surprisingly was the effects of alcohol and street drugs. None of the officers felt that they had received adequate mental health training before they took on the custody role. Most reported that the training was focused on the provisions of section 136 MHA (1983). As was openly acknowledged, they were very reliant on the street experience and guidance from their more senior colleagues. This appears to remain the case. For example, Inspector Michael Brown won an award from the mental health charity MIND (2007) for his blog *Mentalhealthcop*, which became a forum for discussing issues related to mental health and policing. One of the reasons for the success of the blog was the fact that officers were using it as a source of real practice advice that was not available in official protocols and procedures. Another key theme that ran through these interviews was the frustration that was felt with the bureaucratic demands of the role and, from the police perspective, the failure of community mental health services to provide adequate and timely support. These failures led to delays in specialist mental health assessments. One of the perverse outcomes was that those identified as being at risk actually spent more time in custody. This increases rather than decreases the risks involved. The custody environment will never be a therapeutic one. The physical surroundings, the sense of isolation and perhaps the realisation of the seriousness of the offence mean that it has a potentially damaging impact on the mental health of detained persons. The custody sergeant has to decide which of those who are booked in at every shift are most at risk. The final point that the officers emphasised was the limited range of options open to them when they had concerns. At the time that this study was carried out, there were few examples of schemes where mental health or social work staff members were attached to custody settings.

Two further studies (Cummins 2008; 2012(c)) examined how the police responded to incidents of self-harm or cases where there were concerns about the mental state of the detained person. The first study explored incidents of self-harm. There were 168 recorded incidents in an eight-month period. This study was based on anonymised records so it is important to acknowledge the potential scope for under recording. In the period of the study, over 45,000 people went through police custody. Such incidents thus appear relatively rare. The records contained basic demographic information such as age, gender, ethnicity (not self-recorded) and employment status. The police also record other information, for example status on arrest – this was often "drunk". As far as the actual incidents are concerned, there was a brief description, followed by the action taken. The most common method was attempted strangulation – ligatures were fashioned from either their own clothing or the paper suits that the police use if there are concerns or the detained person's clothes are being forensically examined. Other methods included punching or head butting walls, swallowing toilet paper or cutting with cutlery. One of the most significant findings was that women appeared to be at much greater risk in custody. Alcohol and drugs were a consistent factor in these cases. These findings do need to be approached with some caution – obviously this is a small sample. However, it is also important to recognise that the risk factors for self-harm – such as a history of substance misuse, unemployment, adults survivors of childhood sexual abuse – are all much higher in this cohort than the general population.

The study confirmed that the police tackle this issue with relatively few resources and frequently no other information than what is provided at the point of arrest. The Police National Computer (PNC) may contain some information; for example, the police can put a warning on the individual's record that there has been a previous incident of self-harm. The police did not have access to the health records or other information. The options open to the police were also limited. In the most serious incidents, the detained person was taken to hospital because of their injuries. This was rare. In the overwhelming majority of cases, these incidents were dealt with in the custody setting – certainly for a period before specialist help arrived. The police ensured that the person was safe, that is not in a position to harm themselves. They then would remove objects such as cutlery that could be used in other incidents. In a number of cases, the detained person was placed in a paper suit. The most common response was then to increase observations or in some cases have one officer sitting outside the cell with the door open. It should be clear that this is not a criticism of the staff involved; the issues here are structural ones. From the information on the records, it was also possible to identify periods when the risks were increased. The first hour – possibly when the impact of custody is strongest – was a key stage. The number of incidents tailed off after this but increased after the six-hour period when detention was reviewed. In addition, it appears that those charged with sexual or violent offences are also at increased risk. One has to be careful when looking at the alleged offence – a minor shoplifting offence might have much more profound implications for some individuals. It should also be noted that the majority of people leave custody – they are either bailed or there is no further action. There was not a systematic approach for dealing with the aftermath of these incidents. A record was entered on the PNC but there was no system for making referrals to other agencies. The force also required the custody sergeant to record any changes that might be made to avoid such incidents in future.

As has been noted above, if a custody officer has sufficient concerns about a detained person's mental health then they will arrange for an assessment to be carried out by a Forensic Physician (FP). In the Cummins (2012c) study, arrangements were made for information to be collected in all cases where a detained person was assessed by a FP because of police concerns about their mental health. In the month of the project, there were 59 such assessments. There were many more cases where the doctors were called to treat physical health issues. From this sample, as well as basic demographic information, details of contacts, if any, with community mental health services were collected. Only six of the 59 had any contact with mental health services but this was very limited. The study raises the possibility that there is a cohort of individuals with complex needs who would benefit from support from mental health services but are not receiving it. If being in custody leads to an incident of self-harming then there are other stressful situations that might lead to this. What is clear is that custody can be a key point of intervention for mental health services. A model of ideal service provision would see custody as a vital cog in comprehensive provision. Recent policy initiatives in England have acknowledged this.

12.6 Conclusion

The current landscape of mental health services is a bleak one. Community mental health services are under increased strain and facing financial pressures. Such issues are dramatically explored in Nathan Filer's *The Shock of the Fall* (2013) in which 18 year old Matthew is suffering from a psychotic breakdown linked to the death of his younger brother in a childhood accident. The novel brings to life the landscape of despair that Knowles (2000) and others have described in academic work: people at the margins, in poor housing, being supported by embattled staff. The staff are battling in an economic climate where resources are being cut. At the same time, the approach to the caring role has been replaced by a managerialist approach focusing on risk assessment and bureaucratic care plans. Matthew finishes his memoir just in time as the day centre where he writes it is closed as part of a programme of spending cuts. The progressive ideals of community care have failed to be realised. The current period of austerity has added to these difficulties and these problems are deeply entrenched (Beresford 2013). The result of these changes has not been deinstitutionalisation but rather *transinstitutionalisation*: the asylum has gone – most likely converted into desirable properties – to be replaced by a poorly furnished flat and a day centre on the point of closure. One of the indirect consequences of these changes in mental health policy has been to change to the role of the police in this field. Lurigio and Watson (2010) refer to the "porous boundaries" between the CJS and Mental Health systems. The police increasingly find themselves part of both. This creates tension on both an organisational and an individual level. Despite the fact that the maintenance of social order has always been a key part of policing, the focus has always been on law and order. There is some evidence of a shift away from this. Senior managers certainly accept this. The whole ethos of neighbourhood policing is to recognise that the police have a much wider role to play. As the research considered in this chapter demonstrates, officers still lack confidence in their ability to manage these situations.

At the start of 2014, there are grounds for some cautious optimism that these long-standing issues will finally be addressed. The recognition as in Lord Adebowale's (2013) report that mental health is core police business is long overdue. There are a number of initiatives such as mental health triage, the placement of mental health nurses in police custody suites and new approaches to the management of section 136 MHA (1983) that taken together could signal a new beginning. These should be regarded as one of the key features of mental health services. But the police role is not a replacement for what is really needed and was the goal of its original proponents: genuine community care.

References

Adebowale, Lord. 2013. *Independent Commission on Mental Health and Policing Report.* London: Independent Commission on Mental Health and Policing.

Barr, H. 2001. Policing Madness: People with Mental Illness and the NYPD in Quality of Life and the New Police Brutality in New York City. New York. NYU Press Mcardle, A. and Erzen, T (eds).

Bauman, Z. 2003. *Wasted lives: Modernity and its outcasts.* Oxford: Polity.

Beresford P. 2013. https://theconversation.com/mental-health-is-in-no-fit-state-whatever-the-politicians-say-15743.

Bradley K. 2009. *The Bradley Report: Lord Bradley's review of people with mental health problems or learning disabilities in the criminal justice system.* London: Department of Health.

Corston J. Baroness. 2007. *The Corston Inquiry.* www.justice.gov.uk/publications/docs/corston-report-march-2007.pdf.

Cross S. 2010. *Mediating madness: mental illness and cultural representation.* Basingstoke, UK: Palgrave.

Cummins I. 2007. "Boats against the current: Vulnerable adults in police custody". *Journal of Adult Protection* 9(1): 15–24.

Cummins I. 2008. "A Place of Safety: Self-harming behaviour in police custody". *Journal of Adult Protection* 10(1): 36–47.

Cummins I. 2010. "Mental health services in the age of neoliberalism". *Social Work and Social Policy in Transition* 1(2): 55–74.

Cummins I. 2012a. "Policing and mental illness post Bradley". *Policing: A Journal of Policy and Practice* 6(4): 365–376.

Cummins I. 2012b. "Using Simon's '*Governing through crime*' to explore the development of mental health policy in England and Wales since 1983". *Journal of Social Welfare and Family Law* 34(3): 325–337.

Cummins I. 2012c. "Mental health and custody: A follow on study". *Journal of Adult Protection* 14(2): 73–81.

Cummins I. and Jones S. 2010. "Blue remembered skills: Mental health awareness training for police officers". *Journal of Adult Protection* 12(3): 14–19.

Filer N. 2013. *The Shock of the Fall.* London: HarperCollins.

Foucault M. 1988. *Madness and Civilisation.* New York: Random House.

Godfredson J., Thomas S., Ogloff J. and Luebbers S. 2011. "Police perceptions of their encounters with individuals experiencing mental illness: A Victorian survey". *Australian and New Zealand Journal of Criminology* 44: 180–195.

Goffman E. 1968. *Asylums.* London: Penguin.

Howard J. 2013 (first published 1777 and 1784). *The state of the prisons in England and Wales.* Cambridge: Cambridge University Press.

Knowles C. 2000. *Bedlam on the Streets.* Oxford: Routledge.

Laing R. 1959. *The Divided Self.* London: Tavistock.

Laing R. 1967. *The politics of experience and the bird of paradise.* Harmondsworth, UK: Penguin.

Lamb H. R., Weinberger L. E. and DeCuir W. J. 2002. "The police and mental health". *Psychiatric Services* 53(10): 1266–1271.

Large M. and Nielssen O. 2009. "The Penrose hypothesis in 2004". *Psychology and Psychotherapy: Theory, Research and Practice* 82: 113–119.

Lurigio A. and Watson A. C. 2010. "The Police and people with mental illness: New Approaches to a longstanding problem". *Journal of Police Crisis Negotiations* 10 (1–2): 3–14.

Marcuse H. 2002. *One-dimensional man: Studies in the ideology of advanced industrial society.* London: Routledge Classics.

McKinnon I., Srivasta S., Kaler G. and Grubin D. 2013. "Screening of psychiatric morbidity in police custody: results from the HELP-PC project". *The Psychiatrist Online* 37: 389–394.

Mental Health Act. 1983. London: Her Majesty's Stationery Office

MIND. 2007. *Another assault: Mind's campaign for equal access to justice for people with mental health problems.* London: MIND.

Moon G. 2000. "Risk and protection: the discourse of confinement in contemporary mental health policy". *Health and Place* 6(3): 239–250.

Morabito M. 2007. "Horizons of context: Understanding the police decision to arrest people with mental illness". *Psychiatric Services* ps.psychiatryonline.org 58(12): 1582–1587.

Ogloff J., Warren L., Tye C., Blaher F. and Thomas S. 2011. "Psychiatric symptoms and histories among people detained in police cells". *Social Psychiatry and Psychiatric Epidemiology* 46: 871–880.

Ogloff J., Thomas S., Luebbers S., Baksheev G., Elliott I., Godfredson J., Kesic D., Short T., Martin T., Warren L., Clough J., Mullen P., Wilkins C., Dickinson A., Sargent L., Perez E., Ballek D. and Moore E. 2013. "Policing services with mentally ill people: Developing greater understanding and best practice". *Australian Psychologist* 48(1): 57–68.

Penrose L. S. 1939. "Mental disease and crime: Outline of a comparative study of European statistics". *British Journal of Medical Psychology* 18: 1–15.

Penrose L. S. 1943. "A note on the statistical relationship between mental deficiency and crime in the United States". *American Journal of Mental Deficiency* 47: 462.

Pinfold V., Huxley P., Thornicroft G., Farmer P., Toulmin H. and Graham T. 2003. "Reducing psychiatric stigma and discrimination. Evaluating an educational intervention with the police force in England". *Social Psychiatry and Psychiatric Epidemiology*. 38(6): 337–344.

Police and Criminal Evidence Act. 2004. London: Her Majety's Stationery Office.

Powell E. 1961. www.canehill.org/history/enoch-powells-1961-speech.

Pogrebin M. 1986. "Police responses for mental health assistance". *Psychiatric Quarterly* 58: 66–73.

Prins H. 2010. *Offenders, deviants or patients? Explorations in clinical criminology*, 4th edn. Hove, UK: Routledge.

Rivlin A., Hawton K., Marzano L., Fazel S. 2010. Psychiatric disorders in male prisoners who made near-lethal suicide attempts: case-control study. *Br J Psychiatry 2010*; 197: 313-319.

Robertson G. 1988. "Arrest patterns among mentally disordered offenders". *British Journal of Psychiatry* 153: 313–316.

Robertson G., Pearson R. and Gibb R. 1995. *Entry of mentally ill people into the criminal justice system.* London: Home Office.

Sainsbury Centre for Mental Health. 2008. www.centreformentalhealth.org.uk/pdfs/briefing36_police_and_mental_health.pdf.

Scull A. 2004. "The Insanity of Place". *The History of Psychiatry* 15: 417–436.

Seddon T. 2007. *Punishment and Madness.* Oxford: Routledge.

Steadman H. J., Deane M. W., Borum R. and Morrissey J. P. (2000). "Comparing outcomes of major models of police responses to mental health emergencies". *Psychiatric Services* 51(5): 645–649.

Szasz T. 1974. *The myth of mental illness: Foundations of a theory of personal conduct* (revised edition). New York: Harper and Row.

Teplin L. 1984. "Criminalising mental disorder". *American Psychologist* 39: 794–803.

Wolff N. 2005. "Community reintegration of prisoners with mental illness: a social investment perspective". *International Journal of Law and Psychiatry* 28(1): 43–58.

Wood J., Swanson J., Burris, J. D. and Gilbert A. 2011. *Police interventions with persons affected by mental illnesses: A critical review of global thinking and practice.* New York: Rutgers University, Center for Behavioral Health Services and Criminal Justice Research.

13 Mental health and the courts

Ronald D. Francis

13.1 Introduction

This chapter sets out to deal with the various aspects of mental health and crime. In particular it deals with the establishment of the crime: mental health connection, court matters, special courts for the mentally ill, sentencing matters, psychological issues and human rights. Courts deal with various offences against both the criminal and the civil law. Where they do so, particularly in the criminal jurisdiction, the ascription of responsibility is seen as a major problem. Those who bear adult responsibility take the consequences of their actions; for those with a mental illness, or with intellectual impairment, that responsibility may be absent. Although there may be aspects of mental health that are conducive to crime they are not the same thing. Crime is one form of behaviour, mental illness may generate another. What is being asserted is that some forms of mental illness have criminal implications.

13.2 The crime–mental health connection

One of the early empirical studies that established the connection was that of Penrose. Writing in 1939 he demonstrated the relationship between prison beds and hospital beds in psychiatric institutions; his conclusion was that they appear to have a complementary relationship. It is almost as if the prison and mental hospital accommodation is a constant: when one goes up, the other goes down. Penrose does make the point that the situation is not necessarily simple. He noted (1939, 12) that "attention to mental health may help to prevent the occurrence of serious crimes, particularly deliberate homicide".

A later study by Biles and Mulligan (1973) presented a similar analysis and conclusion for the six states of Australia (it did not include the two Territories), concluding that Penrose's finding is supported in an Australian context. Both the Penrose and the Biles and Mulligan studies suggested differences in administrative procedures in the various jurisdictions (countries or states) as a possible explanation of the results. For example, if a particular jurisdiction places emphasis on psychiatric care, then individuals convicted of a crime and showing some sign of mental disorder are more likely to be institutionalised in a mental hospital than sent to prison. Additionally, there is a greater likelihood in such a jurisdiction of the early detection and institutionalisation of anyone suffering from mental illness.

More recent studies have shown the Penrose hypothesis to have qualified explanatory power. For example, Kelly (2007) in Ireland found an inverse relationship between the annual censuses of psychiatric inpatients and prison statistics. The Large and Nielssen (2009) study examined the relationship between the numbers of psychiatric beds and prisoners, covering 158 countries. There the relationship was positive in low and middle-income countries, but not for high income countries, for which there is no doubt an explanation. Since that time it has become understood that there is a clear connection between particular cases of mental health and of crime. It is an observation now so commonplace that it has warranted the setting up of diversion programmes that deal specifically with that issue.

By way of contrast there is the seminal case: the 1843 M'Naghton case from Britain. Daniel M'Naghton killed, in error, the secretary of the British Prime Minister of the day (Sir Robert Peel), his intended victim being in fact the Prime Minister. At M'Naghton's the trial the issue was that "the party accused was labouring under such a defect of reason, from disease of the mind, as not to know the nature and quality of the act he was doing, or as not to know that what he was doing was wrong" (M'Naghton rule. see: http://en.wikipedia.org/wiki/M'Naghten_rules). In principle this amounts to having no moral sense, no remorse, or such limited reasoning power that there could be little regard for the consequences. That test is still in operation, with its basic premise that a criminal defendant cannot be convicted of a crime if, at the time of committing the offence, the act was the result of a mental disorder.

The Supreme Court of Victoria in Australia in 2007 deliberated on the issue of the mental health of the accused at the time of the offence. Those principles go to the heart of moral responsibility (as distinct from legal liability); it notes the issues of general and specific deterrence, and considers the effect of imprisonment on those with a mental health problem. The issue that they confronted was whether or not psychiatric dysfunction, but not amounting to insanity, should be a factor in statement about outcome. It is the reduction of blameworthiness that was the issue. Deliberating impaired mental functioning at the time of the offence is guided by several principles:

- The condition may reduce the moral culpability of the offending conduct, as distinct from the offender's legal responsibility Where that is so, the condition affects the punishment that is just in all the circumstances and denouncing the individual is less likely to be a relevant sentencing objective.
- The condition may have a bearing on the kind of sentence that is imposed and the conditions in which it should be served.
- Whether general deterrence should be moderated or eliminated as a sentencing consideration likewise depends upon the nature and severity of the

symptoms exhibited by the offender, and the effect of the condition on the mental capacity of the offender, whether at the time of the offending or at the date of sentence or both.

- Whether specific deterrence should be moderated or eliminated as a sentencing consideration likewise depends upon the nature and severity of the symptoms of the condition as exhibited by the offender, and the effect of the condition on the mental capacity of the offender, whether at the time of the offending or at the date of the sentence or both.
- The existence of the condition at the date of sentencing (or its foreseeable recurrence) may mean that a given sentence will weigh more heavily on the offender than it would on a person in normal health.
- Where there is a serious risk of imprisonment having a significant adverse effect on the offender's mental health, this will be a factor tending to mitigate punishment (for a statement of principles see Verdins 2007).

It is clear that there is a connection between crime and mental health but that connection falls short of being an identity. The recognition of the connection has, in recent times, led to the establishment of special courts that deal with the mentally ill. The justification for the establishment of such courts is that diversion programmes for special cases are both legally just and also preventative of further offending by way of treating the causative factors.

The issue of mental illness, specific behaviour and distorted cognitions has been canvassed by Rogers and Pilgrim (2010). They discussed various notions, such as the statistical notion, the ideal notion, the presence of specific behaviours, and distorted cognitions, all placed in the context of the legal framework. An inability to perceive situations as do 'normal' people could generate behaviour that might be regarded as criminal. Such a situation could then lead to being 'labelled' and, as such, they may take on the persona that they regard as fitting (such as 'criminal' or 'mentally ill').

13.3 Court matters

Deciding on whether or not there is mental illness challenges legal decision-makers. In most Western, and many Eastern, countries there are tiers of courts. At the lowest level there is the magistrates' court (in British derived background countries). In those countries, the adversarial approach applies: the magistrate or judge acting as a kind of referee to the opposing sides. In countries that use the Napoleonic Code there is the inquisitorial system, allowing a more active role in eliciting information. It also assumes that the accused is guilty until proved innocent. One readily recognises that culture will dictate different styles in court.

In countries which use the Napoleonic Code, the judicial officer will have a much more direct say in how the trial is conducted; they may require particular sorts of expert evidence, may decline to accept some, and will take a much more controlling interest in the conduct of the trial. In the adversarial system, counsel for prosecution and defence call their witnesses with the judge refereeing their conduct. As such, those countries which use the Napoleonic Code will have the determination of mental well-being being decided more by the judge. It is by the means of judicial control that variations in outcome may occur. Where, in adversarial countries, the counsel for each side is equal the outcome may be just; that is less so for cases where counsel for one side is vastly more skilled. In this respect Napoleonic Code countries have the advantage that a judge led court makes it a more even contest.

One of the several complications in trials is that cultural differences should be distinguished from mental health problems. The concept of the 'reasonable man' may culturally involve seeing women as subservient to men, and considered as property. In Westernised countries this is an unacceptable proposition. The critical point here is that of a belief so firmly held that it may come to be regarded as an indisputable proposition. The question is how the belief is held, the utter conviction of its rectitude, and an unwillingness to see another side. When it becomes too extreme it might be regarded as irrational, and the loss of rationality is one of the considerations made by mental health courts. A similar position applies to the notion of religious beliefs. The notion that a particular religious outlook has primacy over others, and must be fostered, is one of those debatable propositions. That shading of belief and action is one of the difficulties experienced by judicial officers.

It is common to find courts mentioned in hierarchical order. Where countries have special courts (as happens in Australia, the UK, Canada, the USA, Germany, etc.) they tend to be filter courts that deal specially with the mentally ill offender. Cases that progress to the higher courts may accept an 'unfit to plead' case for disposition, or may test the case using the M'Naghton test or some recent development. What is most noticeable is the existence of special courts in many countries: one dealing with, for example, bankruptcy, divorce or mental health. It is by way of precedent that one might argue, as has been argued, the case for special mental health courts.

One might examine the notion of the accountability of judges. That topic has been addressed by Shetreet *et al.* (2013). Their account examines the independence and accountability of the English judiciary. While the system works as well as it does, it is not without safeguards, and checks and balances. Court judgements depend upon the character of those making them and the bench must not only have integrity but also to be seen to have it. By way of contrast it is interesting to know what judges and lawyers think about expert testimony. Four conclusions emerged: that they preferred psychiatrists to psychologists, the main interest of the court was in clinical diagnosis, a lesser interest was in research findings, and that the kinds of response are affected by the role that they occupy in the adversarial system (see Redding *et al.* 2001).

In addition to the strain on defendants one must also consider the strain on court officials. In a recent account, a Victorian Supreme Court judge noted prevalence of depression and anxiety in the legal profession (Warren 2013). Such consequences flow from being a member of an adversarial and combative profession. It is no surprise that the mental well-being of those charged should be echoed by that of the legal profession who represent them. Here, the general idea that court trials impose a burden on the legal professional is one that should be accommodated. ✓

13.4 Special courts

Mental health courts are a relatively recent phenomenon. Their main function is to lessen the problems that bring offending individuals into recurring contact with the criminal justice system. That brief is particular to those whose offending problems relate to mental ill health. As Frailing (2010, 51) put it "mental health courts divert willing and eligible offenders from incarceration towards mental health and related treatment". Here one might debate the use of the word "willing".

Most recently there have been special courts set up that deal specifically with mental disorder problems; this applies most strongly to the lower tier of courts where cases are referred. In the more senior court trials the process is more likely to be dictated by the circumstances of the case: the court calling appropriate witnesses as needed. From the point of view of this chapter, of special interest to us is the recent development of courts that deal with mental health issues. Goldcamp and Irons-Guynn, in their report for the National Criminal Justice Reference Service (2000), nominated some jurisdictions in the USA that are introducing such courts. Australia is well advanced in that respect wherein every state has mental health courts. Those who are mentally ill may be disadvantaged in court by any one of several factors: among them are a lack of rational understanding of the case, a lack of knowledge of the court process and, in some cases, the prospect of deportation.

There have been a number of reports on mental health courts: among them is, in Britain, Winstone and Pakes (2010). Their evaluation of the Mental Health Court confirms that mental health courts are a developing feature of the criminal law process. Their analysis provides a glossary and policy considerations as well as a conclusion. Their understanding was that there was a need for a clear model, and an analysis of costs to both the criminal justice system and the health service. Their main recommendation was to have the Health Ministry provide, and be accountable for, the health of prisoners. That recommendation noted the need for special courts as a part of the criminal justice system, and is now so firmly accepted that it has been the basis of models in the UK (Winstone and Pakes 2010). Redlich *et al.* (2006) give the features that distinguish early versions of the courts from later court versions: the felony/misdemeanour acceptance, pre- versus post-adjudication models, the merits of jail as a sanction, and types of court supervision. That work has provided valuable information about the mental health courts, and is based upon an extensive national survey. It is worth noting that not only have different countries and various jurisdictions introduced special mental health courts, but also the WHO through its European Network on Prison and Health has an expert group: the Stewardship of Prison Health (see www.euro.who.int/).

Trials are often greatly distressing, particularly for the new offender. Those who are mentally fragile could well find themselves distressed beyond endurance at the prospect. An essential part of the court is due process such that evidence is adduced in a prescribed order, including the testimony of psychological experts (see Faust 2012, for example). In giving appropriate weight to evidence of psychological experts, the judicial officer must consider the relevance of some factors while ignoring others. Instances are noting such factors as age and gender, but not race or skin colour. Among the many factors to be taken into account in sentencing are: the demeanour of the accused, the availability of remedial services and, perhaps of substantial importance, contrition. The lack of remorse for an offence is often a serious consideration in the sentencer's mind. Remorse is often taken as a sign by the judge that the offender has understood what they have done, and regrets the offence. It is by such means that the judge knows that the consequences of the offending action are now understood by the offender, and that a recurrence is thus less likely. That discrimination is taken by sentencers to indicate an insight that the individual with a mentally disorder may not have.

Many countries have set up special mental health courts, which use diversionary programmes, taking the criminality out of the offence and dealing with treatment. Crucial to this role are the provision of a sympathetic judge and the availability of expertise. Here the role of the psychological professional is essential in providing diagnosis and recommended disposition for the court to consider. It is by such means that the twin aims of both prevention and rehabilitation would seem to be simultaneously served.

13.5 Factors in sentencing

When the bench sentences they need to keep relevant factors firmly in mind, excluding things that they know but are irrelevant to sentencing. Among the issues to be considered is that of the formal charge, which may have been bargained to a lesser charge – permissible in some jurisdictions, but not in others. Here one makes a distinction between plea bargaining, 'sentence bargaining' and 'fact bargaining' (see Findlaw – http://criminal.findlaw.com/criminal-procedure/plea-bargains-in-depth.html). Such bargaining may involve 'unfit to plead'. There is a case to be made for unfitness to plead, one that is in contrast to the equally persuasive seminal argument of Wootton (1963) that the trial take place first to determine culpability and then the sentence take into account the mental state of the defendant. To such considerations we might also add the concern of distinguishing the irresistible impulse from the unresisted impulse.

Where a court decides that therapy is appropriate, one would wish to be assured that such help is available and professionally qualified. It is worth noting that where disorders are culturally loaded the disorder may be related to one language and not another. Providing therapy for mental health problems also requires cultural sensitivity. For example, Knipscheer and Kleber (2004) found evidence that sharing a similar worldview with those who treat them may be more important for patients in therapy than sharing the same ethnic background. The authors of the research concluded that "culturally sensitive indigenous therapists may treat ethnic minorities just as well as therapists with matching cultural backgrounds" (2004, 552). In providing a custodial sentence, one must be aware of the several consequences. Alan *et al.* (2011), in their analysis of linked inpatient and prison data, found that one-fifth of adults released from prisons in Western Australia (2000–2002) were admitted to hospital within a year following release. This translated to 12,704 inpatient beds. The article recounted that mental health disorders (such as schizophrenia and depression) and injuries to head and face accounted for nearly 59 per cent of all beds. In comparative terms, this amounted to a rate of 1.7 times the comparable non-incarcerated population.

The risks of hospitalisation and of death have also been canvassed by Katelaris (2011) who noted that ex-prisoners are dying quite out of proportion to their representation in the community – at about ten times the rate of those in the comparable wider community, with many dying of drug-related disorders. Andrews *et al.* (2011) and Kinner *et al.* (2011) both provide evidence of the relatively high mortality rate of ex-prisoners dying within a short time after release. Those freed from psychiatric facilities and sent in to the community are less likely than average to cope with ordinary social life. This runs to the heart of the problem of consequences of sentencing. It is thus seen as one of the most difficult areas of decision-making.

What is critical here is the need for similar information on the consequences of a case being assigned to a special mental health court, and to the consequences of each disposition, such as therapy or incarceration in a mental hospital. It is only by such empirical information that hearing and sentencing may be improved.

13.6 Psychological matters

Whether one calls a psychologist or a psychiatrist to testify in court depends upon the type of expertise required. The evidence adduced in court will have a significant bearing on the way in which testimony is regarded and handled. Psychiatrists bring qualifications in medicine; psychologists have clinical training in individual and interpersonal functioning. Given psychiatrists are qualified in the medical model, and are dysfunction-oriented, they may (or may not) be disposed to see the world in such terms. Whilst psychologists are not qualified in medicine and have the drawback of not having insight into medical matters, they have some advantage that may confer a margin of wider perspective. The diagnoses of those before the courts require professional input in order to determine their status. One of the common findings of studies is that of mental illness and intellectual disability being more common among prisoners than in the corresponding external population. In this connection an indispensable part of classification is that of good identification and record keeping; as such it is not only an aid to understanding but may also be valuable in dealing with recurring cases.

Defining mental health is problematical. Among the many complications are: intellectual disability, the social milieu of offenders, and those who lack insight and empathy, the latter largely described in terms of psychopathy (see American Psychiatric Association DSM 5). To such analyses we might add such issues as brain damage and drug usage.

When needing a diagnosis, the reference point is commonly the International Classification of Diseases model (WHO ICD 10) or the American Psychiatric Association Diagnostic and Statistical Manual of Mental Disorders (DSM 5). In such cases, the diagnosis is commonly based on the medical model of disorders. That model may work substantially well in many cases but, in some cases, is less appropriate, the problem being that it is often just a description of the disorder (as distinct from a disease diagnostic). Further, it is a medical diagnosis, and does not always accommodate the existential aspects of life.

Brain injury has been shown to be more prevalent among prisoners than it is among the corresponding external population. Williams *et al.* (2010), using a large sample of prisoners with a report rate of 43 per cent, showed that over 60 per cent reported head injuries with 16 per cent reporting moderate to severe traumatic brain injury. It had already been shown that the prevalence of long-term disability in the general population was associated with head trauma, with a prevalence of 1.1 per cent (Zaloshnja 2008). By whatever standard one measures, it is clear that the prevalence of head trauma is much higher in the prison population than it is in the general population, and does point to the need for brain injury assessment to be part of the assessment and management of offenders. It is worth noting that the same conclusion was drawn about prisoners in New Zealand (McClure 2013).

Other aspects of mental health related problems are those of substance abuse. Those who are drug dependent, as a result of being substance affected, may commit offences; they may also engage in theft offences as a means of funding their drug habit, thus there is a double driver to crime when there is drug addiction.

Individuals with intellectual disability may be vulnerable to offending behaviour because of their struggles with judgement and/or a low sense of risk. Moreover it is noted that many offenders before the courts may live on the margins of the community before imprisonment, with little education and socio-economic disadvantage. Many social inequalities may have precipitated the offending behaviour. Those variables include unemployment, unstable accommodation, poverty, limited prospects and reluctance to use (or unavailability of) community support services – which continues and potentially worsens upon release. Overall this results in stigmatisation and limited post-release resources, which serve to raise the risk of recidivism.

Giving evidence in court rests upon several factors, apart from having been either a common witness or an expert. In the case of common witnesses the presumption is one of both recall and cognitive ability. In the case of a professional witness, their brief is not to be an advocate but, rather, to be an independent expert. That idea has been examined by Murrie *et al.* (2013) whose study involved over 100 American experts, examining whether or not the psychologists showed a bias toward those who retained them. It emerged that there was an unconscious bias towards the retainer (prosecution or defence). The point here is that that expert witnesses should not have an orientation towards those who commissioned them. They are there to give professional opinions in order to assist the trial. What is also apparent is that bias might be stronger for subjective judgements, such as the assessment of emotional harm. The type of expert called may sway the case in a different direction, given the world outlook of different professionals may vary sufficiently to give a case a particular inclination (see Melton *et al.* 2007).

13.7 Human rights and moral dilemmas

The human rights of prisoners are a telling problem: that is particularly so for those with a mental disability in that they may be treated as a non-responsible person, and thus treated with patronage. Having been sentenced by an independent judiciary, they have lost some rights. That is no reason for them not to be treated with consideration of those rights that remain. While remand prisoners have a vote in the UK, in some countries (including Armenia, Bulgaria, Estonia, Hungary and Romania) prisoners do not have a vote. The European Court of Human Rights noted that it was for individual nations to determine which prisoners could vote, but that a blanket ban was not acceptable.

The issue of sentencing is replete with moral dilemmas. One basic one is whether or not there should be special courts for the mentally ill. This issue goes to the heart of the issue of due recognition of special problems – and the allocation of finite resources. Should one, for example, provide mental health care for defendants that may be superior to that used by those not sentenced? The general proposition of the allocation of scarce resources is always fraught with difficulty. As such, the issue of patient protection and affordable care was the subject of the US Government Report on Patient Protection and Affordable Care (2010). A yet more vexing problem is that of general deterrence. For the courts to deal more harshly with a defendant simply because the court wishes to deter others could be severely detrimental to those of marginal mental stability. The use of medication to calm individual defendants may impair their rationality; while containing behavioural problems and making them more amenable. It could also erode the individual's autonomy. Such dilemmas require careful and considered judgement.

13.8 Conclusion

The notion of special courts is deserving of cautious support. One can readily see the need for monitoring and evaluation to assess their effectiveness. Alternatively one could consider adapting Wootton's (1963) seminal point, that of special courts hearing a case conventionally and then, and only then, deciding on the disposition. If the aim of courts is to be both punitive and affording preventive and remedial action one cannot help but support the notion of special courts for the mentally ill.

If it may be argued that special courts are needed for issues such as bankruptcy, family matters and marine matters, then it is equally compelling to have such for the mentally ill. It is clear that incarceration to protect the public is a worthy motive, and so too is the notion that special cases require special treatment.

While the system of legal and judicial appointments is always capable of improvement, it must evolve in a considered way rather than through political expediency. Where such debates occur there is a clear need for advocacy, particularly in what may seem an unpopular cause. Such recommendations must be considered for their serious and long-term implications.

References

Alan J., Burmas M., Preen D. and Pfaff J. 2011. "Inpatient hospital use in the first year after release from prison: A Western Australian population-based record linkage study". *ANZ Journal of Public Health* 35(3): 264–269.

American Psychiatric Association. 2013. 5th edn. *Diagnostic and Statistical Manual of Mental Disorders 5*. Arlington, Va: American Psychiatric Association.

Andrews J. Y., Forsyth S., Wade J. and Kinner S. A. 2011. "Sensitivity of a national coronial database for monitoring unnatural deaths among ex-prisoners in Australia". *BMC research notes* 4: 450. See: www.biomedcentral.com/1756–0500/4/450.

Biles D. and Mulligan G. 1973. "Mad or bad – the enduring dilemma". *British Journal of Criminology* 13: 275–279.

Faust D. (based on an original work by J Ziskin) 2012. *Coping with psychiatric and psychological testimony*. New York: Oxford University Press.

FindLaw. "Plea bargaining: in depth". See: http://criminal.findlaw.com/criminal-procedure/plea-bargains-in-depth.html.

Frailing K. 2010. "Mental health courts". In M. French, S. Jackson and E. Jokisuu (eds) *Diverse engagement: Drawing in the margins*. Proceedings of the interdisciplinary graduate conference. Cambridge University, England, June 2010, 51–56.

Goldcamp J. S. and Irons-Guynn C. 2000. *Emerging judicial strategies for the mentally ill in the criminal caseload: Mental health courts in Fort Lauderdale, Seattle, San Bernardino, and Anchorage: A report on community justice initiatives.* Report for Bureau of Justice Assistance, Washington DC: US Crime and Justice Research Institute.

Katelaris A. 2011. "Why are prisoners dying after their release". *Medical Journal of Australia* 195(2): 59.

Kelly B. 2007. "Penrose's Law in Ireland: An ecological analysis of psychiatric inpatients and prisoners". *Irish Medical Journal* 100(2): 373–374.

Kinner S. A., Preen D. B., Kariminia A., Butler T., Andrews J. Y., Stoove M. and Law M. 2011. "Counting the cost: Estimating the number of deaths among recently released prisoners in Australia". *Medical Journal of Australia* 195(2): 64–68.

Knipscheer J. W. and Kleber R. J. 2004. "A need for ethnic similarity in the therapist–patient interaction? Mediterranean migrants in Dutch mental-health care". *Journal of clinical psychology* 60: 543–554.

Large M. and Nielssen O. 2009. "The Penrose hypothesis in 2004". *Psychology and psychotherapy: theory, research and practice*. 82: 113–119.

M'Naghton rule: http://en.wikipedia.org/wiki/M'Naghten_rules.

McClure T. 2013. "Traumatic Brain Injury". See: www.stuff.co.nz/national/health/9335492/Most-prison-inmates-have-brain-injuries.

Melton G. P., Petrila J., Poythress N. G. and Slobogin C. 2007. 3rd edn. *Psychological evaluation for the courts: A handbook for mental health professionals and lawyers.* New York: Guilford Press.

Murrie D. C., Boccaccini M. T., Guarnera L. A. and Rufino K. A. 2013. "Are forensic experts biased by the side that retained them?" *Psychological Science* 24(10): 1889–1897.

Napoleonic Code. See: http://europeanhistory.about.com/od/thenapoleonsandempire/a/Napoleonic-Code-Code-Napoleon.htm.

Patient Protection and Affordable Care Act. 2010. (USA). www.gpo.gov/fdsys/pkg/BILLS-111hr3590enr/pdf/BILLS-111hr3590enr.pdf. US Congress.

Penrose L. S. 1939. "Mental disease and crime: Outline of a comparative study of European statistics". *British Journal of Medical Psychology* 18: 1–15.

Redding R. E., Floyd M. Y. and Hawk G. L. 2001. "What judges and lawyers think about the testimony of mental health experts: a survey of the courts and bar". *Behavioral Sciences and the Law* (Special Issue: The Practice of Forensic Psychology and Psychiatry) 19(4): 583–594.

Redlich A. D., Steadman H. J., Monahan J., Robbins P. and Petrila J. 2006. "Patterns of practice in mental health courts: a national survey". *Law and human behaviour* 30(3): 347–362.

Rogers A. and Pilgrim D. 2010. 4th edn. *The sociology of mental health and illness.* Maidenhead, Berks: Open University Press.

Shetreet S. and Turenne S. 2013. *Judges on trial: The independence and accountability of the English judiciary.* Cambridge: Cambridge University Press.

Verdins principles: *Summary of Judgment R* v. *Verdins, R* v. *Buckley, R* v. *Vo* [2007] VS CA 102. 23 May 2007. See: http://assets.justice.vic.gov.au/scv/resources/23c35d9d-998d-4c80–932a-a5278efeccd4/summary_verdins.pdf.

Warren M. 2013. "When the black dog bites". *Law Institute Journal of Victoria*, 87(11): 20.

Williams W. W., Mewse A. J., Tonks J., Mills S., Burgess C. N. W. and Cordan G. 2010. "Traumatic brain injury in a prison population: Prevalence and risk for re-offending". *Brain injury.* 24(10): 1184–1188.

Winstone J. and Pakes F. 2010. *Process evaluation of the Mental Health Court pilot.* Ministry of Justice Research Series 18/10, September 2010. London: Ministry of Justice.

Wootton B. F. 1963. *Social science and social pathology.* London: Allen and Unwin.

World Health Organisation. Health in Prisons Program. See: www.euro.who.int/en/health-topics/health-determinants/prisons-and-health/who-health-in-prisons-programme-hipp.

World Health Organisation. 2010. International statistical classification of diseases and related health problems. (ICD10 [10th revision]).

Zaloshnja E., Miller T., Langlois J. and Selassie A. W. 2008. "Prevalence of long-term disability from traumatic brain injury in the civilian population of the United States". *Journal of head trauma rehabilitation* 23(6): 394–400.

14 Vulnerability and resilience in the criminal justice system

Peta Barry, Julie Ann Pooley and Maryam Omari

14.1 Introduction

Staff working within the criminal justice system are employed in a variety of roles to assist with all aspects of offender management, including policing, courts, prisons and community corrections. These staff face occupational challenges as a result of working with victims, offenders and their families, managing people's responses to the aftermath of crimes, and the continuing risk of harm that some offenders pose to the community.

This chapter examines work in corrections service environments; challenges and risks faced by staff in offender rehabilitation roles; factors associated with staff vulnerability; and poses the question who is currently most vulnerable and at risk within corrective service environments, offenders or staff? Recommendations for support of staff are outlined, which may have implications for the range of staff employed within the corrections environment.

14.2 Work in corrections environments

Work in corrections environments places significant demands on its employees (Ghaddar *et al.* 2011). Armstrong and Griffin (2004, 577) comment that: "few other organisations are charged with the central task of supervising and securing an unwilling and potentially violent population". Assaults, injuries and self-harm do occur; however, a more common risk is to the psychosocial health of both the offenders and staff who reside and work within these environments (Lambert *et al.* 2009). For offenders, the impact of the correctional service environment is well documented. It is recognised that a restrictive and punitive environment; long prison sentences; limited meaningful activities; and exposure to criminal peers all impact negatively on offender outcomes (Australian Institute of Health and Welfare 2013).

It is important, however, to acknowledge that staff also experience negative outcomes from working within a corrections environment. Previous studies have generally been limited to examining the experiences of prison officers and parole/probation officers (Lambert *et al.* 2008). This overlooks the many other staff who work with offenders: in rehabilitation, health, as cultural consultants and religious/spiritual representatives, about whom there is negligible research within the corrections environment (Howells *et al.* 2004). The lack of attention to the experiences of these staff means there is little understanding both of potential risks to staff and of what makes staff vulnerable in the corrections environment, thus limiting the capacity of organisations to provide such staff with adequate support and training (Biere 2012).

14.3 Corrections culture

The correctional services work environment is shaped by some key influences, affecting both offenders and staff. They are environments which are highly structured and controlled, in order to reduce risk of harm to both groups (Biere 2012). Physical and emotional strength, dominance, intimidation, threats and violence are tools used by offenders to survive, to defend themselves, and ensure a safe physical and psychological distance from others; offenders and staff are forced to become emotionally tough to survive (Karp 2010).

A socially contrived hierarchy amongst offenders exists according to age, abilities, crimes, sexual preference, culture and peer associations (Karp 2010). A hierarchy also exists among correctional staff, with those employed in roles of prison officer and community corrections officers (parole and probation) having additional legal powers to direct offenders. At times, these staff also guide the behaviour of others, particularly for reasons of safety and managing offender compliance with court/order requirements.

The majority of offenders within correctional services environments are male and the majority of staff has traditionally been male (Karp 2010). Significant increases in both female offender and female staff populations have had an impact on the corrective services environment. This includes: increasing knowledge of female offending; developing services for women; and influencing the way offenders are managed, with women found to have contributed a more caring and calming approach when working with offenders.

The work of staff is influenced by the vulnerability of offenders, particularly those within prisons. Vulnerability refers to the potential for people to be harmed, and to foresee, manage, and recover from stress (Dhami *et al.* 2007). Offenders are affected both by 'imported vulnerability', which refers to pre-prison experiences of trauma, abuse and disadvantage (Liebling *et al.* 2005, 44); and 'deprivation vulnerability', which refers to the negative consequences from living in custody (Dhami *et al.* 2007, 1086). Females, mentally ill, and cognitively impaired offenders have been acknowledged as having higher levels of 'imported vulnerability', due to their levels of disadvantage, and therefore require additional support, placing extra demand on staff (Liebling 2009).

As well as gender, ethnicity is an influencing factor in corrective services environments, yet corrections programmes are still largely drawn from approaches to male white offenders (Heseltine *et al.* 2011). Within the Australian context, this presents particular challenges given the over-representation of Indigenous Australians within the criminal justice system (Weatherburn and

Holmes 2010). As a group of offenders, they have higher rates of arrest, conviction, and incarceration; experience more physical and mental health problems; and are more likely to self-harm or attempt suicide than non-Aboriginal offenders (Butler *et al.* 2007). In addition, Aboriginal offenders residing away from their communities and supports are particularly vulnerable; they lack access to their lands, community and supports. A limited understanding of Aboriginal culture, family connections and social protocols also creates barriers between offenders and staff and at times places offenders in unsafe and culturally compromising situations when discussing offending, victims, and the impact on their community (Macklin and Gilbert 2011).

These cultural influences affect how staff in corrective services environments experience their work and interact with offenders and other staff, affect the delivery of offender programmes and present challenges in terms of managing safety and well-being within these environment for both offenders and staff (Ghaddar *et al.* 2011).

14.4 Offender rehabilitation

Rehabilitation broadly refers to the restoration of something to its former or proper condition; in the corrections services environment it refers specifically to efforts to restore offenders to a non-offending lifestyle and to adopt good lives (Ward 2011). Offender rehabilitation primarily involves structured group programmes, and/or individual counselling. The benefit of a group programme rather than individual counselling lies in the additional social learning offenders gain from staff role-modelling; peer feedback of pro-social attitudes, beliefs and behaviours; and challenging of anti-social attitudes and behaviours by staff and peers (Dowden and Andrews 2004).

Programmes target specific areas of offending, related to issues of violence, sexual assault, substance use, general offending and offence related thinking (cognitive skills programmes). The aim is to improve offenders' understanding of the factors associated with their offending, and to develop strategies which may assist them to remain offence-free in the future. Programme content broadly addresses: offence details; offence related thinking, emotions, and behaviours; high-risk situations; communication; relationship skills; self-management; and future goals and plans to prevent a return to crime (Andrews and Bonta 2003; McGuire 2002). Offenders are assessed as suitable for these programmes due to their offence type, their level of risk to re-offend, and their level of treatment needs, such as attitudes supportive of crime (Andrews and Bonta 2003). This also enables staff to deliver longer and more intensive programmes as required with higher risk and higher need offenders. Additional factors are considered when recommending suitable programmes for offenders, such as gender, culture, denial of offending and cognitive ability (Andrews and Bonta 2003).

Offender rehabilitation has at times been portrayed as 'simple' psychological work, yet there is considerable complexity in the work, and staff deliver programmes in a therapeutic way, within anti-therapeutic environments (Drapeau 2005). Offenders participating in rehabilitation programmes are also mandated clients, and may not be interested or willing to engage in these offender programmes. Attendance however, is coerced (court ordered) rather than voluntary; failure to participate in a programme may result in order sanctions. Participation can therefore feel forced or considered as a form of punishment (Trotter and Ward 2013; Day and Ward 2010).

Services provided for offenders are sometimes perceived to be at the expense of victims or re-directing focus from victim services. The primary client of offender rehabilitation, however, is the community; improving the quality of offenders' lives assists to prevent further harm to others (Ward *et al.* 2006).

14.5 Offender rehabilitation staff

Staff delivering offender rehabilitation programmes are usually clinically trained (e.g. psychologists, social workers), have specific cultural knowledge (Aboriginal programme staff), or are prison officers. It can be difficult, however, to recruit qualified, experienced and/or suitably trained staff as they can be reluctant to work in these environments (Howell *et al.* 2009).

Staff face a number of challenges in their role. Actively engaging offenders in programmes can be difficult, especially when offending might be justified and minimised, when offending is denied or there is reluctance to disclose details (Ward *et al.* 2006). Offenders themselves may be disruptive or display antisocial behaviours, have mental health concerns, cultural and language barriers, or cognitive impairment, all of which will challenge effective programme functioning and outcomes for participants (Pankow and Knight 2012). Safety concerns around offenders who have a history of violence or predatory behaviour are common among staff; female rehabilitation staff may also experience opposition from offenders with negative attitudes towards women and authority, especially those who have been convicted of violent crimes against women (Gordon *et al.* 2012).

The delivery of community-based programmes has its own challenges, trying to maintain offender attendance often complicated by employment, transport, homelessness, illness and other factors. These problems are exacerbated in regional areas, with fewer numbers, a more transient population, and limited transport (Coverdale 2011). Where participants come to community-based programs aggressive, intoxicated or substance affected it heightens the risk for potential harm (Pankow and Knight 2012).

Listening to details of offences can be emotionally challenging for staff, particularly details about ways that victims and others have suffered (Hatcher and Noakes 2010). While some offenders are remorseful, others may show no concern for others and these discussions compound the difficulty staff will have hearing and responding to this information. Equally offender accounts of their own victimisation and trauma histories will have an impact on rehabilitation staff (Hatcher and Noakes 2010). The way staff manage their responses to these situations is referred to as 'emotional labour' (Crawley 2004, 471). They have to mask their reactions and respond professionally, working in a supportive way, seeking feedback from the offenders (Crawley 2004).

Grooming and manipulation can be a feature in interactions between offenders and rehabilitation staff, with offenders trying to evoke empathic responses from staff to influence staff perceptions of the offender and their risk of re-offending (Cornelius 2009). Such manipulation is heightened when staff members are inexperienced or stressed. Yet it is important not to misconstrue politeness or friendliness from offenders towards staff, where offenders are seeking to extend pro-social behaviours as part of rehabilitation. Mackain *et al.* (2010) also remind staff not to become complacent with the routine of delivering programmes, noting the individual and varying needs of offenders for rehabilitation, and potential for risk.

While offender rehabilitation work has many challenging aspects, it also involves mundane tasks, including significant amounts of reporting and administrative tasks; repetition of programmes and concepts; and work with similar offender types or offending issues for an extended period of time. This can impact on dissatisfaction and intent to leave (Mackain *et al.* 2010).

14.6 Risk and work in offender rehabilitation

Risk refers to the likelihood of negative outcomes for that individual as a result of stressful or traumatic situations (Masten 2011). While the impact of working in an offender rehabilitation role is not well understood, some outcomes noted for staff working in correctional services have been identified as: absenteeism, turnover; stress; negative emotions and thinking; depression; reduced self-efficacy; relationship instability/divorce; substance use; a loss of interest in, and energy for the work; a higher risk of suicide (Morgan 2009). Corrections staff considered at most risk of suicide and post-traumatic stress include those who report high levels of stress, exhaustion, hyperactivity, depersonalization, avoidance and intrusive thoughts (Severson and Pettus-Davis 2013). Forensic health care professionals including psychologists and social workers have also been identified as experiencing high levels of stress-related conditions (Elliot and Daley 2013).

It is acknowledged that listening to stories of crime, trauma, and the distress and suffering of others is associated with harm to staff, and can increase risk of experiencing burnout, compassion fatigue and vicarious trauma (Hatcher and Noakes 2010). Burnout involves a decline in the professional and personal functioning of an individual over a period of time through their exposure to stress (Morgan *et al.* 2002). It is typified by exhaustion, disconnection and withdrawal from the work and from others, loss of confidence, a lack of care about work, and devaluing their work (Figley 2002; Keinan and Malach-Pines 2007). Vicarious trauma, however, involves a rapid change in functioning as a result of exposure to a client who has been involved in a traumatic event, or discloses details of traumatic incidents to staff. It is a form of psychological distress, and symptoms include intrusive thoughts, hypervigilance, anxiety and depression (Stamm 1995).

While the vulnerability of offenders and current risks are assessed from initial contact and monitored throughout their contact with correctional services, this does not happen for staff (Liebling 2009). Offender assessment includes consideration of historic and current factors including trauma, physical/mental health, self-harm, suicide attempts and current thoughts, strategies to manage stress, substance use, relationships, support, and future plans (AIHW 2013). These are all identified at entry into corrective services environments. All staff have systems in place to raise an alert about an at risk offender, arrange a risk assessment, and provide supports including counselling, cultural, and religious support, as well as from peers, family and friends.

The vulnerability of staff is not always assessed when first employed within a correctional services environment. Few personal background factors are known about staff in relation to past trauma and current personal circumstances (mental health, substance use, self-harm/suicidal ideation) unless self-disclosed, even though these may directly impact on their work with offenders, particularly in responding to sexually inappropriate behaviours and aggression (Drapeau 2005). While formal and informal supports are available to staff – which will include peer support, line supervision and management, and employee assistance programmes – staff may be reluctant to admit they are having personal difficulties, and unwilling to identify their problems to supervisors and managers. Colleagues may also be reluctant to disclose these issues, as they are concerned about placing additional pressure on the other person (Bearse *et al.* 2013). This maintains staff vulnerability and places them and others at further risk; it can also negatively impact on the work undertaken with offenders (Clarke 2011; Hatcher and Noakes 2010).

On the question of whether offenders or staff members are the more vulnerable, staff can move away from their workplace at the end of their working day, removing themselves from the workplace stressors. As well as being able to disengage from work, they have access to leisure activities, can socialise with others, and use health services and other supports to mediate some of the negative effects of their work (Sonnentag 2012). This assumes that the homelife of staff provides a respite from this stress, rather than adding to and compounding stress. If in fact home life is also stressful, staff may be more vulnerable at work. On the other hand, offenders are generally more vulnerable than staff. They are exposed to more sources of risk over longer periods, and may have little option to reduce their exposure to situations which increase their vulnerability. This may arise either from incarceration and the associated stresses with being in prison, or from continuing risks within their home environment such as substance use or violence.

While no specific risk factors have been clearly identified for offender rehabilitation staff, the risks for staff working within corrective service environments have been outlined within the literature, and are presented in Table 14.1. They include personal, professional, relational, organisational and other factors.

Table 14.1 Factors that contribute to vulnerability of staff working within corrective services environments

Personal	Professional	Relational	Organisational	Other
• Age (young and older workers more at risk) • Biology (injury, disability) • Health (physical or mental) • Gender, race, ethnicity • Personality • Personal experiences, including past trauma • Personal values and needs being unmet; dissatisfied with work, and intent to leave • Current circumstances and life changes (includes marital status, parenting) • Fear of harm/injury at work • Fatigue • Substance abuse	• Employment status • Education • Experience in corrections • Working overtime • Role (authoritative or caring/helping role) • Professional values/ mismatch with perceived organisational practices • Strategies for managing stress and change • Perceptions of status • Conflicts between other staffing groups • Concerns regarding efficacy/valuing of work • Concerns regarding re-offending by some offenders, with limited control over this • Deterioration in performance at work	Quality of relationships with: • Offenders (impacted by hostility, inappropriate sexual behaviours, or poor boundaries) • Colleagues • Partner • Family • Friends • Community networks • Professional networks and supports available	• Location (regional versus metropolitan) • Prison or community corrections • Security rating of facility • Gender/health of offenders – females and mentally ill offenders are more vulnerable and place more demands on staff • Contact hours with offenders • Overcrowding • Caseload/Workload • Vacancy and leave management • Perceived organisational support • Supervision and management approaches • Organisational policy and procedures	• Broader political and social pressures (including punitive, reactive, and 'political' decision making) • Fiscal pressures • Media coverage and impact on community attitudes about crime, offenders, punishment, rehabilitation and reintegration into the community

Personal factors influence how the individual is able to tolerate and manage stress at work, given their past experiences, current circumstances, abilities and strengths (Leip 2013). *Professional factors* influence how the individual perceives themselves in their role; how others see them; how they perceive their organisation; how organisational practices fitted with their own personal and professional values; and how this influences the individual's capacity to manage challenges inherent in their role (Gordon *et al.* 2012; Lahm 2009). *Relational factors* include the quality of interactions with others inside and outside work, and how these impact on performance at work (Bough and Williams 2007; Crawley 2004). *Organisational factors* include specific pressures related to managing work within a highly controlled, high demand environment (Dowden and Andrews 2004; Liebling 2009). *Other factors* include sources of influence from within the community such as media; community perceptions of criminal justice work, and how they impact on decision making; financial resourcing for organisations; and perceived support for and valuing of offender management and rehabilitation work by the community (Ashforth and Kreiner 1999; Lambert *et al.* 2009).

All these factors can contribute to staff vulnerability when working within a corrective services role (Lambert *et al.* 2009). It is unclear, however, who among staff may be most at risk. This gap in knowledge therefore presents a problem for organisations. Without clear guidance about what contributes to vulnerability of staff, who may be at risk, and how to address these needs, particularly when there is often limited budget to do so, it reduces the capacity for organisations to support staff effectively (Clarke 2011).

14.7 Positive adaptation to stress

While exposure to work related stress and trauma can have negative effects, there are other ways that staff may respond to these experiences, including recovery, growth and resilience. Recovery refers to the process whereby the person is able to return to their original level of functioning before the stressful experience; this occurs following rest, support, returning to normal routines, distracting from thoughts about work, and having time to come to terms with the events (Sonnentag 2012).

Growth is also a possible outcome following periods of stress and trauma; following recovery, individuals can actually improve on their original functioning, as the stressful or traumatic event can stimulate new knowledge, awareness of skills and strengths that may not have been previously acknowledged, and increased confidence in ability to cope. They thus learn new positive adaptation and self-care strategies (Morgan *et al.* 2012).

Resilience is defined in many ways, and is considered the ability to function well, despite exposure to stressful and potentially harmful situations. Pooley and Cohen (2010, 34) define resilience as: "the potential to exhibit resourcefulness by using available internal and external resources in response to different contextual and developmental challenges". There are many factors or processes which may increase the risk of harm (risk factors), or provide a level of protection from harm (protective factors); these factors do differ, however, according to the person's environment, current influences, culture, gender and other individual circumstances (Masten 2011).

Protective factors identified as important for adult resilience include positive emotion, self-esteem, happiness and satisfaction, optimistic thinking, a sense of competence, connected relationships and social support (Dainese *et al.* 2011; Lee *et al.* 2013). Protective factors related to work (including corrective services environments, and specifically for offender rehabilitation staff) are relatively unexplored. Yet some strategies to improve resilience of offender rehabilitation staff have been proposed, such as: managing energy levels; reflecting on meaning and value of the work; understanding risks, strengths and vulnerabilities; acknowledging personal impacts of the work on thinking and emotion; and planning to exit the role in a staged way to assist in managing emotional connection to the work (Clarke 2011). Further understandings of factors related to the resilience of offender rehabilitation staff require additional exploration.

More broadly within the resilience research, it is recognised that positive emotions play a key role in developing resilience. Tugade and Frederickson's (2002) 'Broaden and Build' theory states that negative emotions increase arousal and narrow thinking and options for actions, so that people can react to threats in quick and decisive ways for survival, such as through the fight or flight response. Positive emotions, however, have a calming effect on the body, reducing the arousal that negative emotions generate; and expand thinking, enabling people to think in more creative and flexible ways (Tugade and Frederickson 2002). This develops resilience by building personal resources and skills, which will be available to the person in future, and have an upward spiral effect of assisting the person to manage challenging situations in future (Frederickson and Branigan 2005).

In addition to positive emotions, there are other factors argued as important. In his 'Well-being Model', Seligman (2011) outlines aspects which contribute to well-being and resilience, which he refers to as PERMA. These are: Positive Emotion, Engagement, Relationships, Meaning and Accomplishment. By encouraging positive emotions, fun, enjoyment and satisfaction; fully engaging in a task for its enjoyment, and building enthusiasm and momentum to a point where the task seems to 'flow' easily; developing and strengthening supports; connecting with values and beliefs that are important and give meaning; and working towards and achieving goals, individuals can build their well-being and resilience (Seligman 2011). As a foundation for learning the PERMA skills, character strengths assessments are used to: identify areas of existing personal resources; align personal goals with their strengths and values; and use these to overcome challenges and foster a sense of accomplishment (Peterson and Seligman 2004).

14.8 Building resilience with corrections staff

Staff resilience is associated with improved outcomes for managing both challenging times and times of stability, new experiences and change at work, stress and critical incidents; and strengthening the inherent resources, capacities and competencies of staff, making them more adaptable over the longer term (Bardoel *et al.* 2014).

Resilience programmes have therefore been introduced into a variety of workplaces and schools as a way of promoting psychological health, growth and resilience. These programmes have initially used positivity and optimism concepts, and then later adopted content related to the PERMA model.

The Penn Resiliency Programme (PRP) and the Strath Haven Positive Psychology Programme (PPP) are two programmes which have been implemented in schools. Results from PRP include reduced depression, hopelessness, anxiety and behavioural problems such as aggression; the PPP improved enjoyment, engagement, and social skills, including empathy, cooperation, assertiveness, self-control (Seligman *et al.* 2009). As a consequence, programmes using PERMA content have been introduced into Australian schools to train staff, students and families to learn and adopt these skills (Seligman 2009; Waters 2011).

The US Army introduced a Master Resilience Training (MRT) programme in 2009 to prepare soldiers for the psychological challenges of combat, reduce trauma related issues, and enhance well-being and resilience. MRT focused on core modules related to PERMA and evaluations in 2011 and 2013 yielded results which demonstrated reduced diagnoses for post-traumatic stress related conditions, mental health, and substance abuse problems; and improvements in the areas of adaptability, character, coping, optimism, friendship, and reducing catastrophic thinking (Harms *et al.* 2013; Lester *et al.* 2011).

These programmes offer guidance on some approaches which could be used within the workplace. What is clear is that implementation of resilience programmes in correctional services environments could develop skills to manage work related stress more effectively, thus increasing staff capacity to manage work related challenges. Such a resilience plan in this work context would include key constructs of assessment, training, support supervision, and management. *Assessments* identify areas of potential risk, character strengths, and protective factors, to provide a basis for skill building, and assist in monitoring staff well-being (Peterson and Seligman 2004; Adamson *et al.* 2012). *Training* increases staff awareness of resilience, risks and protective factors, impact of work stress, and core skills of PERMA to manage stress and build resilience (Seligman 2011). *Support* needs to be multi-faceted and include supervision, collegial/peer support, mentoring, professional networking, employee assistance programmes, critical incident support, and referral to community agencies and mental health services as required (Adamson *et al.* 2012; Clark 2011).

Supervision should be provided on a regular basis to reflect on personal and professional impacts of the work; review critical incidents; anticipate and develop strategies to manage future incidents; promote positivity, and provide support and encouragement; recognise/value work from staff; and monitor any changes to work performance (Clarke 2011). *Management* strategies recommended include: diversity management and inclusive employment practices; flexible work arrangements; work–life balance practices; assessment of staff functioning and risk management plans; safety and well-being training; mediation; change management; periods of non-contact with offenders as required; leave plans; and return to work plans (Adamson *et al.* 2012; Badoel 2014).

These strategies are supported by the development of resilience goals at an individual, team and organisational level but require identification of steps to achieve these goals and tracking of progress (Seligman 2011). This approach ensures the development of a workplace culture which promotes positivity, optimism and hope, which are important to counter the effects of burnout and vicarious trauma. They are also supportive of staff adaptability, health, recovery and resilience (Tugade and Frederickson 2002).

14.9 Conclusion

This chapter has provided an understanding of staff experiences of working within corrective services environments, and specifically the role of offender rehabilitation staff. It has also considered the vulnerability and risk to staff; protective factors; and strategies to improve the resilience of staff, including resilience programmes, assessments, supports, supervision and management strategies.

Given the acknowledged stressors of work in corrective services environments, it is important to have an understanding of factors that may increase vulnerability and risk to staff, and to find ways of strengthening and supporting staff so they can maintain their health and perform well. Without this knowledge, staff working in corrective services environments, though not as vulnerable as offenders, are currently at more risk of harm than necessary as there is limited potential to identify risk and act effectively to reduce negative effects on staff. Organisations without an understanding of risk to staff, and well developed resilience strategies to manage this, face continued difficulty attracting and maintaining a stable workforce and on-going problems associated with absenteeism, turnover and stress related conditions among staff.

A framework has been provided within this chapter to guide organisations to implement strategies to improve the well-being of staff, enhance their resilience and increase their capacity to manage the challenges inherent within their roles both in the present and in the future. This will be important for the future delivery of services within the criminal justice system and ultimately impact on how well staff cope within these workplaces.

References

Adamson C., Beddoe L. and Davys A. 2012. "Building resilient practitioners: Definitions and practitioner understanding". *British Journal of Social Work* doi: 10.1093/bjsw/bcs142.

Andrews D. and Bonta J. 2003. *The Psychology of Criminal Conduct.* 3rd edn. Cincinnati OH: Anderson Publishing Company.

Armstrong G. and Griffin M. 2004. "Does the job matter? Comparing correlates of stress among treatment and correctional staff in prisons". *Journal of Criminal Justice* 32(6): 577–592.

Ashforth B. E. and Kreiner G. E. 1999. "How can you do it? Dirty work and the challenge of constructing a positive identity". *Academy of Management Review* 24(3): 413–434.

Australian Institute of Health and Welfare. 2013. *The Health of Australia's Prisoners 2012.* Cat. no. PHE 170. Canberra: AIHW.

Bardoel E. A., Pettit T. M., De Cieri H. and McMillan L. 2014. "Employee resilience: An emerging challenge for HRM". *Asia Pacific Journal of Human Resources* 52(2): 1–19.

Bearse J. L., McMinn M. R., Seegobin W. and Free K. 2013. "Barriers to psychologists seeking mental health care". *Professional Psychology, Research and Practice* 44(3): 150–157.

Biere D. M. 2012. "The impact of prison conditions on staff well-being". *International Journal of Offender Therapy and Comparative Criminology* 56(1): 81–95.

Butler T., Allnutt S., Kariminia A. and Cain D. 2007. "Mental health status of Aboriginal and non-Aboriginal Australian prisoners". *Australian and New Zealand Journal of Psychiatry* 41(5): 429–435.

Brough P. and Williams J. 2007. "Managing occupational stress in a high-risk industry: Measuring the job demands of correctional officers". *Criminal Justice and Behavior* 34: 555–567.

Clarke J. 2011. "Working with sex offenders: Best practice in enhancing practitioner resilience". *Journal of Sexual Aggression, An International, Interdisciplinary Forum For Research, Theory And Practice* 17(3): 335–355.

Cornelius G. 2009. *The art of the con: Avoiding offender manipulation.* 2nd edn. Alexandria Va: American Correctional Association.

Coverdale R. 2011. "Postcode justice: Rural and regional disadvantage in the administration of the law". *Deakin Law Review* 16(1): 155–187.

Crawley E. 2004. *Doing Prison Work: The public and private lives of prison officers.* Cullompton, Devon: Willan Publishing.

Dainese S. M., Allemand M., Ribeiro N., Bayram S., Martin M. and Ehlert U. 2011. "Protective factors in midlife – How do people stay healthy?" *Journal of Gerontopsychology and Geriatric Psychiatry* 24: 19–29.

Day A. and Ward T. 2010. "Offender rehabilitation as a value-laden process". *International Journal of Offender Therapy and Comparative Criminology* 54(3): 289–306.

Dhami M. K., Ayton P. and Loewenstein G. 2007. "Adaptation to imprisonment: Indigenous or imported?". *Criminal Justice and Behavior* 34: 1085–1100.

Dowden C. and Andrews D. A. 2004. "The importance of staff practice in delivering effective correctional treatment: A meta-analytic review of core correctional practice". *International Journal of Offender Therapy and Comparative Criminology* 48(2): 203–214.

Drapeau M. 2005. "Research on the processes involved in treating sexual offenders". *Sexual Abuse: A Journal of Research and Treatment* 17: 117–125.

Elliott K. A. and Daley D. 2013. "Stress, coping, and psychological well-being among forensic health care professionals". *Legal and Criminological Psychology* 18(2): 187–204.

Figley C. R. 2002. "Compassion fatigue: Psychotherapists' chronic lack of self care". *Journal of Clinical Psychology* 58(11): 1433–1441.

Fredrickson B. L. and Branigan C. 2005. "Positive emotions broaden the scope of attention and thought–action repertoires". *Cognition and Emotion* 19(3): 313–332.

Ghaddar A., Ronda E. and Nolasco A. 2011. "Work ability, psychosocial hazards and work experience in prison environments". *Occupational Medicine* 61: 503–508.

Gordon J. A., Proulx B. and Grant P. A. 2012. "Trepidation among the 'keepers': Gendered perceptions of fear and risk of victimization among corrections officers". *American Journal of Criminal Justice* 38: 245–265.

Harms P. D., Krasikova D., Vanhove A., Herian M. and Lester P. 2013. "Stress and emotional well-being in military organizations". *Research in Occupational Stress and Well-being* 11: 103–132.

Hatcher R. and Noakes S. 2010. "Working with sex offenders: The impact on Australian treatment providers". *Psychology, Crime and Law* 16(1–2): 145–167.

Heseltine K., Sarre R. and Day A. 2011. *Correctional offender treatment programmes: The 2009 national picture in Australia.* Canberra: Australian Institute of Criminology.

Howells K., Heseltine K., Sarre R., Davey L. and Day A. 2004. *Correctional offender treatment programmes: The national picture in Australia.* Canberra: Criminology Research Council.

Karp D. R. 2010. "Unlocking men, unmasking masculinities: Doing men's work in prison". *The Journal of Men's Studies* 18(1): 63–83.

Keinan G. and Malach-Pines A. 2007. "Stress and burnout in Israeli police officers during a Palestinian uprising (Intifada)". *International Journal of Stress Management* 14(2): 160–174.

Lahm K. M. 2009. "Inmate assaults on prison staff: A multilevel examination of an overlooked form of prison violence". *The Prison Journal* 89(2): 131–150.

Lambert E., Hogan N. and Tucker K. 2009. "Problems at work: Exploring correlates of role stress among correctional staff". *The Prison Journal* 89(4): 460–481.

Lambert E. G., Hogan N. L. and Griffin M. L. 2008. "Being the good soldier: Organizational citizenship behavior and commitment among correctional staff". *Criminal Justice and Behavior* 35: 56–68.

Lee J. H., Nam S. K., Kim A., Kim B., Lee M. Y. and Lee S. M. 2013. "Resilience: A meta-analytic approach". *Journal of Counseling and Development* 91(3): 269–279.

Leip L. A. 2013. "Should I stay or should I go?: Job satisfaction and turnover intent of jail staff throughout the United States". *Criminal Justice Review* 38(2): 226.

Lester P. B., Harms P. D., Bulling D. J., Herian M. N., Beal S. J. and Spain S. M. 2011. *Evaluation of relationships between reported resilience and soldier outcomes.* Arlington Va: Department of Defense.

Liebling A. 2009. "Women in prison prefer legitimacy to sex". *British Society of Criminology Newsletter* 63: 19.

Liebling A., Tait S., Durie L., Stiles A. and Harvey J. 2005. "Safer Locals Evaluation". Cambridge, UK: Cambridge Institute of Criminology.

MacKain S. J., Myers B., Ostapiej L. and Newman A. 2010. "Job satisfaction among psychologists working in state prisons: The relative impact of individual facets assessing economics, management, relationships, and perceived organizational support". *Criminal Justice and Behavior* 37: 306–318.

Macklin A. and Gilbert R. 2011. *Working with indigenous offenders to end re-offending.* Indigenous Justice Clearinghouse, Brief 11. Canberra: Australian Institute of Criminology.

McGuire J. (ed.) 2002. *Offender rehabilitation and treatment: Effective programmes and policies to reduce re-offending.* Chichester, UK: Wiley.

Management and Training Corporation. 2008. *Women professionals in corrections: A growing asset.* Centerville, UT: Management and Training Corporation Institute.

Masten A. S. 2011. "Resilience in children threatened by extreme adversity: Frameworks for research, practice, and translational synergy". *Development and Psychopathology* 23: 141–154.

Morgan R. D., Van Haveren R. and Pearson C. A. 2002. "Correctional officer burnout: Further analyses." *Criminal Justice and Behavior* 29(2): 144–160.

Morgan W. 2009. "Correctional officer stress: A review of the literature 1977–2007". *American Jails* 23(2): 33–34.

Pankow J. and Knight K. 2012, "Asociality and engagement in adult offenders in substance abuse treatment". *Behavioral Sciences and the Law* 30: 371–383.

Peterson C. and Seligman M. E. P. 2004. *Character Strengths and virtues: A handbook and classification.* Washington DC: APA Press.

Pooley J. A. and Cohen L. 2010. "Resilience: A definition in context". *Australian Community Psychologist* 22(1): 30–37.

Seligman M. E. P. 2011. *Flourish: A visionary new understanding of happiness and wellbeing.* New York: Free Press.

Seligman M. E. P., Gillham J., Reivich K., Linkins M. and Ernst R. 2009. "Positive Education". *Oxford Review of Education* 35(3): 293–311.

Severson M. and Pettus-Davis C. 2013. "Parole officers' experiences of the symptoms of secondary trauma in the supervision of sex offenders". *International Journal of Offender Therapy and Comparative Criminology* 57(1): 5–24.

Sonnentag S., Unger D. and Naegel I. J. 2013. "Workplace conflict and employee wellbeing: The moderating role of detachment from work during off-job time". *International Journal of Conflict Management* 24(2): 166–183.

Stamm B. H. (ed.) 1995. *Secondary traumatic stress: Self care issues for clinicians, researchers, and educators.* Lutherville, MD: Sidran Press.

Trotter C. J. and Ward T. 2013. "Involuntary clients, pro-social modelling and ethics". *Ethics and Social Welfare* 7(1): 74–90.

Tugade M. M. and Fredrickson B. L. 2002. "Positive emotions and emotional intelligence". In L. Feldman Barrett and P. Salovey (eds) *The Wisdom of Feelings.* New York: Guilford.

Ward T. 2011. "Human rights and dignity in offender rehabilitation". *Journal of Forensic Psychology Practice* 11(2–3): 103–123.

Ward T., Day A. and Casey S. 2006. "Offender rehabilitation down under". *Journal of Offender Rehabilitation* 43(3): 73–83.

Waters L. 2011. "A review of school-based positive psychology interventions". *The Australian Educational and Developmental Psychologist* 28(2): 75–90.

Weatherburn D. and Holmes J. 2010. "Rethinking indigenous over-representation in prisons". *Australian Journal of Social Issues* 45(4): 559–576.

Part IV
Rehabilitation and recovery

15 The recovery environment

Health, homelessness and criminal justice

William Holt and Jacqueline Blatt

15.1 Introduction

Behavioural health disorders such as substance abuse, mental illness and trauma play significant roles in urban homelessness causing personal and societal costs. As a population, these individuals often come into contact with the criminal justice system. Traditional addiction treatment programmes have failed to attract, engage, retain and effectively treat this population, leaving homeless persons excluded from addiction treatment or constituting a chronically recycling segment of the treatment population. This chapter describes the design and outcomes of a specialised homelessness initiative that is part of a broader recovery-focused systems transformation in the city of Philadelphia, Pennsylvania USA. This approach emphasises sustained recovery through partnership, collaboration and building of recovery capital. Emerging and evidence-based practices for responding to the needs of individuals with addiction disabilities are outlined, as well as the legal and ethical challenges and implications for systemic changes. The service designs described and the service outcomes reported underscore the need to alter traditional service models radically to achieve enhanced long-term recovery outcomes with this population.

15.2 The impact of homelessness

Homelessness is a worldwide problem. In major US cities there is a lack of 0.1 to 2.1 per cent of housing stock at any point in time (Eyrich-Garg *et al.* 2008). Housing problems increased in the US during the second half of the twentieth century in the wake of urban gentrification projects that reduced the availability of low-income housing, saw the mass de-institutionalisation of persons with severe mental illness or developmental disabilities, and saw the diminished personal support from families and kinship networks, with the loss of what had once been close-knit neighbourhoods (National Alliance to End Homelessness 2007). Ongoing problems for people who are chronically homeless are exacerbated by co-occurring medical, psychiatric and substance use disorders embedded within a larger array of personal, social and legal problems; these are exacerbated by a categorically segregated system of health and human services severely challenged to respond to problems of such scope, intensity and duration.

Most individuals who experience homelessness do so for a short period of time (weeks to months), but a small percentage of the homeless are considered to be chronically homeless, meaning they have been homeless for more than one year or have experienced four or more episodes of homelessness for a month or longer in the past three years (National Alliance to End Homelessness 2007). Although people who are chronically homeless represent a very small proportion of the homeless population, they use a majority of the available beds in shelters and consume a disproportionate quantity of health and human service resources (Kuhn and Culhane 1998).

However, a large percentage of the chronically homeless population does not utilise services. As such, new cost-effective measures need to be developed to assist that portion of the chronically homeless population (Poulin *et al.* 2010). There is a significant concentration of substance use and psychiatric disorders within the homeless population (Eyrich-Garg *et al.* 2008), and those with pro-longed homelessness present to addiction treatment with complex needs that often compromise short and long-term recovery outcomes (Milby *et al.* 2005). Ways to develop addiction treatment and related recovery support services that address the needs of this population continue to be explored.

It is no surprise that research supports the interrelatedness of homelessness, addiction, offending, trauma and mental illness. In 1996, the National Survey of Homeless Assistance Providers and Clients found that 49 per cent of the currently homeless individuals reported an experience of spending five or more days in a city or county jail (Burt *et al.* 1999). More recent studies also found that 20 per cent of the incarcerated population diagnosed with mental illness were homeless (Malone 2009). Of imprisoned individuals who were homeless in the year prior to their incarceration, 79 per cent exhibited symptoms of addiction, 75 per cent exhibited symptoms of mental illness, 31 per cent had been physically or sexually abused, 46 per cent had been shot at and 49 per cent had been attacked with a knife or other sharp object (Greenburg and Rosenheck 2008).

15.3 Homelessness in Philadelphia

Past approaches have proven ineffective in addressing the problems of those with mental illness and addiction, and have directly resulted in the growing rates of homelessness, suicide and incarceration for the past 20 years. During the early to mid-1990s, the growing homeless population in the city prompted the govern-ment of Philadelphia to appoint a homeless 'czar' who initiated a strategic plan to eliminate homelessness in their city.

A review of scientific studies and a vast inventory of past experiences with homeless initiatives in Philadelphia led to the following conclusions and greatly influenced the design of the chronically homeless treatment model:

- Homeless persons with severe substance use disorders rarely enter addiction treatment on a voluntary basis, but can be engaged in treatment through assertive outreach programmes (Fisk *et al.* 2006; Tommasello *et al.* 1999).

- Duration of addiction treatment is a significant predictor of post-treatment outcomes, particularly for those with high problem severity/complexity/chronicity and low recovery capital (internal and external assets to initiate and sustain recovery) (White 2008b).
- Providing addiction treatment for the homeless is inseparable from the larger needs for assistance with permanent housing and employment or income assistance (Kertesz *et al.* 2007; Milby *et al.* 2000, 2005).
- Integrating housing assistance with addiction treatment and ancillary support services is more effective than providing either in isolation (Tsemberis *et al.* 2003, 2004; Padgett *et al.* in press).
- In addition to housing and addiction treatment, long-term recovery is contingent upon reducing the social isolation and community disconnection of the homeless (Hawkins and Abrams 2007).
- The costs of assertive recovery management services provided to the homeless are offset by savings in reductions in public service utilisation such as the criminal justice system (Larimer *et al.* 2009; Sadowski *et al.* 2009; White 2008b).

On the whole, this body of research steers us toward treatment programmes which address homeless individuals' tangible needs (e.g. housing, employment) as well as their addiction. These programmes need to be initially flexible and non-demanding, targeting specific needs of subpopulations, and providing longer-term, continuous intervention (Zerger 2002). These treatment programmes need to incorporate these elements into their treatment model:

- offer individuals a safe and dependable residential recovery environment that will *support people for an extended period of time* post incarceration tailored to the individual's needs and recovery goals;
- provide extended care supports to *ensure continued participation in treatment* and other recovery activities, including employment;
- create opportunities for *supported housing* for individuals who successfully complete the therapeutic experience, but who require transitional housing supports, especially those re-entering from the criminal justice systems;
- establish the unique *social and psychological approach of the therapeutic community* (TC) to foster the continuous interaction between participants and the recovery community (De Leon 2000);
- *facilitate interagency collaboration and community integration* driven by the participants' individual needs and supported by peer support specialists and other staff;
- *collaborate with community, self-help organizations* and advocacy groups to access and cultivate relationships and develop resources;
- *enhance* the recovery support capacities of *families and kinship networks* (White *et al.* 2006).

One of the most consistent findings in this research is the direct association between the length of time spent in treatment and positive outcomes. Furthermore, programmes which provide housing have consistently lower drop-out rates and have reduced recidivism. Overall, the research finds appropriately modified therapeutic communities to be cost-efficient and effective for homeless persons with co-occurring disorders. In order to meet the population's multiple needs, an integrated system of care that reduces barriers and fosters interagency collaboration is critical (White and Kurtz 2006; Zerger 2002).

The integration of mental health and physical health into a treatment system reduces the barriers and the stigma associated with behavioural health issues. Feedback from outreach workers and case managers working within systems serving homeless persons in Philadelphia indicated that it was extremely difficult to refer a client from one system to the other. As the numbers of homeless individuals on the streets of Philadelphia increased, these systems sought new and innovative ways to provide assistance. Members of the Department of Behavioral Health and Intellectual Disabilities, the Office of Supportive Housing and other important stakeholders in the homeless prevention and intervention community worked to identify methods to improve homeless outreach services and increase more effective systems collaboration. Outreach teams, which generally consisted of two or three outreach workers in a van, began incorporating members from the addiction recovery field, mental health field, and even psychiatrists and psychologists in their outreach teams and efforts. This proved to be an extremely valuable technique and helped train members of the outreach teams. Through such collaborations, homeless persons' access to addiction treatment increased (White and Kurtz 2006).

Traditionally in the US, recovery has been perceived as an event rather than a journey. Individuals who 'graduate' are discharged from treatment without taking into consideration post-treatment recovery supports. Without the availability of long-term assertive continuing care, people completing treatment have high rates of relapse. The majority of people completing addiction treatment resume use within one year following treatment (Wilbourne and Miller 2003) with more than half of all relapses occurring within 30 days of discharge and 80 per cent within 90 days of discharge (Hubbard *et al.* 2001). However, new models are challenging this compartmentalised view. Addiction is a chronic disorder and should be addressed through continuity of treatment, including engagement prior to treatment and transition back into the community post treatment (White *et al.* 2006).

Both William White (2006) and George De Leon (2000) describe recovery in terms of a change in lifestyle, involving 'habilitation' and 'rehabilitation'. Rehabilitation is the re-establishing of the capacity to sustain positive living and regaining emotional and physical health. Habilitation is, for the first time, learning the behavioural skills, attitudes and values associated with socialised living. For both White and De Leon, recovery is a multidimensional change which occurs through a process of social learning and is contributed to by peers, family and significant others in a therapeutic environment that is supportive of recovery.

Building an individualised recovery foundation begins in the modified therapeutic community, by developing a dependable, peer and social community in which participants can initiate healing, change perceptions about identity and lifestyle, and develop plans for sustaining wellness and recovery. White (2008b) outlines three primary goals for linking individuals in addiction treatment to recovery support groups and the larger recovery community: establishing a commitment to recovery; connection to a community in which they are able to share their experience, strength and hope; and connection to communal guidance towards recovery maintenance.

15.4 The Journey of Hope Project: a recovery-treatment model

The Department of Behavioral Health and Intellectual Disabilities (DBHIDS), Office of Addiction Services (OAS), in collaboration with the Office of Supportive Housing and local homeless outreach and advocacy agencies coordinated efforts to transform four identified inner city residential addiction treatment programmes into programmes specialising in the treatment of individuals with histories of prolonged homelessness. This initiative is now known as the Journey of Hope (JOH) Project. In the weeks and months leading up to the opening of the first specialised addiction treatment sites, outreach workers began communicating to homeless individuals that a new programme was soon starting that would allow up to a year's stay in treatment, with subsidised housing provided upon completion. The promise of housing upon programme completion was a key component to having individuals accept the treatment services. Every effort was made to develop these programmes utilising evidence-based practices, feedback and input from chronically homeless individuals within Philadelphia County.

Traditionally, treatment approaches are passive and needs for housing, medical and psychiatric treatment and legal resolutions are addressed on an emergency basis. The JOH programmes offer a proactive approach that incorporates prolonged outreach and support to individuals through life events. Formerly, barriers preventing access to treatment included long waiting lists and denial of treatment due to lack of identification or multiple prior admissions. With JOH programmes, treatment is accessible within four to eight hours of interest with no identification requirement for admission. Previously, high rates of attrition were commonplace, as participants left against medical advice early in treatment. JOH programmes have low attrition rates due to a focus on relationship engagement, service partnership, personalisation of services and continuity of care.

In the past, the medical model pathologised homelessness and addiction. JOH offers a treatment approach based on research and focused on lifestyle reconstruction rather than clinical pathology. Throughout the city, a newly developed programme trained recovering individuals to become paraprofessional. These 'Certified Peer Specialists' help those entering treatment 'walk the walk' of recovery. Additionally, the programmes welcome adjunct indigenous healers from the community, including Twelve Step sponsors, clergy and alumni. Conventional focus has been on screening, assessment, diagnosis and treatment. JOH focuses on building long-term recovery partnerships, emphasises individuals' choice, utilises community-developed rules and assumes a collaborative stance in counselling.

Over ten to 20 years, treatment has seen lengths of stay decrease to fewer than 90 days. JOH programmes offer lengths of stay that routinely are six to 12 months, which allow a broader range of services supporting lifestyle reconstruction: identification and clothing; medical treatment with an emphasis on wellness; permanent housing assistance; education and vocational training. JOH offers an open door drop-in policy, alumni support, and assertive staff outreach after discharge.

One of the JOH programmes, Horizon House's Susquehanna Park, offers long-term treatment to 19 men. As the programmes evolved over the first two years, it became apparent that additional support was needed for those who had re-entered the community through subsidised independent living. This led to the development of the second Susquehanna Park programme, offering two month short term treatment for six men, who are in their apartments and need help re-establishing stability post relapse to prevent a reoccurrence of their homelessness. Our programmes incorporate the following recovery management best practices to enhance the potency of treatment:

- Stages of Change model (Proschaska *et al.* 1992)
- Strategies for Motivational Enhancement (Miller and Rollnick 2012)
- active peer culture and participant government
- clinical practice in recovery management (White *et al.* 2006)
- responsiveness to the distinct needs of homeless individuals struggling with addiction (De Leon 2000)
- Men's Trauma Recovery and Empowerment Model (Harris 1998)
- harm reduction to abstinence (White *et al.* 2005)
- intensive post stabilization monitoring and supports (White *et al.* 2006)
- Cognitive Behaviour Therapy (Alford and Beck 1998)
- Motivational Interviewing (Miller and Rollnick 2012)
- Recovery Star (Triangle Consulting Social Enterprise Limited 2012)
- integration of treatment for co-occurring substance abuse and mental disorders
- as people of colour are disproportionately represented in the criminal justice system and in the homeless population, an emphasis on culturally competent services (Bell 2002)
- networking with family members, natural supports and community resources to enhance the ability of participants to establish and maintain in-community status
- active involvement of the family in service planning, educational and employment goals.

15.5 Recovery management: core components

Engagement is the first core component. Individuals targeted by JOH have substantial personal, social and environmental obstacles to recovery, due to long periods of homelessness, unsatisfactory experiences in prior treatment and suspicion and doubts about the benefits of residential treatment. Assertive outreach and engagement is an essential step for connecting with individuals to invite them into treatment (Zerger 2002). Outreach is carried out in partnership with homeless outreach teams, DBHIDS, case managers, peer specialists and alumni. Eligible individuals are screened for major health and psychiatric issues by a local assessment centre.

Services begin with the modified therapeutic community. Individuals entering the therapeutic community are experiencing health risks and social crises. Their drug use is recently out of control and they have little ability to maintain abstinence on their own. Their social and interpersonal functioning is often diminished and their drug use is either embedded in, or has eroded into, a socially deviant lifestyle. Although individuals differ in the severity of their problems, they are offered interventions to stabilise and reverse their self-destructive and self-defeating lifestyle behaviours. Susquehanna Park's recovery goals include sobriety, socialisation and healthy living. The staff and participants collaborate on these goals, with an emphasis on stabilising psychological and social functioning and initiating a long-term process of personal and lifestyle change (De Leon 2000).

De Leon (2000) defines recovery as a change in lifestyle and personal identity. Change begins when an individual makes a commitment to recovery, which is then sustained by the community of recovering persons who are key supports in the individual's change process. The individual is committed to self-help and the therapeutic community is committed to mutual self-help which creates a therapeutic milieu that initiates and sustains recovery. The three main factors in the change process are:

- internal motivation: the individual's pain concerning the negative aspects of their life and the hope for a more positive future;
- readiness to change: the individual's acceptance of the community's expectations and approach to recovery; and
- commitment to change: the person's willingness to commit to the TC's goals and to a sustained process for recovery.

Furthermore, the milieu helps participants develop shared assumptions and beliefs about healthy personal and social living, establishes expectations for participation in all activities, recognises responsible behaviour, completes all obligations and offers peer role modelling in values of honesty, self-reliance and work ethic. The daily practice of living healthily over time evolves into a changed life style and personal identity. De Leon (2000) suggests that the construct of community promotes change across moral, personal and recovery dimensions, which helps to integrate the ideological and psychological views of the TC perspective into a participant's lasting lifestyle and identify changes.

The TC uses social context to help individuals change themselves by participating in a healing, learning and change process facilitated by daily structure, social organisation and a daily regimen of groups, meetings, work and recreation. Healing is promoted by individuals feeling psychologically safe to be seen, heard and accepted by others. Learning is promoted by the individual's acquisition of knowledge and skills as well as by learning from one's own observation and experience with others. The milieu of the TC becomes the method of change through the social context of roles and relationships, community assessment of the individual and the person's response to that assessment (De Leon 2000).

Susquehanna Park invites and relies on suggestions endorsed by service experts: people in recovery. To obtain this valuable input, Horizon House established an internal and external Recovery Advisory Council, the third core component. Council members include staff, family and people in recovery, who meet monthly to assist in this process. The Council assists with Susquehanna Park programme development and provides continuous guidance in the implementation and on-going operations.

As individuals enter the TC, they collaborate with their Drug and Alcohol Specialist on the development of an individualised recovery plan, with goals that they agree to work toward. Each stage of their involvement is shaped by prescribed goals of expected change and the service expectations for each of the tasks. The TC stages convey the process of change in terms of individual movement within the organisational structure and planned activities. Participants are supported to complete all stages in a six to nine month period.

Change in the individual evolves incrementally as a process of developmental learning. The TC stages mark an individual's passage through the learning process, which is supportive of participants who have difficulty making and keeping commitments, defining goals and completing tasks, and pursuing social and personal growth. The stages define clear points and expectations for goal attainment based on explicit community expectations.

The stage format reframes the long-term change objectives into short-term goals that can be defined, understood and pursued in manageable learning and training increments (De Leon 2000). The three major stages in Susquehanna Park are based on De Leon's stages: Assimilation, Primary Treatment and Re-entry (2000).

Stage 1 "Getting Back on Your Feet" (assimilation). The primary objective of Stage 1 is the person's rapid assimilation into the community. This is crucial in the early days of a person's enrolment when they are ambivalent about the long-term commitment and are most vulnerable to dropping out. In addition to assessing the person's need for immediate supports regarding health care, detoxification, entitlements and possible criminal justice involvement, the principal Stage 1 focus is on the person's affiliation within the milieu. Staff and residents help new participants assimilate over the course of one to two months through relative isolation, crisis intervention, focused orientation and supportive counselling.

Relative Isolation (Focus) offers new participants a break from unhealthy relationships. Problems from the person's life outside can distract from their ability to concentrate on what must be learned for life in the milieu, and involvement with outside relationships can undermine and delay establishing relationships in the TC. New participants are introduced formally and informally to other participants. Informal contacts include established TC members introducing the new person, escorting the new participant on business appointments, talking about their experiences and goals, and countering any comments about leaving the TC. Staff provide initial crisis intervention to address pressing immediate needs related to legal, medical, family, financial and other matters. Attention to these pressing needs is intended to mitigate the acute nature of problems that could subvert the person's retention and is not intended to provide the person with longer-term solutions. Focused orientation sessions are facilitated by staff, offering information on the structure and general functioning of the community. Peers and staff provide informal counselling aimed at alleviating the person's anxiety about living in the community, addressing self-doubts and reducing worry about the future. Counselling sessions with the Drug and Alcohol Specialist focus on the person's short-term needs related to helping the person connect with peers, what must be learned during orientation, difficulties the person has in assimilating and how to use peers effectively for support in the community.

Stage 2 is "Walking the Walk" (primary treatment). The primary objective of Stage 2 is to address the person's recovery needs for socialisation, personal growth and psychological awareness within the structure provided by the TC, resources and activities. Many individuals receiving services from public behavioural health systems have histories of interpersonal violence, abuse and neglect that began in childhood often leading to involvement with child welfare, juvenile justice and the adult criminal justice system. Unless acknowledged and treated, childhood trauma may have a residual effect and become a barrier to recovery, treatment and services. Furthermore, a recovery wellness curriculum provides education for the life domains of self-care, addiction and trauma recovery, social relationships, family relationships, home and financial management and spiritual health. Peer supports and professional staff offer experience, strength and hope through encouraging role modelling, storytelling, mentoring, mutual support and the inclusion of peer volunteers. As the participant becomes more involved in treatment, the milieu gradually increases expectations for assuming leadership roles. Over the next four to five months, as one learns how to "Walk the Walk", community expectations increase significantly for participants in all activities and roles, as do the expectations for the intensity of mutual-help and peer and staff counselling.

Working with other staff, volunteers and members of the community, Susquehanna Park Case Managers and Certified Peer Specialists have the lead responsibility for developing community resources and facilitating community integration through linkage of the participants to those community resources. As an element of the personal recovery plan, each individual will have a community integration plan that will be initiated in the primary treatment stage. Based on a person's long-term community reintegration goals, case managers will work with the treatment team to identify in-community supports for the person that will be part of his community support network after transition.

Stage 3 is Walking out the Door (re-entry). The primary objectives of Stage 3 are to prepare the person for their independence and separation from the TC community and to assure a successful transition into the public community. Participants remain in the TC while they pursue goals that reduce dependency on the milieu for learning and support, and while they increase connections and supports in the public community. Participants' goals focus on adjustment to social living, strengthening daily living skills, and maintaining sobriety and healthy living within the public community. Participants who complete all stages will have achieved a period of continuous sobriety and resolved housing, legal, health and family matters. They will have a firm commitment to the recovery process, including a commitment to continue working on challenging areas and to maintain treatment and mutual self-help relationships. People who complete the TC component of the Susquehanna Park programme are recognised in a transition event. All alumni are encouraged to maintain a relationship with Susquehanna Park by involving themselves with new participants in mentoring and sponsorship roles, and within an expanding network of supports in the community.

15.6 Assertive continuing care

As previously mentioned, engagement begins when an individual considers entering treatment. But that connection, developed at the beginning and strengthened throughout treatment, is most tested as participants re-enter the public community. After discharge from services, staff continue to connect with alumni to offer support, encouragement and celebration as they continue to "Walk the Walk." And if they stumble, staff are available for early intervention to it is hoped reduce the intensity and duration of a relapse and re-orient the participant toward recovery and, if needed, a return to treatment.

An individual's recovery from addiction is not stabilised until they have sustained remission lasting four to five years (White *et al.* 2005). Our experience has been that this population needs a level of support beyond that which exists in the traditional behavioural health system as they transition to independent living settings and/or treatment settings, sustained long beyond discharge. Susquehanna Park has found that supporting individuals who have applied for permanent housing or other types of specialised housing has been challenging and at times difficult due to a number of factors.

Susquehanna Park I alumni reported that they had experienced a number of difficulties while residing in their permanent housing settings. Some of these have relapsed into substance abuse because of their inability to mobilise their recovery capital or utilise the community of supports that they developed while in treatment. Living independently and alone has also affected others who felt isolated in their apartments or have struggled maintaining day to day activities. While some of these individuals maintained their affiliation with Susquehanna Park and received support sufficient to their needs, it became apparent that for some individuals a return to treatment was warranted.

Susquehanna Park II was developed to better support JOH alumni in transitioning from treatment to permanent housing, with a focus on preventing a recurrence of homelessness. As a group, these individuals present with numerous high risk factors that compromise their ability to transition to or sustain permanent housing including greater personal vulnerability due to early age of addiction onset, chronic medical conditions and histories of intergenerational violence, trauma, addiction and poverty. Furthermore, these men are often from disempowered communities with limited resources that are adversely affected by cultural oppression and historical trauma and social inequalities. These are coupled with mental illness and the criminal behaviours associated with lifestyles that are the result of long-term, serious substance abuse and periods of incarceration. Clinical and management practices follow the stages above but with a length of stay of one to two months and are moderated to assure a flexible response to individual differences and the need for a menu of varied services. Each individual recovery service plan will be developed collaboratively to meet the individual needs of the participants.

15.7 The Journey of Hope Project: the outcomes

Three basic questions posed at the beginning of the JOH programmes include whether this complex population can be engaged and retained in treatment and what significant changes are necessary to do so.

First, can people with histories of chronic homelessness, severe addiction, co-occurring psychiatric and medical disorders and legal issues be successfully engaged through assertive outreach? Data collected from 2008 to 2010 confirmed high utilisation rates adding to the existing research confirming the value of assertive outreach by indigenous paraprofessionals.

Second, can people with histories of chronic homelessness, severe addiction and co-occurring psychiatric illness be successfully retained in treatment and successfully complete treatment at rates comparable to or exceeding the national average? The National Institute of Drug Abuse recommends a 90-day minimum dose of service, as published in the Principles of Addiction Treatment (NIDA, 1999). Nationally, on average, 39 per cent of those who start addictions treatment successfully complete the programme. Research has also shown that participants with shorter lengths of stay have poorer rates of post-treatment abstinence and higher treatment re-admissions rates. It is impressive that Susquehanna Park's successful treatment completion was 48 per cent in 2008, 52 per cent in 2009, 46 per cent in 2010, 71 per cent in 2011 and 50 per cent in 2012, with average lengths of stay ranging from 146 to 176 days.

Lastly, will the effective treatment of individuals with histories of chronic homelessness, severe addiction and co-occurring psychiatric illness require significant changes in treatment and service relationships? Clearly there have been dramatic changes to traditional treatment in the design of JOH programmes in order to attract, retain, effectively treat and support the on-going recovery process of our participants. This results in the positive outcomes well above the national norm for successful completion of treatment as cited above.

On a programmatic level, there were several factors that made the Horizon House Susquehanna Park programme successful:

- incorporating trauma treatment to address its impact on various dimensions of our participants' lives;
- creating a culture of inclusiveness and diversity e.g. lesbian, gay, bisexual, transgender, questioning and intersex community and varying cultural perspectives;
- community partnerships and collaborations (medical, recovery, education, vocational, religious);
- integrating physical health care into behavioural health treatment (Horizon House's federally qualified health clinic and the Abbottsford Falls Family Practice);
- lengths of stay spanning six months to one year;
- abandoning the practice of administrative discharges for "confirming a diagnosis" (alcohol/drug relapse);
- facilitating individuals obtaining personal Identification Documents (Pennsylvania driving licence or other ID);
- transitioning from a clinical orientation to a collaborative orientation;
- effectively varying programme structure based on each individual's needs;
- recognising that homelessness is a personal identity that must be replaced through treatment and recovery support;
- recognising that the threat of programme dismissal and homelessness has no potency for those with extensive street survival skills;
- discovering that life skills training may be more important as an early stage emphasis than traditional therapy (independent living skills, budgeting/finances, nutrition/cooking);
- shifting from going through "the Programme" to a menu of services and activities specific to each individual's Strengths, Needs, Abilities and Preferences (SNAP);
- abandoning concept of service/relationship termination following "graduation" and focusing on post-treatment recovery support process;
- emphasising the importance of a transition from a culture of homelessness to the culture of the therapeutic milieu to the culture of community recovery.

15.8 Challenges and proposed system changes

For many people, finding affordable and safe community housing was initially a major challenge. Throughout the literature on working with homeless individuals struggling with addiction, the availability of housing is cited as an essential component for successful outcomes. The Mayor of the City of Philadelphia, the OAS, and the Philadelphia Housing Authority designated housing vouchers for successful completion of JOH Programmes. Participants who successfully complete a JOH programme but need other types of housing due to behavioural health needs are provided with supported housing in an array of other programmes e.g. recovery houses, halfway houses.

Further challenges included budgetary constraints that impacted on multiple levels of the transformation system. As word on the street spread, soon there were not enough JOH beds to address the large homeless population, creating waiting lists resulting from the increased lengths of stays and programmes operating at full capacity. The 2012 elimination of state government sponsored cash assistance created monumental challenges for participants who successfully complete treatment, obtain subsidised housing and need means for basic necessities such as toiletries, cosmetics, household products etc. to sustain themselves in their apartments. This lack of personal funding also further stressed JOH provider budgets, which now had to supply those items throughout the treatment stays. Another long-term challenge affected by budgets is having a sufficient number of housing subsidies to support this treatment model. This includes variety of integrated services as well housing options, including accessible or senior housing.

Lastly, it is important to note that not all staff members working at the pilot sites successfully adjusted to the transformation in clinical philosophy and treatment strategies, due in part to their own entrenched experience in traditional addiction treatment philosophies.

15.9 Summary

During its first seven years, Horizon House Susquehanna Park has developed a unique approach to treatment for this complex population. Key strategies include assertive continuing care, comprehensive and ongoing assessment and collaborative counselling. With an emphasis on the integration of medical, behavioural and addiction services, Susquehanna Park offers rapid access to treatment, extended duration of treatment, person-focus, a therapeutic milieu for learning pro-social behaviour, development of recovery capital and linkage to recovery community resources. Discharge no longer is the end of the therapeutic relationship, but instead is merely a transition to sustained post-treatment monitoring, support and, if necessary, early intervention within the individual's current environment.

Acknowledgement

This chapter is dedicated to the late Bill Dinwiddie whose vision and direction inspired the development of the chronically homeless drug and alcohol treatment program at Horizon House.

References

Alford B. A. and Beck A. T. 1998. *The integrative power of cognitive therapy*. New York: The Guilford Press.

Bell P. 2002. *Chemical dependency and the African American: Counseling and prevention strategies, 2nd Edn.* Center City, Minn: Hazelden Publishing.

Burt M., Aron L., Douglas T., Valente J., Lee E. and Iwen B. 1999. *Homelessness: Programmes and people they serve*. Washington DC: Urban Institute.

De Leon G. 2000. *The therapeutic community: Theory, model and method*. New York: Springer Publishing Company.

Eyrich-Garg K. M., Cacciola J. S., Carise D., Lynch K. G. and McLellan A. T. 2008. "Individual characteristics of the literally homeless, marginally housed, and impoverished in a US substance abuse treatment-seeking sample". *Social Psychiatry and Psychiatric Epidemiology* 43(10): 831–842.

Fisk D., Rakfeldt J. and McCormack E. 2006. "Assertive outreach: An effective strategy for engaging homeless persons with substance use disorders into treatment". *The American Journal of Drug and Alcohol Abuse* 32(3): 479–486.

Greenberg, G. A. and Rosenheck R. 2008. "Jail incarceration, homelessness, and mental health: A national study". *Psychiatric Services* 59(2): 170–177.

Harris M. 1998. *Trauma recovery and empowerment*. New York: The Free Press.

Hawkins R. L. and Abrams C. 2007. "Disappearing acts: The social networks of formerly homeless individuals with co-occurring disorders". *Social Science and Medicine* 65(10): 2031–2042.

Hubbard R. L., Flynn P. M., Craddock G. and Fletcher B. 2001. "Relapse after drug abuse treatment". In F. Tims, C. Leukfield and J. Platt (eds) *Relapse and recovery in addictions*. New Haven, Conn: Yale University Press, 109–121.

Kertesz S. G., Mullins A. N., Schumacher J. E., Wallace D., Kirk., K. and Milby J. B. 2007. "Long-term housing and work outcomes among treated cocaine-dependent homeless persons". *Journal of Behavioral Health Services and Research* 34(1): 17–33.

Kuhn R. and Culhane D. 1998. "Applying cluster analysis to test a typology of homelessness by pattern of shelter utilization: Results from the analysis of administrative data". *American Journal of Community Psychology* 26(2): 207–232.

Larimer M. E., Malone D. K., Garner M. D., Atkins D. C., Burlingham B., Lonczak H. S., Tanzer K., Ginzler J., Clifasefi S. L., Hobson W. G. and Marlatt A. 2009. "Health care and public service use and costs before and after provision of housing for chronically homeless persons with severe alcohol problems". *Journal of the American Medical Association* 301(13): 1349–1357.

Malone D. K. 2009. "Assessing criminal history as a predictor of future housing success for homeless adults with behavioral health disorders". *Psychiatric Services* 60(2): 224–230.

Milby J. B., Schumacher J. E., Wallace D., Freedman M. J. and Vuchinich R. E. 2005. "To house or not to house: The effects of providing housing to homeless substance abusers in treatment". *American Journal of Public Health* 95(7): 1259–1265.

Milby J. B., Schumacher J. E., McNamara C., Wallace D., Usdan S., McGill T. and Michael M. 2000. "Initiating abstinence in cocaine abusing dually diagnosed homeless persons". *Drug and Alcohol Dependence* 60(1): 55–67.

Miller W. R. and Rollnick S. 2012. *Motivational Interviewing: Helping people change (applications of motivational interviewing), 3rd edn*. New York: The Guilford Press.

NIDA. 1999. *Principles of drug addiction treatment* (NIH Publication No. 00–4180).

Rockville, MD: National Institute on Drug Abuse. www.nida.nih.gov/PODAT/PODATIndex.html.

Padgett D. K., Stanhope V., Henwood B. F. and Stafancic A. (in press). "Substance use outcomes among homeless clients with serious mental illness: Comparing housing first with treatment first programmes". *Community Mental Health Journal.*

Prochaska J. O., DiClemente C. C. and Norcross J. C. 1992. "In search of how people change. Applications to addictive behaviors". *American Psycho*logist 47: 1102.

Poulin S. R., Maguire M., Metraux S. and Culhane D. P. 2010. "Services use and costs of persons experiencing chronic homelessness: A population-based study of sheltered and unsheltered persons in Philadelphia". *Psychiatric Services* 61: 1093–1098.

Sadowski L. S., Kee R. A., VanderWeele T. J. and Buchanan D. 2009. "Effect of a housing and case management programme on emergency department visits and hospitalizations among chronically ill homeless adults: A randomized trial". *Journal of the American Medical Association* 301(17): 1771–1778.

Tommasello A. C., Myers C. P., Gillis L. Treherne L. L. and Plumoff M. 1999. "Effectiveness of outreach to homeless substance abusers". *Evaluation and Programme Planning* 22(3): 295–303.

Triangle Consulting Social Enterprise Limited™ 2012. *Outcomes Star, Mental Health Recovery Star (2012).* Brighton, UK: Preston Park House.

Tsemberis S., Gulcur L. and Nakae M. 2004. "Housing First, consumer choice, and harm reduction for homeless individuals with a dual diagnosis". *American Journal of Public Health* 94(4): 651–656.

Tsemberis S. J., Moran L., Shinn M., Asmussen S. M., and Shern D. L. 2003. "Consumer preference programmes for individuals who are homeless and have psychiatric disabilities: A drop-in center and supported housing programme". *American Journal of Community Psychology* 32(3–4): 305–317.

White W. L. 2008. *Recovery management and recovery-oriented systems of care: Scientific rationale and promising practices.* Pittsburgh, PA: Northeast Addiction Technology Transfer Center, Great Lakes Addiction Technology Transfer Center, Philadelphia Department of Behavioral Health and Mental Retardation Services.

White W. and Kurtz E. 2006. *Linking addiction treatment and communities of recovery: A primer for addiction counselors and recovery coaches.* Pittsburgh, PA: IRETA/NeATTC.

White W., Kurtz E. and Sanders M. 2006. *Recovery Management.* Chicago, IL: Great Lakes Addiction Technology Transfer Center.

White W., Scott K., Dennis M. and Boyle M. 2005. "It's time to stop kicking people out of addiction treatment". *Counselor* 6(2): 12–25.

Wilbourne P. and Miller W. (2003). "Treatment of alcoholism: Older and wiser?" *Alcoholism Treatment Quarterly* 20(3/4): 41–59.

Zerger S. 2002. *Substance abuse treatment: What works for homeless people?* Nashville, TN: National Health Care for the Homeless Council. www.nhchc.org/Publications/SubstanceAbuseTreatmentLitReview.pdf.

16 Mental health services in prison

Sheila Howitt and Lindsay Thomson

16.1 Introduction

Institutional penal services worldwide have always faced the challenge of providing care to those suffering from mental disorders. Historically, and in some developing countries today, those with learning difficulties and severe mental illness have been inappropriately detained in prison due to poor understanding of mental illness; a perception that those with mental disorder are dangerous; and a lack of an alternative resource. In modern Western societies prison mental health teams are required to detect, diagnose and treat mental disorder in a socially disadvantaged cohort with complex needs.

In 2001 the World Health Organisation published *Mental Health: New Understanding, New Hope* (The World Health Report 2001) which stated that during their lifetime one in four people develop one or more mental disorders; and that the prevalence of mental disorder in the prison environment is much higher than in the community, as will be discussed in this chapter.

There are a number of challenges to the delivery of effective and comprehensive mental health care in prison, and for the purpose of discussion these can be divided into extrinsic and intrinsic factors. Extrinsically those aiming to design and deliver services can encounter opposition at times from financially and morally reluctant politicians and members of the public, encouraged by the media, who believe that prisoners are less deserving of care and consequently funding than the general population. Intrinsically the team delivering care can be fragmented and often the trained members of the mental health team, including psychiatrists, psychologists and nurses, will rely on prison staff for monitoring and day-to-day management of mental health issues. This can lead to delays in the diagnosis and suboptimal management of mental disorder. The physical environment and prison rules are necessary to maintain order and safety but can cause difficulties by limiting access to prisoners to set, and often short, periods. The high rate of substance misuse within the prison population can also complicate the presentation of problems and the diagnostic process. Furthermore mental health services face the paradoxical challenges of drug seeking behaviour in those without mental illness and poor compliance by those most in need of care.

Table 16.1 Cross-national prison population rate 2013

Country	Prison population rate (per 100,000 of national population)
USA	716
England and Wales	101
Scotland	147
Germany	79
Australia	130
New Zealand	192

In 2013 there were more than 10.2 million people held in penal institutions worldwide and incarceration rates are increasing. Over the last 15 years the world prison population rose by 25 to 30 per cent, while the global population rose by only 20 per cent. Incarceration rates vary widely across the globe, reflecting politics, legal codes and socio-economic factors.

In this chapter we will discuss prevalence of mental disorder in the prison population, models of mental health care in prisons, the principle of equivalence and 'ideal' services.

16.2 Mental disorder in the prison population

There have been numerous studies to ascertain the prevalence of mental disorder within the prison population and some are summarised in Table 16.2.

In 2012 Fazel and Seewald published a systematic review of 81 publications from 24 countries encompassing 33,588 individuals and established the prevalence rates for psychosis and depression as set out in Table 16.3. In contrast to previous studies, they were able to include data from eight low, middle-income countries: Brazil, Dubai, India, Iran, Kuwait, Malaysia, Mexico and Nigeria. This supplemented the 2002 systematic review by Fazel and Danesh of 62 surveys from 12 western countries encompassing 22,790 individuals.

There is a plethora of reasons for the increased morbidity of mental disorder in the incarcerated population. As a demographic group, prisoners are predisposed to mental disorder due to socio-economic adversity, substance misuse and high rates of trauma. The prison environment itself is known to be detrimental to mental health with lack of meaningful activity, lack of privacy or conversely enforced solitude, limited future prospects and isolation from social networks all factoring.

Alongside mental disorder, rates of substance misuse are significantly higher among prisoners than the general population. A UK Office of National Statistics prison survey (Singleton *et al.* 1998), found that over three-quarters of prisoners were dependent on drugs, and a similar percentage of those assessed as hazardous drinkers also had two or more mental disorders. Fazel *et al.* (2006) conducted a systematic review of 13 studies totalling 7,563 prisoners and found the estimated prevalence of drug dependence to be 10–48 per cent of male prisoners and 30–60 per cent of female prisoners.

Table 16.2 Prevalence studies of mental disorder in prison

Authors	Country	Study cohort	Results
Singleton *et al.* 1998	UK	1,250 male remand prisoners	10% Psychosis 59% Neurotic disorder 58% Alcohol abuse 51% Drug dependence
Singleton *et al.* 1998	UK	1,121 male convicted prisoners	7% Psychosis 40% Neurotic disorders 63% Alcohol abuse 43% Drug dependence
Davidson *et al.* 1995	Scotland	389 male remand prisoners	2.3% Psychosis 24.8% Neurotic disorders 22% Alcohol abuse dependence 73% Drug abuse/dependence
Victorian Prisoner Health Study 2003	Australia	451	7.5% Schizophrenia 9.7% Manic depression 20.5% Depression 40%+ Alcohol abuse 70%+ Drug abuse
Andreoli *et al.* 2014	Brazil	1,809	3.4% Schizophrenia 2.9% Bipolar affective disorder 14.2% Depression 18.5% Alcohol related disorder 26.5% Drug related disorder
Falissard *et al.* 2006	France	799	22.9% Major depressive disorder 1.3% Bipolar disorder 15.4% Generalised anxiety disorder 6.2% Schizophrenia 8.9% Drug dependence 8.7% Alcohol dependence

Table 16.3 Prevalence of mental disorder: systematic review

Disorder	Prevalence in males %	Prevalence in females %
Psychotic illness (2012)	3.6	3.9
Major depression (2012)	10.2	14.1
Any personality disorder (2002)	65	42
Antisocial personality disorder (2002)	47	21
Borderline personality disorder (2002)	–	25

Crawford and Crome (2001) reported that a dual diagnosis of mental illness and substance misuse increases the likelihood of the development of a range of mental, physical and social problems as listed below, compared to those with a sole diagnosis of mental illness:

- increased suicide risk
- more severe mental health problems
- homelessness/unstable housing
- increased risk of being violent
- increased risk of victimisation
- poorer general health
- more contact with criminal justice system
- family and relationship problems
- history of childhood abuse (physical and sexual)
- more likely to fall through the net of care
- less likely to be compliant with medication and other treatments.

Of additional concern is the high rate of suicide within the prison population. Fazel *et al.* (2008) published a meta-analysis which revealed suicide to be five times more common in male prisoners than the community male population, and 20 times higher in females. They identified the following risk factors:

- occupation of a single cell
- recent suicidal ideation
- a history of attempted suicide
- history of alcohol problems or a psychiatric diagnosis
- being on remand.

The risk of suicide is particularly high during early custody and Shaw *et al.* (2004) found in a study of 172 suicides that occurred in prisons in England in Wales in 1999 and 2000 that 32 per cent occurred within the first week of custody and 11 per cent within the first 24 hours.

Recognition of the high rates of suicide has led to the implementation in many prisons of suicide awareness campaigns and policies, which will be discussed later in this chapter.

16.3 Special groups

Women in prison

There are more then 500,000 women held in penal institutions across the world. According to the World Health Organisation (Walmsley 2013), this typically constitutes between 2 and 9 per cent of a country's prison population, making women a small but important minority. Furthermore they note that the rate of increase of women in prison is higher than that of men. Due to the small number of women prisoners, there are few female prisons and consequently women convicted of a wide range of violent and non-violent offences are imprisoned together. This heterogeneous group has high rates of mental disorder and has complex needs, presenting a range of challenges to those aiming to deliver mental health care.

Women in prison have high rates of trauma, childhood abuse, socio-economic disadvantage and substance misuse which predispose them to mental disorder. For rates of specific mental disorder see Table 16.3. Plugge *et al.* (2006) recruited 505 women from two busy remand prisons in England and found that 42 per cent of responders drank in excess of government guidelines before imprisonment compared to 22 per cent of women in the general population. Furthermore 75 per cent of women had taken an illicit substance in the six months prior to imprisonment.

The prevalence of self-harm and suicidal behaviours is higher in female than male prisoners and the World Health Organization (2009) report *Women's Health in Prison* states that one-third of men and half of the women who self-harm in prison do so repeatedly. The Corston Report (2007) stated that, in England and Wales, women in prison were found to be 14 times more likely to harm themselves than men. In 2005, despite the small number of women in prison compared with men, 56 per cent of all recorded incidents of self-harm occurred in the female estate. Special note should be taken of mothers with young children. For those living in the community, motherhood can serve as a protective factor against suicide; this does not apply to mothers separated from their children in prison, especially where a lengthy sentence is anticipated or has been bestowed.

Prisoners with learning disability

In the general population the number of people with an IQ of less than 70 is said to be 2 per cent. Estimates of the prevalence of a learning disability in the prison population vary widely but are in the main significantly larger than this number. Hayes *et al.* (2007) found that 7.1 per cent of prisoners randomly sampled at one UK prison had an IQ of less than 70 and a further 23.6 per cent had an IQ of less than 80. In 1998 Singleton *et al.* found 11 per cent of male remand prisoners had an IQ of less than 70, 5 per cent of male sentenced prisoners had an IQ of less than 70 and 17 per cent had an IQ between 70 and 75.

The Prison Reform Trust Report *No One Knows* (Loucks 2007) found that people with learning disabilities are not routinely identified before entry to prison. Within the prison they are more likely to experience bullying and exploitation from other prisoners. There is evidence that they are five times more likely to be subjected to control and restraint procedures and three times more likely to be placed in a segregation unit.

Elderly

The population of older prison inmates is growing in Western countries and the Human Rights Watch Report (2012) *Old Behind Bars* found that the number of sentenced federal and state prisoners in the US who are aged 65 or older increased by 63 per cent between 2007 and 2010, while the total prison population grew by 0.7 per cent. This reflects an aging general population, and is compounded by an increase in convictions for historic offences including sexual offences. Elderly prisoners have increased social, physical and mental health needs as compared to their younger counterparts. Depression and anxiety are common in this group, with issues of social isolation and the prospect of death within the prison pertinent. Furthermore with increasing numbers of older inmates and high levels of vascular risk factors there will be greater demands on mental health services to detect cognitive changes and to deliver treatment and support inmates with dementia.

Typically prison buildings and internal environments are designed to accommodate young men, without physical or cognitive impairments. In some states of America there are purpose built prison units designed specifically to meet the needs of elderly, frail and dementing inmates. These have the additional benefits of protecting older vulnerable prisoners from exploitation and victimisation.

In the community, older adults are typically cared for by specialist mental health teams with expertise in the diagnosis and treatment of dementia. It should be argued that elderly inmates should have access to an equivalent service, especially as the majority of forensic psychiatrists will have limited knowledge and expertise in this field. Although not currently available in most jurisdictions, specialist mental health services for elderly prisoners are likely to be developed as need grows.

Young offenders

The majority of young offenders entering the penal system come from socially disadvantaged backgrounds and as a group they have higher rates of social care involvement in childhood than non-incarcerated peers. In a majority of cases of youth offending, efforts are made to avoid incarceration, to prevent separation from family supports and institutionalisation. Where this is not possible and a custodial sentence is bestowed, young offenders are typically accommodated in specialised units.

Youth offenders have distinct mental health needs including high rates of alcohol and substance misuse, prodromal and emerging psychotic illnesses and Attention Deficit Hyperactivity Disorder (ADHD). Rosler *et al.* (2004) found the prevalence of ADHD in a young offending population to be 45 per cent. ADHD is hypothesised to be a contributing factor in criminal behaviours and Lichtenstein *et al.* (2012) studied a cohort of 25,656 Swedish patients with ADHD and found that medication reduced criminality significantly. Despite this there is currently a reluctance to prescribe ADHD medications in prison due to concerns around drug misuse, and further research is required to evaluate the long-term effects of ADHD treatment in the prison population. It is the authors' belief that if a prisoner is identified via a robust diagnostic assessment as having ADHD, appropriate medication, including stimulants, should be available to them within the prison environment under appropriate supervision.

16.4 Models of mental health care in prisons

Mental health services for prisoners vary in availability, structure and quality across the globe. In many countries (including the Netherlands, the US, Germany, Australia and Sweden) general responsibility for prison heath care provision lies with the country or state's Ministry of Justice or Prison Administrator, while in other countries it lies with the Ministry of Health or National Health Service (including the UK, France and Norway). This can have important implications for available resources, levels of bureaucracy and delivery of cohesive care. It should be noted that wherever the general responsibility for care lies, there is likely to be a substantial contribution of external psychiatric care, for example by mental health professionals visiting the prison or by use of external inpatient beds. In the majority of regions basic mental health assessment and care can be delivered within the prison. However, there are exceptions to this, such as Denmark, Italy and Spain, where prisoners are referred to external services.

For prisoners suffering from some forms of mental illness, most commonly severe psychotic disorders, it may be necessary for the prisoner to be cared for in an inpatient setting. As part of gold standard care, this would include staff with specific training and expertise in treating psychotic patients. The European Commission (Salize and Dreβing 2007) report *Mentally Disordered Persons in European Prison Systems: Needs, Programmes and Outcomes* (EUPRIS) identified three models by which this can be provisioned for prisoners:

- psychiatric inpatient treatment within a prison hospital or prison medical ward;
- referral and transfer to forensic psychiatric hospital or ward;
- referral and transfer to general psychiatric hospital or ward.

Many countries operate a model of care whereby inpatient assessment and treatment is delivered either within the prison system or general psychiatric inpatient services (including Germany, Finland and Portugal). In others (including Sweden, England and Wales, France) inpatient care is delivered either in a forensic or a general psychiatric hospital. In the US and Belgium those requiring inpatient care remain within the prison system and will receive this care in either a prison hospital or a medical ward.

The referral of a mentally disordered prisoner to an external inpatient service can be challenging for a number of reasons as discussed in the *Healthcare Improvement Scotland: National Prisoner Healthcare Network Report* (2013). A legal framework must be in place whereby a prisoner can be transferred to a suitable bed promptly. Typically this takes place under the country's mental health legislation. This will certainly require liaison between prison and health services, but may require additional approval from government or justice departments. For those being transferred to general psychiatric services, bed availability and stigma attached to patients from prison can lead to delays in this process. Special consideration must be given to issues of security in this instance, and it is unlikely that a prisoner will be treated in an unlocked ward without additional resources. Where a prisoner is to be transferred to a specialist Forensic Psychiatric Service, consideration must be given to the level of security required for the prisoner, taking into account the nature of the index offence, previous offending and current level of aggression displayed. For those convicted of serious offences such as murder or rape, a high secure hospital environment would normally be appropriate.

The mental health needs of the prison population are heterogenic and as such the prison mental health services must encompass primary, community and specialist care. As in the community, anxiety and mood disorders are common (see Tables 16.2 and 16.3) and should be treated according to local guidelines such as the NICE guidelines in the UK (National Institute for Health and Care Excellence). Ideally a general prison doctor, responsible for the primary care needs of the prison population, should manage those suffering from mild to moderate mental illness, as would typically occur in a community setting. Where available and appropriate, they should prescribe such treatments as self-help, antidepressant medication or psychological therapies, such as cognitive behavioural therapy (CBT). Modern computer based self-help or CBT programmes may be of particular use in this group, and have the benefit of reduced staff input, allowing limited resources to be utilised in other areas.

It should be noted that psychological therapies are not currently available to prisoners in many regions, reflecting limited resources and historic prioritisation of services towards treatment of psychosis. Where psychological therapies are available, these are typically low level and delivered in a group setting, such as a relaxation group. For those with more severe mood disorders or psychotic illnesses, review by a psychiatrist should be available, alongside indicated biological treatment and ongoing care and monitoring by a mental health nursing team. As discussed above, specialist inpatient care may be required and specialist consideration must be given to those who are unable, or unwilling, to consent to treatment.

16.5 Treatment without consent

The treatment of prison inmates without their informed consent is a contentious issue. It can be argued that, as prisoners are deprived of their liberty, they are unable to provide valid consent; however, by following established human rights principles prisoners should have the right to refuse treatment, where they have the mental capacity to do so, even if this may cause them harm. Across the globe there are a number of approaches to the problem of the prisoner who is refusing or unable to consent to treatment, and this can be complicated by legal differences between sentenced prisoners and those on remand. In many countries, such as Scotland, England and Wales, and Norway, involuntary treatment for mental disorder can only be given in an inpatient setting outside the prison, e.g. in a general or forensic psychiatry setting. At the other extreme, in Hungary, according to prison law, a prisoner has no right to refuse medical treatment. In many countries, such as Portugal and the Netherlands, involuntary care can be delivered, when indicated, in either a prison setting or a psychiatric one. It is important to note that wherever involuntary treatment is utilised prisoners must be treated in accordance with Article 10(1) of the *International Covenant on Civil and Political Rights* which states "All persons deprived of their liberty shall be treated with humanity and with respect for the inherent dignity of the human person".

16.6 Principle of equivalence

As previously described there are a number of challenges to delivering effective mental health care in the prison environment. This can be compounded by a perception that prisoners are 'less deserving' of resources. Levy (1997, 1394) proposed that "prison health services should be as good as those in the general community". Article 12 of the 1966 United Nations *International Covenant on Economic, Social and Cultural Rights* recognises the right of every individual to "the enjoyment of the highest attainable standard of physical and mental health". This should be assessed by a well-defined framework for health care that examines what is available, accessible, acceptable and of good quality (AAAQ). The AAAQ framework has four key components:

- Availability: the sufficient supply and appropriate stock of health workers with the competencies and skill mix to match the mental health needs of the population;
- Accessibility: the equitable distribution of these health workers taking into account the demographic composition, rural-urban mix and under-served areas or populations;
- Acceptability: health worker characteristics and ability (such as sex, language, culture, age) to treat all patients with dignity, create trust and promote demand for services;
- Quality: health workforce, competencies, skills, knowledge and behaviour, as assessed according to professional norms and as perceived by others.

Exworthy *et al.* (2012) proposed that allocating resources by this model goes beyond the principle of equivalence of care due to the higher level of clinic need in the prison system: given the higher prevalence of mental disorder, socio-economic adversity and personal trauma, the prison population requires greater resources than the community.

16.7 Ideal prison mental health services

As identified, there is a range of issues that must be considered in developing an ideal model of prisoner mental healthcare:

- the principle of equivalence
- high level of need

- recognition of the unique challenges of the prison environment
- recognition of the need for partnership working with Criminal Justice Services
- challenge of co-morbid disorder and substance misuse.

Figure 16.1 summarises the components of an ideal prison mental health service. In order for appropriate care to be delivered, those in need must first be identified. Due to the high levels of social problems and substance misuse, those entering prison are less likely to have engaged with community health services than the general population; thus even those living with significant psychiatric problems may not have been diagnosed. Screening at time of reception offers the opportunity not only to identify problems, but also to promote engagement in this population. It is of particular import when the high rate of suicide in early custody is considered.

At time of reception to prison, a comprehensive assessment of physical and mental health should be conducted by healthcare staff. This should include establishing the presence of current or past symptoms of mental disorder, treatment and any hospital admissions. Ideally screening questionnaires should be

Screening

Referral system

Standardised assessment, including diagnosis and formulation

Treatment planning

Contribution to Suicide Awareness Policies and Procedures

Access to psychological therapies

Access to programmes that cover both clinical and criminogenic needs, such as substance misuse

Access to hospital beds or prison inpatient facilities

Access to independent advocacy

Liaison with family and carers

Throughcare

Developed standards and an inspection regime

Defined core competencies of staff

Provision of educational programme for prison staff

Figure 16.1 Components of a prison mental health service.

employed and these should enquire about current or previous suicidal thoughts or behaviours.

In order to meet the diverse range of needs, the prison mental health team must be multidisciplinary and should ideally have the following components: mental health, addiction and learning disability nursing staff; general practitioners; psychiatrists; and allied health professionals, such as social workers, occupational therapists and psychologists. There must also be close working with the prison services including liaison with governors and operational staff. Third party organisations and prison chaplaincy services are also of vital importance in providing support and pastoral care to the prison population. Each region should consider their own prison population and develop their mental health team/services accordingly, taking into account prevalence of disorder, available resources and environmental conditions. Within the team there must be clear leadership and supervision. Mental health staff must have the opportunity for continued professional development, with regular appraisal and training opportunities. There must also be regular workforce planning meetings and service auditing to ensure optimal team performance.

A range of treatment options should be available for use within the prison environment including psychotropic medication, psychological therapies and occupational therapies. Self-help and modern tele-mental health resources should be utilised, and have the additional benefit of reduced cost and security implications, for example less disruption to prison routine and increased access to off-site, highly skilled mental health practitioners.

For those identified as requiring transfer to hospital, due to acute or chronic disturbance or non-compliance with medication, the prison mental health team must have access to hospital beds and a clear transfer and admission policy, within a local legislative framework. Transfers should be performed without unnecessary delay and ensure appropriate handover of key issues. The multidisciplinary prison mental health team must have links with community services to ensure continuity to community care; this is of particular importance when high rates of homelessness and limited social networks are considered. Ideally there should be in-reach work to help improve engagement on discharge.

16.8 Communication

Regular and effective communication is integral to the success of any health service, but is of particular import in prison environments, where working between health, criminal justice and other services can be complex. This encompasses oral, written and procedural communication. As a patient group, prisoners may hold anti-authoritarian views and may be mistrustful of healthcare professionals. This can make it difficult to establish a rapport and to differentiate paranoid delusions from dissocial attitudes. Skilled communication by the clinician, both with the patient and to gather collateral history, is key to establishing a therapeutic relationship.

Beyond the therapeutic interaction with the prisoner, communication between health professionals and prison staff is vital to ensure that when a health need arises prison staff are equipped to identify it and liaise appropriately with the mental health team. Furthermore they may be called upon to monitor mental state on a day-to-day basis and ensure appropriate treatment is administered. This can only be done effectively when appropriate training is delivered to prison officers and other operational staff. Observed symptomatology and behaviour should be clearly recorded in written notes alongside resultant decisions and the rationale behind them. Within the prison system, an electronic tracking system should be utilised to ensure mental health records are transferred with prisoners and care is continuous.

16.9 Learning disabilities

The British Psychological Society (2000) gives three core criteria for learning disabilities:

- significant impairment of intellectual functioning
- significant impairment of adaptive/social functioning
- age of onset before adulthood.

Those living with learning disabilities are known to have greater health and social care needs. It is important therefore that prisons have robust systems in place to ensure regular review of physical health in this population, e.g. annual general physical assessment. Consideration must be given to the specific challenges in delivering mental health care to the learning disabled population, including difficulties in understanding and describing symptoms, difficulties in understanding information provided and complex care needs on release. Rates of epilepsy and brain injury are significantly higher in those with learning disabilities than the general population and for this reason organic psychosis must be considered especially when atypical psychotic symptoms are present.

At time of entry prisoners should be screened for learning disability. The LD Screening Questionnaire (McKenzie and Paxton 2006) is currently being utilised by the Criminal Justice Services in England and Wales. This questionnaire takes a maximum of five minutes and is useful in identifying learning difficulties. Training to raise awareness and understanding of learning disability should be delivered to all mental health and procedural staff. Psychological therapies and offending work should be tailored to a format appropriate and accessible to those with learning disabilities.

16.10 Co-morbid substance misuse

Given the increased prevalence of co-morbid substance misuse, and the increased care needs associated with this, prisons must deliver effective, cohesive and holistic care to those who use illicit substances. This should involve an evidence-based process by which substance misuse is identified at time of entry to prison. There should then be agreed operational and clinical policies by which cohesive care is delivered to those with a dual diagnosis. In many prison services this care is delivered by two different teams: addictions, and mental health. Specialist addictions teams should have expertise and protocols to safely deliver detoxification, substitute prescribing and psychological therapies. These should be aimed at reducing drug use, promoting abstinence and understanding the links between substance use and offending. It is likely that addictions teams will have less knowledge and experience of managing mental illness. Similarly, mental health teams may have limited knowledge of the management of substance misuse. For this reason it is important that appropriate training is delivered and that addictions and mental health teams work in partnership, or that services are amalgamated, to provide optimal care utilising available expertise.

16.11 Suicide awareness policies

As previously discussed, rates of suicide within penal institutions are significantly higher than in the community. In response to this the International Association for Suicide Prevention Task Force on Suicide in Prison published guidelines in 2007 which outlined key components of a model suicide prevention programme for all correctional facilities, regardless of size (Konrad *et al.* 2007). The key components of these guidelines are as follows:

- **Training:** All correctional, health care and mental health staff should receive suicide prevention training with subsequent yearly refresher training. In addition staff who have routine contact with inmates must receive appropriate first aid and resuscitation training.
- **Intake Screening:** All inmates should be screened for suicidal ideation as soon as practically possible on entrance to the institution. Screening questionnaires should enquire about static (historical demographic) and dynamic (situational and personal) variables. If an increased risk of suicide is identified, this should be recorded in the individual's file and communicated to all relevant parties.
- **Post-Intake Observation:** After initial screening there must be on-going vigilance for the development of suicidal ideation in all inmates. This should be achieved by routine security checks with attention paid to any change in behaviour or mood. Special attention should be paid around times of court appearance or any change in circumstance.
- **Monitoring:** This should be proportionate to perceived risk. Those felt to be at high risk of suicide will require constant supervision.
- **Communication:** This includes communication of identified risk with all relevant staff, referral to mental health team and regular multidisciplinary team meetings to review risk and associated precautions. There should be written documentation of precautions being taken and any subsequent changes.
- **Social Intervention:** Ideally inmates at risk of suicide should be housed in shared dormitories or cells, but where segregation is necessary they should

be monitored constantly. Some institutions have programmes whereby other prisoners take on the role 'buddies' or 'listeners', and the suicidal inmate may feel more able to trust these fellow inmates than staff.

- **Physical Environment and Architecture:** The physical environment of an institution should be designed to minimise potential ligature points and access to lethal materials. For some inmates with active suicidal thoughts and behaviours it may be necessary to utilise protective clothing and restraint. There should be clear policy around this and an understanding that least restrictive alternatives be used first.
- **Mental Health Treatment:** Those identified to be at risk of suicide should have a comprehensive mental health assessment and access to appropriate treatments, including psychopharmacological.

16.12 Management of high-risk offenders

Within any penal institution there will be a cohort of prisoners who have committed serious violent and sexual offences, and who pose a significant risk of committing further offences on release. Some of these offenders will suffer from one or more mental disorders, including antisocial personality disorder or psychopathy. Justice authorities around the globe have different strategies to reduce the risk of re-offending on release, if indeed release is considered. In some jurisdictions the death penalty can be imposed for those convicted of the most serious crimes and those who repeatedly commit serious violent crimes. The majority of western countries are able to impose life sentences, which may involve conditional release. In the US, some states have sexual predator laws that allow a patient to be civilly detained at the end of a custodial sentence if they are still deemed to pose a risk due to mental disorder. In Scotland, Orders of Lifelong Restriction came into operation in 2006 and provide indeterminate detention and life-long risk management for offenders deemed to pose an on-going risk of serious harm because "the nature of, or the circumstances of the commission of, the offence of which the convicted person has been found guilty either in themselves or as part of a pattern of behaviour are such as to demonstrate that there is a likelihood that he, if at liberty, will seriously endanger the lives, or physical or psychological well-being, of members of the public at large" (*Criminal Justice (Scotland) Act 2003*). A Risk Assessment Order can be applied by the court to an offender convicted of a serious violent or sexual offence, or an offence that endangers life. The emphasis in Scotland is on clinical risk assessment and there have been eight times more indeterminate public protection orders in England where there is no professional assessment of risk.

Special consideration must be taken of the psychological impact of facing an indeterminate or lengthy sentence and the prospect of death within custody. As with elderly inmates, this group should be considered to be at high risk of suicide. The European Court of Human Rights (2013) ruled in the Case of *Vinter and Others* v. *The United Kingdom* that whole-life sentences without any prospect of release amounts to inhuman and degrading treatment of prisoners. This ruling is being appealed, but if upheld will lead to revision in sentencing in affected European countries.

Prison offers the opportunity to engage high risk individuals in offending work and to address risk factors linked to offending, such as drug and alcohol misuse. From the point of sentencing a thorough risk assessment, ideally including scenario planning, is required to identify health, social and criminogenic needs.

16.13 Conclusion

Rates of imprisonment and rates of mental disorder in prisoners are high. We face a major challenge in the provision of mental health care within our prisons. In almost all jurisdictions the provision of mental health care in prisons is poorer than the equivalent found within the community. This must be challenged. Prisons require fully functioning and multidisciplinary mental health teams able to meet the demands of their populations. The provision of additional resources to prisoners may not be initially politically appealing but may become so if the argument regarding a potential reduction in recidivism with adequate treatment and through care is progressed. These needs and arguments apply to specialist populations such as those with autistic spectrum disorders or learning disability, and also to the increasing number of female and elderly prisoners.

Internationally there are significant differences in where and how prisoners with major mental disorder receive psychiatric treatment and whichever model is utilised health needs and security requirements must be considered. Those offenders suffering from major mental illness should be transferred to a health setting, ideally a Forensic Psychiatric Hospital. There they can receive expert care and appropriate medical treatment in an environment with a level of security proportionate to the individual's current and past offences, and where risk can be assessed and managed appropriately.

Prison mental health teams should engage with the training of correctional staff in basic mental health and suicide prevention strategies; they should look beyond their traditional roles of detecting and managing major mental illness, to the development of more sophisticated care for those with neurotic disorders or personality disorders. For example, there is good evidence that psychological therapies can be made available via tele-medicine and this allows their on-going use when an individual moves to the community. Similarly, joint work between mental health and criminal justice or correctional services for those presenting with problematic behaviours can improve outcomes.

References

British Psychology Society. 2000. *Learning disability: Definitions and contexts*. Leicester: British Psychology Society.

Corston J. 2007. *The Corston Report: A review of women with particular vulnerabilities in the criminal justice system*. London: Home Office.

Crawford V. and Crome I. 2001. *Co-existing problems of mental health and substance misuse ("dual diagnosis"): A review of relevant literature.* London: Royal College of Psychiatrists.

Criminal Justice Scotland Act. 2003. *Order of Lifelong Restriction.* Available at www. legislation.gov.uk/asp/2003/7/section/1.

Docherty J. 2009. *The healthcare challenges of older people in prisons: a briefing paper.* Prison Health Research Network. www.ohrn.nhs.uk.

European Court of Human Rights. 2013. *Case of Vinter and Others* v. *The United Kingdom.* Available at http://hudoc.echr.coe.int/sites/eng/pages/search.aspx?i=001–12 2664#{"itemid":["001–122664"]}.

Exworthy T., Samele C., Urquia N. and Forrester A. 2012. "Asserting prisoners' right to health: Progressing beyond equivalence". *Psychiatric Services* 63(3): 270–275.

Fazel S. and Danesh J. 2002. "Serious mental disorder in 23,000 prisoners: a systematic review of 62 surveys". *The Lancet* 359 (9306): 545–550.

Fazel S. and Seewald K. 2012. "Severe mental illness in 33,588 prisoners worldwide: systematic review and meta-regression analysis". *The British Journal of Psychiatry* 200: 364–373.

Fazel S., Bains P. and Doll H. 2006. *Substance abuse and dependence in prisoners: A systematic review.* Addiction 101(2): 181–191.

Fazel S., Cartwright J., Norman-Nott A. and Hawton K. I. 2008. "Suicide in prisoners: A systematic review of risk factors". *Journal of Clinical Psychiatry* 69(11): 1721–1731.

Hayes S., Shackell P., Mottram P. and Lancaster R. 2007. "The prevalence of intellectual disability in a major UK prison". *British Journal of Learning Disabilities* 35: 162–167.

Healthcare Improvement Scotland. 2013. *National prisoner healthcare network report.* Edinburgh: Health Improvement Scotland.

Human Rights Watch. 2012. *Old behind bars. The aging prison population in the United States.* New York: Human Rights Watch. See: www.hrw.org/sites/default/files/reports/usprisons0112webwcover_0.pdf.

Konrad N., Daigie M., Daniel A., Dear G., Frottier P., Hayes L., Kerkhof A., Leibling A. and Sarchiapone M. 2007. "Preventing suicide in prisons, Part 1. Recommendations from the international association for suicide prevention task force on suicide in prisons". *Crisis* 28(3): 113–121.

Levy M. 1997. "Prison Health Services". *British Medical Journal* 315(7120): 1394–1395.

Lichtenstein P., Halldner L., Zettergvist J., Sjolander A., Serlachius E., Fazel S., Langstrom N. and Larsson H. 2012. "Medication for attention deficit-hyperactivity disorder and criminality". *New England Journal of Medicine* 367(21): 2006–2014.

Loucks N. 2007. *No One Knows: Offenders with learning difficulties and learning disabilities.* London: Prison Reform Trust.

McKenzie K. and Paxton D. 2006. *Learning Disability Screening Questionnaire.* Edinburgh: GCM Records.

National Institute for Heath and Care Excellence. *Guidelines.* See: http://guidance.nice. org.uk/CG/Published.

Plugge E., Douglas N. and Fitzpartick R. 2006. *The health of women in prison: Study findings.* Oxford: Department of Public Health, University of Oxford.

Rosler M., Retz W., Retz-Junginger P., Hengesch G., Schneider M., Supprian T., Schwitzgebel P., Pinhard K., Dovi-Akue N., Wender P. and Thome J. 2004. "Prevalence of attention deficit/hyperactivity disorder (ADHD) and comorbid disorders in young male prison inmates". *European Archives of Psychiatry and Clinical Neuroscience* 254(6): 265–371.

Salize H. J. and Dreβing H. 2007. *Mentally disordered persons in European prison systems – needs, programmes and outcomes (EUPRIS) final report*. European Commission: The SANCO Directorate General. Central Institute of Mental Health. See: www.antoniocasella.eu/archipsy/Salize_EU_psy-prisons_31oct2007.pdf.

Shaw J., Baker D., Hunt I., Moloney A. and Appleby L. 2004. "Suicide by prisoners. National Clinical Survey 2004". *The British Journal of Psychiatry* 184: 263–267.

Singleton N., Meltzer H., Gatward R., Coid J. and Deasey D. 1998. *Psychiatric morbidity among prisoners in England and Wales*. London: Office for National Statistics.

Walmsley R. 2013. *World Health Population List, 10th edn.* International Centre for Prison Studies. www.prisonstudies.org/research-publications?shs_term_node_tid_depth=27.

World Health Organization. 2009. *Women's health in prison. Correcting gender inequity in prison health.* World Health Organization. See: www.euro.who.int/__data/assets/pdf_file/0004/76513/E92347.pdf.

The World Health Report. 2001. *Mental health: new understanding, new hope.* World Health Organisation. www.who.int/whr/2001/en/whr01_en.pdf?ua=1.

17 After prison

Managing re-integration, mental health and desistance from offending

Flora I. Matheson, Amanda Brazil and Pamela Forrester

17.1 Introduction

For women leaving prison, the process of community reintegration is one that involves preparation on multiple dimensions. Women need assistance during this transition period to improve their chances of living prison-free. This chapter presents a framework for understanding the conditions that 'ready' a woman for her transition to the community. This framework, entitled 'reintegration readiness', consists of both contextual and person-specific conditions. It is the interconnection between these conditions which can help 'ready' a woman for release. Barriers to reintegration are also discussed, as barriers can significantly derail any efforts which have been made towards readiness. Correctional jurisdictions and service providers must be aware of these interrelated conditions which make up reintegration readiness to help women succeed upon release from prison. Brief suggestions for practice are presented.

The majority of people in prison, regardless of their sentence length, will one day return to the community. Release planning is essential to ensure people being released from prison receive appropriate social and medical services that will enable them to be healthy and to remain prison-free. Therefore, it is important that the necessary supports are in place to help facilitate safe re-entry into our communities. "Inadequate transitional supports may increase the risk of recidivism for inmates, undermining a key goal of corrections..." (Gaetz and O'Grady 2006, 1). This amounts to a failure of the system to create a process that addresses the health and safety of those leaving jails and prisons.

The research community, health practitioners and policy-makers are well aware of the influence of social determinants on health and overall well-being. Social and personal conditions – social status, income, employment, social support, access to services, personal health practices, coping skills, childhood development, gender, culture and ethnicity – all influence health and well-being. These same social determinants of health are also very clearly the social determinants of imprisonment. Those incarcerated in prisons have a complexity of health and social needs, including personal experiences of poverty, violence and trauma, addiction, mental illness and homelessness. A majority of people in prison in the US, UK and Canada suffer from serious drug and/or alcohol problems (Belenko

1998; Correctional Investigator 2012; Light *et al.* 2013) and close to half have mental health concerns (Derkzen *et al.* 2012; Halliwell *et al.* 2007; James and Glaze 2006). Traumatic brain injury among prison populations (estimated at 50 per cent) is also higher than among the general population and this type of impairment can often make confinement and treatment extremely difficult (Colantonio *et al.* 2007). Likewise, the lifetime rate of injection drug use and rate of hepatitis C infection is higher among people in prison than among the general population (Zakaria *et al.* 2010). In a Canadian study, self-reported prevalence of hepatitis C infection was 31 per cent, a rate that increased by 50 per cent between 2000 and 2008 (Zakaria *et al.* 2010). Homelessness is also an issue for those leaving prison with an estimated one-quarter homeless at the time of imprisonment (Kellen *et al.* 2010).

The lack of a national strategy on homelessness and poverty in Canada creates undue difficulties in coordinating care for those with serious mental illness, addictions and criminal histories. Inability to be economically independent through conventional activities limits options and perpetuates the cycle of poverty, homelessness, mental illness and drug abuse. Anyone with a criminal record is exposed to considerable social stigma and few businesses are interested in employee candidates with a criminal history. The dehumanisation of the prison experience and rejection from mainstream society places someone leaving prison in a very precarious situation with few options to make positive life changes aimed at staying out of prison, especially when there is no national agenda to reduce or eliminate poverty and homelessness. Few available social and health services along with discrimination, including racial profiling (Wortley and Owusu-Bempah 2011; Wortley and Tanner 2005), create serious limitations to recovery from prison and drug abuse.

Gender is a particularly salient social determinant of health. Gender roles are tied to issues of powerlessness, access to resources and constrained roles; these are conditions that are particularly exacerbated in the lives of people in prison, especially women. Prior victimisation is a very real experience for women entering prisons in North America, the UK and Australia. Childhood physical and sexual abuse and neglect is high among women in prison ranging anywhere from 25 to 90 per cent depending on the sub-sample and definition of trauma (Browne *et al.* 1999; Cook *et al.* 2005; Green *et al.* 2005; Harlow 1999). Trauma is associated with serious, complex and interconnected health and social needs among women in prison: mental and physical illnesses, drug and alcohol addiction, unemployment and low educational attainment. Being gender-responsive to this complexity of need is essential to break the cycle of re-incarceration for women (Harris and Fallot 2001a, 2001b) and to enable them to overcome a social context of instability that influences overall quality of life and ability to sustain healthy behaviours.

While there is a large body of literature on effective treatment practices in prison like cognitive behavioural therapy and dialectical behavioural therapy (Andrews *et al.* 2011; Andrews and Kiessling 1980; Dowden *et al.* 2003), there are fewer studies and less knowledge on how to support people returning to the community after incarceration. Studies that do focus on the transition from prison to the community point to some of the pathways that may make re-entry easier for women who are leaving prison. Desistence from crime often means making lifestyle choices that may differ from previous experiences such as giving up old social networks, adopting the mother role, finding employment and engaging in treatment for addiction (Gobeil 2008; Kruttschnitt and Gartner 2003; Richie 2001; Stuart and Brice-Baker 2004). Being able to view oneself outside the label of 'prisoner' and create a new self-identity is also critical to help women desist from crime (Gobeil 2008; LeBel *et al.* 2008; Rumgay 2004). The time immediately after release from prison can be very challenging but with the appropriate health and social supports this transition can become an important turning point where positive change can begin (Michalsen 2013).

One of the most difficult challenges for women in prison is addiction. There is awareness in the field that addiction treatment for women is best delivered within a holistic model and one that appreciates the specific relational needs of women (for example their roles as mothers) and trauma-related experiences (Green *et al.* 2005; Kassebaum 1999; Matheson *et al.* in press). For women, effective timely aftercare programmes can further help them manage their addiction through either abstention or harm-reduction approaches. Managing the addiction allows them to focus on other need areas that will promote overall success in developing a normative, pro-social lifestyle (Prendergast *et al.* 1996; Strauss and Falkin 2001). But when addiction is coupled with mental health problems this creates further demand and challenges on their ability to develop these more normative lifestyles and can impact negatively on reintegration efforts. Women leaving prison with concurrent addiction and mental illness can have difficulty securing and retaining jobs and maintaining social support from family and friends. These life stressors can ultimately create vulnerability to homelessness and further criminal justice involvement (Benda 2005; Mallik-Kane and Visher 2008).

17.2 Addiction, criminality and change

How does change occur within the context of addiction and criminality? One of the most well known theories of change, developed by Prochaska *et al.* (Prochaska and DiClemente 1986; Prochaska *et al.* 1993) is the trans-theoretical model of change (TTM). This theory formulates behavioural change as happening in stages. These stages are not linear – a person may move back and forth (regress) between stages, and each stage is characterised by one's degree of readiness to engage in the change process. The TTM of change is often employed in prison treatment settings (D'Sylva *et al.* 2012). There are parallels between the TTM and the community reintegration process which itself can be iterative and marked by some successes and some disappointments along the pathway. The re-conceptualisation of the self from 'prisoner' to community member, mother, and/or daughter takes time and is made more difficult by broader societal issues like stigma and discrimination. Imprisonment itself shatters self-esteem and self-efficacy and reinforces and entrenches both the individual and collective labelling of people as 'prisoner' or 'drug user'. This then becomes the primary lens through which people leaving prison are viewed while citizen, mother, daughter or employee are secondary (Becker 1967). It is daunting to leave prison and face a world of stigma and discrimination. Transforming one's identity as 'prisoner' is imperative to build a full and productive life and women require special supports to succeed in this process.

Research shows that the desire, readiness or commitment to change is only part of the key to successful transition to community after prison. Therefore, there is more to the process than just what the TTM of change would suggest. Social environment (context) during this transition is also of central importance (Mallik-Kane and Visher 2008; Visher and Travis 2003). Internal attitudes, cognitions and emotions play a role in successful change but so too does the context in which a woman finds herself upon release. The neighbourhood of re-entry, meaningful opportunities (employment, volunteering, mothering), resources (access to health and social/community services, housing, disability income and food) and interpersonal supports (coping styles, instrumental supports, family networks) all work together to make the reintegration experience positive or negative and ultimately can determine whether the woman will have a successful reintegration experience. The available evidence suggests that readiness is developed through a synthesis of personal, interpersonal and contextual influences and the combination of these factors will enable women to successfully shift their identity from 'prisoner' to citizen (Visher and Travis 2003).

There are some precipitating conditions that create vulnerability for women and increase the likelihood of return to prison. These include depression, loneliness, and frustration; contact with family and friends who use drugs; and economic hardship (Harm and Phillips 2001). Given the difficulties faced by women leaving prison, readiness should be viewed as multifaceted and informed by internal and external processes. Prison initiatives and interventions that consider both the personal and contextual components of women's reintegration needs would be considered best practice.

The reintegration of women leaving prison requires strategies that can address the social, employment, behavioural, physical and mental health and housing needs of this population. Integrated pre-release planning and post-release case management could play a pivotal role in achieving better outcomes for women as they leave prison. It would enable women to develop tools and connections that will help them establish and maintain healthy lifestyles and stay out of the prison system. We employ the concept of 'reintegration readiness' in similar fashion to Doherty *et al.* (2014) as a conceptual framework for the re-entry needs of women leaving prison, building upon previous research on community reintegration for women leaving prison. This framework encapsulates the person and context specific conditions that enable women leaving prison to successfully re-engage with the community after imprisonment (Cobbina 2010; Dodge and Pogrebin 2001; Doherty *et al.* 2014; Gobeil 2008; Graffam *et al.* 2005; Mallik-Kane and Visher 2008; Severance 2004; van Olphen *et al.* 2006).

17.3 The reintegration readiness framework

'Reintegration readiness' (as illustrated in Figure 17.1) begins with the idea that women need to ready themselves for release. As conceptualised by Doherty *et al.* (2014) reintegration readiness consists of several interconnected themes: desire to change, self-esteem, institutional treatment, family and professional support and continuity of care. The concept of reintegration readiness can be viewed as the presence of both person-specific conditions (i.e. desire to change and self-esteem) and context-specific conditions (i.e. access to institutional treatment, family and

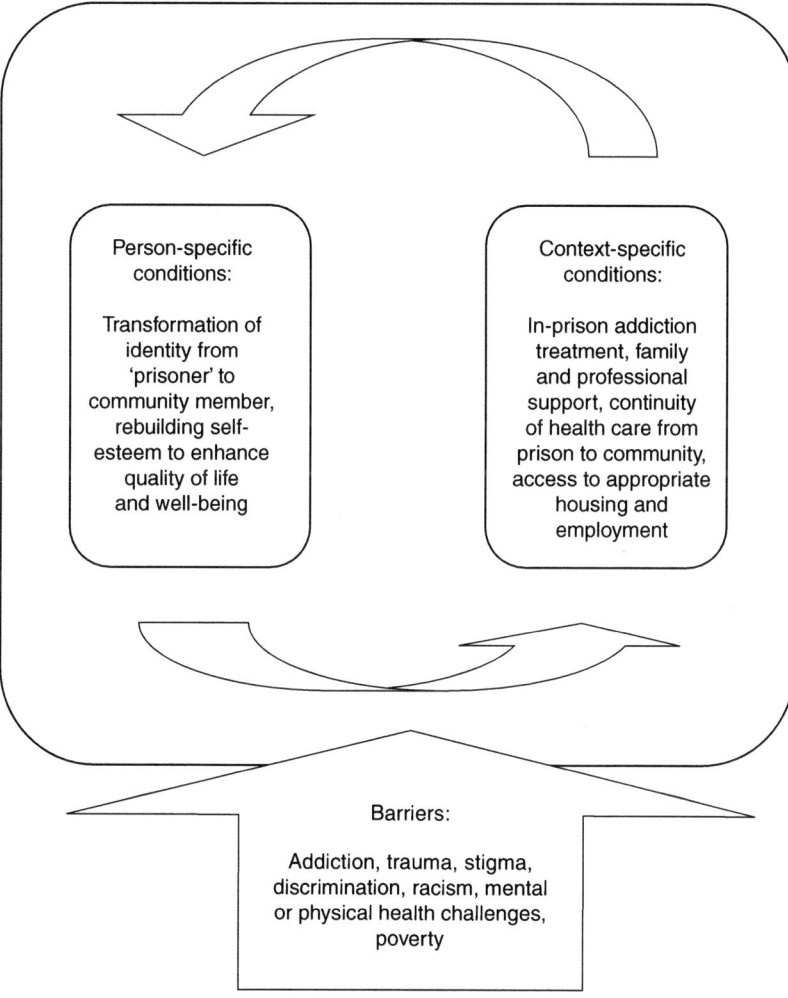

Figure 17.1 Reintegration readiness: the interaction between person-specific and context-specific conditions which facilitate readiness, while also recognising and addressing barriers to reintegration.

professional support, and continuity of care) that support the transition of a woman from prison to the community. This framework, first conceptualised by Doherty *et al.* (2014) emerged out of conversations with women who were in prison and who had left prison and were living in the community. It reflects women's thoughts about leaving prison and what would facilitate a positive reintegration experience.

Reintegration readiness may seem a straightforward concept, but in reality it encompasses complex personal and contextual processes. Navigating these processes is critical for women leaving prison as evidence shows that readiness influences the level of success achieved in the transition from a criminal behaviour to a healthy life position (Mallik-Kane and Visher 2008; Visher and Travis 2003). Figure 17.1 illustrates aspects of reintegration readiness (those originally formulated by Doherty *et al.* (2014) and additional aspects that have been identified from other literature on this subject and which will be addressed in later sections of this chapter.

17.4   Person-specific conditions and reintegration readiness

The person specific conditions within the proposed framework include a desire to change and self-esteem. Desire to change begins with the recognition of the need for alternative life choices and a personal belief that change is possible. Belief in one's ability to change is recognised as integral to the reintegration process for women leaving prison (Buchanan *et al.* 2011) and is connected to the desire to reshape identity. For example, Rumgay (2004) suggests that desistance from crime is tied to enduring and stable cognitive variables like personal identity, self-narratives and mindsets. She notes that change, within the context of the lives of women who spend time in prison, entails a shift in personal identity from 'criminal' or 'prisoner' to conventional identities like mother, student, or wife. First and foremost, a person must have the internal belief that an alternative identity is possible to achieve. If this is present then there must be valid opportunities to reach the new identity or identities (Rumgay 2004). The personal belief that you have the ability to create a new life and situational opportunities to do so are critical to recovery from prison (LeBel *et al.* 2008). Self-efficacy is also an important aspect of change. It is the belief that one can succeed in a given situation (Bandura 1977). For example, self-efficacy is known to be one of the most important predictors of stable remission from addiction among women (Moos *et al.* 2006).

Intricately linked to identity is self-esteem. Doherty *et al.* (2014) found that low self-esteem was a salient feature in the lives of women in prison. Past experiences of trauma, criminal behaviour, drug and alcohol addiction and imprisonment all contributed to the erosion of self-esteem among women in prison. Women in their study reflected on the links between feelings of low self-esteem and their drug use and criminal involvement. The authors also found that drug abuse was symptomatic of past traumatic life events – most notably childhood abuse and neglect, but also violence in adulthood – acting as a panacea to self-criticism and discrimination. Addiction and trauma are salient issues in the lives of women with criminal justice involvement (Clark 2002; Green *et al.* 2005; Grella *et al.* 2005; Herman 1997; Matheson *et al.* in press; Messina and Grella 2006; Moloney *et al.* 2009), and act as person-specific barriers to reintegration readiness. Most important for practice is the interconnectedness of the identified person-specific and context-specific conditions and the need to have these conditions addressed holistically to facilitate readiness. ✓

17.5 Context-specific conditions and reintegration readiness

The Doherty *et al.* (2014) framework also includes contextual conditions that impact on reintegration readiness. These include factors such as prison-based addictions treatment e.g. cognitive and dialectical behavioural therapy, family and professional supports/services and continuity of care. There is ample evidence that women who participate in addiction treatment are less likely to have further criminal justice involvement (Hall *et al.* 2001, 2004; Pelissier and Jones 2006). Experiential evidence shows that women want, and need, access to in-prison treatment which provides skills that help them to manage emotions and cope with cravings (Doherty *et al.* 2014; Matheson *et al.* 2009; Matheson *et al.* 2011; Prendergast *et al.* 1996).

Family support is essential for women leaving prison (Doherty *et al.* 2014). Supportive families help to encourage women to establish connections with law-abiding citizens and conventional institutions, while simultaneously providing them with a legitimate identity (Bazemore and Erbe 2004; Buchanan *et al.* 2011; Dodge and Pogrebin 2001; Golden 2005; Green *et al.* 2005). Familial and social support networks have also been found to be paramount to successful reintegration by helping women overcome substance use problems (Bazemore and Erbe 2004; Maidment 2006).

People leave prison with multiple health issues including addictions and chronic physical and mental illness (Derkzen *et al.* 2012; Freudenberg 2001; Green *et al.* 2005; Grella and Rodriguez 2011; Shantz and Frigon 2009; Wilper *et al.* 2009). Ensuring that women are connected with appropriate health and social services after leaving prison is challenging due to the complexity of needs, yet continuity of care is imperative to improve their chances to remain in the community (Hammett *et al.* 2001). Evidence from women in prison suggests that reintegration planning should be inclusive, such that prison staff and the women to be released from prison work together to design the re-entry plan (Doherty *et al.* 2014). Done in this way, the planning process can better meet the unique needs of each woman. An important part of this planning process is timely referrals and entry into community-based treatment as evidence suggests that community aftercare for addictions reduces the likelihood that a woman will return to prison (Grella and Rodriguez 2011; Matheson *et al.* 2011).

After leaving prison women often go to a new community, which can evoke anxiety (Doherty *et al.* 2014). Release planning that includes an orientation to the new community, and establishment of links to health and social services can help to alleviate fear of community life after prison (Doherty *et al.* 2014) and enhance women's chances to remain prison-free (Hammett *et al.* 2001; Prendergast *et al.* 1996; Robbins *et al.* 2009).

17.6 Barriers to reintegration readiness

Doherty *et al.* (2014) describe personal challenges faced by women leaving prison that can make the re-entry process more formidable. For those with childhood histories of trauma (neglect and abuse), drug use often becomes a maladaptive coping mechanism, a way to dull extremely painful memories. A woman's feelings of shame related to childhood abuse combined with those related to her own drug use and imprisonment coalesce, making it difficult for women to seek treatment. This can be very detrimental to her recovery and can have a negative impact on her ability to make the transition from prison to community. For some women it may seem they are swimming in a sea of addiction and trauma that thwarts progress towards recovery. Constant vigilance and ongoing care is integral so that women leaving prison have the social and health care supports to ensure their safety and recovery.

In addition to the barriers expressed by the women interviewed by Doherty *et al.* (2014) additional factors have been identified in the literature as barriers to successful community re-entry. These include poverty, access to safe and affordable housing; educational training and employment services; experiences of stigma and discrimination; family reunification (child custody and rejection by family) problems; and physical health concerns (Cobbina 2010; Dodge and Pogrebin 2001; Gobeil 2008; Graffam *et al.* 2005; Mallik-Kane and Visher 2008; Metraux and Culhane 2004; Severance 2004; Wormith *et al.* 2007; Zurhold *et al.* 2011) While a woman may have her sights set on successful re-entry, personal fortitude alone is not sufficient to ensure recovery from prison. Societal conditions may not afford a woman the ability to make positive changes while contextual conditions such as lack of housing, insufficient finances and lack of education and employment skills further impede reintegration.

17.7 Supporting and enhancing reintegration readiness: promising approaches for women

Building on previous research we have argued that reintegration readiness is a process that can be conceptualised as starting before women leave prison and which continues into the community. Conditions that impact on reintegration readiness and hence women's success in the re-entry process reflect a mix of person-specific and context-specific factors. We further argue that addressing context-specific barriers to success is imperative to ensure that women leaving prison can achieve health and well-being. For example, access to affordable housing is generally accepted as a first step in achieving health especially among those with mental illness, addictions and who suffer chronic homelessness (Goering *et al.* 2011; Kirst *et al.* 2014; Tsemberis *et al.* 2004). The housing first models are predicated on the notion that housing is a fundamental need and right and a primary social determinant of health. Getting people reliably housed creates a base for interventions that can address complex health issues including addiction and mental health problems that are paramount among women leaving prison.

The reintegration readiness model may be best supported with a holistic intensive case management model that provides support to the women in all aspects of the social determinants of heath. Intensive case management is defined as a single point of planning, monitoring and accountability for services for seriously mentally ill people in the community (thought to be beneficial for people leaving prison and who are facing complex service needs) (Solomon and Draine 1995) The fact that many women leaving prison have been heavily traumatised in childhood, often again in adult relationships and yet again by the experience of imprisonment speaks to the need for system-wide provision of services that are trauma informed (Green *et al.* 2005; Harris and Fallot 2001a; Matheson *et al.* in press; Messina and Grella 2006).

Case Management in itself is also often used to bridge clients between services and, in doing so, offer a more holistic and comprehensive approach to care. Case Management can also provide a focal point for a woman leaving prison especially if she has one consistent person with whom she can build rapport and develop trust. This consistent relationship can also help to promote self-esteem and a sense of control and reduce anxieties related to trauma, which are important person-specific components of change. A case manager may also minimise the need for a woman to have to retell her story to a myriad of service providers when seeking assistance. Ideally, community services would work together through formalised partnerships, funding initiatives or bundled (e.g. one-stop shop) services to meet the contextual needs of women upon release while the case manager or social worker can help her address person-specific conditions.

The reintegration readiness framework forces us to look critically at our social, health and justice systems and to move towards system-wide integration of services for women leaving prison, paying attention to the woman's multiple needs and her own understanding of the services and solutions that will aid in her journey to full health and well-being. If reintegration readiness is a synthesis of person- and context-specific conditions that enable success, then reintegration planning might be considered as a practice of case management, which simultaneously addresses all components of reintegration readiness. For example helping women to re-build self-esteem and overcome the repercussions of trauma may be the focus of social and mental health professionals, while lack of housing and employment opportunities are larger policy issues that need to be addressed at the political and societal level.

We argue that the reintegration readiness model must be supported with coordinated and holistic case management practices and systems integration. Only then will women receive the social, human services and health supports that will sustain them in their journeys to health. Such integration of services and systems needs to begin in prison, continue into the community and be sustained over the life course. One model that has been put into practice in a comparable population is Housing First (Goering *et al.* 2011; Kirst *et al.* 2014; Tsemberis *et al.* 2004). It reflects a more integrative approach to recovery for people with mental illness and addictions and is founded on subsidised housing as the first priority towards health improvement. The focus is on the provision of housing to those who are homeless, coupled with supports for mental illness and addictions. For people with more severe mental illness/addictions, the Housing First model employs assertive community treatment teams with intensive case management for those with less severe problems. Another component of Housing First is the belief in consumer choice – housing is not contingent on abstinence or medication compliance. Denying access to treatment and services or expelling people from treatment or services for relapse to substance use or non-compliance with medication is particularly paternalistic and puts people at additional risk of adverse health outcomes. The criminal justice model, for the most part, does not tolerate substance use relapse, putting people in jeopardy of being returned to prison, which places it outside such non-traditional approaches to treatment.

Yes, the idea that treatment and services need to be tailored to need is already embedded in criminal justice philosophy. Andrews *et al.* (2011) formulated the risk–need–responsivity model as a way to organise entry into prison interventions. Predicated on reducing future criminal activity the model reflects an approach that matches people in prison to interventions based on their risk of reoffending, the need to address modifiable risk factors to reduce reoffending and use of approaches to treatment that adopt social and behavioural learning theories to create change. The trauma literature argues that, for women, recovery happens when the consumer-survivor of trauma can regain her sense of mastery, control and autonomy (Harris and Fallot 2001a, 2001b) and be part of the recovery process. Trauma itself might be better situated as a risk factor for criminal justice involvement. Indeed, trauma is an almost universal experience for people who seek public services for mental illness, substance use, social services, homelessness and those with criminal justice involvement (Substance Abuse and Mental Health Services Administration 2014). If we situate trauma within the risk-need-responsivity model then it becomes an additional risk factor for criminality (Ardino 2010) ensuring that women are screened for trauma and supports and services are designed with the impact of trauma in mind. Identification of trauma prior to release and integration of trauma-informed practice into coordinated care would enhance health improvements among women leaving prison (Matheson *et al.* in press).

In terms of contextual needs, in the world of practice the issue of clients 'falling through the cracks' seems more often the rule than the exception. There is growing recognition that siloed approaches do not work for populations with multiple vulnerabilities – mental illness, criminal justice involvement, addictions, homelessness and family estrangement. Some collaborative services have emerged in response to this need: either informal community partnerships among service providers, or more formalised and documented collaborations. One example is the Allegheny County Jail Collaborative "which is arguably the most advanced and comprehensive collaboration-based social services reintegration programme in the United States" (Yamatani and Spjeldnes 2011, 54). This programme was established with the goal of increasing successful reintegration and reducing recidivism. The programme begins during incarceration and continues through release with seamless transitioning with services available from over 60 community-based agencies through the programme. It has proven successful and considered best practice boasting recidivism rates which are reduced by half (Yamatani and Spjeldnes 2011). Ohio's department of rehabilitation and corrections also developed community-based partnerships called citizens' circles. These circles challenge pro-criminal behaviour and are made up of a coordinator from the justice system and prisoner's support network and members of the community. As a group and in coordination with the release plan for each person leaving prison, an accountability plan is developed which addresses the social and personal needs of each person (Kane 2009). In developing policy recommendations for governments, communities and service providers to improve responses to people with mental illness involved in the criminal justice system, the Mental Health Consensus project found demonstrated success in partnerships (Council of State Governments 2002). "Identifying and engaging others with a stake in the problem builds a support network for its solution. Partnerships create a framework for moving forward" (Council of State Governments 2002, 9). Partnerships can help a fragmented service system work together to ensure the needs of the people they serve are addressed holistically. Collaborative roles have been proposed across the realm of helping services (Wormith *et al.* 2007).

17.8 Conclusion

To truly help women to succeed when they leave prison, reintegration planning must be viewed as a process that incorporates both the person-specific and the context-specific elements as identified by Doherty *et al.* (2014) and others (Bazemore and Erbe 2004; Cobbina 2010; Dodge and Pogrebin 2001; Gobeil 2008; Graffam *et al.* 2005; Mallik-Kane and Visher 2008; Metraux and Culhane 2004; Severance 2004; van Olphen *et al.* 2006; Walker 2009; Wormith *et al.* 2007; Zurhold *et al.* 2011). Services striving to support women must be cognisant that a holistic approach is necessary to address the complexity of needs of women upon release from prison. Such an approach will enhance women's motivation and their ability to make positive life changes. Release planners should also be aware of the impact of trauma and addictions on reintegration readiness and work with each woman to develop coping strategies that will offset the intense emotions brought on by traumatic life events and personal experiences of stigma, discrimination and marginalisation. The person- and context-specific factors that have been discussed in this chapter often are not explicitly embedded into release planning, but are central to readiness and to positive change.

References

Andrews D. A. and Kiessling J. J. 1980. "Program structure and effective correctional practices – a summary of the CaVIC (Canadian Volunteers in Corrections) research." In R. R. Ross and P. Gendreau (eds) *Effective Correctional Treatment*. Toronto: Butterworths, 441–463.

Andrews D. A., Bonta J. and Wormith J. S. 2011. "The risk–need–responsivity (RNR) model: Does adding the Good Lives Model contribute to effective crime prevention?". *Criminal Justice and Behavior* 38(7): 735–755.

Ardino V. 2010. "PTSD and criminal behaviour: Biology, emotion and cognition". *Conference Proceeding. In ESTSS workshop: The two sides of trauma. Victim and offender experience*. London, UK: London Metropolitan University.

Bandura A. 1977. "Self-efficacy: Toward a unifying theory of behavioral change". *Psychological review* 84(2): 191–215.

Bazemore G. and Erbe C. 2004 "Reintegration and restorative justice: Towards a theory and practice of informal social control and support". In S. Maruna and R. Immarigeon (eds) *After crime and punishment: Pathways to offender reintegration*. Cullompton, Devon: Willan, 27–66.

Becker H. S. 1967. *Outsiders: Studies in the sociology of deviance*. New York: The Free Press.

Belenko S. 1998. *Behind Bars: Substance abuse and America's prison population*. Columbia, OH: Columbia University, the National Center on Addiction and Substance Abuse.

Benda B. B. 2005. "Gender differences in life-course theory of recidivism: A survival analysis". *International Journal of Offender Therapy and Comparative Criminology* 49(3): 325–342.

Browne A., Miller B. and Maguin E. 1999. "Prevalence and severity of lifetime physical and sexual victimization among incarcerated women". *International journal of law and psychiatry* 22(3–4): 301–322.

Buchanan M., Murphy K., Martin M. S., Korchinski M., Buxton J., Granger-Brown A., Hanson D., Hislop G., Macaulay A. C. and Martin R. E. 2011. "Understanding incarcerated women's perspectives on substance use: Catalysts, reasons for use, consequences and desire for change". *Journal of Offender Rehabilitation* 50(2): 81–100.

Clark C. 2002. *Addressing histories of trauma and victimization through treatment*. Delmar, New York: The National GAINS Centre for People with Co-Occurring Disorders in the Justice System.

Cobbina J. E. 2010. "Reintegration success and failure: Factors impacting reintegration among incarcerated and formerly incarcerated women". *Journal of Offender Rehabilitation* 49(3): 210–232.

Colantonio A., Stamenova V., Abramowitz C., Clarke D. and Christensen B. 2007. "Brain injury in a forensic psychiatry population". *Brain Injury* 21 (13–14): 1353–1360.

Cook S. L., Smith S. G., Tusher C. P. and Raiford J. 2005. "Self-reports of traumatic events in a random sample of incarcerated women". *Women and Criminal Justice* 16(1–2): 107–126.

Correctional Investigator. 2012. *Annual Report of the Office of the Correctional Investigator 2011–2012*. Ottawa: The Correctional Investigator, Canada.

Council of State Governments. 2002. *Criminal Justice/Mental Health Consensus Project*. New York: Council of State Governments.

D'Sylva F., Graffam J., Hardcastle L. and Shinkfield A. J. 2012. "Analysis of the stages of change model of drug and alcohol treatment readiness among prisoners". *International *Journal of Offender Therapy and Comparative Criminology* 56(2): 265–280.

Derkzen D., McConnell A. and Taylor K. 2012. *Mental health needs of federal women offenders.* Ottawa: Correctional Service of Canada.

Dodge M. and Pogrebin M. R. 2001. "Collateral çosts of imprisonment for women: Complications of reintegration". *The Prison Journal* 81(1): 42–54.

Doherty S., Forrester, P., Brazil A. and Matheson F. I. 2014. "Finding their way: Conditions for successful reintegration among women offenders". *Journal of Offender Rehabilitation* 53(7).

Dowden C., Antonowicz D. and Andrews D. A. 2003. "The effectiveness of relapse prevention with offenders: A meta-analysis". *International Journal of Offender Therapy and Comparative Criminology* 47(5): 516–528.

Freudenberg N. 2001. "Jails, prisons, and the health of urban populations: A review of the impact of the correctional system on community health". *Journal of Urban Health* 78(2): 214–235.

Gaetz S. and O'Grady B. 2006. *The missing link: Discharge planning, incarceration and homelessness.* Toronto: The John Howard Society of Ontario.

Gobeil R. 2008. *Staying out: Women's perceptions of challenges and protective factors in community reintegration.* Ottawa: Correctional Service of Canada.

Goering P. N., Streiner D. L., Adair C., Aubry T., Barker J., Distasio J., Hwang S. W., Komaroff J., Latimer E., Somers J. and Zabkiewicz D. M. 2011. "The At Home/Chez Soi trial protocol: a pragmatic, multi-site, randomised controlled trial of a Housing First intervention for homeless individuals with mental illness in five Canadian cities". *BMJ Open* 1(2) e000323.

Golden, R. 2005. *War on the family: mothers in prison and the families they leave behind.* New York: Routledge.

Graffam J., Shinkfield A., Lavelle B. and McPherson W. 2005. "Variables affecting successful reintegration as perceived by offenders and professionals". *Journal of Offender Rehabilitation* 40(1–2): 147–171.

Green B. L., Miranda J., Daroowalla A. and Siddique J. 2005. "Trauma exposure, mental health functioning, and program needs of women in jail". *Crime and Delinquency* 51(1): 133–151.

Grella C. E. and Rodriguez L. 2011. "Motivation for treatment among women offenders in prison-based treatment and longitudinal outcomes among those who participate in community aftercare". *Journal of psychoactive drugs* Suppl 7: 58–67.

Grella C. E., Stein J. A. and Greenwell L. 2005. "Associations among childhood trauma, adolescent problem behaviors, and adverse adult outcomes in substance-abusing women offenders". *Psychology of Addictive Behaviors* 19(1): 43–53.

Hall E. A., Baldwin D. M. and Prendergast M. L. 2001. "Women on parole: Barriers to success after substance abuse treatment". *Human organization* 60(3): 225–233.

Hall E. A., Prendergast M. L., Patten M., Cao Y. and Wellisch J. 2004. "Treating drug-abusing women prisoners: An outcomes evaluation of the Forever Free Program". *The Prison Journal* 84(1): 81–105.

Halliwell E., Main L. and Richardson C. 2007. *The Fundamental Facts: The latest facts and figures on mental health.* London: Mental Health Foundation.

Hammett T. M., Roberts C. and Kennedy S. 2001. "Health-related issues in prisoner reentry". *Crime and Delinquency* 47(3): 390–409.

Harlow C. W. 1999. *Prior abuse reported by inmates and probationers.* Washington DC: Dept. of Justice, Office of Justice Programs: Bureau of Justice Statistics.

Harm N. J. and Phillips S. D. 2001. "You can't go home again: Women and criminal recidivism". *Journal of Offender Rehabilitation* 32(3): 3–21.

Harris M. and Fallot R. D. 2001a. "Envisioning a trauma-informed service system: A vital paradigm shift." *New Directions for Mental Health Services* 2001(89): 3–22.

Harris M. and Fallot R. D. 2001b. *Using trauma theory to design service systems.* San Francisco: Jossey-Bass.

Herman J. L. 1997. *Trauma and recovery.* New York: BasicBooks.

James D. J. and Glaze L. E. 2006. *Mental health problems of prison and jail inmates.* Washington DC: Bureau of Justice Statistics.

Kane L. 2009. "Partnerships between states and CFBOs: Challenges and opportunities". *Corrections Today* 71: 68.

Kassebaum P. 1999. *Substance abuse treatment for women offenders: Guide to promising practices.* Rockville, MD: US Department of Health and Human Services.

Kellen A., Freedman J., Novac S., Lapointe L., Maaranen R. and Wong A. 2010. *Homeless and jailed: Jailed and homeless.* Toronto: The John Howard Society of Toronto.

Kirst M., Zerger S., Wise H. D., Plenert E. and Stergiopoulos V. 2014. "The promise of recovery: Narratives of hope among homeless individuals with mental illness participating in a Housing First randomised controlled trial in Toronto, Canada". *BMJ Open* 4 (3).

Kruttschnitt C. and Gartner R. 2003. "Women's Imprisonment". *Crime and Justice* 30: 1–81.

LeBel T. P., Burnett R., Maruna S. and Bushway S. 2008. "The 'chicken and egg' of subjective and social factors in desistance from crime". *European Journal of Criminology* 5(2): 131–159.

Light M., Grant E. and Hopkins K. 2013. *Gender differences in substance misuse and mental health amongst prisoners: Results from the Surveying Prisoner Crime Reduction (SPCR) longitudinal cohort study of prisoners.* London: Ministry of Justice Analytical Services.

Maidment M. R. 2006. *Doing time on the outside: deconstructing the benevolent community.* Toronto: University of Toronto Press.

Mallik-Kane K. and Visher C. A. 2008. *Health and prisoner reentry: How physical, mental, and substance abuse conditions shape the process of reintegration,* Washington DC: Urban Institute, Justice Policy Center.

Matheson F. I., Doherty, S. and Grant B. 2009. *Women offender substance abuse programming and community reintegration.* Ottawa: Correctional Service of Canada.

Matheson F. I., Doherty S. and Grant B. A. 2011. "Community-based aftercare and return to custody in a national sample of substance-abusing women offenders". *American Journal of Public Health* 101(6): 1126–1132.

Matheson F. I., Brazil A., Doherty S. and Forrester P. 2014. "A call for help: Women offenders' reflections on trauma care". *Women and Criminal Justice.*

Messina N. and Grella C. 2006. "Childhood trauma and women's health outcomes in a California prison population". *American Journal of Public Health* 96(10): 1842–1848.

Metraux S. and Culhane D. P. 2004. "Homeless shelter use and reincarceration following prison release". *Criminology and Public Policy* 3(2): 139–160.

Michalsen V. 2013. "A cell of one's own? Incarceration and other turning points in women's journeys to desistance". *International Journal of Offender Therapy and Comparative Criminology.* Published online 1 September 2013: DOI: 10.1177/0306624X13498211: 1–20.

Moloney K. P., van den Bergh B. J. and Moller L. F. 2009. "Women in prison: The central issues of gender characteristics and trauma history". *Public health* 123(6): 426–430.

Moos R. H., Moos B. S. and Timko C. 2006. "Gender, treatment and self-help in remission from alcohol use disorders". *Clinical medicine and research* 4(3): 163–174.

van Olphen J., Freudenberg N., Fortin P. and Galea S. 2006. "Community reentry: Perceptions of people with substance use problems returning home from New York City jails". *Journal of Urban Health* 83(3): 372–381.

Pelissier B. M. M. and Jones N. 2006. "Differences in motivation, coping style and self-efficacy among incarcerated male and female drug users". *Journal of substance abuse treatment* 30(2): 113–120.

Prendergast M. L., Wong M. M. and Wellisch J. 1996. "Residential treatment for women parolees following prison-based drug treatment: Treatment experiences, needs and services, outcomes". *The Prison Journal* 76(3) 253–274.

Prochaska J. O. and DiClemente C. C. 1986. "Toward a comprehensive model of change". In N. Heather and W. R. Miller (eds) *Treating addictive behaviors: Processes of change.* New York: Plenum Press, 3–27.

Prochaska J. O., DiClemente C. C. and Norcross J. C. 1993. "In search of how people change: Applications to addictive behaviors". *Journal of Addictions Nursing* 5(1): 2–16.

Richie B. E. 2001. "Challenges incarcerated women face as they return to their communities: Findings from life history interviews". *Crime and Delinquency* 47(3): 368–389.

Robbins C. A., Martin S. S. and Surratt H. L. 2009. "Substance abuse treatment, anticipated maternal roles, and reentry success of drug-involved women prisoners". *Crime and Delinquency* 55(3): 388–411.

Rumgay J. 2004. "Scripts for safer survival: Pathways out of female crime". *The Howard Journal of Criminal Justice* 43(4): 405–419.

Severance T. A. 2004. "Concerns and coping strategies of women inmates concerning release: 'It's going to take somebody in my corner'". *Journal of Offender Rehabilitation* 38(4) 73–97.

Shantz L. R. and Frigon S. 2009. "Aging, women and health: From the pains of imprisonment to the pains of reintegration". *International Journal of Prisoner Health* 5(1) 3–15.

Solomon P. and Draine J. 1995. "One-year outcomes of a randomized trial of case management with seriously mentally ill clients leaving jail". *Evaluation Review* 19(3): 256–273.

Strauss S. M. and Falkin G. P. 2001. "Social support systems of women offenders who use drugs: A focus on the mother-daughter relationship". *The American Journal of Drug and Alcohol Abuse* 27(1): 65–89.

Stuart B. and Brice-Baker J. 2004. "Correlates of higher rates of recidivism in female prisoners: An exploratory study". *Journal of Psychiatry and Law* 32(1): 29–70.

Substance Abuse and Mental Health Services Administration. 2014. *Creating a trauma-informed criminal justice system for women: WHY AND HOW.* GAINS Center. http://gainscenter.samhsa.gov/cms-assets/documents/62753–983160.ticjforwmn.pdf.

Tsemberis S., Gulcur L. and Nakae M. 2004. "Housing First, consumer choice, and harm reduction for homeless individuals with a dual diagnosis". *American Journal of Public Health* 94(4): 651–656.

Visher C. A. and Travis J. 2003. "Transitions from prison to community: Understanding individual pathways". *Annual Review of Sociology* 29: 89–113.

Walker L. 2009. "Modified restorative circles: A reintegration group planning process that promotes desistance". *Contemporary Justice Review* 124: 419–431.

Wilper A. P., Woolhandler S., Boyd J. W., Lasser K., McCormick D., Bor D. H. and Himmelstein D. U. 2009. "The health and health care of US prisoners: Results of a nationwide survey". *American Journal of Public Health* 99(4): 666–672.

Wormith J. S., Althouse R., Simpson M., Reitzel L. R., Fagan T. J. and Morgan R. D. 2007. "The rehabilitation and reintegration of offenders: The current landscape and some future directions for correctional psychology". *Criminal Justice and Behavior* 34(7): 879–892.

Wortley S. and Owusu-Bempah A. 2011. "The usual suspects: Police stop and search practices in Canada". *Policing and Society* 21(4): 395–407.

Wortley S. and Tanner, J. 2005. "Inflammatory rhetoric? Baseless accusations? A response to Gabor's critique of racial profiling research in Canada". *Canadian Journal of Criminology and Criminal Justice/La Revue canadienne de criminologie et de justice pénale* 47(3): 581–610.

Yamatani H. and Spjeldnes S. 2011. "Saving our criminal justice system: The efficacy of a collaborative social service". *Social Work* 56(1): 53–61.

Zakaria D., Thompson J. M., Jarvis A. and Borgatta F. 2010. *Summary of emerging findings from the 2007 National Inmate Infectious Diseases and Risk-Behaviours Survey.* Ottawa: Correctional Service of Canada.

Zurhold H., Moskalewicz J., Sanclemente C., Schmied G., Shewan D. and Verthein U. 2011. "What affects reintegration of female drug users after prison release? Results of a European follow-up study". *Journal of Offender Rehabilitation* 50(2): 49–65.

18 Substance abuse and offending

Pathways to recovery

David Best and Michael Savic

18.1 Introduction

In the conclusion to *Making Good*, Maruna (2001, 166) argues that "societies that do not believe that offenders can change will get offenders who do not believe that they can change". This quotation comes from the description of the sample in the Liverpool Desistance Study (LDS), in which it is clear that desistance from offending and addiction recovery are frequently the same thing. Indeed, in describing his sample of desisting and continuing offenders, Maruna observes that "almost every LDS participant ... admitted to regular drug use at some point in their lives and two-thirds ... said they had at some point been dependent or addicted to alcohol or drugs" (Maruna 2001, 62). This is particularly worrying where Maruna describes a concern that the US is employing a 'waste management' model of corrections in which the aim of interventions is neither to correct nor punish but rather is to incapacitate and control. Similar anxieties have been expressed in the treatment of illicit drugs, where substitute prescribing has provoked fears about the low aspirations of indefinite treatments.

Maruna (2001) also makes the point – and cites one of the Liverpool participants – that there is no shortage of services and support available while you are offending or using; however once you have started a desistance journey, there is almost no support available. This is compounded by the concern, expressed in the context of youth offenders, that while incarceration provides a space where young people generate desistance narratives, the youth justice space does not offer them the supports or resources to develop the links and skills needed to build on the foundations of imagined desistance (Soyer 2014). So young offenders can imagine a future free from crime, but they are not offered the skills or supports to make this a reality.

However, Maruna's work is not pessimistic and describes the successful self-narratives of those managing to achieve desistance (or recovery), based on the premise that desistance from crime necessitates making sense of a new identity that in turn requires a successful self-narrative of change. The successful ex-offenders "need a coherent, prosocial identity for themselves" (Maruna 2001, 7). This process may result in the evolution of a 'redemption' script or a generative story in which the person turns bad to good by giving back to their families or communities. Indeed, Maruna cites Alcoholics Anonymous (AA) as a powerful example of sustaining the desistance journey by 'giving back' and the important role of this form of growth in sustaining desistance.

This chapter will examine the recovery or desistance journey, primarily from the perspective of alcohol and drug recovery, in terms of the impact of community factors – societal beliefs and responses to recovery – on individual beliefs and experiences about what is possible in a recovery pathway or journey. This will be illustrated using two pilot projects in two Australian states: the first in the Magistrates Court in Dandenong, in south-east Melbourne, Victoria, and the second in Dooralong, an alcohol and drug rehabilitation centre on the Central Coast in New South Wales. The aim of the chapter will be to outline how communities – including professionals' attitudes – can act as facilitators or barriers to personal recovery and what impact such beliefs and attitudes have on recovery pathways and trajectories. The central aim is to outline an ecology of recovery or desistance that is based on environmental factors that create the 'ground' for the personal challenges of identity change. The chapter assumes a parallel between addiction recovery and criminal desistance that is in part predicated on the observation that, as Maruna (2001) points out, we are often talking about the same people in any case.

18.2 What is addiction recovery?

In the US, the Betty Ford Institute Consensus Group produced a definition of recovery as "a voluntarily maintained lifestyle characterised by sobriety, personal health and citizenship" (Betty Ford Institute Consensus Panel 2007, 222): the subsequent UK definition from the UK Drug Policy Commission (UKDPC) is broadly similar in both scope and composition. According to the UKDPC, recovery is "voluntarily sustained control over substance use which maximises health and well-being and participation in the rights, roles and responsibilities of society" (UK Drug Policy Commission (UKDPC) 2008, 6). In the context of mental health recovery, Deegan (1998, 11) argues that: "recovery refers to the lived experience of people as they accept and overcome the challenge of disability ... they experience themselves as recovering a new sense of self and of purpose within and beyond the limits of the disability". This latter definition is important as it asserts the subjective as a key component of the recovery experience.

The US Substance Abuse and Mental Health Services Administration (SAMHSA 2012) identified four major dimensions of recovery: health (overcoming or managing one's symptoms); home (a safe place to live); purpose (meaningful daily activities); and community (social networks that provide support, friendship, love and hope). In the ten guiding principles that SAMHSA identify, four are socially or community focused: recovery is supported by peers and allies; recovery is supported through relationships and social networks; recovery is culturally-based and influenced; and recovery involves individual, family and community strengths and responsibility.

Although there have been concerns about the operationalisation of recovery, recovery rates have been estimated in a number of studies. In a review of the existing evidence, Sheedy and Whitter (2009) estimated that 58 per cent of those who have lifetime substance dependence will eventually achieve full recovery. White (2012) has reviewed overall remission rates in a review analysis of 415 scientific reports between 1868 and 2011, and has concluded that an average of 49.9 per cent of those with a lifetime substance use disorder will eventually achieve stable recovery (and this rate increases to 53.9 per cent in studies published since the year 2000). White also argues that between 5.3 and 15.3 per cent of the adult population of the US are in recovery from a substance use disorder. This suggests a high prevalence of recovery in the general population and a rate of recovery that exceeds the lay expectation.

18.3 Personal, social and community recovery capital

It does not, however, answer the question of who will recover and who will not. There is a strong argument that the transition to recovery from substance use involves identity change, echoing the view of Maruna (2001) above. The idea of identity change as central to recovery was first advanced by Biernacki (1986) who argued that, in order to achieve recovery, "addicts must fashion new identities, perspectives and social world involvements wherein the addict identity is excluded or dramatically depreciated" (Biernacki 1986, 141). Building on this theme, McIntosh and McKeganey's (2002) analysed the recovery stories of 70 ex-addicts. They concluded that, through substance misuse, the addicts' "identities have been seriously damaged by their addiction" (McIntosh and McKeganey 2002, 152) and that recovery necessitates the restoration of a spoiled identity. This restoration would appear to have a strong social quality, in which identity is embedded in social activities and social networks.

Litt and colleagues (2007; 2009) assigned individuals who completed residential detoxification from alcohol use to either standard aftercare or to a 'network support' intervention that involved developing a relationship with at least one non-drinking peer. Those who added at least one non-drinking member to their social network showed a 27 per cent increase in the likelihood of treatment success at 12 months post-treatment (defined as being without alcohol 90 per cent of the time) compared to people receiving standard after-care. This is consistent with the findings of Beattie and Longabaugh (1999) that while both general and abstinence-specific support predicted abstinence in alcoholics at three months post-treatment, only social support for abstinence goals predicted longer-term abstinence (at 15 months post-treatment).

The importance of social factors is illustrated in the concept of 'recovery capital' (Granfield and Cloud, 2001), which referred to four types of capital: personal, physical, cultural and social, to cover material possessions, personal skills and capabilities, support and friendship networks, and community resources. The concept of recovery capital offers a tantalising possibility of a metric for the quantification of recovery, but this development remains at an early stage.

Underpinning this idea is the concept of social capital described by Putnam (2000) as the supports and resources that an individual has access to and perceives themselves as able to make use of. The notion of social capital also refers to the relational quality involved; in other words, social capital is not simply a 'reserve' of resources, rather it is the embedding of the individual in social relationships and bonds that are dynamic and binding. This is particularly important for the concept of community or cultural capital, as at this level it will refer not only to what the resources available in the community are, but also to the extent that they are perceived as both accessible and desirable by the person in recovery.

The idea of cultural capital is particularly important for the concept of addiction recovery as it relates to the supports and resources available in the community. At one level, these are practical resources like houses and jobs, and other tangible resources that make a community accessible and available. It is linked to social capital in the need to have bridging to resources in the community and the accessibility and availability of supports. But cultural capital also relates to the level of community integration or disintegration that make such resources accessible and available to people. And these resources are not equivalent for everyone. Those who are excluded or stigmatised may not come to know about such resources because they may have low bridging capital. Putnam (2000) discussed two types of social capital: (1) bonding capital refers to the connections between people who belong to the same group (e.g. connections between supporters of the same sporting team); and, (2) bridging capital relates to connections between people of different groups (e.g. supporters of different sporting teams). People who are socially excluded may have a social network consisting of other socially excluded people and so their network has limited bridges to resources available in the community.

Thus, in a study of drug-using offenders assertively engaged in sports activities in the north-east of England, as a form of diversion from custody, one of the key success factors was building not only a new set of social bonds and relationships, but relationships with people who had access to community supports and resources (Landale and Best 2012). In this study, young drug-using offenders were offered a diversion programme called Second Chance that enabled them to engage in sports activities, primarily a soccer team, to build self-esteem and resilience (personal capital) as well as a sense of belonging and a positive identity (social capital). However, one of the major successes of the programme was creating new links to community resources such as housing and employment opportunities (cultural capital) that allowed the young people to translate the gains made in the programme to sustainable life improvements.

18.4 Societal attitudes and barriers to recovery

The importance of the cultural capital component of recovery capital is that it reflects the community's response to substance use and recovery and the extent to which recovery is perceived as a meaningful transition to long-term well-being.

There is considerable evidence (WHO 2001; UKDPC 2011) to show that stigma is a major problem for users of alcohol and other drugs and their families. The World Health Organisation found that illicit drug dependence is the most stigmatised health condition in the world, and alcohol dependence the fourth most (WHO 2001). In social capital terms, this stigmatisation and exclusion results in barriers to community capital and so a self-perpetuation of social exclusion. In criminology, Braithwaite (1989) has argued, in his work on reintegrative shaming, that "stigmatisation is disintegrative shaming in which no effort is made to reconcile the offender with the community" (1989, 101).

There is also evidence that individual recovery does not result in a change in perceptions of stigma or exclusion. In the US, Phillips and Shaw (2013) have shown that, relative to smoking and obesity, substance users are more stigmatised both when active users and when they are in recovery, suggesting that stigma persists even when active addiction is left behind. In this study, participants were asked about scenarios involving working beside individuals and having the individual marry into their family, with only marginal differences reported in social distance between active substance users and those in recovery. The stigmatised attitudes towards problem substance use and the public failure to differentiate between active use and recovery represents a significant barrier to effective reintegration for individuals attempting to achieve lasting recovery. As Maruna (2001, 166) has concluded "societies that do not believe that offenders can change will get offenders who do not believe that they can change". Indeed, the perception that they cannot change is reinforced to all parties by social exclusion that prevents access to the tools that would enable such changes to happen.

18.5 Visible recovery and the contagion of hope

Within the field of health geography, there is increasing interest in the concept of 'therapeutic landscapes' described as "changing places, settings, situations, locales and milieus that encompass the physical, psychological and social environments associated with treatment or healing" (Williams 1999, 2). This has been applied to recovery from alcohol and drug dependence and the importance of context in recovery. Wilton and DeVerteuil (2006) describe a cluster of alcohol and drug treatment services in San Pedro, California, as a 'recovery landscape': a foundation of spaces and activities that promote recovery. This is done through a social project that extends beyond the boundaries of the addiction services into the community through the emergence of an enduring recovery community in which a sense of fellowship is developed in the wider community.

Thus, AA programmes provide ongoing support to people in recovery in San Pedro, but there are public actions to promote recovery as well. In San Pedro, for one day a year, all of those in recovery wear red shirts and there was a public recovery rally at which around 300 people participated in a recovery celebration event. This challenges stereotypes and stigma as "programme advocates positioned themselves and their programmes in opposition to other groups who were unable to strive for norms of responsibility and productivity" (Wilton and

DeVerteuil 2006, 659). Although AA is an anonymous organisation, this does not preclude its members from engaging in visible recovery activities and the more effective AA networks have active links with formal treatment services through Hospital and Institution Committees. Thus, the therapeutic landscape of recovery will include not only the hubs of recovery but also the nodes that link them.

In one local example – in Barnsley in South Yorkshire in England – an initial training programme for workers and peers in recovery and interested community members led to the development of a voluntary Barnsley Recovery Coalition. This initially set out a recovery vision and mission for the area and then set about planning a series of activities that started with a float in the Lord Mayor's Parade, followed by a Recovery Walk and a sports fun day (Best *et al.* 2013). This is consistent with a much wider movement to recovery visibility in the UK that has been driven by 'recovery-oriented' Government drug strategies in both Scotland and England (Scottish Government 2008; HM Government 2010), promoting visible and accessible recovery groups and communities. Roth and Best (2013) outline the innovations in this approach around public events and celebrations of recovery, the emergence of grass-roots organisations and the development of community linkages. In the UK, the notion of developing 'therapeutic landscapes' is enshrined in alcohol and drug policy. However, this is based on relatively little evidence for the spread of recovery through public activity and little indication of how the 'recovery champions' outlined in the UK Drug Strategy can successfully disseminate the idea of a recovery contagion. There is also a disparate and poorly connected conceptual framework for the development of community support for recovery.

What exists is partly based on the ideas of asset-based community development (what is known as the 'ABCD' model: Kretzmann and McKnight 1993). In this model, the most important resources in a local community are its people, informal groups and formal organisations, all of which represent community (or cultural) capital. McKnight and Block (2010) have argued that building integrated and supportive communities rests on "more individual connections and more associational connections" (McKnight and Block 2010, 132), which in turn relies on identifying those who have the capacity to connect others in our communities. McKnight and Block (2010) refer to such people as community connectors, and they argue that, to make more accepting and integrated communities, "we want to make more visible people who have this connecting capacity. We also want to encourage each of us to discover the connecting possibility in our own selves" (2010, 132). This last point is crucial in that, within this model, the development of connections and communities is essentially an act of co-production between professionals and members of the community; it is not done by professionals to communities, and it is not done by community members alone – it is essentially and at heart a partnership. The remaining sections of this chapter provide basic information on the two pilot studies mentioned above (one in Dandenong, in South-East Melbourne, and the other in the Central Coast of New South Wales) that have attempted to engage in community connections activity to challenge discrimination and stigma and to create the bridges to community recovery capital for those in early recovery.

18.6 Therapeutic jurisprudence and recovery

Without support to engage in meaningful activities, or social groups that are supportive of their recovery, offenders find it difficult to achieve lasting recovery, and may relapse and re-offend. Although services and caseworkers assist offenders with referral to formal services post-release or as part of their sentencing conditions, without peer assistance people are unlikely to participate in informal community support groups, such as AA. As a consequence they may have little or no connection to the groups in the community which can provide social support, meaningful activity and a positive sense of social identity. This in turn is likely to reinforce a sense of marginalisation.

Based on a therapeutic jurisprudence model (Wexler 1999), magistrates in Dandenong (an outer suburban area of Melbourne, Victoria) engaged with Turning Point (a Victorian alcohol, drug and behavioural addiction research and treatment centre) to develop a model for continuity of care for offenders with substance use histories who were completing their sentences. The aim of the community linkage project was to identify appropriate community connectors drawn from three primary pools: substance using offenders in the community, professionals working in relevant services and other members of the community, all of whom could act as 'bridges' between offenders and community groups, such as AA, sporting clubs and other groups. This approach is underpinned by an asset-based model of community development which attempts to utilise strengths and resources that already exist in the community to achieve sustainable change. In this case, the change we are referring to includes: (1) supporting offenders' own changes in substance use and offending behaviour at the *individual* level; and (2) promoting *communities* that are welcoming and supportive of recovery as opposed to communities that stigmatise and marginalise people with substance use problems and offending histories.

Initial pilot work involved court observations and mapping community groups in the Dandenong area to examine whether we could identify offenders who might benefit from the community linkage programme, and to explore whether there were sufficient groups in the community to which offenders could be linked.

Dandenong is a suburb 30 kms south-east of Melbourne, Victoria. The Greater Dandenong area has a population of just over 135,000 and has a greater proportion of people born overseas compared to Victorian and Australian averages (Australian Bureau of Statistics, 2013). Greater Dandenong also has a higher unemployment rate and lower median income as compared to Victorian and national averages (Australian Bureau of Statistics, 2013), and has a higher crime rate than the Victorian average (Community Indicators Victoria, 2013).

Observations of public court proceedings to record substance use involvement were completed. This involved observing court proceedings from the public gallery on four different days and collecting data on the characteristics of offenders, particularly where there were clear indications of substance use problems. The court proceedings observed were a mixture of bail and bail review hearings, judicial monitoring, suspended sentence and breach of order hearings, as well as guilty plea hearings. Substance use was mentioned in just over a quarter ($n=19$, 27.9 per cent) of the 68 cases observed, with alcohol, amphetamine-type stimulants and cannabis being the most commonly mentioned substances. In most of these cases, substance use was considered to be a major underlying reason for offending. This means that around one in four cases at the Dandenong Magistrates' Court might benefit from the proposed community linkage programme.

All the individuals involved in court hearings where substance use was mentioned (except one) were male, the average age was 36 years (SD=10.4), and all had prior criminal histories. Whatever prior criminal justice responses they had received had not been a deterrent to further offending, reinforcing the need for innovative responses. Past use of substance use treatment services was mentioned in under half of the cases ($n=8$, 42.1 per cent), although 55.6 per cent of people ($n=10$) were currently engaged in some form of treatment, and in 72.2 per cent ($n=13$) of cases a recommendation for treatment was provided by the magistrate. The focus on therapeutic jurisprudence at the Dandenong Magistrates' Court was also borne out in sentencing/recommendations, where the most common outcome was a community corrections order (50 per cent) followed by bail (12.5 per cent) and deferred sentence (12.5 per cent). Imprisonment was rare in instances where substance use was involved and was limited to one case only. Family members or friends were present in only one of the 19 cases where substance use was mentioned, suggesting that this group of offenders may lack immediate social capital and might benefit from engagement in community groups.

Having identified a need for community linkage, our next task was to map community assets in the Dandenong region to understand the community groups to which offenders could potentially be linked. A number of formal health and welfare services exist in Dandenong and case managers work with people who are involved in the criminal justice system to facilitate access to these. While health and welfare services are important (and are indeed community assets) they do not always facilitate connections to broader community. Our interest was, therefore, in mapping peer-led and informal groups in the community.

We did this by searching online community directories and talking to magistrates in Dandenong. We identified 97 informal community groups in Dandenong and the diversity and scope of these is illustrated in Figure 18.1. The majority of groups identified were either sporting clubs (47.4 per cent, $n=46$) or recreation groups (33.0 per cent, $n=32$), such as fishing clubs and community bands (see Figure 18.1). Training and support groups, which were often attached to formal services, included regular group programmes on community gardening, cooking, computers, art and craft etc. and these accounted for 9.3 per cent ($n=9$) of groups. Importantly, there were also 10 (10.3 per cent) addiction recovery groups identified. These provided peer support and mutual aid for people with substance use and mental health issues, including groups like AA and SMART Recovery (a mutual aid group based on the principles of cognitive behavioural therapy).

As illustrated in Figure 18.1, recovery groups (and some training and support groups) had the specific purpose of supporting people to desist from problematic substance use and crime. Recovery groups are likely to have the most experience of, and be the most welcoming to, people who either are currently or were previously involved in the criminal justice system. These may be ideal targets for community linkage initially, and indeed there is a literature around assertive linkage to mutual aid groups (e.g. Manning *et al.* 2012), but they may not be sufficient for all individuals and across all stages of the recovery journey. As people's confidence, social networks and ability to participate in diverse group situations grow, there are a wide range of non-recovery specific groups available in Dandenong which could be accessed. Whether these groups would be welcoming of people with prior substance use issues or offending histories will require further investigation, and this will impact on the willingness and openness of the people in recovery both to be open about their recovery and to feel safe and comfortable in non-specific recovery groups. Critically we will need to explore how any barriers and stigma can be overcome.

The next steps in this project involve the identification and recruitment of community connectors whose job it will be to make this link. The connectors group will be recruited from a combination of professionals, peers in recovery and members of the local community, overseen by a coordinating committee, akin to the group in Barnsley (Best *et al.* 2013) described above.

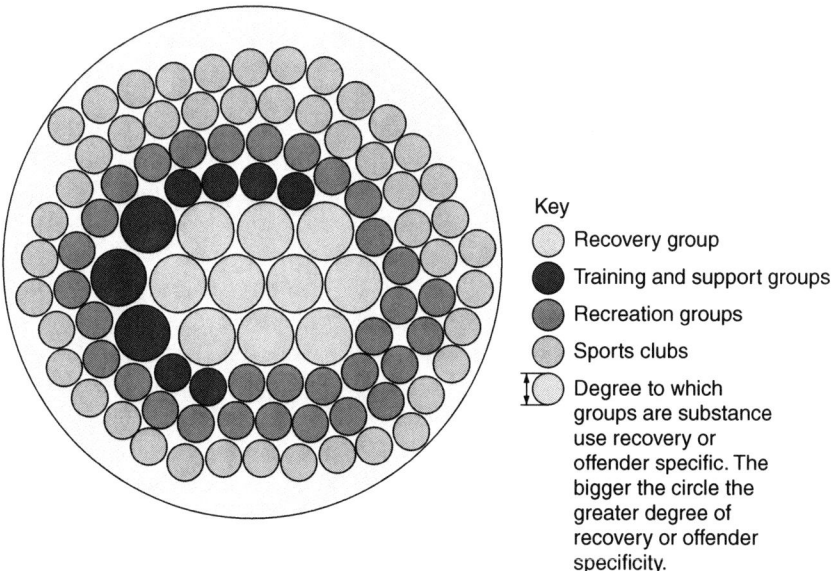

Key
- Recovery group
- Training and support groups
- Recreation groups
- Sports clubs
- Degree to which groups are substance use recovery or offender specific. The bigger the circle the greater degree of recovery or offender specificity.

Figure 18.1 Community asset map of community groups (*n*=97) in Dandenong, Victoria.

18.6 RECOVERY COMMUNITY DEVELOPMENT

Dooralong is a 110-bedded residential rehabilitation service run by the Salvation Army in the Central Coast area of New South Wales, Australia, that offers a Therapeutic Community intervention (De Leon 2000) to substance-users with entrenched substance use history (many of whom have co-occurring offending and mental health histories). The Dooralong Transformation Centre opened not long prior to the start of the initiative and is set in a large estate of 350 acres with extensive opportunities for sport as well as a broad range of therapeutic activities.

As such, the Transformation Centre represents not only a potential hub for recovery activity, but also an asset for the community. Such a centre moves from a model of asset mobilisation to one of asset provision and so can be more appropriately referred to as a Reciprocal Community Development model, where the aim is not only to access existing connectors and resources in the community but also to ensure that the Centre, its staff and clients take on the role of providing assets to the wider community and playing an active role in engaging with and improving community life. The use of the Centre, its staff and residents as community assets is part of an attempt not only at asset development but also at building proximity and linkage between the treatment Centre and the community, and through doing this, challenging discriminatory practices and beliefs.

The pilot project at Dooralong was a partnership with the Salvation Army to identify community connectors from within the Therapeutic Community and to utilise this initial cohort to engage the wider community actively in recovery-oriented activities including those associated with challenging stigma and discrimination.

The model in Dooralong is based on four connected concepts:

- **recovery capital:** as the sum of personal, social and community resources that an individual can draw on to support them in their recovery journey;
- **assertive linkage:** although this has primarily been used in the past to link clients into AA groups, the philosophy is applied here to link in to other community resources including sports and recreation activities, education and training, peer activities and volunteering;
- **ongoing peer participation:** based on the idea that generating a growing community of peer champions increases the visibility and feasibility of recovery in the community and strengthens that community by its presence and its activities;
- **asset-based community development:** is the idea that communities have strengths and resources that are available and accessible to support recovery pathways and journeys, and tapping into those resources is essential for bridging people through transitions to their own communities.

The initial sessions recruited 15 volunteer community connectors and an asset map identified a further group of around 50 candidate community connectors or supports. This group constitutes the basis for the therapeutic landscape of recovery (Wilton and DeVerteuil 2006) but with the additional element of actively engaging the community as partners. The visibility of a recovery community is limited if it seeks only to grow through its membership and this model is about active engagement through attraction and through the promotion of recovery as beneficial to communities, and of recovery groups and individuals as important assets in a community.

18.7 Communities and the ground for recovery

Based upon the ideas and pilot work we have discussed thus far, we imagine a therapeutic landscape of recovery to encompass several key elements as illustrated in Figure 18.2.

This conceptualisation integrates both the formal systems that attempt to help people with substance use and offending histories and the community, in which people desist, relapse and live their lives (often in the face of considerable stigma and marginalisation). Our pilot work in Dandenong and Dooralong is predicated on the notion that recovery involves both individual and community level change. A person's individual behaviour change in treatment can be threatened when they enter corrosive community environments: environments that continue to exclude and stigmatise. However, too often the treatment and community worlds are viewed in isolation and separately. By virtue of being members of community groups and their willingness to engage with the treatment/criminal justice worlds, community connectors can act as the vital bridge between the treatment/criminal justice-worlds and the community. They facilitate access to groups in the community from which people may derive support, and a sense of belonging and ultimately wellbeing. These may be recovery groups in the first instance but as the social networks of people who have stopped using grow through participation in recovery groups,

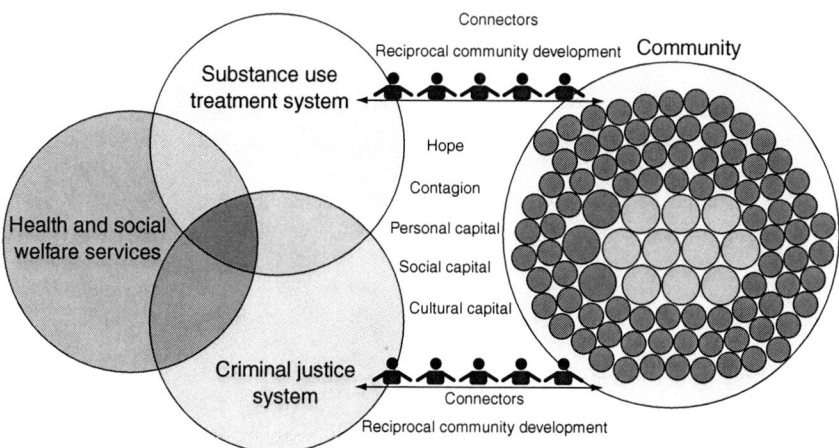

Figure 18.2 Therapeutic landscape of recovery among people with histories of substance use and offending.

opportunities for participation in other groups are also likely to grow. Importantly, however, if community connectors operate under a reciprocal community development model, they are also likely to decrease stigma and effect community level change. Together these reciprocal actions may contribute to a contagion of hope that recovery is possible and ultimately increase both the personal and social capital of the individual, and also the community's cultural capital in supporting recovery.

Acknowledgements

We would like to thank the staff at the Dandenong Magistrates' court and at the Salvation Army's Dooralong residential rehabilitation service for their support and assistance with pilot work. We would also like to thank our colleagues – Dylan Smith and Laura Abbey – who were involved in collecting data as part of the Dandenong pilot.

References

Australian Bureau of Statistics. 2013. 2011 Census Quick Stats: Greater Dandenong. Australian Bureau of Statistics. www.censusdata.abs.gov.au/census_services/getproduct/census/2011/quickstat/LGA22670.

Beattie M. and Longabaugh R. 1999. "General and alcohol-specific support following treatment". *Addictive Behaviours* 24: 593–606.

Best D., Loudon L., Powell D., Groshkova T. and White W. 2013. "Identifying and recruiting recovery champions: Exploratory action research in Barnsley, South Yorkshire". *Journal of Groups in Addiction and Recovery* 8(3): 169–184.

Biernacki P. 1986. *Pathways from heroin addiction: Recovery without treatment.* Philadelphia PA: Temple University Press.

Braithwaite J. 1989. *Crime, shame and reintegration.* New York: Cambridge University Press.

Community Indicators Victoria. 2013. *Greater Dandenong Wellbeing Report.* www.communityindicators.net.au/wellbeing_reports/greater_dandenong.

Deegan P. 1998. "Recovery: The lived experience of rehabilitation". *Psychosocial Rehabilitation Journal* 11: 11–19.

De Leon G. 2000. *The Therapeutic Community: Theory, model and method.* New York: Springer Publishing Company.

Granfield R. and Cloud W. 2001. "Social context and natural recovery: The role of social capital in overcoming drug-associated problems". *Substance Use and Misuse* 36: 1543–1570.

HM Government. 2010. *Drug Strategy 2010: Reducing demand, restricting supply, building recovery: Supporting people to live a drug-free life.* London: Her Majesty's Stationery Office.

Kretzmann J. and McKnight J. 1993. *Building communities from the inside out: A path toward finding and mobilising a community's assets.* Skokie, IL: ACTA Publications.

Landale S. and Best D. 2012. "Dynamic shifts in social networks and normative values in recovery from an offending and drug using lifestyle". In C. D. Johnston (ed.) *Social Capital: Theory, measurement and outcomes.* New York: Nova Science Publishers, 219–236.

Litt M. D., Kadden R. M., Kabela-Cormier E. and Petry N. 2007. "Changing network support for drinking: Initial findings from the Network Support Project". *Journal of Consulting and Clinical Psychology* 75(4): 542–555.

Litt M. D., Kadden R. M., Kabela-Cormier E. and Petry N. M. 2009. "Changing network support for drinking: Network Support Project 2-year follow-up". *Journal of Consulting and Clinical Psychology* 77(2): 229–242.

Manning V., Best D., Faulkner N., Titherington E., Morinan A., Keaney F., Gossop M. and Strang J. 2012. "Does active referral by a doctor or 12-step peer improve 12-step meeting attendance? Results from a pilot Randomised Control Trial". *Drug and Alcohol Dependence* 126(1): 131–137.

Maruna S. 2001. *Making Good: How ex-convicts reform and rebuild their lives.* Washington, DC: American Psychological Association.

McIntosh J. and McKeganey N. 2002. *Beating the dragon: The recovery from dependent drug use.* Harolow, UK: Pearson Education.

McKnight J. and Block P. 2010. *The abundant community: Awakening the power of families and neighbourhoods.* San Francisco: Berrett-Koehler Publishers.

Phillips L. and Shaw A. 2013. "Substance use more stigmatised than smoking and obesity". *Journal of Substance Use* 18(4): 247–253.

Putnam R. 2000. *Bowling alone: The collapse and revival of American community.* New York: Simon and Schuster.

Roth J. and Best D. 2013. *Addiction and recovery in the UK.* Abingdon, Oxon: Routledge.

Scottish Government 2008. *The road to recovery: A new approach to tackling Scotland's drug problem.* Edinburgh: Scottish Government.

Sheedy C. K. and Whitter M. 2009. *Guiding principles and elements of recovery-oriented systems of care: What do we know from the research?* HHS Publication No. (SMA) 09–4439. Rockville, MD: Center for Substance Abuse Treatment, Substance Abuse and Mental Health Services Administration.

Soyer M. 2014. "The imagination of desistance: A juxtaposition of the construction of incarceration as a turning point and the reality of recidivism". *British Journal of Criminology* 54: 91–108.

Substance Abuse and Mental Health Services Administration. 2012. http://blog.samhsa.gov/2012/03/23/definition-of-recovery-updated/.

UK Drug Policy Commission. 2008. *The UK Drug Policy Commission Recovery Consensus Group: A vision of recovery.* London: Her Majesty's Stationery Office.

UK Drug Policy Commission. 2011. *Getting serious about stigma in Scotland: The problem with stigmatising drug users.* London: Her Majesty's Stationery Office.

Wexler D. 1999. "Therapeutic Jurisprudence: An overview". Presentation at Thomas Cooley Disabilities Law Review Lay Symposium, East Lansing MI, 29 October 1999.

White W. 2012. *Recovery/remission from substance use disorders: An analysis of reported outcomes in 415 scientific reports, 1868–2011.* Philadelphia PA: Philadelphia Department of Behavioural Health and Intellectual Disability Services and the Great Lakes Addiction Technology Transfer Center.

Wilton R. and DeVerteuil G. 2006. "Spaces of sobriety/sites of power: Examining social model alcohol recovery programs as therapeutic landscapes". *Social Science and Medicine* 63: 649–661.

Williams A. 1999. "Introduction". In A. Williams (ed.) *Therapeutic landscapes: The dynamics between place and wellness.* Lanham MA: University Press of America, 1–11.

World Health Organization. 2001. *The World Health Report. Mental Health: new understanding, new hope.* Geneva: World Health Organization.

19 Balancing legal, cultural and human rights with the forensic paradigm

James Ogloff and Rosemary Sheehan

Like any book, the preparation of *Working within the Forensic Paradigm: Cross-discipline approaches for policy and practice* has presented the typical range of challenges. In addition, however, complications arose due to still developing constructs that underlie the forensic paradigm. While some mental health professions have a long history of working within the forensic context (e.g. medicine generally and psychiatry specifically) for other professions it is still quite novel. Some professions, such as social work (see Chapter 1, this volume) and psychology (Otto and Ogloff 2013), while also having long histories of involvement in forensic areas, are still considered rather esoteric fields of specialisation in their disciplines. In some health professions, such as occupational therapy, the forensic specialisation is still very much developing, having begun development in the 1980s (Farnworth *et al.* 1987). Taken together, while many mental health professionals across the disciplines work within forensic services, few specialist academic education programmes exist and practice standards are either non-existent or generally so broad as to be ineffective.

The many topics covered in this book reflect the breadth of the forensic field. Contributions from many professionals from a range of backgrounds provide an opportunity to explore the diversity not only of topics covered but also methodologies and forms of discourse. Despite the diversity which enriches our work, we firmly believe that the forensic mental health domain has evolved to a point where core competencies are emerging and standards can and must be developed. An exploration of the topics covered in the book and the questions they raise enables a consideration of the areas where core knowledge has emerged or is required. Moreover, the information presented points to the need for ongoing development of standards.

Looming largest over the forensic field, of course, is the stark reality of law and policy. Very often the law and related policies are inconsistent with the empirical and experiential realities of mental health professionals. These realities present particular challenges. For example, the law and order movement has led to the implementation of laws that are not supported by the empirical realities. Popovic (see Chapter 7) uses examples from Victoria, Australia, which is experiencing a surge in building prison beds, directly as a result of changes in government policy and law, at a time when the overall crime rate has been decreasing over a ten-year period. It is incumbent on those of us who work in the forensic paradigm to ensure that where possible correct information is provided to policy-makers. In addition, in our clinical and front line work we must uphold our obligations to our clients.

As so many of the authors have articulated or demonstrated, bringing the work of mental health professionals into the forensic arena has the inescapable effect of taking our work into the public forum – which can be a particularly uncomfortable place to be. The public spotlight can bring focus to the limitations of our work and all too often highlights anomalies with the effect of raising concerns about our practices and the clients with whom we work.

By way of example, at the time of writing this chapter, a patient of the Victorian Institute of Forensic Mental Health (Forensicare) failed to return to the hospital one evening following a period of unescorted leave. As is their practice, Forensicare notified the police who in turn notified the community. The media spotlight was immediately focused on the 'failure' of the service and the risk the patient posed to the community. Facts mattered not. The actions of the man which brought him into a forensic hospital involved a family member; he was not seen to be a risk to the general community. The act occurred many years ago and the man was imprisoned and then hospitalised for more than seven years. Of the almost 29,000 occasions of unescorted leave taken by patients from the Thomas Embling Hospital in the past five years, there were only two occasions where the patients did not return; this represents an astonishingly low 'failure rate' of 0.0069 per cent. Moreover on both occasions, as with the current one, the patients were returned to the hospital in short order without adverse incident to anyone. Facts matter not, however, when the media grabs hold of a news story that fits within its fear campaign.

The matters raised in this book are drawn from the expertise and experience of the authors who come from a range of backgrounds: mental health practitioners, legal practitioners, policy contributors, advocates and researchers in mental health, welfare, law, criminology, policing and health. Thus, the issues go well beyond mental health practitioners alone. This again emphasises that matters arising within the forensic paradigm go beyond the mental health professions and broadly permeate all the disciplines and agencies in the legal system.

The chapters in Part I of the book, that examine contemporary policy and paradigmatic underpinnings of the forensic domain, challenge contemporary views on a broad range of matters. Rosemary Sheehan, in Chapter 1, emphasises the breadth of the mental health disciplines, particularly social work, that interface with the legal system and related human services systems. She notes the need to ensure that the developing forensic field is one built upon specialist knowledge and training.

Chapters 2 (Andrew Carroll), 3 (Chris Trotter), 4 (Gloria Kirwan) and 5 (Katie Seidler, Emma Collins, Rima Nasr and Chris Lennings) all address the broad issue of risk, safety and containment. In their own way, the authors of each chapter challenge many of the assumptions underlying the increasing focus in society on risk and containment. Andrew Carroll (Chapter 2) emphasises that mental health professionals must face the reality that questions of risk assessment and management raise, questions both of empirical evidence and values. Chris Trotter (Chapter 3) challenges some of the assumptions that underlie evolving criminal justice policy. He argues that more focus on client needs (broadly stated) and the provisions of support can more effectively reduce the level of risk that people in the criminal justice system pose. Gloria Kirwan (Chapter 4) notes the absence of a consistent understanding of risk management. She reviews the many conceptualisations of risk management, noting that each has implications for services and service systems. Finally, Lennings and colleagues (Chapter 5) address issues generally consistent with the other chapters in this section by focusing on the unique area of sexual offending. They note, convincingly, that a continuity of care and services is required between the prison system and community and that sexual abuse needs to be seen as a community problem or public health concern that requires a multi-pronged approach leading to remediation.

Taken together the chapters in Part I of the book raise significant challenges regarding the prevailing risk framework and note that to truly enhance public safety a very different framework is required. Public policy and practice in criminal justice and forensic mental health services require a significant reframing if efforts to reduce offending are to be more effective. More work is required pertaining to so-called 'risk management' and individual agency needs to be considered a vital element of recovery among both forensic mental health consumers and offenders.

The chapters in Part II of the book each challenged contemporary notions of fairness and justice, including responses to offending. Paul Garrett (Chapter 6) draws convincing parallels between the rise in prison populations in most western countries and the rise of neoliberalism. He convincingly shows how public policy is shifting from one of respect for people to one that treats people with contempt, particularly for those who depend upon the welfare system. Garrett concludes by reminding social workers that theirs is a profession in which human rights and social justice are fundamental principles. This is an important message for all professionals. Jelena Popovic (Chapter 7) challenges the rise in harsher penalties and tougher approaches to criminal behaviour. Drawing on an emerging evidence base, she demonstrates how 'solution focused justice' – including problem-solving courts – is both cost-efficient and effective in reducing crime.

The next three chapters in Part II explore specific areas of concern. In Chapter 8, Grant Burkitt, Daniel Kinston and Ronan McLoughlin examine the complexities of facilitating forensic mental health consumers from custodial care to the community. With the movement away from indefinite detention and asylum to community care comes the need to focus on the expanding role of forensic mental health services to assist with the transition to the community.

Focusing on the challenge of policing young people, Stuart Thomas (Chapter 9) explores the knowledge base concerning police contacts with young people. Given the burden that they present to the justice system, Thomas emphasises the importance of developing mechanisms to assist the police working with youth. He concludes that there is a significant gap in understanding police decision-making in their interactions with young people. In particular police discretion needs to be enhanced to afford them the opportunity to refer young people to health, social and welfare services that can assist the young person to make positive change.

James Ogloff and Margaret Cutajar (Chapter 10) address the vexing question of whether experiences of child sexual abuse (CSA) lead victims to later offend and be re-victimised. Included in this question is whether those who are sexually abused as children are more likely than those who were not to go on to commit sexual offences. They conclude, following a review of a programme of research on the topics, that the vast majority of children who are sexually victimised do not go on to offend (particularly girls). Sadly, though, those boys who were sexually abused were more likely to commit sexual offences later in life. Male and female victims of CSA were more likely than others to engage in criminal offending and to be re-victimised over time.

The chapters in Part III brought focus to different aspects of mental health and wellbeing. Anna Gupta begins in Chapter 11 with a focus on the question of when maltreatment of children in families rises to the threshold of 'significant harm.' She argues that the fact that significant harm is not well defined operationally is positive to the extent that it allows discretion to consider the extremely broad diversity of circumstances of families and their children. Paradoxically, this lack of clarity in the operational definition is problematic insofar as the discretion allows subjective judgments to be made with a lack of transparency. Gupta concludes with a theme raised before by Garrett (Chapter 6), emphasising the importance of practitioners critically evaluating their own values.

In Chapter 12, Ian Cummins draws attention to questions of the role of the police in working with mentally ill people since the deinstitutionalisation movement. He notes that as the model of care for people with mental illnesses shifted from housing them in large asylums to community-based care, the role of police in working with people with psychiatric illnesses has necessarily increased. He argues that mental health services are under terrible strain and financial pressures and need to be enhanced and that police need to reconceptualise their roles to include responding to people with mental illnesses as a core function.

Moving from the role of police when encountering people with mental illnesses to the courts, Ronald Francis (Chapter 13) explores the issues arising for courts dealing with mental health issues. Francis concludes that there is a role for mental health professionals to assist the courts to deal more effectively with people who have mental illnesses. Moreover, similar to some of the points raised by Popovic (Chapter 7), Francis notes that the rise of specialist courts – particularly mental health courts – can be effective in helping to address these matters.

In the final chapter in this Part, Peta Barry *et al.* (Chapter 14) raise questions of well-being from a novel perspective – the need to consider the well-being of staff who work in corrections environments. She focuses in particular on offender rehabilitation staff members. Barry *et al.* argue convincingly for the need to consider the range of vulnerabilities that may jeopardise the well-being of offender rehabilitation staff. She concludes by presenting a framework for corrective services to assist staff to enhance their resilience to work in this challenging environment.

In the final section of the book, Part IV, the authors explore matters pertaining to recovery and transition to the community. William Holt and Jacqueline Blatt (Chapter 15) commence the Part with a description of a novel initiative to address homelessness in Philadelphia that is part of a broader recovery-focused system (The Journey of Hope project). The authors describe the recovery-focused approach to address homelessness, stating convincingly that recovery is a journey rather than an event.

Focusing on the plight of another group of disadvantaged individuals, Sheila Howitt and Lindsay Thomson (Chapter 16) highlight the mental health needs of prisoners. They argue that despite the difference in where and how mentally ill prisoners are treated in different jurisdictions around the world, the prisoners' health needs and security requirements are the same. They also note the importance of moving beyond the detection and treatment of prisoners with psychotic illnesses to those with affective disorders, anxiety disorders and personality disorders.

In Chapter 17, Flora Matheson, Amanda Brazil, and Pamela Forrester write about the challenges of women leaving prison and the need to ensure they are in a state of 'reintegration readiness' prior to release. They touch on issues not dissimilar to those raised in Chapter 8 by Burkitt, Kinston and McLoughlin who discussed issues pertaining to transitioning forensic mental health patients from secure hospital to community. Using the reintegration readiness framework, Matheson and her colleagues show how women can ready themselves for release with the assistance of staff and service providers. By adhering to both person-specific and context-specific factors, the chances of women successfully reintegrating into the community can be maximised.

In the final substantive chapter in this Part and the book, David Best and Michael Savic (Chapter 18) address the pathways to recovery for offenders afflicted with substance abuse. Similar to the points made by Matheson and colleagues in Chapter 17, Best and Savic emphasise the importance of incorporating both individual level and community level (contextual) change. The approach explained also shares similarities with the homelessness initiative described by Holt and Blatt (Chapter 15).

Overarching themes

By its very nature the forensic paradigm and human service interface is broad and diverse. This diversity is reflected in this book. Both the topics and the authors mirror the range of concerns and professions that intersect in the forensic–human service interface. Rising above the diversity, some conclusions can be drawn from the array of chapters presented in this book: the high level of need among prisoners (male and female), forensic mental health patients, those afflicted with substance use disorders, children and families, and those experiencing homelessness; the need for increased human services in the criminal justice system; the rise of risk in the law and order movement; the general lack of evidence base for much criminal justice policy; the need to ensure policymakers are informed; the need for increased responsiveness among institutions in the justice system (courts, prisons, police); the need for ongoing reflection among mental health professionals; and the need for standards and care for those working in the forensic paradigm. Each of the points will be briefly highlighted below.

A theme that runs through many of the chapters in this book is the high level of need among prisoners, forensic mental health patients, those who misuse substances, children and families, and homeless people. As a result of holes in the social net and diminishing resources, the level of need among the populations is great.

To help address the plight of clients in the forensic paradigm, it is important to provide enhanced and more efficient human resources to tackle the plethora of matters raised. Rather than focusing on the underlying causes of crime and adversity, policymakers have focused resources on building prisons and hiring police. This focus lacks an evidence base and has little chance of making the community safer or improving the plight of the increasing numbers of people captured in the broadening net of criminality.

There can be no doubt about the need for increased forensic mental health services; however, equally important is the need for increased research and evaluation of the policy initiatives – and alternatives – in the law and order movement. Only with careful empirical research can the effect of policy change be effectively evaluated. Over time evidence-based approaches are likely to be recognised as they have been in the US with the movement toward justice reinvestment (Kleiman 2011), which can lead to a 'reinvestment' in resources to help further desistance from crime.

Several of the chapters highlight the need for increased responsiveness among institutions in the justice system (courts, prisons, police). The role of therapeutic jurisprudence in courts and the emergence of so-called problem-solving courts have been shown to improve the outcomes of those who come before the courts. In this sense the courts can be more responsive to the needs of those who appear before them. To the extent that many people before the courts have a range of afflictions, approaches are required to provide assistance to them to help address their needs and thereby making them less likely to reoffend. Beyond the courts, police services and prisons also must continue to develop mechanisms to be responsive to the characteristics of those with whom they deal.

In several of the chapters, the need for those mental health professionals who work in the forensic paradigm to monitor their values was emphasised. Similarly it is important that they monitor their own well-being and personal needs. This also raises the need for standards of care and practice guidelines for those who work in the forensic paradigm. As the field continues to evolve, it is important that practice standards are promulgated to ensure that practice is evidence based.

Concluding remark

In closing, it is our hope that the contributions in this book extend debate on the challenges confronting individuals drawn into the forensic domain and continue to further the appreciation of the plethora of issues facing those who work in the forensic paradigm.

References

Farnworth L., Morgan S. and Fernando B. 1987. "Prison-based occupational therapy". *Australian Occupational Therapy Journal* 34: 40–46.

Kleiman M. A. R. 2011. "Justice reinvestment in community supervision". *Criminology and Public Policy* 10: 651–659.

Otto R. K. and Ogloff J. R. P. 2013. "Defining forensic psychology". In I. B. Weiner and R. K. Otto (eds) *Handbook of forensic psychology*, 4th edn. Hoboken, NJ: John Wiley and Sons.

Index

Page numbers in **bold** refer to figures and those in *italics* refer to tables.

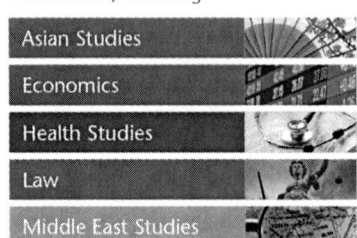